THE

RELIGIOUS ASPECT OF PHILOSOPHY

A CRITIQUE OF THE BASES OF CONDUCT
AND OF FAITH

BY

JOSIAH ROYCE, Ph. D.

INSTRUCTOR IN PHILOSOPHY IN HARVARD COLLEGE

Der Anblick giebt den Engeln Stärke,
Da Keiner Dich ergründen mag.
GOETHE'S *Faust, Prolog.*

BOSTON AND NEW YORK
HOUGHTON MIFFLIN COMPANY
The Riverside Press Cambridge

COPYRIGHT, 1885 AND 1913, BY JOSIAH ROYCE

The Riverside Press

CAMBRIDGE · MASSACHUSETTS

PRINTED IN THE U.S.A.

To

𝔐𝔶 𝔥𝔬𝔫𝔬𝔯𝔢𝔡 𝔉𝔯𝔦𝔢𝔫𝔡,

GEORGE BUCHANAN COALE,

OF BALTIMORE,

I DEDICATE THIS BOOK,

IN EARNEST AND GRATEFUL RECOGNITION

OF HIS KINDNESS, OF HIS COUNSEL,

AND OF HIS WISDOM.

PREFACE.

THIS book sketches the basis of a system of philosophy, while applying the principles of this system to religious problems. The form and order of the treatment depend on the nature of these latter problems themselves, and are not such as a system of philosophy, expounded solely for its own sake, would be free to take. The religious problems have been chosen for the present study because they first drove the author to philosophy, and because they, of all human interests, deserve our best efforts and our utmost loyalty.

A large portion of this discussion seeks to appeal both to the special student of philosophy and to the general reader. A considerable part, again, can with the very best of fortune hope to interest the special student of philosophy, but cannot hope for more. The Preface must therefore tell what sort of appeal is made to each of the two classes of readers.

To begin with the general reader, who may have the curiosity to glance at this philosophic essay, the author must forthwith confess that while on the one hand he desires to trouble nobody with fruitless and blank negations, and while his aim is therefore on the whole a positive aim, yet on the other hand, as he has no present connection with any visible religious body, and no sort of desire for any such connection, he cannot be expected to write an apology for a popular creed. This confession is made frankly, but not for the sake of provoking a quarrel, and with all due reverence for the faith of other men. If the fox who had lost his tail was foolish to be proud of his loss, he would have been yet more foolish to hide it by wearing a false tail, stolen mayhap from a dead fox. The full application of the moral of the fable to the present case is moreover willingly accepted. Not as the fox invited his friends to imitate his loss, would the present writer aim to make other men lose their faiths. Rather is it his aim not to arouse fruitless quarrels, but to come to some peaceful understanding with his fellows touching the ultimate meaning and value and foundation of this noteworthy custom, so widely prevalent among us, the custom of having a religion. If the author ends by stating for his own part a religious doctrine, it will yet be seen upon reading the same that a man could hold that and much more too; so that what is here said is rather proposed as a basis for a conceivable if very far off reconciliation, than as an argument to dissuade those who may think that they can go further than the author, from proving in a philosophical fashion whatever they can prove. Such people may manage to interpret many of the negations that occur in these pages as directed against an inadequate form, or imperfect understanding, of their more elaborate creed. If they can do so, no one will be more heartily delighted than the author, although he may not agree with them.

As to the relation of this book to what is called modern doubt, it is a relation neither of blind obedience nor of unsympathetic rejection. The doctrine of philosophic idealism here propounded is not what in these days is popularly called Agnosticism. Yet doubting everything is once for all a necessary element in the organism of philosophic reflection. What is here dwelt upon over and over again is, however, the consideration that the doubts of our time are not to be apologetically "refuted," in the old fashioned sense, but that taken just as they are, fully and cordially received, they are upon analysis found to contain and imply a positive and important religious creed, bearing both upon conduct and upon reality. Not to have once thoroughly accepted as necessary the great philosophic doubts and problems of our day, is simply not to have philosophized as a man of this age. But to have accepted these doubts without in time coming to find the positive truth that is concealed in them, is to treat them as the innocent favorite of fortune in a fairy tale always at first treats his magic gift. It is something common and dingy, and he lays it carelessly away in his empty house, feeling poorer than ever. But see: handle it rightly, and the fairy gift fills your transfigured home with a wealth of gems and gold, and spreads for you a wondrous banquet. To the author has come the fancy that modern doubt may be some such fairy gift as this. And he would like to suggest to some reader what may possibly prove the right fashion of using the talisman.

The general reader, if very " benevolent," may be able to endure the " First Book " of the present volume in its entirety; but in the " Second Book " he will find much that is meant only for the student whose interests are decidedly technical. Some warnings are given in the text, to help the general reader in skipping. But perhaps it may be well for his purpose to confine himself at once in this Book II., at least upon the first reading, to the following passages, namely : in Chapter VIII., to the introductory remarks and the first and the last sections of the chapter ; in Chapter IX., to the introductory re-

marks, and Sections I., II., III., and V.; in Chapter
X., to the introductory remarks, and Sections I., II.,
and IV.; in Chapter XI., to the introductory remarks, and the concluding section only; and then
he may try the whole of Chapter XII. Thus he
will not be troubled by the technical statement of
the proof of our doctrine, and he will see the trend
of our thought, which may at least amuse him. If
he is then still curious, he may take his own risks
and look farther.

The student of philosophy will find in this volume
a doctrine that undertakes to be in certain significant respects independent and original, but that,
without ceasing to be the author's own system,
frankly belongs to the wide realm of Post-Kantian
Idealism. Of course no true lover of philosophy
ventures, when he calls a doctrine his own, to pretend to more than the very moderate degree of relative originality that the subject in our day permits;
and of course the author for his own part feels very
deeply how much what he has to offer is the product of what he has happened to read and remember
about philosophy and its history. Most of all he
feels his debt to Kant; then he knows how much he
has gained from Fichte, from the modern Neo-Kan-
tians in Germany, and from the revivers of idealism
in recent years in England and America. To Hegel

also he has of course a decided debt to acknowl-
edge.

There are in recent philosophical history two
Hegels : one the uncompromising idealist, with his
general and fruitful insistence upon the great fundamental truths of idealism ; the other the technical
Hegel of the " Logik," whose dialectic method seems
destined to remain, not a philosophy, but the idea
of a philosophy. With this latter Hegel the author
feels a great deal of discontent ; to the other Hegel,
whose insight, as we know, was by no means independent of that of Fichte and other contemporaries,
but who was certainly the most many-sided and critical of the leaders of the one great common idealistic
movement of the early part of the century, — to him
we all owe a great debt indeed. It is, however, a
mistake to neglect the other idealists just for the
sake of glorifying him. And it is an intolerable
blunder to go on repeating what we may have
learned from him in the awkward and whimsical
speech of the wondrous and crabbed master. If
Hegel taught anything, then what he taught can be
conveyed in an utterly non-Hegelian vocabulary, or
else Hegel is but a king of the rags and tatters of a
flimsy terminology, and no king of thought at all.
It is therefore absolutely the duty of a man who
nowadays supposes that he has any truth from He-

gel to propound, to state it in an entirely fresh and
individual form. Of Hegelian language repeated to
us in place of Hegelian thought, we have had by
this time a sickening surfeit. Let us therefore
thank men who, like the late lamented Professor
Green, have at last been free to speak their own
thoughts very much in their own way; and let us be
glad too that the number of so-called Hegelians of
similar independence is daily growing greater. The
author, however, cannot call himself an Hegelian,
much as he owes to Hegel.

Further especial acknowledgments the author
wants to make to Professor William James, to Mr.
Shadworth Hodgson, to Professor Otto Pfleiderer,
to Professor Hans Vaihinger, to Professor Otto
Liebmann, to Professor Julius Bergmann, to Professor Christoph Sigwart, and to Mr. Arthur Balfour, for the valuable helps in thought that, unknown to them, he, as a reader of their works, has
felt, and that he now recognizes as distinctly affecting this book. To Professor William James once
more in particular, and also to Professor George
Palmer, the author owes numerous oral suggestions
that have influenced him more than he now can exactly estimate or fully confess. And then there
remain two thinkers to name, men very different
from each other, but both for the author very valu-

able. Of these one was among the first of the German thinkers in the chance order of the author's early reading, the other was deeply influential both by his spoken words and by his writings; the former is that brilliant and stimulating master of contradictions, Schopenhauer, the other is the now departed Lotze, whose lectures the author will never forget nor disregard, although what is here taught is remote enough from most of Lotze's system.

In outer form this work may be considered by the philosophic student as a sort of roughly sketched and very incomplete Phenomenology of the religious consciousness, first on its moral, and then on its theoretical, side. The parts of the argument that the author supposes to contain most relative originality will be found in Book I., Chapters VI. and VII., and in Book II., Chapter XI. On these chapters all else hinges.

The discussion of the Problem of Evil, as it appears in Chapter XII., is, as the author has seen only since that chapter was in type, very closely parallel to part of the discussion of the same question in the new second edition of Pfleiderer's " Religionsphilosophie." Yet, as the thoughts of this new edition of Pfleiderer's argument were indicated in his first edition, although not so clearly expressed, the author claims little originality here, save in the form of presentation, in the illustrations used, and in the reference of the whole to the arguments of Chapter XI. This last matter seems to him, of itself indeed, quite important.

The work as it here appears is an outgrowth of several separate lines of study. The questions of the present Chapter XI. were first attempted by the author in a thesis for the Doctor's degree of the Johns Hopkins University in 1878. The argument has since been essentially altered. Several fragments that are here used as organic parts of the whole book have appeared separately, in various degrees of incompleteness, in the "Journal of Speculative Philosophy," in "Mind," and elsewhere. The present form of the book has grown out of lectures on religious questions to the students of Harvard College; but only a small portion of the manuscript of these lectures has entered into the structure of the book, which, for its own part, tries to be no patchwork, but a single united, if incomplete, study of its chosen problem.

CAMBRIDGE, MASS., *January* 11, 1885.

TABLE OF CONTENTS.

CHAPTER I.

BOOK I.

THE SEARCH FOR A MORAL IDEAL.

CHAPTER II.

CHAPTER III.

CHAPTER IV.

CHAPTER V.

CHAPTER VI.

CHAPTER VII.

BOOK II.

THE SEARCH FOR A RELIGIOUS TRUTH.

———◆———

CHAPTER VIII.

b

CHAPTER XII.

CHAPTER I.

INTRODUCTION ; RELIGION AS A MORAL CODE AND AS A THEORY.

Auch bezweifl' ich, dass du glaubest,
Was so rechter Glaube heisst,
Glaubst wohl nicht an Gott den Vater,
An den Sohn und heil'gen Geist.

HEINE.

INTENDING in the following pages to sketch certain philosophic opinions that seem to him to have a religious bearing, the author must begin by stating what he understands to be the nature of religion, and how he conceives philosophy to be related to religion.

We speak commonly of religious feelings and of religious beliefs ; but we find difficulty in agreeing about what makes either beliefs or feelings religious. A feeling is not religious merely because it is strong, nor yet because it is also morally valuable, nor yet because it is elevated. If the strength and the moral value of a feeling made it religious, patriotism would be religion. If elevation of feeling were enough, all higher artistic emotion would be religious. But such views would seem to most persons very inadequate. As for belief, it is not religious merely because it is a belief in the supernatural. Not merely is superstition as such very different from

1

religion, but even a belief in God as the highest of
beings need not be a religious belief. If La Place
had needed what he called " that hypothesis," the
Deity, when introduced into his celestial mechanics,
would have been but a mathematical symbol, or a
formula like Taylor's theorem, — no true object of
religious veneration. On the other hand, Spinoza's
impersonal Substance, or the Nirvâna of the Bud-
dhists, or any one of many like notions, may have,
either as doctrines about the world or as ideals of
human conduct, immense religious value. Very
much that we associate with religion is therefore
non-essential to religion. Yet religion is something
unique in human belief and emotion, and must not
be dissolved into any lower or more commonplace
elements. What then is religion ?

I.

So much at all events seems sure about religion.
It has to do with action. It is impossible without
some appearance of moral purpose. A totally immoral religion may exist ; but it is like a totally un-
seaworthy ship at sea, or like a rotten bank, or like
a wild-cat mine. It deceives its followers. It pretends to guide them into morality of some sort. If
it is blind or wicked, not its error makes it religious,
but the faith of its followers in its worth. A religion may teach the men of one tribe to torture and
kill men of another tribe. But even such a religion
would pretend to teach right conduct. Religion,
however, gives us more than a moral code. A moral

code alone, with its " Thou shalt," would be no more
religious than is the civil code. A religion adds something to the moral code. And what it adds is, first,
enthusiasm. Somehow it makes the faithful regard
the moral law with devotion, reverence, love. By
history, by parable, by myth, by ceremony, by song,
by whatever means you will, the religion gives to the
mere code life and warmth. A religion not only
commands the faithful, but gives them something
that they are glad to live for, and if need be to die
for.

But not yet have we mentioned the element of religion that makes it especially interesting to a student of theoretical philosophy. So far as we have
gone, ethical philosophy would criticise the codes of
various religions, while theoretical philosophy would
have no part in the work. But, in fact, religion always adds another element. Not only does religion
teach devotion to a moral code, but the means that
it uses to this end include a more or less complete
theory of things. Religion says not merely *do and
feel*, but also *believe*. A religion tells us about the
things that it declares to exist, and most especially it
tells us about their relations to the moral code and
to the religious feeling. There may be a religion
without a supernatural, but there cannot be a religion without a theoretical element, without a statement of some supposed matter of fact, as part of
the religious doctrine.

These three elements, then, go to constitute any
religion. A religion must teach some moral code,
must in some way inspire a strong feeling of devo-

tion to that code, and in so doing must show something in the nature of things that answers to the code or that serves to reinforce the feeling. A religion is therefore practical, emotional, and theoretical; it teaches us to do, to feel, and to believe, and it teaches the belief as a means to its teaching of the action and of the feeling.

II.

We may now see how philosophy is related to religion. Philosophy is not directly concerned with feeling, but both action and belief are direct objects of philosophical criticism. And on the other hand, in so far as philosophy suggests general rules for conduct, or discusses the theories about the world, philosophy must have a religious aspect. Religion invites the scrutiny of philosophy, and philosophy may not neglect the problems of religion. Kant's fundamental problems: *What do I know?* and *What ought I to do?* are of religious interest no less than of philosophic interest. They ask how the highest thought of man stands related to his highest needs, and what in things answers to our best ideals. Surely no one ought to fear such questions, nor ought any philosophic student to hesitate to suggest in answer to them whatever after due reflection he honestly can suggest, poor and tentative though it may be. In fact there is no defense for one as sincere thinker if, undertaking to pay attention to philosophy as such, he willfully or thoughtlessly neglects such problems on the ground that he has no time for them. Surely he has time to be not merely a student of philosophy, but also a man, and these things are among the essentials of humanity, which the non-philosophic treat in their way, and which philosophic students must treat in theirs.

When, however, we say that the thinker must study and revere these questions, we must not fancy that because of their importance he may prejudge them. Assumptions, postulates, *a priori* demands, these indeed are in all thinking, and no thinker is without such. But prejudice, *i. e.* foregone conclusions in questionable matters, deliberate unwillingness to let the light shine upon our beliefs, all this is foreign to true thought. Thinking is for us just the clarifying of our minds, and because clearness is necessary to the unity of thought, necessary to lessen the strife of sects and the bitterness of doubt, necessary to save our minds from hopeless, everlasting wandering, therefore to resist the clarifying process, even while we undertake it, is to sin against what is best in us, and is also to sin against humanity. Deliberately insincere, dishonest thinking is downright blasphemy. And so, if we take any interest in these things, our duty is plain. Here are questions of tremendous importance to us and to the world. We are sluggards or cowards if, pretending to be philosophic students and genuine seekers of truth, we do not attempt to do something with these questions. We are worse than cowards if, attempting to consider them, we do so otherwise than reverently, fearlessly, and honestly.

III.

The religious thought of our time has reached a position that arouses the anxiety of all serious thinkers, and the interest of many who are not serious. We are not content with what we learned from our fathers; we want to correct their dogmas, to prove what they held fast without proof, to work out our own salvation by our own efforts. But we know not yet what form our coming faith will take. We are not yet agreed even about the kind of question that we shall put to ourselves when we begin any specific religious inquiry. People suggest very various facts or aspects of facts in the world as having a religious value. The variety of the suggestions shows the vagueness of the questions that people have in mind when they talk of religion. One man wants to worship Natural Law, or even Nature in general. Another finds Humanity to be his ideal object of religious veneration. Yet another gravely insists that the Unknowable satisfies his religious longings. Now it is something to be plain in expressing a question, even if you cannot give an answer. We shall do something if we only find out what it is that we ought to seek. And the foregoing considerations may help us in this way, even if what follows should be wholly ineffective. For we have tried to give a definition that shall express, not merely what a Buddhist or a Catholic or a Comtist or an Hegelian means by his religion, but what all men everywhere mean by religion. They all want religion to define for them their duty, to give them the heart to do it, and to point out to them such things in the real world as shall help them to be steadfast in their devotion to duty. When people pray that they may be made happy, they still desire to learn what they are to do in order to become happy. When saints of any creed look up to their God as their only good, they are seeking for guidance in the right way. The savages of whom we hear so much nowadays have indeed low forms of religion, but these religions of theirs still require them to do something, and tell them why it is worth while to do this, and make them more or less enthusiastic in doing it. Among ourselves, the poor and the lonely, the desolate and the afflicted, when they demand religious comfort, want something that shall tell them what to do with life, and how to take up once more the burdens of their broken existence. And the religious philosophers must submit to the same test that humanity everywhere proposes to its religions. If one tries to regulate our diet by his theories, he must have the one object, whatever his theory, since he wants to tell us what is healthful for us. If he tells us to eat nothing but snow, that is his fault. The true object of the theory of diet remains the same. And so if men have expressed all sorts of one-sided, disheartening, inadequate views of religion, that does not make the object of religious theory less catholic, less comprehensive, less definitely human. A man who propounds a religious system must have a moral code, an emotional life, and some theory of things to offer us. With less we cannot be content. He need not, indeed, know or pretend to know very much about our wonderful world, but he must know something, and that something must be of definite value.

To state the whole otherwise. Purely theoretic philosophy tries to find out what it can about the real world. When it makes this effort, it has to be perfectly indifferent to consequences. It may not shudder or murmur if it comes upon unspeakably dreadful truths. If it finds nothing in the world but evil, it must still accept the truth, and must calmly state it without praise and without condemnation. Theoretic philosophy knows no passion save the passion for truth, has no fear save the fear of error, cherishes no hope save the hope of theoretic success. But religious philosophy has other objects in addition to these. Religious philosophy is indeed neither the foe nor the mistress of theoretic philosophy. Religious philosophy dare not be in opposition to the truths that theory may have established. But over and above these truths it seeks something else. It seeks to know their value. It comes to the world with other interests, in addition to the purely theoretic ones. It wants to know what in the world is worthy of worship as the good. It seeks not merely the truth, but the inspiring truth. It defines for itself goodness, moral worth, and then it asks, *What in this world is worth anything?* Its demands in this regard are boundless. It will be content only with the best it can find. Having formulated for itself its ideal of worth, it asks at the outset: *Is there then, anywhere in the universe, any real thing of Infinite Worth?* If this cannot be found, then

and then only will religious philosophy be content
with less. Then it will still ask : *What in this world
is worth most?* It cannot make realities, but it is
determined to judge them. It cannot be content
with blind faith, and demands the actual truth as
much as theoretic philosophy demands it ; but religious philosophy treats this truth only as the material
for its ideal judgments. It seeks the ideal among
the realities.

Upon such a quest as this, we ask the reader to accompany us in the following pages. We have not
space to be exhaustive, nor in fact to offer much
more than suggestions ; but we want the suggestions
to be explicit, and we hope that they may stimulate
some reader, and may perhaps help him in complet-
ing his own trains of thought.

IV.

People come to such questions as these with certain prejudices about the method and spirit of inquiry ; and all their work may be hampered by these
prejudices. Let us say yet a little more of what we
think as to this matter. There are two extremes to
fear in religious philosophy : indifference that arises
from a dogmatic disposition to deny, and timidity
that arises from an excessive show of reverence for
the objects of religious faith. Both of these extreme
moods have their defective methods in dealing with
religious philosophy. The over-skeptical man looks
with impatience on all lengthy discussions of these
topics. There can be nothing in it all, he says:

nothing but what Hume, in an eloquent passage, called sophistry and delusion. Why spend time to puzzle over these insoluble mysteries? Hence his method is: swift work, clear statement of known difficulties, keen ridicule of hasty assumptions, and then a burning of the old deserted Moscow of theology, and a bewildering flight into the inaccessible wintry wastes, where no army of religious philosophers shall follow him. Now for our part we want to be as skeptical as anybody; and we personally always admire the freedom of motion that pure skepticism gives. Our trouble with it all, however, is that, after we have enjoyed the freedom and the frosty air of pure philosophic skepticism for a while, we find ourselves unexpectedly in the midst of philosophic truth that needs closer examination. The short and easy agnostic method is not enough. You must supplement skepticism by philosophy; and when you do so, you find yourself forced to accept, not indeed the old theology of your childhood, but something that satisfies, oddly enough, certain religious longings, that, as skeptic, you had carefully tried to forget. Then you find yourself with what you may have to call a religious doctrine; and then you may have to state it as we are here going to do, not in an easy or fascinating way, such as the pure skeptic can so well follow, but at all events with some approach to a serious and sustained effort to consider hard questions from many sides. The skeptical method is not only a good, but also a necessary beginning of religious philosophy. But we are bound to go deeper than mere superficial agnosticism. If, however, any reader is already sure that we cannot go deeper, and that modern popular agnosticism has exhausted all that can be said on religious questions, then we bid him an immediate and joyous farewell. If we had not something to say in this book that seems to us both foreign to the popular modern agnostic range of discussion, and deeper than the insight of popular modern skepticism, we should say nothing. The undertaking of this book is not to wrangle in the old way over the well-known ordinary debates of to-day, but to turn the flank of the common popular thought on these topics altogether, by going back to a type of philosophic investigation, that is nowadays familiar indeed to a certain school of specialists, but forgotten by the general public. In this type of investigation, we have furthermore something to offer that seems to us no mere repetition of the views of other thinkers, but an effort to make at least one little step in advance of the thoughts that the great masters of philosophy have given to us. Yet we know indeed that the range of any useful independent thought in philosophy must be, in case of any one individual, very narrow.

The other mood and its method remain. It is the mood of excessive reverence. It wastes capital letters on all the pronouns and adjectives that have to do with the objects of religious faith; but it fears to do these objects the honor to get clear ideas about them. Now we respect this mood when it appears in men who do well their life-work, who need their religious faith for their work, and who do not feel any calling as truth-seekers. No man has any business

to set up his vocation as the highest one; and the
man for whom truth is useful in his actual life-work
as an inspiration, revealed to him only in feeling, is
welcome to his feelings, is worthy of all regard from
those whose vocation is philosophy, and shall not be
tormented by our speculations. He is careful and
troubled about many things; the world needs him,
and philosophy does not. We only lay claim to our
own rights, and do not want to interfere with his.
Our right to clear thought, we must insist upon.
For looked at philosophically, and apart from the necessary limitations of the hard worker, all this dumb
reverence, this vague use of vague names, has its serious dangers. You are reverent, we may say to the
man who regards philosophic criticism as a dangerous
trifling with stupendous truths; you are reverent,
but what do you reverence? Have a care lest what
you reverence shall turn out to be your own vague
and confused notions, and not the real divine Truth
at all. Take heed lest your object of worship be only
your own little pet infinite, that is sublime to you
mainly because it is yours, and that is in truth about
as divine and infinite as your hat. For this is the
danger that besets these vague and lofty sentiments.
Unreflected upon, uncriticised, dumbly experienced,
dumbly dreaded, these, your religious objects, may
become mere feelings, mere visceral sensations of
yours, that you have on Sunday mornings, or when
you pray. Of course, if you are a worker, you
may actually realize these vague ideas, in so far as
they inspire you to work. If they do, they shall be
judged by their fruits. Otherwise, do not trust too

confidently their religious value. You, individually regarded, are but a mass of thought and feeling. What is only yours and in you, is not divine at all. Unless you lift it up into the light of thought and examine it often, how do you know into what your cherished religious ideal may not have rotted in the darkness of your emotions? Once in a while, there does come to a man some terrible revelation of himself in a great sorrow. Then in the tumult of anguish he looks for his religious faith to clothe his nakedness against the tempest; and he finds perhaps some moth-eaten old garment that profits him nothing, so that his soul miserably perishes in the frost of doubt. Such a man has expected God to come to his help in every time of need; but the only god he has actually and consciously had, has been his own little contemptible, private notion and dim feeling of a god, which he has never dared fairly to look at. Any respectable wooden idol would have done him better service; for then a man could know where and what his idol is. Such is only too apt to be the real state of the man who regards it as profanity to think clearly and sensibly on religious topics.

We claim, then, the right to criticise as fearlessly, as thoroughly, and as skeptically as may be, the foundations of conduct and faith. For what we criticise are, at the outset, our own notions, which we want to have conform to the truth, if so be that there is any truth. As for doubt on religious questions that is for a truth-seeker not only a privilege but a duty; and, as we shall experience all through this study, doubt has a curious and very valuable place in philosophy. Philosophic truth, as such, comes to us first under the form of doubt; and we never can be very near it in our search unless, for a longer or shorter time, we have come to despair of it altogether. First, then, the despair of a thorough-going doubt, and then the discovery that this doubt contains in its bosom the truth that we are sworn to discover, however we can, — this is the typical philosophic experience. May the memory of this suggestion support the failing patience of the kindly disposed reader through some of the longer and more wearisome stretches of dry skeptical analysis over which we must try to journey together. Whatever may be the truth, it must lie beyond those deserts.

BOOK I.

THE SEARCH FOR A MORAL IDEAL.

CHAPTER II.

THE GENERAL ETHICAL PROBLEM.

"Certain spirits, by permission, ascended from hell, and said to me, 'You have written a great deal from the Lord, write something also from us.' I replied, 'What shall I write?' They said, 'Write that every spirit, whether he be good or evil, is in his own delight, — the good in the delight of his good, and the evil in the delight of his evil.' I asked them, 'What may your delight be?' They said that it was the delight of committing adultery, stealing, defrauding, and lying. . . . I said, 'Then you are like the unclean beasts.' . . . They answered, 'If we are, we are.' " — SWEDENBORG, *Divine Providence*.

"There's nothing, either good or bad, but thinking makes it so." — *Hamlet*.

WITH which of the two considerations mentioned in our introduction shall a religious philosophy begin? Of its two chief considerations, the moral code, and the relation of this code to reality, which is the one that properly stands first in order? We have already indicated our opinion. The philosophy of religion is distinguished from theoretic philosophy precisely by its relation to an ideal. If possible, therefore, it should early be clear as to what ideal it has. The ideal ought, if possible, to be studied first, since it is this ideal that is to give character to our whole quest among the realities. And so the first part of religious philosophy is properly the discussion of ethical problems.

2

I.

The theoretic philosopher might interpose just here, and insist that as one can be moral only in a real world, the philosopher has a theoretical right and duty to point out, first of all, wherein consists the reality of the world and whereon is based our assurance of this reality. Yet this strictly logical order we must decline, in the present discussion, to follow. Our interest is, first of all, with the ideal in its relation to human life. So much of the world of commonplace reality as we have to assume in any and every discussion of the ideal, we accept in this first book wholly without theoretical question. For such questions, in their relation to religious philosophy, the proper place will come later. But at the outset we will suppose a moral agent in the presence of this concrete world of human life in which we all believe ourselves to exist. Beyond the bright circle of these commonplace human relations, all shall for the present remain dark to this moral agent. His origin, his destiny, his whole relation to nature and to God, if there be a God, he shall not at the outset know. But he shall be conceived as knowing that he is alive in the midst of a multitude of living fellows. With them he is to have and to define and to develop certain moral relations. For his life, or for human life in general, he is to form his ideal. Then later, after forming and striving to realize this ideal of his, he is to come to the real physical world, and to ask of it how it stands related to these, his moral needs. In the answer to this question he is to find, if at all, the completion of his religious philosophy. When he comes to this second stage, which our second book is to treat, he may find himself obliged to analyze afresh and skeptically the *naïve* theoretic notions that he has possessed concerning nature, and so even concerning his own fellow-men. But for his analysis itself he will have a fresher courage, because he will have filled himself with the love of an ideal, whose realization he will be hoping somehow to find all through all the tedious wanderings of his theoretic study. If the order of his whole thought is thus not the order of the truth itself, still his little inconsequence in beginning his religious philosophy with assumptions that he proves only after he has gone some distance in his investigation, may be a useful concession both to his own human weakness and to the needs of his practical nature.

With the search for the ideal, then, we begin, expressly assuming, in this part of the first book, without proof, as much of the world of daily life as may be necessary to a study of the moral law in its application to this daily life. Yet, with this explanation, we are only at the beginning of the troubles that arise in examining the relation between the basis of ethics and the real world. These troubles form a great part of the obscurity of moral doctrine.

II.

In treating of ethical doctrine, it is common to avoid by all sorts of devices the main and most difficult problem of all. Men like to fill half a volume

with a description of the "moral sentiments," or
with a panegyric of the "moral principle in man," or
in these days especially, with a great deal of talk
about savages and about the "evolution of the moral
sense." Having occupied so many pages in enter-
taining digressions, when they come, if they ever do
come, to the central problem, namely, the nature of
moral distinctions considered purely as such, such
writers have no time to do more than to appeal to
the common sense of readers, and then to pass on to
consequences. It seldom occurs to them that a description of the "moral faculties" in this man or in
that, or a history of moral and immoral notions and
practices as they have come up among men in the
order of evolution, is no more a "moral philosophy,"
in the proper sense, than is a description of the coin-
age or of the products of any country or of the world
a true explanation of the difference between commercial solvency and insolvency.

We for our part shall be obliged, however, by our
limited space, to aim forthwith at the heart of the
problem of a philosophical ethic. What is the real
nature of this distinction between right and wrong?
What truth is there in this distinction? Is this
truth relative to particular conditions, or independent thereof? What ideal of life results? These
things we want to know; and we do not want to
spend our time more than we shall be obliged to do
in irrelevant descriptions of the mental states of this
or that man. All mental states now interest us only
in so far as we first see what logical bearing they
may have upon our problem. We shall have to de-

scribe a good deal, but that work will have only its proper subordinate place.

As for the main problem itself, we can best bring its nature home to ourselves by considering forthwith some aspects of an old and often neglected question, namely, the very question before referred to about the proper relation of one's moral ideal to the reality that he may have recognized.

We are to form a moral ideal apart, as we have said, from any theory of the physical universe outside of man. But is this practicable? Is not every moral theory dependent in truth on a theory of things? Is it possible for us to make for ourselves our ideal, and only afterwards to go to the real world and to see if our ideal is realized? Must not rather our ideal be founded, in the very nature of the case, on what we know, or think we know, about the world? Is not then this whole undertaking of ours a blunder? Is a rational moral distinction possible save through a knowledge of the facts about the world? Can the ideal say to the world: " I demand that thou shouldst be like me?" Must not the ideal rather humbly say: " Thus and thus it is in truth, and therefore I am what I am?"

The nature of moral ideals and distinctions is plainly involved just here. We must look closely at these questions; for to answer them aright is to answer the fundamental questions of all ethical philosophy.

To understand then more justly the nature of this difficulty, let us consider more closely the two possible answers to the foregoing questions. Let us call

a man who insists in spite of all upon going to the
real world, to find there in some way the sole basis
for his ideal distinctions between good and evil, an
ethical realist. Let us on the other hand call him
who would somehow demonstrate if he could some
ideal as the true and only moral ideal, without in any
wise making it depend upon physical reality, a moral
idealist. Let us then let the two parties discuss, in
their opposing ways, the question at issue. Let us
hear their views briefly stated and argued. First the
view of the extreme ethical realists : " Go to real
ity," they say, " and to whatever reality you need to
consider. Thence derive your notion of duty. Morality must not be built in the air, but on a solid
foundation of natural fact. Your moral doctrine
may have to depend upon all that you can find out
about the universe." — On the other hand we have
the idealistic doctrine : " Morality," say the supporters of this view, " is for the first an ideal. From
reality one learns the relations that are to be judged
by the ideal, but cannot by any searching find the
ideal itself. From reality one can learn the means;
the End of action is an Ideal, independent of all reality save the bare existence of our choice of this End.
As Prometheus defied Zeus, so the moral consciousness could and must defy the forces of nature in case
they made the ideal forever hopeless. If the good
be unattainable, that makes it no less the good. If
the existent world were the worst world imaginable,
it would not be justified by the mere fact that it was
the real world. Ideals must be realized in so far as
we can realize them, but what can be realized need

not therefore turn out to be the ideal. The judgments : *This is*, and, *This is good*, are once for all
different; and they have to be reached by widely different methods of investigation." — Such are the two
opposing views. We cannot yet repeat in detail the
arguments for each, but we can suggest a few of
them.

" See," says the supporter of the first view, " how
absurd it is to evolve moral theories out of one's
inner consciousness. What happens to such theories?
Either nature favors them, and then they survive in
the struggle for life, or they are unequal to the tasks
of the real world, and then their supporters go mad,
or die. But in the first case they are merely such
theories as could have been much better reached by
a process, not of guessing at truth, but of studying nature's laws. In the second case, the result is
enough for common sense people. The moral theory
that is destined to die out for want of supporters can
hardly triumph over more useful opinions. If we
want a moral theory, we must therefore consider what
kind of action, what rule of life, wins in the battle
of existence, and tends most to outlive its rivals.
That rule is the one destined to become universal."

The maintainers of the second view are ready with
their answer. " What sort of morality is this?" they
say. " Is this the morality of the martyrs? Is this
an ideal that can satisfy us? The preservation of
truly valuable life may indeed be an end in itself,
and therefore an action that tends, on the whole, to
destroy rather than to save such life may be bad from
any point of view ; but the moral thinker is not, on

that account, bound to choose a code that will make its believers survive. The believers are not all who are affected by obedience to the code, and it may be the believer's place to be sacrificed, either because his life is worth less than his ideal, or because the unbelievers may somehow be bettered through his death. And, in general, what would be the consequence of the consistent following out of the principle that the true goal is conformity to reality? Assume that, for instance, a man in society is to regulate his actions solely according to the demands that society as a real power makes upon him, in view of his place in the social organism, and that morality thus expresses simply the requirements that the individual must meet if he is to remain a successful member of this social organism. Then, to get your moral code, you are to examine the facts of social life. You are to see, for example, what each man must nowadays do if he is to be tolerable to his fellows. You will find something of this sort: It will not do for him to kill his fellows, or to steal from them, or openly to insult them. It will be unprofitable for him to be caught in cheating them, or in lying to them. He will do well to help them as far as his means allow, and so to get a reputation for kind-heartedness and public spirit, as well as for strict integrity. For such, at least in our society, are some of the requisite or useful kinds of adjustment to our environment. On these is founded our moral code, if it is to be founded on reality alone.

" But these requirements are not equally good in all societies. Once a power to kill certain kinds of people was a necessary condition to happy social life. A reputation for fearlessness, for prowess, for military skill, for a certain kind of cunning, for perfect willingness to take your weaker enemy's property ; all this was a part of the necessary adjustment to one's environment. Was all this then for that society true morality? If morality were the body of rules governing successful adjustment to the social environment, then morality would be relative to the environment, and would vary with it. So even now such rules vary with one's social position. Ministers of religion are considered to be best adjusted to the environment if they are outwardly meek, save when defending their creeds against heretics. But politicians are best adjusted when they are aggressive and merciless. A poet or artist is best adjusted if he has a reputation for very ideal and impersonal aims, and he can then even afford to leave his debts unpaid ; but a business man must be very concrete in behavior, severely definite in his dealings with his fellows. And so runs the world away. Find your place, and farm it cleverly, for that is the whole duty of man.

" Such would be," say our idealists, " the consequences of looking simply to reality for a definition of the moral code. There would no longer be a difference between morality and cleverness. Practical skill in the art of living is what survives in this world ; and if it is survival, or tendency to survival, that distinguishes a true from a false moral code, then universal cleverness as a moral code would on the whole tend to survive, with its adherents."

But a realistic opponent is not t
" Such caricatures," he insists, " do not
sent my doctrine." He, too, has an id
wholly dependent on reality. What b
conformity to reality as the foundation
code is properly expressed by the more
advocates of the doctrine of evolution —
ment to one's real surroundings is alway
" one very important element in mor
there are higher and lower forms of
Cannibals, or conquerors, or bad politici
sufficiently adjusted to their environmen
mentarily successful; but true philanth
truly great statesmen are better than the
statesmen and philanthropists have a hig
adjustment than have the others, and are
in the scale of progress. There is in t
constant evolution of higher out of lowe
life. This applies also to society. And
of evolution depends the true morality.
morality is that form of adjustment of
man to his environment towards which so
progress forever tends." How then shall
our moral code? " Why, once more," say
lutionist, " by the facts. Do not make
first and then judge the world. You wi
to accept the universe even if you did not
But examine the world to see in what way
ing. Then conform yourself to that tend
to hasten the realization of the coming ide
tion. Progress does not depend on you, bu
do well to assist progress. So, by exper

not therefore turn out to be the ideal. The judgments : *This is*, and, *This is good*, are once for all
different; and they have to be reached by widely different methods of investigation." — Such are the two
opposing views. We cannot yet repeat in detail the
arguments for each, but we can suggest a few of
them.

" See," says the supporter of the first view, " how
absurd it is to evolve moral theories out of one's
inner consciousness. What happens to such theories?
Either nature favors them, and then they survive in
the struggle for life, or they are unequal to the tasks
of the real world, and then their supporters go mad,
or die. But in the first case they are merely such
theories as could have been much better reached by
a process, not of guessing at truth, but of studying nature's laws. In the second case, the result is
enough for common sense people. The moral theory
that is destined to die out for want of supporters can
hardly triumph over more useful opinions. If we
want a moral theory, we must therefore consider what
kind of action, what rule of life, wins in the battle
of existence, and tends most to outlive its rivals.
That rule is the one destined to become universal."

The maintainers of the second view are ready with
their answer. " What sort of morality is this?" they
say. " Is this the morality of the martyrs? Is this
an ideal that can satisfy us? The preservation of
truly valuable life may indeed be an end in itself,
and therefore an action that tends, on the whole, to
destroy rather than to save such life may be bad from
any point of view ; but the moral thinker is not, on

that account, bound to choose a code that will make
its believers survive. The believers are not all who
are affected by obedience to the code, and it may be
the believer's place to be sacrificed, either because
his life is worth less than his ideal, or because the
unbelievers may somehow be bettered through his
death. And, in general, what would be the consequence of the consistent following out of the principle that the true goal is conformity to reality?
Assume that, for instance, a man in society is to regulate his actions solely according to the demands
that society as a real power makes upon him, in view
of his place in the social organism, and that morality
thus expresses simply the requirements that the individual must meet if he is to remain a successful
member of this social organism. Then, to get your
moral code, you are to examine the facts of social
life. You are to see, for example, what each man
must nowadays do if he is to be tolerable to his
fellows. You will find something of this sort: It
will not do for him to kill his fellows, or to steal
from them, or openly to insult them. It will be unprofitable for him to be caught in cheating them, or
in lying to them. He will do well to help them as
far as his means allow, and so to get a reputation
for kind-heartedness and public spirit, as well as for
strict integrity. For such, at least in our society,
are some of the requisite or useful kinds of adjustment to our environment. On these is founded our
moral code, if it is to be founded on reality alone.

"But these requirements are not equally good in
all societies. Once a power to kill certain kinds of

people was a necessary condition to happy social life. A reputation for fearlessness, for prowess, for military skill, for a certain kind of cunning, for perfect willingness to take your weaker enemy's property; all this was a part of the necessary adjustment to one's environment. Was all this then for that society true morality? If morality were the body of rules governing successful adjustment to the social environment, then morality would be relative to the environment, and would vary with it. So even now such rules vary with one's social position. Ministers of religion are considered to be best adjusted to the environment if they are outwardly meek, save when defending their creeds against heretics. But politicians are best adjusted when they are aggressive and merciless. A poet or artist is best adjusted if he has a reputation for very ideal and impersonal aims, and he can then even afford to leave his debts unpaid; but a business man must be very concrete in behavior, severely definite in his dealings with his fellows. And so runs the world away. Find your place, and farm it cleverly, for that is the whole duty of man.

"Such would be," say our idealists, "the consequences of looking simply to reality for a definition of the moral code. There would no longer be a difference between morality and cleverness. Practical skill in the art of living is what survives in this world; and if it is survival, or tendency to survival, that distinguishes a true from a false moral code, then universal cleverness as a moral code would on the whole tend to survive, with its adherents."

But a realistic opponent is not thus silenced. "Such caricatures," he insists, "do not fairly represent my doctrine." He, too, has an ideal but it is wholly dependent on reality. What he means by conformity to reality as the foundation of a moral code is properly expressed by the more thoughtful advocates of the doctrine of evolution. "Adjustment to one's real surroundings is always," they say, "one very important element in morality. But there are higher and lower forms of adjustment. Cannibals, or conquerors, or bad politicians, may be sufficiently adjusted to their environment to be momentarily successful; but true philanthropists and truly great statesmen are better than they, since the statesmen and philanthropists have a higher form of adjustment than have the others, and are thus higher in the scale of progress. There is in the world a constant evolution of higher out of lower forms of life. This applies also to society. And on this fact of evolution depends the true morality. The ideal morality is that form of adjustment of the social man to his environment towards which society in its progress forever tends." How then shall we define our moral code? "Why, once more," says the evolutionist, "by the facts. Do not make your code first and then judge the world. You will do well to accept the universe even if you did not make it. But examine the world to see in what way it is tending. Then conform yourself to that tendency; try to hasten the realization of the coming ideal perfection. Progress does not depend on you, but you will do well to assist progress. So, by experience, we are to find the direction in which society is moving, we are to discover the goal toward which this movement tends, and this object of life, once formulated, is to give us our moral code."

Again, however, the idealist objects. This, he admits, is a view higher, no doubt, than the preceding; but is it a clear and consistent view? Will it bear criticism? In one respect, as appears to him, it fails badly. However certain and valuable the facts about evolution may be, the theory that founds morality wholly upon these facts of evolution is defective, because it confuses the notion of evolution with the notion of progress, the conception of growth in complexity and definiteness with the conception of growth in moral worth. The two ideas are not necessarily identical. Yet their identity is assumed in this theory. How does it follow that the state toward which a physical progress, namely, evolution, tends, must be the state that is to meet with moral approval? This is not to be proved unless you have already done the very thing that the doctrine of evolution wishes to teach you to do, that is, unless you have already formed a moral code, and that independently of what you know of the facts of natural evolution. Why is the last state in an evolution better than the former states? Surely not because it is the last stage, surely not because it is physically more complex, more definite, or even more permanent; but solely because it corresponds to some ideal that we independently form. Why should my ideal necessarily correspond with reality? Why should what I approve turn out to be that which exists? And why, if any correspondence is to exist, should that particular bit of reality that comes at the end of a physical process called evolution be just the one bit that is to answer my ideal demands? It will be very satisfactory if such correspondence between the real and the ideal is found to result; but how can I know beforehand that it must result?

Evolution and progress: what do the terms respectively mean? Evolution, we learn, is an increase in the complexity, definiteness, individuality and organic connection of phenomena. But progress is any series of changes that meets with the constantly increasing approval of somebody. The growth of a tree or of a thistle is an evolution. The climbing of a hill for some purpose may throughout be a progress. Evolution may or may not meet with the approval of anybody; and a pessimist might fully accept some proposed law of evolution. But unless there is some approval from some source, we have no progress. How thoughtless then it is, our idealist insists, to confound such different notions. But is a case of evolution ever a process of degeneration? Certainly. You want to eat asparagus before it is full grown. Hence every moment of its evolution after a certain point is for you distinctly a degeneration. You want the potatoes in your cellar to keep fresh. If they sprout, a process of evolution has begun, but every moment of it is for you the reverse of progress. The egg that begins to incubate is in full course of evolution; but what if it is wanted for market? Might not the evolution of the whole world conceivably be for the moral consciousness what such cases of evolution are for the purposes of ordinary life?

"But," the realist may say, "in fact the world does grow better. The course of evolution is on the whole a progress." "Be it so," the idealist answers, "but how can we know it? Only by first setting up our moral ideal, and then comparing the facts with this ideal. If we know what we mean by better, we can judge whether the world is growing better. But we may not pretend to determine what is better by simply observing how the world grows. Growth and improvement are not identical ideas. One may grow while growing ever worse."

And thus a moral code, according to our idealist, does not, as a code, depend on physical facts; tells us nothing of what does exist, but tells us solely what ought to exist. If the ideal either does exist, or some day will exist, so much the better; but through all the changes of fate the terrible *ought* remains, and judges fearlessly the world, whether it be good or whether it be evil. But here the realist, to whom the moral code that is not built on natural fact is just a dream, interposes what shall just here be his final objection. "Be it so," he says, "judge after your heart's desire; but remember this, that some other idealist beside you will be judging the world in his own way, after what will seem to you the folly of his heart, and his judgment and yours will differ, as the dreams of any two dreamers must differ. Did Plato's ideal agree with Paul's? or did Byron judge the world after the same fashion as Wordsworth? Even so in the present day the

ideals war their wars, shadowy struggles, such as one
would expect the tedious ghosts of Ossian's heroes
to carry on in their cloudy cars; but reality will
never be one whit the wiser for all such deeds.
For when you forsake the real world you have no
basis left for your ideals but individual caprice,
and every idealist will be his own measure of all
things, and an elastic measure at that."

To this, how can the idealist answer? Only, if at
all, by the fact of his success in establishing such a
criterion as shall be independent of his own caprice,
without being realistic.

We have let the contending doctrines fight some
part of their old battles over again. How shall we
decide between them? Alas! the decision is the
whole labor of founding a moral doctrine. We have
not yet seen deeply enough into their opposition.
They may both be one-sided. The truth may lie in
the middle. But as yet we have no right to dogmatize. This capriciousness in the choice of ideals
seems a grave defect in a moral system; we cannot
submit to the objection that our boasted ideal is just
our whim. Yet how shall we escape this? Equally
unsatisfactory it seems to say: "I believe in such
and such ideal solely because I see it realized."
That is too much like saying, "Might is right."
And thus we should come to an equal capriciousness
on this side; for if might makes right, then another
and opposing might, if triumphant, would make another and opposing right. And in this wise there
would be no true distinction at all between right and
wrong. There seems in fact so far only an acciden-

tal distinction. This ideal or that is the highest because somebody chances to choose it for his, or because the physical world chances to realize it. This
is a perfectly empty distinction.

But difficulties must not discourage us so early in
the day. The world has talked of these matters before. Let us turn to the history of some of the speculations about the ideal. They may suggest something to us.

CHAPTER III.

THE WARFARE OF THE MORAL IDEALS.

Sure, if I find the Holy Grail itself,
It too will fade, and crumble into dust.
TENNYSON, *Holy Grail.*

The spirits I have raised abandon me,
The spells which I have studied baffle me —
The remedy I recked of tortured me.
I lean no more on superhuman aid.
BYRON, *Manfred.*

WE are yet without an ideal, and as we come
nearer to our task, its difficulties increase. We have
described above the remarkable position in which
every moral idealist finds himself. He says that
his moral doctrine is to be more than a mere bit of
natural history. He wants to find out what ought
to be, even if that which ought to be is not. Yet when
some man says to him: "Thy ideal is thus but thy
personal caprice, thy private way of looking at
things," he does not want to assent. He wants to
reply: "My ideal is the true one. No other rational
ideal is possible." Yet to do this he seems to need
again some external support in reality. He seems to
require some authority based upon facts. He must
somewhere find his ideal in the world of truth, external to his own private consciousness. He must
be able to say: "Lo, here is the ideal!" He must

be able to show it to us, so that we shall see it to be more than his whim. But thus he is in danger of forsaking his idealism. His position so far has therefore seemed to us an uncertain one. We have felt the force of his needs; but we have not been able to see as yet just how they are to be satisfied. The satisfaction of them would in fact be a complete ethical doctrine. And the foundation of such a doctrine is just what we here are seeking.

It is incumbent upon us yet further to show how the search for a moral ideal has in the past been hindered by the weight of this doubt about the exact relation of the real and the ideal. The controversy that the last chapter considered is a controversy endlessly repeated in the history of moral doctrines. Everywhere we find a moral ideal maintained by some devoted idealist as the one perfectly obvious aim for human life. Everywhere there stands over against this ideal some critic who says: "The choice of this aim for life is an accident. I reject this boastful ideal. For where in reality is found the firm basis of fact on which the ideal is founded?" Then possibly the idealist, relaxing the rigor of his idealism, points out in the external world some real or mythical support for his ideal. And thereupon either his critics reject the creed about the external world thus offered to them, or they deny the moral force of the supposed realities, or, again, themselves assuming an idealistic attitude, they reproach the idealist with his unworthy desertion of his own high faith, in that he has yielded to realistic demands, and has founded the lofty *Ought* on the paltry *Is*. And thus the controversy continues.   Often it seems to us that the struggle must be endless.   At all events we must here look at some of its phases.

I.

In the days of the Sophists, Greek thought had reached its first great era of ethical skepticism.   This skepticism was directed against the ideals of popular morality.   " They are not self-evident and necessary ideals," said in substance the Sophists.   " They are conventions.   They are private judgments."   The popular ideals were of course popularly defended against such assaults by the use of the national religion.   " The gods made these distinctions," it is replied.   " The gods are able to enforce them ; therefore, fear the gods."

Skepticism had two answers to this defense.   The one answer was simple : " Who knows whether there are any gods, or what the gods, if they exist, may choose to do "   The other answer was more subtle, because it really expressed in skeptical guise a new form of moral idealism.   It is best preserved to us in a fine passage in the second book of Plato's Republic.   Here the young men, Glaucon and Adeimantos, confess that certain sophistic objections to the reality of moral distinctions are deeply puzzling to themselves.   They ask Socrates to discuss the matter in some such fashion as to remove these doubts. They sum up the doubts in substance as follows : Grant that the gods are of irresistible might, and that they are disposed to enforce some moral law ;

still does that fact give any true distinction between good and evil as such? For whoever urges us to do right merely to get the favor of the gods, urges us in reality just to do what is prudent. Such doctrines make justice not desirable in itself, but desirable solely for what it brings in its train. And thus there would be no difference between good and evil as such, but only between what brings reward and what brings punishment. "Therefore, O Socrates," they in effect say, " do thou defend for us justice in itself, and show us what it is worth in itself, and how it is different from injustice. But put us not off with stories about reward and punishment." Such is a brief summary of their two speeches.

No better could either the need or the difficulty of the task of moral idealism be set forth than in these eloquent statements. How does Plato lay the ghosts that he has thus raised? How does he give an independent foundation to the ideal of justice? He surely felt how hard a problem he was undertaking. He has, in fact, attempted several answers to it. But the main answer, given in the Republic itself is insufficient, though noble. This answer is, in effect, that the properly balanced, fully and harmoniously developed soul, absorbed in the contemplation of eternal truth, cannot possibly desire injustice; that only the tyrannical soul, in which the desires have the upper hand, where nothing is secure, whose life is like the life of an ill-governed or even anarchic community, tumultuous, wretched, helpless before passion, only such a soul can desire injustice. Injustice, then, means desire for discord, it means the victory of the desires over the reason, it is inconsistent with the life of the soul that is given to blessed contemplation of the eternal ideas. For such a blessed soul its blessedness is, in the fine phrase that Spinoza long afterwards created, not the reward of virtue, but virtue itself ; so that such a soul will not do the right as a means by which it may procure the blessed contemplation of the eternal, but, being engaged in this blessed contemplation, it is thereby enabled to do right.

But to the wicked soul of the unjust man Plato seemingly has no inducement to offer in order to persuade it to become just, save the eloquent statement of the pains that accompany injustice, the picture of the warfare of desires, the proof of the wretched instability and of the possibly eternal misery in which the tyrannical soul must live. And thus Plato himself would be in so far open to the objection that his Glaucon and Adeimantos had made to all previous moralists, namely, that they never gave a reason why justice in itself was to be chosen, but always made justice desirable by reason of the rewards that result from it. For Plato's view, as for that of less ideal moralists, the unjust man should seek to become just because, until he does become just, he will be wretched. Can no other basis for the virtue of justice be found save this one ? If none can be found save this, then whenever a soul exists that prefers the tumult of desire, with average success in injustice, to the solemn peace of the contemplation of ideal good apart from the satisfaction of sensuous desires, for that soul Plato's argument will be worth-

less. Such a tyrannical man will delight to remain
a tyrant, and that will be the end of life for him.

The suggestiveness, the deeper significance of this
Platonic doctrine, we do not deny. But, as it stands,
the doctrine is not complete nor consistent. For
Plato himself has given us as the support for his
ideal, a fact, or a supposed fact, of human nature.
A moral skeptic will deal with it as Glaucon and
Adeimantos had dealt with the popular morality.
The supposed fact, they will say, may be doubted.
Perhaps some tyrant will actually feel happier than
some struggling and aspiring soul far higher up in
the heavens. But, leaving that doubt aside, there is
the other objection. The ideal justice has come to
be founded on a bare physical fact, namely, on the
constitution of the soul, which might, for all we can
see, have been different.

Important as he is in concrete ethical questions,
Aristotle does nothing of importance to remove this
fundamental difficulty, since his position as to this
matter is too near to Plato's. Still less do the Epi-
cureans, for whom in fact just this difficulty does not
exist. Plainly they declare that they merely state
physical facts. Generosity, fidelity to friends, and
other idealistic activities they indeed regard as the
part of the wise man, but the end of all is very
frankly declared to be his selfish advantage. As
Cicero expresses their view : [1] " Cum solitudo et
vita sine amicis insidiarum et metus plena sit, ratio
ipsa monet amicitias comparare, quibus partis con-

[1] *De Fin.*, I. 20, 66. Quoted in Zeller's *Philos. d. Griechen*, Th
S, Abth. I. (3d ed.) p. 460.

firmatur animus et a spe pariendarum voluptatum
sejungi non potest."

The Stoics have a new thought to offer, one that
would have been as revolutionary as Christianity itself, if they could but have grasped and taught its
full meaning. But that was for them impossible.
Their new thought, which gave foundation to their
moral ideals, was the thought of the perfect equality
of all men in the presence of the universal Reason,
to which all alike ought to conform. Everyone, they
said, ought to be rational; everyone ought to try to
extend the empire of reason. If one's neighbor is
a rational being, one can and must try to realize the
rational in him almost as much as in one's own self.
Hence one's duty to do good to men. This duty, to
be sure, commonly did not for the Stoics extend to
the point of very great practical self-sacrifice. But
at any rate they gave a new foundation for justice.
One works not only to conform one's self to the
ideal, but also to realize the ideal here in this world
in others as well as in himself. The ideal Reason
can be realized in yonder man through my efforts,
much as, through my acts, it can be realized in me.
All men are in so far brothers, members of one family, children of one Father, and so all alike objects
of moral effort for every one of their number.[1]

[1] For a collection of the passages illustrative of this doctrine,
see the quotations in Zeller's *Philos. d. Griechen*, Th. 3, Abth. I.
p. 285, *sqq.* (3d ed.). Marcus Aurelius is prominent in the list.
Epictetus is responsible for the deduction of human brotherhood
from the common fatherhood of God. Seneca has frequent expressions of similar thoughts. Yet for all that the wise man is to be
independent and separate. In his respect for humanity, he is not
to lose himself.

II.

This thought was indeed a deep one, and if the Stoics gave but an imperfect practical realization of it to the world, they prepared thereby the way for the reception of the higher thought of Jesus, when that thought appeared. We may therefore more readily suggest the skeptical criticism of the Stoical thought by first looking at the well known completion of the notion of God's fatherhood in the doctrine of Jesus.

Jesus founded his morality in his theology, yet he did not make moral distinctions dependent on the mere fact of divine reward or vengeance. An act is for him wrong, not because outside the kingdom of heaven there is weeping and gnashing of teeth; rather should we say that because the act is opposed to the very nature of the relation of sonship to God, as Jesus conceives this relation, therefore the doers of such acts cannot be in the kingdom of heaven, all whose citizens are sons of the King. And outside the kingdom there is darkness and weeping, simply because outside is outside. Therefore, if Jesus gives us a theological view of the nature of morality, he does not make morality dependent on the bare despotic will of God, but on a peculiar and necessary relation between God and his creatures. So long as God is what he is, and they remain his creatures, so long must this relation continue. Jesus in fact, as we know, gives us a higher and universal form of the morality of the prophets. They had said, Jahveh has saved his people, has chosen them from all the earth, has fed them with his bounty, has treated them as his well-beloved vineyard, has taken the nation as it were to wife. And so, if the people offend against the law of righteousness that is written in their hearts and known through the words of prophecy, they are guilty not alone of dangerous revolt against irresistible might, but also of something far worse, namely, of the basest ingratitude. Their sin is unheard of in all the earth. The heathen forsake not their wretched gods, that are yet no gods, and shall Israel turn against the will of its living, almighty lover? The waste vineyard, the unfaithful wife, these are the types of the iniquity of the people. Their sin is a miserable state of utter corruption. What the very beasts do, to know the masters that feed them, Israel forgets, whose master is not only the maker of all things, but also the loving spouse of his chosen nation.

This sanction for morality, not the might so much as the tender love of God, is by Jesus extended in range and deepened in meaning. Every man stands before God as beloved son. If he wanders, the Father would fain seek him as the shepherd would a lost sheep; would fain, like the prodigal's father, fall upon his neck and kiss him, if he will but return; would fain feed and clothe him with the best; would not forget him amid all his sins. And the Father's rain and sunshine are for just and unjust. Deeper and tenderer is this thought than the prophetic idea, because the relation is no political one, but a close personal one. To be conscious of it means, according to Jesus, to wish to live in accordance with it, so as to return to the Father love for love. Hence, in knowing this relation, one has the highest sanction for all good acts. The ultimate motive that Jesus gives to men for doing right is therefore the wish to be in harmony with God's love. So the Father in his holiness wills for each of us, and so each son, conscious of the love of the Father, also desires, as soon as he is aware of the Father's will. One cannot know of this infinite love without wishing to be in union with it. Even without knowing of the love, the very consciousness of the wretchedness of the lonely, separate life of selfish wickedness must lead one to want to forsake the husks and find the Father, even if he should be but the angry Father. Much more then if one has found the Father, has found him caring for the sparrows, and for the lilies, and for the least and the worst of his children, must one, thus knowing the Father, desire to submit to him. One is lost in the ocean of divine love. Separate existence there is no more. One is anxious to lose his life, to hate all selfish joys, to sell all that one has, to be despised and rejected of all the world, if so be that thereby one can come into accord with the universal life of God's love, in which everything of lesser worth disappears.

Duty to one's neighbor is but a corollary to all this. In the first place one's neighbor is no longer a mere fact of experience, a rival, a helper, an enemy; but he is, instead of all this, a child of God. Every other aspect of his life is lost in this one. As child then he represents the Father. The highest messenger of God will say in God's name at the last: *Inasmuch as ye did it unto the least of these my brethren, ye did it unto me.* And so each brother is the ambassador of God. When Job had spoken of his duty towards the lowly, he had given the sanction for it in the thought : *Did not one fashion us ?* Jesus gives a higher sanction : Does not one Father love you all ? In the presence of the Father the children are to lose their separateness. They are to feel the oneness of their life. There is no longer any rival or enemy, any master or slave, any debtor or creditor here, for all are in infinite debt to the Infinite One, and all in his sight brethren.

The Stoics had conceived of a common Father. But they regarded him as an impersonal, all-pervading Reason. The thought of Jesus gave to his idea of the fatherhood of God a warmth and life unknown to any previous thought. And in this warmth and life he intended the idea of Duty to grow. The highest principle of the doctrine is : Act as one receiving and trying to return an Infinite Love. To thy neighbor act as it befits one so beloved to act towards his brother in love. And thus is Duty explained.

For our present skeptical inquiries this doctrine of Jesus in its original form is no longer enough. For one thing, Jesus himself did not intend it as a philosophy, but always expresses it as an insight. And in our time this insight is clouded by many doubts that cannot be lightly brushed away. This idea of God as a Father, — it is exactly the idea that our philosophy finds most difficulty, nowadays, in establishing.

For many in all the future history of our race this idea will be harder to establish than will be the moral doctrine that was deduced by Jesus from it. For many who with steadfast faith accept the doctrine of God's fatherhood, their ultimate reason will rather be that, first accepting the morality of Jesus, they find it most natural to accept therewith what they understand to be his theology. His moral doctrine will be to them the insight, the theology will be taken on trust. Many others will accept indeed the morality, but be unable to accept the theology. In ethical faith they will be Christians, in theology Agnostics. And therefore, to the philosophic student, who must prove all things, and hold fast only what he finds sure, it is impossible to take the theology of Jesus on simple faith, and not profitable to postpone the discussion of the moral problems until he first shall have established a theology. Morality is for us the starting-point of our inquiry. Theology comes later, if at all. And, as we shall presently see, the theology, if accepted, would not satisfy all the questions of the ethical inquirer.

Yet if the doctrine of Jesus does not belong among the purely idealistic theories of duty, since it gives duty the fact of God's fatherhood as its foundation, it has one aspect that would make the recapitulation of it necessary even in the course of a study of purely ideal ethics. For, while this doctrine founds duty ultimately on the consciousness that God is a Father, and so on a belief in a physical or metaphysical truth, still the immediate ground of the idea of duty to one's neighbor is the consciousness in each man that his neighbor is his brother. In the teachings of Jesus this latter insight follows from the sense of common sonship that Jesus wants to give to men. But, apart from the theology, the belief in the brotherhood of men, in case it can be made clear and definite, may have just the relation to the idea of duty that Jesus, in his theological ethics, wished the idea of the common sonship to have.

But it is our present purpose to see how doubt follows the track of the moral idealists. And to carry out even here this purpose, it is very important to note that however much the morality of Jesus seems to rest upon his theology, and did, for him, rest upon that theology, for us that basis would be of itself insufficient, even if we could unhesitatingly accept the theology. For the skeptical question might arise in the inquiries of the philosopher, to whom all questions are allowed, Why is it evident that one ought to return the Father's love? Granting the fact of this love, how does it establish the ideal? And this question, easy as seems the answer of it to a believer, is just the question that the " almost persuaded " of all times have been disposed to ask. Any particular individual may believe in the theology of Jesus, and yet fail to feel the force of the moral doctrine. Why does this love constrain me? he may say. In fact the church has always found it necessary to construct for itself a process, or even a series of processes, through which the unbeliever must go, in order to reach the point of development where he could begin to feel the constraining force of the divine love. It has been recognized as a fact

that the unregenerate could believe and even tremble and yet remain unregenerate. The saving faith
was seen to be not identical with the mere belief in
God as Father. For the saving faith, divine grace
was necessary, adding to the unregenerate recognition of the bare truth the devotion of the loving
child of God. And therefore the church has never
been content with the doctrine of Jesus in its undeveloped simplicity.

But if all this is so, then for us the morality of
Jesus, considered as morality, is founded, not on the
theological theory alone, but also on a peculiar insight
that each man is to have into the duty of returning
the divine love. That the divine love is real, gives a
basis for all duty in case and only in case one first
sees that it is one's duty to return the divine love.
And wherein is this insight as such any clearer than
the direct insight into the duty of loving one's neighbor? If a man loves not his brother whom he has
seen, how shall he love God whom he has not seen?
Is not the duty of gratitude first evident, if at all, in
man's relations to his fellows? Is not love given first
as a duty to one's companions, and only secondarily
as a duty to God, and then only in case one believes
in God? In other words, are we not here, as in the
discussion with the realist at the outset, led to the
view that not a physical doctrine, nor yet even the
sublimest metaphysical doctrine, as such, but only an
ethical doctrine, can be at the base of a system of
ethics? The doctrine that God loves us is a foun
dation for duty only by virtue of the recognition of
one yet more fundamental moral principle, the doc-

trine that unearned love ought to be gratefully returned. And for this principle theology as such
gives no foundation. But on the other hand, upon
what should the ideal principle itself be founded?
Why is unearned love to be gratefully returned? Is
this principle founded once more on some doctrine
of the constitution of human nature? The same objection would again appear. A physical fact is no
ideal. So, then, this insight is just an insight, the
acceptance of an ideal wholly for its own sake? But
then returns the old objection. What is such an
unfounded ideal but the individual caprice of somebody? Let the faithful be never so devoted; still
there are the unregenerate, who are somehow to be
convinced of a truth that they do not recognize. And
how are they convinced, if at all? Not by showing
them the facts, which they have already known without conviction; but by arousing in them a new feeling, namely, gratitude. Thus the Christian ideal
seems to have for its sole theoretical foundation the
physical fact that man often feels gratitude. It is true
that no one can accuse Jesus of expressly giving this
or any other theoretical foundation to his doctrine.
He was necessarily wholly free from the theoretical
aim in his dealings with the people. But for us now
the point is the theoretical point. If the foundation
of Christian ethics as popularly understood be not
the physical fact of the Father's love, then is it not
just the physical fact of the frequent existence of
gratitude? And is either of these a satisfactory foundation for an ethical theory as such? Nay, if Christian ethics be the highest from the practical point of

view, still must we not dig much deeper to find the
theoretical foundation on which this glorious structure rests?

III.

We have been seeking to illustrate our fundamental difficulty in ethics, — one that is too frequently concealed by rhetorical devices. The uncertainty here illustrated results from the difficulty
of giving any reason for the choice of a moral ideal.
Single acts are judged by the ideal; but who shall
judge the judge himself? Some one, as Plato, or
some Stoic, or Jesus, gives us a moral ideal. If we
are of his followers, the personal influence of the
Master is enough. Then we say: "I take this to be
my guide," and our moral doctrine is founded. But
if we are not of the faithful, then we ask for proof.
The doctrine says: "Behold the perfect Life, or the
eternal Ideas, or the course of Nature, or the will of
God, or the love of the Father. To look on those
realities is to understand our ideal. If you remember those truths, you will hesitate not to do as we
say." But still the doubter may be unwilling to
submit. He may say to Plato: "The tyrant is easy
to find who will laugh at you when you talk of the
peace of philosophic contemplation, who will insist
that his life of conflict and of danger is fuller and
sweeter in its lurid contrasts and in its ecstasies of
sensuous bliss, than are all your pale, stupid joys of
blank contemplation. And if the tyrant says so,
who shall decide against him? Has not many a
man turned with eagerness from the dull life of the

thinker, once for a while endured, to the richer joys and sorrows of the man of the world? Have not such men actually held the pleasures of life, however dearly bought, to be better than the superhuman calm of your philosophic ideal?" Even so to the Stoic, the objector may say: "Granted that your eternal Reason does pervade all things and is our common Father, why should that cause me, who am one of his creatures, to do otherwise than I like? Who can escape from his presence? Even if I live irrationally, am I not still part of the Universal Reason? The bare fact that there is an Eternal Wisdom does not make clear to me that I must needs be very wise. My destiny may be the destiny of a being made solely to enjoy himself." And, to the Christian doctrine, the skeptic may oppose the objection that if the truth does not at once spiritually convert all who know it, the proof is still lacking that the Christian Ideal actually appeals to all possible natures. "If I feel not the love of God," the objector will say, "how prove to me that I ought to feel it?" Or, as human nature so often questions: "Why must I be loving and unselfish?"

Now, the simple, practical way of dealing with all such objectors is to anathematize them at once. Of course, from the point of view of any assumed ideal, the anathema may be well founded. "If you do not as I command," so says any moral ideal, "I condemn you as an evil-doer." "He that believeth not shall be damned." But anathemas are not arguments. To resort to them is to give up theoretic ethics. We who are considering, not whom we shall

practically condemn, but what we can say in favor
of any moral theory, must be unwilling to be put off
with mere oratorical persuasion, or to mistake practical adhesion for theoretical conviction.   We want
a code that shall seem not only admirable, but, if so
it may be, demonstrable.

Such objections, then, blocking the path of our
idealist, what is he to do with them?   Is there any
direction in which he can successfully seek a foundation for his ideals ?

We have, indeed, much seeking yet to do ere we
can find the right direction.   For, in the next place,
we shall have to show how just such objections as
we have applied to other ethical doctrines will apply
to all those doctrines that put the basis of morals in
the often-used mass of instincts called Conscience.
Conscience undoubtedly expresses the results of civilized ancestry and training.   It no doubt must always prove an indispensable aid in making practical
moral decisions ; but if it be used to give a theoretical basis to ethics, one can say of it what has
been already said of other realities.   Its universal
and uniform presence among men can be doubted,
and its value where it is present can be called in
question whenever it is employed to give a basis for
ethics; since as a mere physical fact of the constitution of human nature, conscience is not yet an ideal,
nor an obvious foundation for an ideal.   Both of
these objections have been frequently urged.   Let
us venture to repeat the old story.

4

IV.

Instincts in general are useful, not because they are infallible, much less because they are rational (for they are neither), but because they work quickly and are less capricious than are our less habitual impulses, and so, in common life, are our substitutes for reason. But, in theory, no act is good merely because the instinct called conscience approves of it; nor does conscience in any man always instinctively approve of good acts. Therefore conscience is, for the purpose of founding an ethical theory, as useless as if it were a mere fiction. It gives no foundation for moral distinctions.

To be sure, we must be understood as referring here not to the moral consciousness of man in its highest rational manifestations; for that there is a rational and well-founded moral consciousness we ourselves desire to show. The conscience that we criticise is conscience as an instinct. When people say that so and so is the right because the immediate declaration of conscience shows it to be the right, they generally mean that so and so is right because it feels right. And when moralists found their ethical doctrine on conscience, they are in great danger of making their whole appeal to mere feeling. But such mere feeling can only give us problems; it cannot solve problems. To illustrate by a notable case: When Butler, in analyzing the data of conscience, in his "Dissertation of the Nature of Virtue," comes upon the fact that benevolence, or the effort to increase the general happiness, is, for our common pop·

ular conscience, only a part of virtue, not in any sort the whole of it, he really discovers nothing positive about the nature of virtue, but only gives us a very interesting problem about the nature of virtue. If benevolence were the sole basis of virtue, then, says Butler, for our conscience treachery and violence would be "no otherwise vicious than as foreseen likely to produce an overbalance of misery to society." Therefore, he continues, "if in any case a man could procure to himself as great advantage by an act of injustice as the whole foreseen inconvenience likely to be brought upon others by it would amount to, such a piece of injustice would not be faulty or vicious at all." Even so, it would not be wrong, he points out, to take A's property away and give it to B, if B's happiness in getting it overbalanced A's inconvenience and vexation in losing it. But since conscience disapproves of such actions, therefore, continues Butler, "the fact appears to be that we are constituted so as to condemn falsehood, unprovoked violence, injustice, and to approve of benevolence to some preferably to others, abstracted from all consideration, which conduct is likely to produce an overbalance of happiness or misery." Were God's "moral character merely that of benevolence, yet ours is not so." All this now shows how full of problems our uncriticised conscience is. It is the starting-point, not the guide, of moral controversies. Conscience approves benevolence, and it also approves the repression of benevolence in cases where justice, distributive or retributive, seems to the popular mind to be opposed to benevolence. And when

some moralist tries to reduce justice in all its forms
to benevolence, the natural conscience is dissatisfied.
Retribution it approves, not because retribution may
ultimately increase happiness, but because retribution seems good to it. And if the natural conscience
is again appealed to, and is at last brought to admit
that benevolence is, after all, really the highest end,
and punishment only a means, then this appeal is
simply a setting of conscience against itself. The
popular conscience is, as an instinct, once for all
confused and uncertain about the true relations of
justice and benevolence. It is useless to ask this
instinct to do what the natural conditions that made
it never prepared it to do, namely, to make a system
of morals. A thinker like Butler, with his serious-
ness and depth of insight, defends the claims of conscience only by analyses which bring home to us
that our conscience is a mystery, and that its assertions about all the deepest ethical questions become
uncertain or confused as soon as we cross-question it.
An instinct is, in short, like any other habit. You
run fast down a familiar flight of stairs so long as
you do not think what your feet are doing. Reflect
upon your running, and ten chances to one you shall
stumble. Even so conscience is a perfectly confident
guide as long as you ask it no philosophical questions.

The objections here in question have been so
frequently urged that it is hardly worth while for
those who can feel their force to dwell on them very
long. It is enough for the present purpose to add
what all the moral skeptics from the time of the
Sophists have insisted upon, namely, that the con-

sciences of various men, nations and races, are conflicting in their judgments of acts. This objection, worthless when urged against a well-founded theory of the moral consciousness, is fatal to any theory that makes morality dependent upon a particular emotional or intellectual "constitution" of human nature, that declares morality to be known by men through one faculty or "sense" of a peculiar character. If there are many consciences, each claiming rank as the true conscience, and all conflicting, then the choice among these can only be made on the ground of something else than a conscience.

The caprices of moral instinct are not exhausted when one has enumerated, as nowadays men often do, as many practices as one can find approved or demanded by the consciences of filthy savages. Among civilized men, yes, in our own hearts, each of us can find numberless conflicting and capricious estimates of actions, and it has only a psychological interest to study them in detail, or to try to reduce them to any semblance of principle. Such conscience as we have about common matters is too easily quieted ; and, as a mere feeling, the conscience that can be called moral is not readily distinguishable in this, or in any other respect, from a mere sense of propriety, from a reverence for custom, or from the fear of committing an offense against etiquette. That certain blunders hurt us more than our lesser crimes, and that our remorse for them is like our remorse for venial immorality, only more intense, is nowadays a matter of frequent remark. You ride using another man's season-ticket, or you tell a white lie, or speak an unkind word, and conscience, if a little used to such things, never winces. But you bow to the wrong man in the street, or you mispronounce a word, or you tip over a glass of water, and then you agonize about your shortcoming all day long, yes, from time to time for weeks. Such an impartial and independent judge is the feeling of what you ought to have done. Shall ethics be founded on feeling, which to-day is and to-morrow is cast into the oven?

The traditional answer of the advocates of conscience, when these facts are urged against them, is well known. They say, various less dignified mental tendencies may at times be mistaken for conscience; but the moral sense is real and trustworthy notwithstanding all these mistakes. Shame, or love of praise, or sense of propriety may pass themselves off as conscience; but the genuine conscience, when you find it, is infallible. But we may still rejoin that, if the difficulty is of this nature, the consequence must be very much the same as what we are insisting upon. For if the question can arise whether a given impulse in me, which I take to be conscience, really is the voice of the infallible conscience or not, then this question cannot be decided by appeal to conscience itself; since the very problem then is: " Of two impulses, both pretending to represent conscience, which is the genuine conscience?" And questions of this sort must be appealed to some higher tribunal than the conflicting impulses themselves. It will not be enough to apply even Antigone's sublime test to the warring impulses, and to

say : This impulse is not of to-day nor of yesterday,
and no man can tell whence it came, therefore it is
the voice of infallible conscience. For, fine as that
saying is, when applied to a genuine eternal truth,
the test is not a sufficient one for us in our weakness
to apply to the impulses that we find in our poor
selves. For we soon forget whence came our prejudices and even our bad habits, and we can fancy that
to be of immemorial antiquity which has begun to
be in our own parish, and within the memory of the
old men. A child born in one of our far western
settlements grows up amid a community that is a
few years older than himself, and not as old as his
eldest brother. Yet he shall look upon all these
rickety, wooden houses, and half-graded streets, full
of rubbish, as the outcome of an immense past; he
shall hear of the settlement of the town as he hears
of ancient history, and he shall reverence the oldest
deserted, weather-beaten, rotting log-cabin of the
place, with its mud chimney crumbling to dust, quite
as much as a modern Athenian child may reverence
the ruins of the Parthenon. A time when all these
things were not, shall be beyond his conception.
Even so, if moral truth be eternal, we yet dare not
undertake to judge what it is by merely examining
ourselves to see what customs or tastes or moral
judgments feel to our present selves as if they must
have been eternal. Such absolute validity one might
possibly feel as belonging to his mother's way of making plum-pudding. Snow, to use a comparison of
Aristotle's, is as white after one day as if it had
been lying untouched and unmelted for a thousand

years. And high judicial authority lately expressed the opinion, *a propos* of a change in standard time, that usage may alter itself in a day as well as in a century, and be as authoritative in one case as in the other. Nothing feels older than a well-established custom, however recent it may be.

Conscience then cannot be recognized as infallible merely through the test of antiquity as judged by our feeling. Conscience furthermore, or emotions that pretend to the authority of conscience, may be found counseling or approving contradictory ways of action. Therefore conscience is no sufficient moral guide.

But even if all this were waived, if conscience were in actual agreement among all men, and if there were no difficulty in distinguishing the voice of conscience from the voice of passion, or from other prejudices or sentiments, it would remain true that no ultimate theory of the difference between right and wrong could be founded on the assertions of any instinct. Why an individual should obey his conscience unless he wishes to do so, cannot be made clear by conscience itself alone. Nor can the necessity and real truth of a distinction be made clear by the assertions of a faculty that, however dignified it may be, appears in the individual as a personal emotion, a prejudice or choice, determined by an impulse in him. Even if other people actually have this same impulse, that does not make their common prejudice necessary or rational. Conscience, if universal, would still be only a physical fact. If there are actually no differences among various consciences

it is still impossible to see why there might not be.
And the possibility is as fatal to the authority of bare
conscience as the reality would be. In conscience
alone, without some higher rational test, there is no
ground evident wherefore its decisions might not
have been other than they are. But what the moralist wants is such a distinction between right and
wrong as does not depend upon any mere accident of
reality, even upon the accidental existence of a moral
sense. He wants to find the eternal ethical truth.
We insist then that one of the first questions of the
moralist must be, *why conscience in any given case
is right*. Or, to put the case otherwise, ethical doctrine must tell us why, if the devil's conscience approves of the devil's acts, as it well may do, the
devil's conscience is nevertheless in the wrong.

The discussion has, we imagine, after all, a practical importance in a way not always sufficiently remembered. In the name of conscience many crimes
have been done. In the name of conscience men
condemn whatever tends towards true moral progress, so long as this new element is opposed to popular prejudice. In the name of conscience they kill
the prophets, and stone every one that is sent unto
them. In the name of conscience wars are waged,
whole tribes are destroyed, whole peoples are oppressed. If conscience is the great practical guide
in common life, conscience is also, in many great
crises, the enemy of the new light. It is the sensitive and penetrating eye of the heart, but it is often
blind before the coming day, even because it has
been so useful to us in finding our way in the night.

It ought to be a commonplace of morals that there are certain times when the moral reason must cast aside the moral instinct, when the lover of the right must silence the voice of conscience. The more dangerous such moments are, the more dreadful the mistakes that people at such times are apt to make, the more necessary it is that the moralist should discover some criterion whereby to decide when instinct fails. And this criterion cannot be conscience itself. We must seek yet deeper.

V.

Our criticism of conscience is only another example of the method before applied to the criticism of the moral ideals. You make a distinction between right and wrong, you give to this distinction the dignity of a principle, you deduce special moral judgments therefrom. But then some one asks you for any foundation for the principle, beyond your own caprice. You thereupon seek to produce an ultimate reason for your faith. And your ultimate reason — what is it but some fact external to your choice and to your ideal judgments? But such dead external facts were just what you wanted to avoid. You had said that an ideal must have only an ideal foundation. And now you say that the ideally right thing depends on God's nature, on the existence of the universal Reason, or on the assertions of Conscience. Say thus what you will, have you done what you intended? Have you made evident the necessity of your ideal? If, *per impossibile*, you suppose your present physical beliefs falsified, if the All-Father changed his mind, and came to hate his children, or if, *per impossibile*, the Devil triumphed, or the eternal Ideas melted away like snow, or the universal Reason became insane, or the Consciences of all men grew corrupt, would that alter the ideal for you? If the moral ideal assumes its desired position as judge of all things, then what matters it to the ideal if evil is triumphant in the world? "Fiend, I defy thee with a calm, fixed mind," the idealist will say, after the manner of Shelley's Prometheus, and that however much the real world may threaten him. Therefore how can the *Is* predetermine the *Ought to be?* But if the *Ought to be* be independent of the *Is*, how does discussion about the power of God, or his goodness, about the universality of conscience, or its inner strength as a feeling, affect our judgment of the ideal distinction between right and wrong?

Thus we are thrown back and forth between the conflicting demands of criticism. " Give us a moral system that is no caprice of thine," say the critics of one sort. That seems reasonable. Therefore we affirm, " This system of ours is founded on a rock of eternal truth," namely, on God's will, or on the intuition of universal conscience, or on some like fact of the world. But thereupon other critics say to us: " Wherein do you differ from those who say that might is right, or that success determines the right, or that whatever exists ought to exist? For after all you say, something that is, ought to be, merely because it is." And always still other critics are

present, to doubt whether we are right about God
or conscience as physical facts. Such critics very
plausibly say, "Why found moral truth, which ought
to be so secure and clear, on physical or metaphysical doctrines that are so often doubted and so hard
to establish?"

Such is the general difficulty illustrated in the
warfare of the moral ideals. They want some highest judge to decide among them. If they seek this
judge in the real world, they seem to endanger their
idealism. If they seek their judge among themselves, the warfare begins afresh. For what one of
them can be the sole judge, when they are all judges
one of another?

CHAPTER IV.

ALTRUISM AND EGOISM IN CERTAIN RECENT DIS-
CUSSIONS.

But if the light that is in thee be darkness, how great is that dark-ness!

NOT even yet have we exhausted the perplexities involved in this fundamental difficulty of moral theory. Some one may say: "Let the ideals in general take care of themselves. We are concerned in this world with individual and concrete duties. These at least are plain." But these also involve questions concerning the ideal. Let us see then how the same difficulty that has beset the more general moral doctrines, returns to plague us in case of the theoretical treatment of one of these plain duties. Our discussion will here gain in definiteness what it loses in generality. Let us choose a concrete moral question, namely, the problem of the true ground of the moral distinctions and other moral relations between what people nowadays like to call altruism and what they like to call egoism.

Upon what, then, if upon anything, is founded the moral precept: *Thou shalt love thy neighbor as thy-self?* Or is there any foundation for it at all? To be quite familiar in discussing this problem, let us take it as it appears in recent discussion. The answers of some recent moralists will illustrate for us afresh the great problem of ethics. We shall find two classes of efforts made to solve the difficulty. On the one hand moralists appear whose tendency is mainly, although not always quite wholly realistic. They say that, assuming the selfish aim as from the beginning self-evident, the unselfish aim soon appears as a necessary concomitant and assistant of the self-ish aim. Such writers, from Hobbes to the present day, have insisted upon unselfishness as a more or less refined selfishness, the product of enlightenment. To this view one opposes very naturally the objec-tion that real unselfishness is thus in fact rendered impossible. The moral ideal resulting is therefore, whether right or wrong in itself, at all events at war with other well-known ideals. And hence the expla-nation satisfies nobody. One still lacks a judge to end the warfare.

On the other hand, however, more idealistic mor-alists have tried to make unselfishness dependent on some impulse, such as pity or sympathy, whose dic-tates shall be perfectly definite and self-evident, and yet not, like the supposed dictates of conscience, either abstract or mysterious. But to such a foun-dation one opposes very naturally again the objec-tion that all such judgments of feeling are capri-cious, that pity and sympathy are confused and deceitful feelings, wholly unfit to give moral insight, and that no ideal can be founded on the shifting sand of such realities.

The results of such criticisms will once more be skeptical, but the skepticism on which we are here insisting is so necessary a foundation for ethics, that we make no apology for dwelling upon it yet farther, devoting to the special problems suggested by these recent discussions of selfishness and unselfishness a separate chapter.

I.

In a collection of Servian popular tales may be found one that runs somewhat as follows: Once there lived two brothers, of whom the elder was very incautious and wasteful, but always lucky, so that in spite of himself he grew constantly richer, while the younger, although very industrious and careful, was invariably unfortunate, so that at last he lost everything, and had to wander out into the wide world to beg. The poor wretch, after much suffering, resolved to go to no less a person than Fate himself, and to inquire wherefore he had been thus tormented. Long and dreadful wildernesses were passed, and finally the wanderer reached the gloomy house. Now visitors at Fate's dwelling dare not begin to speak when they come, but must wait until Fate shall address them, and meanwhile must humbly do after Fate whatever he does. So the wanderer had to live in the house for several days, silent, and busily imitating Fate's behavior. He found that Fate lives not always in the same way, but on some days enjoys a golden bed, with a rich banquet and untold heaps of treasure scattered about; on some days again is surrounded with silver, and eats dainty but somewhat plainer food; on some days has brazen and copper wealth only, with coarse food; and on some

days, penniless and ragged, sleeps on the floor, digs
the ground, and gnaws a crust. Each night he is
asked by a supernatural voice: "How shall those
live who have this day been born?" Fate always
replies: "As I have fared this day, so may they
fare."

Thus our beggar found the secret of his own misfortunes; for he had been born on a day of poverty.
But when at last Fate broke the silence, the visitor
begged him to tell whether there could be any way
whereby he might escape from the consequences of
his unlucky birth. "I will tell thee," said Fate.
"Get thee home again, and ask thy brother to let
thee adopt his little daughter. For she was born on
one of the golden days. Adopting her, thou shalt
thenceforth call whatever thou receivest her own.
But never call anything thine. And so shalt thou
be rich." The beggar joyfully left Fate's dreary
house, with its sad round of days, and went back to
the world of labor and hope. There, by following the
advice that he had received, he became in fact very
wealthy; since all that he undertook prospered. But
the wealth was his adopted daughter's. For always
he called his gains hers. One day he grew however
very weary of this, and said to himself: "These fields
and flocks and houses and treasures are not really
hers. In truth I have earned them. They are mine."
No sooner had he spoken the fatal words than lightning fell from heaven and began to burn his grain-
fields, and the floods rose to drown his flocks. So
that terror-stricken the wretch fell on his face and
cried: "Nay, nay, O Fate, I spoke no truth; they

are not mine, but hers, hers alone." And thereupon flame and flood vanished, and the man dwelt thenceforth in peace and plenty.

II.

The really deep thought that imperfectly expresses itself in this little Servian tale may suggest many sorts of reflections. Just now we shall busy ourselves with only one of the questions that are brought to mind by the story. Many who nowadays have much to say about what they call altruism, actually explain all altruism as a kind of selfish evasion of the consequences of cruder selfishness, so that at bottom they really counsel men much as Fate counseled the wanderer. They say in effect : " To make thyself happy, do certain things called duties to thy neighbor. That we call altruism. Thou shalt have thy reward. For what is more useful to a man than a man? If therefore thou dost well to him, thou shalt make him in many ways of great service to thee. And so, to get happiness for thyself, see that thou be not openly merely a seeker of thy happiness ; but call that which thou seekest his happiness. Calling it his will help to make it thine. Be selfish by casting aside grosser selfishness. Live for the others as the means of living for thyself. In co-operation is safety. Act therefore as a good member of the community, and thou shalt prosper. But such action requires altruism. As the man gave his wealth to his adopted daughter, so that he might own it himself and outwit his destiny, so must thou

5

make thy interests into the interests of society, and
by so doing be true to thyself." But now such altruism, as one at once sees, has no right to parade
itself as genuine altruism at all, and if it be the end
of conduct, there is no moral conduct distinct from
cleverness. But if this be true, it is at least incumbent upon the moralist to explain why the popular
ideal of unselfishness is thus so very far wrong.

More or less disguised, the doctrine here generally
stated appears in modern discussion since Hobbes.
Let us follow it into some of its hiding-places, and
to that end let us distinguish selfishness and unselfishness as ideals or ends of conduct, from selfishness
and unselfishness as means, accidentally useful to
get an end.

III.

Altruism is the name of a tendency. Of what
tendency? Is it the result or the intent that makes
a deed altruistic? Was our hero an altruist when
he gave to his adopted daughter the name and the
enjoyment of a possessor of wealth? Or would he
have needed in addition to all this a particular disposition of mind ere he could be called an altruist?

We need not dispute about mere names as such.
Let everybody apply the name Altruism as he will;
but possibly we shall do well to recall to the reader's
mind what ought nowadays to be the merest commonplace of ethics, namely, that we cannot regard
any quality as moral or the reverse, in so far as the
expression of it is an external accident, with which
the man himself and his deliberate aim have nothing

to do. Ethical judgments deal with purposes. On any theory of right and wrong the man himself, not the accident of fortune, determines the moral character of his act; and this view must be held equally whether one believes the man's will to be free or to be bound. Hence the unforeseen or unintended outcome, or any other accidental accompaniment of my act, does not make me egoistic or altruistic in case egoism and altruism are to be qualities that have any moral character at all. If my property is accidentally destroyed by fire, and if the loss causes great damage to my creditors or to people dependent on me, the loss makes me no less or more an altruist, although I can no longer do good as before. If my purely selfish plan chances to do others good, I am no less an egoist, although I have made my fellows happy. In short, he who means anything, and does what he can to realize his intention, must be judged according to his intent. Circumstances control the outcome, and they make of the chance discoverer of the first bit of gold in a California mill - race a greater altruist, to judge solely by consequences, than a hero would be who sacrificed himself in a good cause, and lost the battle. But no moral system could make genuine saintliness out of the deed of the man who by chance has found what the world needed. And to take one more example, the power *die stets das Böse will, und stets das Gute schafft*, is not altruistic in the moral sense, however vast its creations may become.

All this we maintain, because, if you are morally criticising a disposition, you must study what it is,

not what are its accidental surroundings. Moral
distinctions must apply to aims as such. Unless
you are judging men exactly as you judge the north
wind or the value of rain, not as consciously good or
bad, but as mere forces that happen to produce such
and such results under such and such conditions,
you must study, not first the accidental circumstances, but the men. And in fact all moralists,
however much they may condemn the weighing of
mere motives, however much they desire to take just
the consequences into account, as Bentham did, are
nevertheless forced to separate in their moral judgments accidental from expected consequences. We
maintain that this abstraction of a disposition from
its accidental expressions must be rigidly carried
out in order to get a moral doctrine of any significance. Let others study natural forces. We
here are studying men, and are considering what
ideal of a man we can form. Whatever the accidents of the outer world give him in the way of
means, we want to know his real intent, and to judge
that. But if the intent of the man does alone make
him altruistic or the reverse, then what, for example,
is the position, in ethical controversy, of any system
that declares altruism to be morally good *because the
individual needs the social order to assist him, and
must therefore in all prudence try to further the social ends as a means to the furthering of his own?*
Does such a system say anything whatever about
altruism as such? Does it not make enlightened
egoism the one rule of life? And if this is what is
meant, why not say so plainly? If the intent of the

act makes it altruistic or the reverse, then a man who helps his friend, or his neighbor, or society, and who is honest, and kind, and public-spirited solely because he wants to get protection and help in return, is no altruist, but is as egoistic as a Judas or as a Thomassen. He is only clearer-headed than they were. On the other hand, if by any possibility any one makes the good of others his sole end, and with this as end takes care of his own health, or develops his mental powers, or amasses wealth, but all merely for the sake of being able to benefit others, then is such a man not egoistic, even while working for himself, but altruistic throughout. For such a man by hypothesis aims, not at his own personal good, but solely at the good of others.

All this is consequent upon the general doctrine that the distinction between altruism and egoism, as moral qualities, must depend on no external accident, but on the personal deed of the man himself. For, to make special mention of what many forget, the means that you take to get any end are for you merely physical accidents. If things were otherwise, you would with the same intent do other things to get what you seek. Not what you have to do in getting your ends, but what you actually aimed at, is morally significant. Hence the altruism of consequences as such is morally insignificant, and the altruism of intent is alone morally significant. But yet this obvious and seemingly very commonplace distinction is, by the views that we are combating, wholly lost sight of in its further application to human life. We may hear in modern controversy, for instance, of a "conflict between altruism and egoism," such as the one that Mr. Spencer discusses in his "Data of Ethics," and we may draw near to learn how the conflict goes. We shall possibly find the question put thus : If a man in trying to be altruistic were so far to forget himself as to injure his health, or to become so weak as to have no healthy children ; if he were to be careless of his property, to let his mind go untrained, or to narrow his own life too much, why then his own objects would be defeated, he would be unable to help anybody, he might do harm, and he could be no genuine altruist. Therefore altruism must not oppose egoism too much, else altruism will defeat itself. On the other hand, we hear, if egoism is extravagant, it will in its turn fail to get its own great end, self-satisfaction. For it is useful to one to have his fellow-members in the social organism well-contented, efficient, and moral. One must try to make them so, that he himself may enjoy the fruits of their happiness. He pays more taxes, and also higher prices for what he buys, if the community as a whole is not contented and happy, as well as healthy and moral. Enlightened selfishness therefore means for him public spirit. His neighbor's diseases are apt to infect his own family ; hence, if enlightened, he will do what he conveniently can to keep his neighbor well. His neighbor's peace of mind tends to make his own mind peaceful, hence he will help his neighbor out of trouble. Otherwise he would have to live in anxiety, loneliness, weakness, and danger. His life would be hard, and probably his death would

'be early. So egoism must not be too extravagant.
Altruism is " equally imperative." Thus, perhaps,
we should hear the so-called " conflict " discussed.
If such views were urged, what should we say about
them ? We should have to say that they touch in
no wise at all the true moral distinction and warfare
between selfishness and altruism. They show only
that, whatever the opposition in aim, the two principles have after all, in this world of limitation, to
use very much the same means. Surely it is no
new thing to learn that in warfare both parties have
to burn the same quality of gunpowder, and that
even the cats when they fight all have to scratch
with claws that are very much alike. Do such remarks explain or tend to diminish or to end the conflicts in question ?

How insignificant is this way of studying the conflict of egoism and altruism, we shall see if we take
yet other illustrations. In the sense of the foregoing comparison of egoism and altruism, even a
pirate, in his treatment of merchant vessels, would
have to be moderately altruistic ; namely, he had
better not try to do harm to a merchant vessel that
is too well armed for his force to overcome it. On
the contrary, his egoism will in this case counsel him
unselfishly to let it prosper in its own way. Nay,
he may even try to speed it on its course, if it appears disposed to change roles and to attack him.
He may say that in just this case he thinks that this
merchantman ought to have peace, and to be preserved from injury. The other alternative would
just here increase his own bill for repairs, or might

make his own existence less happy, or might even
bring him to the gallows. The happiness of the
crew of the merchantman is therefore just now an
object of concern for him, as perhaps furthering his
own. So he may be willing to compromise the difficulty, even if it should cost him a large sum to persuade the belligerent captain of the armed merchantman to let him alone. Thus he might even add
quite a fortune to what the merchantman's captain
and crew already have of good things, and this
would surely be very marked altruism. Thus egoism and altruism may oppose each other, and thus,
by careful calculation, their opposing claims may be
balanced! Or yet again, suppose that a robber
meets me in the highway, and egoistically demands
my purse. If now I should manage to disarm him,
to present a pistol to his head, and to ask him to
accompany me to the nearest town, evidently the
claims of altruism would for that man have a consid-
erably stronger emphasis than they had the moment
before. He would now be willing not merely to
live and let live in peace for the present; he would
not merely be delighted to recognize my rights of
property and to leave me free to enjoy them; but he
would undoubtedly be glad to increase my happiness
by giving me anything of value that he might have
about him, or any information of value to me that I
might desire, if by such means he could get me to
let him go free. A great altruist would my robber
now be, however great his egoism just before.

Now do such discussions of the claims of egoism
and altruism mean anything for the moralist? But

if somebody tells us of the altruism that leads a man to advocate good drainage lest he himself may have a fever, of the altruism that pays one's debts to the sole end that one may get further credit, of the sublime unselfishness that makes a man civil even to his rivals, because civility in these days is a social requirement, — what have all these wondrous virtues to do in constituting the moral value of altruism as a disposition, more than have the virtues just illustrated? We have two dispositions in us: one ordering us to respect our neighbor as such, to labor in his behalf because he exists and needs help; the other demanding that we regard him as a mere instrument for our personal pleasure. Only the dispositions as such concern the moralist. Surely in fundamental ethics we are discussing what we ought to aim at, not how we can get our aims, so long at least as we confine ourselves to the general principles. Applied morality may have much to say of means. But of principles, this balancing of means can tell us nothing. The means are the physical accidents, nothing more. What we want to know is whether egoism as an aim is morally the worthiest aim, or whether altruism is a morally better aim. And we ask not yet how, *if* one's aim is egoistic, he can most successfully be selfish, but only *whether* one's aim ought to be selfish, and *in how far*. To tell us that if we are sensible and selfish we shall avoid having too much trouble with our fellows, is not to tell us that our aims ought to be altruistic, but only that sensible selfish men are not fools. To tell us that if we are wise and altruistic we shall avoid wasting

our own powers profitlessly, and shall try to preserve
our own health, and to cultivate our own wits in useful ways, all this is to tell us that unselfish wise men
are not fanatics. It may be useful to say this, but
it is not useful to the discussion of fundamental
moral doctrines. We want to know, for the first,
not how successfully to be altruistic, or selfish, but
why the effort to be altruistic or to be selfish is morally right or wrong.

IV.

If now such comparisons of the claims of altruism and egoism throw no light on the fundamental
moral questions, what shall we say of the chance that
the "conflict" may be explained or diminished by
any proof that the evolution of our race will tend in
time to diminish, or even to extinguish, the opposition? If some one shows us that by and by the most
selfish being in the social order will find it his own
bliss to give as much bliss as he can to everybody
else, so that men shall all be even as the people at a
successful party, getting pleasure as freely as they
give it, and giving it because they get it: and if
such predictions seem to anybody to help us to know
what duty is, then what can we say in reply, save to
wonder at the insight that sees the connection between all these facts and our present duty? If a
society ever does grow up in which there are no
moral conflicts, nothing but a tedious cooing of bliss
from everybody, then in that society there will be
no moral questions asked. But none the less we
ask such. If the people of that day no longer dis-

tinguish egoism from altruism, they may all be blessed : but what is that to us? We ask, What ought we to do? We learn in answer that the people of the future will feel no need to ask that question. We desire that duty be defined. We learn in answer that if men ever get perfect, the sense of obligation will vanish, so that nobody will question: What is duty? at all. This may be magnificent, but it is not ethics.

For what do we really learn by hearing about the society of the future? Only that, in the time coming, there will be such and such freedom from moral problems? *Do we then also learn that we ought to do our best to bring about that reign of peace?* Not at all, for we are sure that we shall never live to see that day; and we cannot know why we should work for it so long as we are still in doubt about the value of selfishness. Do we learn that we ought to conform as nearly as is possible to the rules that will govern men in that ideal state? But how then do we learn that? Is it *because the coming form of conduct will be the " highest form of adjustment of acts to ends*," as the modern apostles of evolution teach that it will be? Nay, though we do accept most confidently all that these apostles teach about the future, since surely they must know about it, we still miss anything of moral significance in these physical facts. For why is this coming state the highest? Does any one say: *Because it will come at the end of the physical process of evolution?* Nay then, if every more advanced state is to be more acceptable, by such reasoning the sprouting potato

or the incubating egg would always be more acceptable than the fresh potato or the fresh egg. *Highest*,
as *last*, or as *most complex*, or even as *most permanent*, cannot be in meaning identical with the *morally highest* that we want defined for us. We ought
to work for the realization of that far-off state, if at
all, then, because we see it to be, not merely the last
in point of time, but also actually the best, and that
for some other reason than this physical one. But
once more then, why is it best? And why ought we
to try to realize it? *Because in that state, every
individual will be happiest?* But then we want to
know what we now are to do, and we see that this
future happiness will be at present for us unattainable. If we were in that state we should be happy.
But it is not at all plain that, by trying to approach
it, we shall now be making ourselves any happier.
And why should we do anything unselfish?

Evolution then, as a mere prospect, throws no
light on the real and fundamental meaning of duty.
If we know what we are to try to do, then we can
judge whether we ought to help or to hinder evolution as a means to that end. But unless we know
our duty otherwise, there is nothing in the mere
physical fact of evolution that indicates what is morally higher or lower, better or worse. Why should
I work for future ages, if it is not already quite
plain, apart from any knowledge of evolution, that I
ought to do what I can just now for my brother
here?

After all, however, it is another aspect of evolution upon which nowadays most stress is laid in

ethics. It is said that, the future aside, evolution has made us what we now are, and, in particular, has formed our society, and us for society. Hence not only is our welfare in fact best served by a wise altruism, but this fact is plain to us in our very organization and instincts. Therefore while throughout our aim is our happiness, our nature has been so organized by generations of social evolution as to make pretty certain that our happiness is already dependent on our good character as social beings. Therefore the doctrine of evolution shows that selfishness must itself become even in our day altruistic if it would be successful.

Is this aspect of evolution any more ethical than the other? That is, does it show us, not the means, but the moral End? We must deny that it does. To be sure, if we never actually felt any conflict between egoism and altruism as dispositions, then indeed for us just that ethical problem would not exist. But we do feel a conflict. And since for us our selfishness is not altruistic in aim, it is quite useless to try to make the warring impulses one by declaring that a perfectly enlightened selfishness, even in our own society, would be altruistic, not indeed in aim, but in consequences. For, in the first place, that would actually be a false statement for our present social condition ; since it is still quite possible for a clever selfish man to live very comfortably, by somehow legally wronging and oppressing others. And, in the second place, if the statement were true, it would be ethically worthless. For if good treatment of others is uniformly the behavior that is, selfishly viewed, the

most advantageous, the man who acts upon that principle is still selfish, not altruistic at all, and he has
not solved for himself the conflict between the two
principles, save by utterly disregarding the principle
of altruism. If altruism were the only goodness,
then altruism of aim would be goodness still, whatever the selfish consequences. If altruism needs to
be limited in any way by selfishness, then the limitation must still be a matter of aim, not of accidental
result. Altruism as a means to selfish ends would
however be no aim at all, but only an accidental
tool. If circumstances varied, it would be cast
aside, while the selfish aim itself remained constant.

J. S. Mill, following others, tried to distinguish
the *motive* from the *intent* of an act. According to
this distinction, a selfish act would be altruistic by
intent, if there was in it the deliberate purpose to make
somebody happy, however selfish the *motive* of the
act. So it would be altruism to be deliberately and
selfishly just. But this distinction, however useful
for some purposes, is for our purpose worthless.
The question is: What in the act belongs to the
man, and what is this part of the act worth? Now
whatever belongs not to the actor, but to the conditions under which he works, is morally insignificant. For it is what we have called the physical
accident of his surroundings. But intent, *apart
from motive*, seems to be just such a physical accident; for intent, apart from motive, must relate, not
to the real aim as such, but only to the means. A
man aims to be selfish. If now he lives where his
selfishness requires him to feed and clothe his enemy,

he will, if enlightened, do so, and deliberately too.
And he will show in the act just as much and just as
little charity as he would have shown had he lived
where selfishness was best served by killing his
enemy, and had he killed him. The intent, apart
from the motive of the man, can have reference only
to the means by which he seeks to get his ultimate
aim. And such intent relates to accidental matters.
If by a physical accident the selfish man grows up
where you must speak politely to your antagonist,
and treat him with great show of respect, then the
selfish man will deliberately, and with conscious intent, do so; and if he grows up where you challenge
your antagonist to a duel, he will possibly try that
way of getting rid of an enemy; and if he lives
among the cannibals, the selfish man, no more or
less selfish than in the other cases, only by training
more brutal in tastes, will torture and eat his antagonist. And if the doctrine of evolution shows that
one of these forms of " adaptation " is more complete
than another, or proves to us that we personally shall
be most prudent in adopting one only of the possible
courses, all this can in no wise tell us what aim in
conduct is morally best, but only what means most
exhaustively accomplish the selfish purposes of a
civilized man. So intent is morally valuable only
in connection with motive.

It is hardly worth while to dwell longer on the
curious devices by which certain defenders of the
application of the hypothesis of evolution to questions of fundamental ethics have tried to establish
that the truths of evolution teach us that we ought

to do right. The whole undertaking resembles that of a man who should try to show us that the truth of the law of gravitation clearly indicates that we all ought to sit down. What is evident or doubtful apart from the law of evolution, cannot, in this field, be proved or disproved by the law. Shall we say : " Do good to thy neighbor to-day, because evolution tends to bring into existence a race of future beings who will do good?" To say this is to say something utterly irrelevant. What do we care about remote posterity, unless we already care about our neighbors as they are? Or shall we say : " Do good to thy neighbor because evolution has made thee a social being, whose instincts lead thee to desire thy neighbor's good?" To say this is to say what is only very imperfectly true. One's instincts often lead him to take much selfish delight in thwarting his neighbor. If it were true universally and strictly, it would not show us why to do right, nor yet what is right. For it is not obviously a fundamental ethical doctrine that we ought to follow an instinct as such. And if we follow an instinct because we find it pleasing, our aim is still not to do any right save what pleases us personally. And the whole wisdom of the doctrine of evolution would be reduced to the assurance that we ought to do as we like, with due regard to prudence. Shall we then say : " Do good, because the social order that has evolved is too strong for thee, and will hurt thee unless thou submittest to it?" Still one has the selfish motive insisted upon, and morality is still only prudence. And the doctrine will still have to

admit that whenever one can outwit society prudently, and can gain for himself his selfish aims by
anti-social but for him in this case safe means, then
and there the selfish man may do this anti-social
thing if he likes, the doctrine, with all its good motives, being unable to show why not. For it will not
do to resort to some such subterfuge as this, and to
say : " A man's advantage depends upon the prosperity of the whole. But anti-social acts *ultimately
tend* to weaken society. Hence they ultimately tend
to diminish the prosperity of the whole, and *therefore tend to harm* the selfish individual." All this
is irrelevant, in case the social consequences *cannot
return upon* the selfish individual's head during his
lifetime. The wasteful owners of great forests in
our western mountains, the great and oppressive
capitalists that crush rivals and outwit the public,
the successful speculators, the national leaders whose
possession of the biggest battalions enables them to
demand of weaker neighbors unjust sacrifices, all
these may listen in scorn to talk about their prosperity as dependent upon that of society, their enemies
and victims included. " We eat the fruit," they can
say. " To be sure we consume it by eating, and we
like to waste it so long as we ourselves profit by the
waste, and we could neither eat it nor waste it if
there were no fruit ; but there is enough to last us
and our children for our lifetimes. After us the
social famine, but for others, not for us." The now
famous reply ascribed to one of our great railroad
kings when, some time since, he was asked about the
" accommodation of the public " by a certain train,

6

well illustrates our point. " Damn the public," said the great servant and master of the traveling world. If he really did not say that, very likely there are those who would have meant it. And may the evolutionist condemn them solely on his own grounds?

Or finally, shall the doctrine retreat behind an ancient maxim, and state itself thus : " Evolution shows us what are the ultimate tendencies of acts ; but no act ought to be committed which belongs to a class of acts whose general tendency is bad " ? Would not this be a lamentable surrender of the whole position? Yet such a surrender is found in one or two passages of the book that is nowadays supposed best to represent the doctrine that we have been criticising in the foregoing, namely, in Mr. Spencer's "Data of Ethics." The physical facts of evolution are to give us our ideal. How? By telling us what in the long run, for the world at large, produces happiness. But if my individual happiness in the concrete case is hindered by what happens to be known to help in the long run towards the production of general happiness, how shall the general rule be applicable to my case ? Mr. Spencer replies, in effect, that the concrete consequences for individuals must not be judged, but only the general tendency of the act. Happiness is the ultimate end ; but in practice the " general conditions of happiness " must be the proximate end. But how is this clear ? If I know in a given case what will make me happy, and if the means to my happiness are not the general ones at all, but, in this concrete case, something conflicting therewith, why should I not do as I please ?

Because, Mr. Spencer says, the concrete case must be tested by the general law of Evolution. But once more, why? The only answer is the principle, which Mr. Spencer sometimes tacitly assumes, sometimes very grudgingly acknowledges, sometimes seems to claim as his peculiar property, namely, the well-known Kantian principle, that *nothing should be done which we could not wish to see done universally*, or that *the rule of the single act ought to be a rule adapted to serve as an universal rule for all rational beings*. But if this maxim is essential to the foundation of a moral system, then how poor the pretense that the law of evolution gives us any foundation for ethics at all. The facts of evolution stand there, mere dead realities, wholly without value as moral guides, until the individual assumes his own moral principle, namely, his ideal determination to do nothing that a person considering the order of the world as a whole and desiring universal happiness would condemn, from the point of view of the general tendencies of acts. Grant that principle, and you have an ideal aim for action. Then a knowledge of the course of evolution will be useful, just as a knowledge of astronomy is useful to a navigator. But astronomy does not tell us why we are to sail on the water, but only how to find our way. With Kant's principle assumed, we already have attained, apart from any physical doctrine of evolution, the essentials of an ethical doctrine to start with; and we need no doctrine of evolution to found this ethical doctrine, but need it only to tell us the means. But if we have not already this Kantian principle,

then it is hard indeed to see what the doctrine of
evolution can do to help us to get it.   Mr. Spencer
seems to forget that a doctrine of Means is not a
doctrine of Ends.

In sum then, either the fundamental moral distinctions are clear apart from the physical fact of
evolution, or the physical fact cannot illustrate for
us the distinctions that we do not previously know.
If there is a real moral conflict between egoism and
altruism, then this conflict must concern the aims of
these two dispositions, not the accidental outcome
that we reach, nor the more or less variable means
that we employ in following the dispositions.   And
any effort to reconcile the two tendencies by showing
that through evolution, or otherwise, it has become
necessary for an altruistic aim to be reached by
seemingly selfish means, or for a selfish purpose to
be gained by seemingly altruistic devices, — any such
effort has no significance for ethics.   If the question
were: " Shall we buy mutton or beef at the market
to-day ? " it would surely be a strange answer to the
question, or " reconciliation " of the alternatives, if
one replied, " But whichever you do you must go
over the same road to get to the market."   How
then are we helped by knowing that, in our society,
altruism and egoism, these two so bitterly opposed
moral aims, have very often to hide their conflicts
under a use of very much the same outward show of
social conformity.

There is indeed no doubt that all the knowledge
we may get about the facts of evolution will help us
to judge of the means by which we can realize the

moral ideals that we independently form. But the ideals themselves we apply to the course of evolution as tests of its worth, or hold as aims to be realized through knowledge of nature. We do not get them from studying the course of nature as a mere process. There is no doubt of the reality and of the vast importance of the physical fact of evolution. Its ethical importance, however, has been, we hold, misunderstood. Evolution is for ethics a doctrine not of ends, but of the means that we can use. In fact, there is an applied ethic of evolution, but no fundamental ethical doctrine based upon evolution. Those who investigate evolution are doing much to further the realization of ethical ideals, but they cannot make or find for us our ethical ideals. They show us where lies the path to an already desired goal. For them to try to define the goal merely by means of their physical discoveries, is a great mistake. It can lead only to such labored efforts as we have here been criticising, efforts to prove some such opinion as that altruism is a form of selfishness, or that selfishness is the only possible altruism. Whether we are just in fancying that these latter efforts are really identical with the actual efforts of any recent evolutionists, the reader must judge for himself. Altruism we must, at all events, justify in another way.

V.

But now let us turn from those who define unselfishness as a useful means to a selfish end, and let us consider the effort to make pure unselfishness a self-

evident goal of conduct, by founding unselfishness
on the direct revelation of the emotion of Pity.
Here, as before, we shall meet with the skeptical
criticism that the mere physical fact of the existence
of certain conditions is no proof of the validity of an
ideal moral demand. Just as the physical fact that
a clever self-seeker must pretend to be unselfish, and
must outwardly produce effects that benefit others,
is no foundation for a genuinely unselfish ideal,
just so the presence of a pitiful impulse, a mere fact
of human nature, is no foundation for an ideal rule
of conduct. The feeling is capricious, just as the
social conditions that render public spirit and generosity the best selfish policy are capricious. As
the selfish man would behave with open selfishness
in case he were where unselfishness in outward conduct no longer was worth to him the trouble, even so
the pitiful man would, merely as pitiful, be cruelly
selfish if cruel selfishness, instead of generous deeds,
could satisfy his impulse. In fact, he often is cruelly selfish ; and if sympathy were always unselfish,
still, as a feeling, it is a mere accidental fact of human nature. So again, the effort to found a moral
ideal on a natural fact will fail. But let us look
closer.

Schopenhauer is the best modern representative of
the view that Pity or sympathetic emotion is the
foundation of right conduct. In pity he finds the
only unselfish principle in man, and he insists that
pity is a tendency not reducible to any other more
selfish emotion of our nature. He finds it necessary
to refute as an error the oft repeated opinion that[1]

[1] *Grundlage der Moral*, p. 211 (2d ed.).

"pity springs from a momentary illusion of imagination, so that we first put ourselves in the sufferer's place, and now, in imagination, fancy that we suffer *his* pangs in *our* person." This, replies Schopenhauer, is a blunder. "It remains to us all the time clear and immediately certain, that *he* is the sufferer, not *we ;* and it is in his person, not in ours, that we feel the pain, and are troubled. We suffer *with* him, so *in* him ; we feel his pain as his, and do not fancy that it is ours ; yes, the happier our own state is, and the more the consciousness of it contrasts in consequence with the situation of our neighbor, so much the more sensitive are we to pity." And of this wondrous feeling no complete psychological explanation can be given ; the true explanation, thinks Schopenhauer, must be metaphysical. In pity a man comes to a sense of the real oneness in essence of himself and his neighbor.

This pity is, therefore, for Schopenhauer, the only moral motive, first, because it is the only non-egoistic motive, and secondly, because it is the expression of a higher insight. The first character of pity is illustrated by Schopenhauer in an ingenious passage, by means of a comparison of pity and other motives as exhibited in a supposed concrete instance. We shall find it well to quote the most of the passage in full : —

"I will take at pleasure a case as an example to furnish for this investigation an *experimentum crucis.* To make the matter the harder for me, I will take no case of charity, but an injustice, and one, too, of the most flagrant sort. Suppose two young people, Caius and Titus, both passionately in love, and each with a different maiden. Let each one find in his way a rival, to whom external circumstances have given a very decided advantage. Both shall have made up their minds to put each his own rival out of the world ; and both shall be secure against any discovery, or even suspicion. But when each for himself sets about the preparations for the murder, both of them, after some inner conflict, shall give up the attempt. They shall render account to us, plainly and truthfully, of why they have thus decided. Now what account Caius shall render, the reader shall decide as he pleases. Let Caius be prevented by religious scruples, by the will of God, by the future punishment, by the coming judgment, or by anything of that sort. Or let him [with Kant] say : ' I reflected that the maxim of my procedure in this case would not have been fit to serve as an universal rule for all possible rational beings, since I should have used my rival as means and not at the same time as End in himself.' Or let him say with Fichte : ' Every human life is Means or instrument for the realization of the Moral Law ; therefore I cannot, without being indifferent to the moral law, destroy one who is destined to contribute to that end.' Or let him say, after Wollaston : ' I have considered that the deed would be the expression of an untrue proposition.' Or let him say, after Hutcheson : ' The moral sense, whose sensations, like those of every other sense, are not further to be explained, has determined me to refrain.' Or let him say, after Adam Smith : ' I foresaw that my deed, if I did it, would arouse no sympathy with me in the spectators of the act.' Or, after Christian Wolff : ' I recognized that I should thereby hinder my own growth towards perfection without helping the growth of anybody else.' Or let him say, after Spinoza : ' *Homini nihil utilius homine ; ergo, hominem interimere nolui.*'

In short, let him say what he will. But Titus, whose account of himself I reserve for my choice, let him say:
' When I began to prepare, and so for the moment was
busy no longer with my passion, but with my rival, then
it became for the first time quite clear to me what now
was really to be his fate. But just here pity and compassion overcame me. I grieved for him ; my heart would
not be put down; I could not do it.' I ask now every
honest and unprejudiced reader, which of the two is the
better man ? To which of the two would he rather in-
trust his fate ? Which of them was restrained by the
purer motive ? Where, therefore, lies the principle of
moral action ? " [1]

What shall we say of this foundation for altruism ? Are pity and unselfishness thus shown to be,
for the purposes of ethics, identical ? Schopenhauer's suggestion seems attractive, but from the outset
doubtful. Let us examine it more carefully.

VI.

This Pity is, at all events, for the first just an impulse, no more ; so at least, as we learn, it appears
in the unreflective man.[2] " Nature," Schopenhauer
tells us, has " planted in the human heart that wondrous disposition through which the sorrows of one
are felt by the other, and from which comes the voice
that, according to the emergency, calls to one ' Spare,'
to another, ' Help,' and calls urgently and with authority. Surely there was to be expected from the
aid thus originating more for the prosperity of all

[1] *Grundlage der Moral*, p. 231.
[2] *Grundlage der Moral*, p. 245.

than could have been expected from a strict maxim
of duty, general, abstract, and deduced from certain
rational considerations and logical combinations of
ideas.   For from the latter source one might the less
expect success, because the mass of men must remain what they always have been, rude men, unable,
by reason of their inevitable bodily tasks, to get
time to cultivate their minds, and therefore, being
rude men, must find general principles and abstract
truths unintelligible, so that only the concrete has
meaning for them.   But for the arousing of this
pity, which we have shown to be the only source of
unselfish actions, and so the true basis of morality,
one needs no abstract, but only perceptive knowledge (*bedarf es keiner abstrakten, sondern nur der
anschauenden Enkenntniss*), only the mere understanding of the concrete case, to which pity at once
lays claim, without further reflective mediation."
And, to make his view clearer, Schopenhauer further appeals to passages quoted by him with approval from Rousseau:[1] " Il est donc bien certain,
que la pitié est un sentiment naturel, qui, modérant
dans chaque individu l'amour de soi-même, concourt
à la conservation mutuelle de toute l'espèce. . . .
C'est, en un mot, *dans ce sentiment naturel plutôt,
que dans les argumens subtils, qu'il faut chercher la
cause de la répugnance qu' éprouverait tout homme
à mal faire.*"   Pity, then, is no abstract principle,
but a tendency to do so and so in a concrete case.
For the natural and unlearned man it is a mere
sentiment, a *feeling with* his fellow, no more.

---

[1] "Discours sur l'origine de l'inégalité."   Quoted in the *Grundlage der Moral*, p. 247.

But then does this sentiment exhaust for Schopenhauer the whole meaning of pity? In no wise. Not for this sole reason is pity the whole basis of morality, namely, because it is the only non-egoistic impulse in us; but besides this reason, there is the second reason used by Schopenhauer to give special dignity to pity. This other reason is in fact the deeper basis for him of pity as the principle of conduct. Pity is namely a revelation in concrete form of a great fundamental truth, the one above referred to, the great fact of the ultimate and metaphysical Oneness of all sentient beings. Because pity reveals this, therefore has this sentiment an authority, a depth and a significance that a sentiment, merely as such, could never have.

About this aspect of the matter, Schopenhauer instructs us more than once in his writings. A few quotations from one discussion will serve for present illustration.

" The difference between my own and another's person seems for experience an absolute difference. The difference of space that separates me from my neighbor, separates me also from his joy and pain. But on the other hand, it must still be remarked, that the knowledge that we have of ourselves is no complete and clear knowledge." [1] . . . " Whereon is founded all variety and all multiplicity of beings? On space and time; through these alone is variety or multiplicity possible, since what is *many* can only be conceived as coexistent or as successive. Because the many like things are called *individuals*, I therefore call space and time, as making possible the existence of a *mul-*

[1] *Grundlage der Moral*, p. 267.

titude of individuals, the *principium individuationis.*" [1]
. . . " If anything is undoubtedly true in the explanations
that Kant's wonderful insight has given to the world, then
surely it is the Transcendental Æsthetics." . . . " According to this doctrine, space and time . . . belong only
to the *phenomena.* . . . But if the world in itself knows
not space or time, then of necessity the world in itself
knows nothing of *multitude.*" . . . " Hence *only one identical Being* manifests itself in all the numberless phenomena of this world of sense. And conversely, what appears
as a *multitude,* in space or in time, is not a real thing in itself, but only a phenomenon." . . . " Consequently that
view is not false that abolishes the distinction between
Self and Not-self; rather is the opposed view the false
one." . . . " But the former is the view that we have found
as the real basis of the phenomenon of pity, so that in fact
pity is the expression of it. This view then is the metaphysical basis of ethics, and consists in this : *that one individual directly recognizes in another his own very self,
his own true essence.*" [2]

These passages from Schopenhauer are, as one sees,
interesting not only because they defend the emotion
of pity as the foundation of morals, but also because
they offer an interesting suggestion of an aspect of
the matter not before noticed in our study. Like
so many of Schopenhauer's suggestions, this one is
neither wholly original, nor very complete in itself.
But it is so expressed as to attract attention ; it is
helpful to us by its very incompleteness. It is stimulating, although it proves nothing. This modern
Buddhism brings to our minds the query (which goes

[1] *Grundlage,* p. 267.   [2] *Grundlage,* p. 270.

beyond the present scope of this chapter), whether the altruistic motives, whatever they are, might not somehow be made of evident and general validity as ethical principles, *if we could show that in the moment of pity or in some other altruistic moment there is expressed the nascent discovery of an Illusion*, namely, the Illusion of Selfishness. That is what Schopenhauer supposed himself to have found out. In pity he found an unselfish impulse. But this unselfish impulse was, for the first, just an impulse, a sentiment, beloved of Rousseau, remote from the abstract principles that the philosophers had been seeking. Here was unselfishness, but still seeming to need reflective development and deeper foundation. Schopenhauer thought that he had found such a deeper basis for pity when he suggested that it was an imperfect metaphysical insight. In effect one might sum up his views thus : In deeper truth, he says, you and I are one Being, namely, *the* One great Being, the Absolute Will, which works in us both. But because we both perceive in time and space, therefore you and I seem to ourselves to be different and perhaps warring individuals, like the two halves of a divided worm. Only the sentiment of pity sees through the temporal veil of illusion, and so seeing, in its own intuitive, unreflective way, it whispers to us that the pain of each is in truth the other's pain. And when we really feel thus, we forget the illusion of sense, and act as if we were one. So acting we follow the higher insight, and when metaphysic comes, it will justify us in our view. Such, in our own words, are Schopenhauer's ideas.

We are still not concerned for Schopenhauer's metaphysic, which, God knows, was a rotten enough tub for a wise man to go down to the sea in. But in his character as keeper of beautiful curiosities, Schopenhauer shows us in his literary museum, that is built on the dry land, many very useful thoughts ; and we need not follow him out onto the great deep at present. But we note with interest this suggestion that he adds to his theory of pity. Is that suggestion worth anything? Is pity in fact a detection of an illusion? And does this illusion constitute the basis of selfishness? Perhaps that suggestion will be needed in a future chapter. Meanwhile, however, we have at present to do only with pity as a mere emotion. Surely if pity does discover for us any illusion in selfishness, then it must be a particular form of pity to which this function belongs. For much of pity simply illustrates this illusion. We cannot then do better than first to distinguish the selfish from the altruistic forms of what we popularly include under the one name Pity, or, to use the more general word, Sympathy. We shall have to go over old and commonplace ground, but we need to ; for the illusion of selfishness, to be detected, needs also to be illustrated.

VII.

When one sees his neighbor in pain, does one of necessity come to know that pain as such, to realize its true nature as it is in his neighbor? Or does one often fall into an illusion about that pain, regard-

ing it as somehow not quite real? Schopenhauer
would reply: The heartless man, who has no compassion, falls into a sort of illusion about his neighbor.
He thinks more or less clearly that that pain of his
neighbor's is a sort of unreal pain, not as living as
would be his own pain. But the pitiful man, the
only quite unselfish man, — he perceives the reality
of his neighbor's suffering. He knows that that is
no phantom suffering, but even such pain as his own
would be.

We want to test this idea in a practical way. So
we say: Let us judge of this sympathy by its fruits?
Are we in fact certain to be led to unselfish acts
if in all cases we obey the dictates of sympathy?
Schopenhauer thinks that he has secured altruism
for his sympathetic or pitiful man by remarking that,
in true pity, one feels the pain, not as his own, but
as the other's pain. To follow the dictates of this
sympathy would of necessity lead, one might say,
to the effort unselfishly to relieve the other. But
then does not this depend very much upon the way
in which pity comes to be an object of reflection for
the man that feels it? Pity is often of itself an in-
determinate impulse, that may be capable of very
various interpretation by the subsequent reflection
of the pitiful mind. One may through pity come to
reflect that this feeling stands for a real pain in the
other man, and may act accordingly; or one may
have very different reflections. One may fail to
realize the other's pain as such, and may be driven
back upon himself. For most people the first reflection that follows upon strong pity is no unselfish

one at all. It is very simply the precept : " Get rid of the pain that your neighbor causes you to feel." Sympathy with pain may make you tremble, grow faint, feel choked, weep; and all these sudden emotions are followed perhaps by long-enduring melancholy. All this causes you to forget the reality of the other's pain. This personal trouble of yours, felt in stronger cases in your body as a physical disturbance, as something unnerving, prostrating, overwhelming, turns your reflection upon yourself, and you are very apt to ask : What am I to do to be free from it ? So to ask is already to begin to forget your neighbor. The pain that his pain caused has simply become your pain. You are, even through your pity, bound fast in an illusion. For there are three ways of removing this pain, and of satisfying for you the sympathy that caused it. One way, and often a very hard one, puzzling to follow, full of responsibility and of blunders, would be taken if you did your best, perseveringly and calmly, to get your neighbor out of his trouble. That would doubtless take a long time, you would never be adequately thanked for your trouble, and you might very easily blunder and do harm instead of good to him, thus causing in the end yet more sympathetic pain for you, coupled this time with remorse. The second way is to get used to the sight of pain, so that you no longer feel any sympathetic suffering. The third way is generally the easiest of all. That is to go away from the place, and forget all about the sad business as soon as possible. That is the way that most sensitive people take in dealing with most of the suffering that they meet. The first way gives you the most of hard work to do. The second way, by dulling your sensibilities, makes you less alive to the pleasures that are to be gained in the company of happy men. The stern man, who has seen so much suffering as to be indifferent to it, may be less alive to the bliss of sympathy that gentler natures come to know, in refined and peaceful society. By far the most inviting way is the third. It prevents you from growing callous, cold, and harsh. It leaves you sensitive, appreciative, tender-hearted, freshly sympathetic, an admirable and humane being. But it also saves you from the pangs that to refined natures must be the most atrocious, the pangs of contemplating a world of sorrow which your best efforts can but very imperfectly help. People with a delicate sense of the beautiful surely cannot endure to go about seeing all sorts of filthy and ugly miseries, and if they can endure it, will they not be much happier, as well as more refined, more delicate in taste, much higher in the scale of beautiful cultivation, if they do not try to endure it, but keep themselves well surrounded by happy and ennobling companions? For the sight of pain is apt to make you coarse; it might degrade you even to the level of the peevish sufferer himself. Does a refined soul desire that? No one is a duller, a less stimulating, a less ennobling companion, than the average man when he is suffering atrociously. Pain brings out his native brutishness. He is abject, he curses, he behaves perhaps like a wild beast. Or he lies mute and helpless, showing no interest in what you do for

7

him, hating you possibly, just because you are the nearest creature to him. His gratitude is apt to be a myth. So long as he yet suffers, he does not appreciate what you are doing for him, for why should he thank you while you make him no better? And if you can cure him, what then? Nobody can remember very clearly a very sharp pain once over. Hence he will underrate your services. You can much better appreciate your moderate trouble in helping him than he can afterwards appreciate the very great and agonizing trouble from which you saved him. One forgets in part one's greatest anguish, one's most dangerous diseases. The worst troubles are not favorable to clear memory. Above all, however, his memory will be weak for what you did in his case. He will shock you afterwards by having failed to notice that you took any serious trouble in his behalf at all. But, if he was sick and you nursed him, he will remember very well how you harassed him as you nursed him. He will remember a creaking door or an ill-cooked steak, when he forgets your cups of cold water, your sleepless nights, your toil to secure silence when he needed it, your patience when he complained, your sacrifice of all other present aims in life on his account. All that he will forget, not because he is a bad man, but because he is an ordinary creature whom pain debased and corrupted, so that he became hardly a fit companion for an elevated and refined soul like yours. He is only human. If you were an average man yourself, you would treat your friends that aided you in your worst suffering after much the

same fashion. It is well if the sufferer and his
helper do not begin a quarrel that will last a life-
time, all because of the meddlesome self-sacrifice of
the officious helper. For to the wretched any help
is apt to seem officious, because no help is immediately and unconditionally successful.

So then, if you are tender-hearted, does tender-
heartedness dictate all this waste of sympathy?
Plainly not. Tender-heartedness need not say: *My
neighbor must be relieved*. Tender-heartedness, as
a personal affection of yours, says only: *Satisfy me.*
And you can satisfy this affection if you forget about
all those degraded wretches that are doomed to suffer, and associate with those blessed ones whose innocent joy shall make your tender heart glad of its
own tenderness. Let us rejoice with those that do
rejoice, and those that weep, let them take care of
themselves in everlasting oblivion. Such is the dictate of tender-hearted selfishness; and our present
point is the not at all novel thought, so often elab-
orated in George Eliot's novels, the thought that,
the tenderer the heart, the more exclusively selfish
becomes this dictate of tender-heartedness. Very
sensitive people, who cannot overcome their sensi-
tiveness, are perforce selfish in this world of pain.
They must forget that there is suffering. Their
pity makes them cruel. They cannot bear the sight
of suffering; they must shut the door upon it. If
he is a Dives, such a man must first of all insist that
the police shall prevent people like Lazarus, covered
with sores, from lying in plain sight at the gate.
Such men must treat pain as, in these days of

plumbing, we treat filth. We get the plumber and the carpenter to hide it so well that even our civilized nostrils shall not be offended. That we call modern improvement in house-building. Even so we get the police to hide suffering from us; and, when that help fails, or is inapplicable, we appeal to the natural sense of decency in the sufferers, and demand, on the ground of common courtesy, that they shall not intrude their miseries upon us. Thus we cultivate a tender sympathy for the most delicate emotions of the human heart, as we never could do if we let suffering, as our forefathers used to let filth, lie about in plain sight. Ignore another's suffering, and then it practically becomes non-existent. So says selfishness.

VIII.

If we ourselves are very happy, our lack of willingness to consider suffering may become greater and greater as we get happier. Nobody is colder in shutting out the thought of misery than a joyous man in a joyous company. "If there be anywhere any wretched people (which we doubt) let them keep well away from this place." That is the voice of the spirit of overflowing sympathetic joy, as Schiller so finely expresses it in the hymn *an die Freude:*—

> " He who, proving, hath discovered,
> What it is a friend to own,
> O'er whom woman's love hath hovered,
> Let him here his bliss make known:
> Yea, if but one living being,
> On the earth is *his* to-day, —

> And who ne'er has known such, fleeing,
> Let him weep his grief away." [1]

"Joy," says the enthusiastic young Schiller in this rhapsody, "Joy was bestowed on the worm." "All beings drink joy at Mother Nature's breast." Delightful generosity of the happy man! But what do the crushed worms think about it? "Whoso hath a friend," — but what of the poor wretches in the slums of great cities, beaten, starved, imprisoned, cheated, and cheating, starved and imprisoned again, all through their lifetimes? How many souls do these poor Ishmaelites call their own? But of whom shall the joyful man think, of whom does he or can he think? Of these? No, it is the tendency of selfish joy to build up its own pretty world of fancy. Everything in that world, from cherub to worm, has joy's sympathy, but only in so far as it is also joyous. *Seid umschlungen Millionen! dieser Kuss der ganzen Welt!* But in fact *dieser Kuss* is intended only for the happy world, which in the illusion, beautiful, but yet cruel, of the innocently joyous man, seems to be the whole world. Much good will such kisses do to the *Millionen* that groan and writhe! Joy ignores them, cannot believe them real.

Such then are some of the dictates of sympathy,

[1] Wem der grosse Wurf gelungen
Eines Freundes Freund zu sein,
Wer ein holdes Weib errungen
Mische seinen Jubel ein!
Ja, — wer auch nur *eine Seele*
Sein nennt auf dem Erdenrund!
Und wer 's nie gekonnt, der stehle,
Weinend sich aus diesem Bund.

which often bear to our conduct such relation as, in a saying of Emerson's, the desire to go to Boston bears to the possible ways of getting there. "When I want to get to Boston," says in substance Emerson, "I do not swim the Charles River, but prefer crossing the bridge." Emerson's saying was intended to illustrate his own preference for reading translations of foreign authors rather than the originals. It does illustrate very well the preference that we all have for the shortest way out of our sympathetic troubles. To help your suffering neighbor is hard swimming, perhaps amid ice-blocks ; to go on and find elsewhere merry company is to take the bridge direct to Boston. Sympathy leads therefore often to the ignoring of another man's state as real. And this is the very Illusion of Selfishness itself.

Pity may then turn to selfish hatred of the sight of suffering. It is hardly necessary to dwell at length upon the disheartening reverse aspect of the picture, namely, on the fact that, when pity does not lead us to dread the suffering of others, it may lead us to take such credit for our very power to sympathize with pain, that we come to feel an actual delight in the existence of the events that mean suffering to others. Our hearts may so swell with pride at our own importance as pitiful persons, that we may even long to have somebody of our acquaintance in trouble, so that we can go and pose, in the presence of the sufferers, as humane commentators on the occurrence, as heroic endurers of sorrows that we do not really share. This is the second stage of selfish pity. It is even more enduring and incurable than the first. The dread of the sight of pain may be made to pass away by enough of inevitable experience. But the selfish love of the office of comforter grows with the sense of our personal importance, and with the number of times when we are called upon to exercise our powers. There are people who are always fretful and disconsolate unless they know of somebody who very badly needs consoling. Then they are calm and happy, for they are sure that they are admirable as comforters, they feel themselves the centre of an admiring neighborhood, they are plying their noble avocation in a graceful fashion. This type is surely no very uncommon one. Such people are apt to be intolerable companions for you unless you have a broken leg, or a fever, or a great bereavement. Then they find you interesting, because you are wretched. They nurse you like saints; they speak comfortably to you like angels. They hate to give the little comfort that can be given from day to day to those who are enduring the ordinary vexations of healthy and prosaic life. They rejoice to find some one overwhelmed with woe. The happy man is to them a worthless fellow. High temperature is needed to soften their hearts. They would be miserable in Paradise, at the sight of so much tedious contentment; but they would leap for joy if they could but hear of a lost soul to whom a drop of water could be carried. To them the most blessed truth of Scripture is found in the passage: "For the poor ye have always with you." Yea, blessed are the merciful, for they shall never lack work. They shall be like the sculptor, delighting in the rough blocks of marble that contain his beloved statues. For them the world will doubtless have always a plenty of blocks.

These are not the vulgarly malevolent. Yet they would be disconsolate altogether if evil were to cease. They regard misery as their special property; hence they would be very much disappointed to hear that Paradise had come again, and that misery had been abolished. And we are speaking now, not of the professional enthusiasm that must make the physician interested in the diseases that he studies, but of the pure delight in pity that distinguishes certain unprofessional people whose lives would be almost utterly empty of all joy were their neighbors not subject to serious calamities. Surely it is not this sort of pity that overcomes the illusion of selfishness. Rather does such pity well illustrate that illusion.

IX.

Sympathy then, as an emotion, is not always altruistic, but frequently very selfish. It does not always overthrow, but often strengthens, selfishness. And so deceitful an emotion cannot be trusted with the office of giving moral insight. In so far as pity ever does involve the detection of an illusion of selfishness, we may have occasion to speak of it hereafter. For on that side, Schopenhauer's thought still looks attractive. But if we view pity with reference not to insight but to emotion, if we ask whether a given act was unselfish because it was pitiful, then we can already answer that, in so far as unselfishness constitutes morality, the pitiful character of an act does not insure its unselfishness, and hence not its morality. Schopenhauer's own typical example, quoted above, is indeed interesting, but not conclusive as to this question. "I pitied him," says the lover who has refrained from slaying his rival. "Had he not resembled my father as he slept, I had done it," says Lady Macbeth. Possibly Lady Macbeth's pity was good in itself, but not quite sufficient in quantity. But her words remind us of what the lover might do, if only pity stood in the way of the murder that he desired to commit. He might get somebody else to take care of the whole business, preparations and all, and so save his own tender emotions. In fact, however, Schopenhauer's young lover has something more than a mere emotion of pity in him.

But so far as we have considered sympathy, we have had but another illustration of the difficulty with which we are dealing. Even if sympathy were always unselfish, never capricious, perfectly clear in its dictates, there would remain the other objection. Sympathy is a mere fact of a man's emotional nature. To an unsympathetic man, how shall you demonstrate the ideals that you found upon the feeling of sympathy? And so one returns to the old difficulty. You have an ideal whereby you desire to judge the world. But this ideal you found in its turn on the fact that somebody has a certain sort of emotion. Any one who has not this emotion you declare to be an incompetent judge. And so your last foundation for the ideal is something whose worth is to be demonstrated solely by the fact that it exists.

Thus in this and in the last chapter, in general and in particular discussions, we have found the one problem recurring. The ideal is to have an ideal foundation, yet we seem always to give it a foundation in some reality. And if we then look about us, we always find some skeptic saying, either that he does not feel sure of the existence of any such reality, or that he doubts whether it means what we say that it means, or, again, that in any case there are other people, who have found other realities, and whose moral principles, founded on these other realities, are in deadly opposition to ours. The idealist of our preliminary discussion on the methods of ethical inquiry has so far met with numerous misfortunes. He has continually been enticed over to a sort of realistic position, and then just the same arguments that he used against the realist are used against him. If, however, true to himself, he assaults the realism of the modern descendants of Hobbes with the argument that all their physical hypotheses are worthless without ideals, then he hears the challenge to show an ideal that is not his whim, and that is not founded on a physical doctrine. There seems no refuge for him as yet but to turn skeptic himself.

CHAPTER V.

ETHICAL SKEPTICISM AND ETHICAL PESSIMISM.

Long is the night to him who is awake ; long is a mile to him who is tired ; long is life to the foolish who do not know the true law. — DHAMMAPADA.

To turn skeptic himself, we said, seemed the only way open before our idealist. If only he had placed his standard a little lower! If only he had not insisted on getting his ideal by ideal methods! Then he might have remained safe in some one of the positions that he temporarily assumed. But always he drove himself out of them. Some stupendous external reality, some beautiful mental state, would suggest itself to him, and he would say: "Lo, here is the ideal that I seek." But forthwith his own doubt would arise, accusing him of faithlessness. "What hast thou found save that this or that happens to exist?" the doubt would say, and our idealist would be constrained to answer, "Not because it exists, but because I have freely chosen it for my guide, is it the Ideal." And then would come the repeated accusation that caprice is the sole ground for the choice of this ideal. Skepticism, then, total skepticism as to the foundation of ethics, seems to be the result that threatens us. We must face this skepticism and consider its outcome.

I.

It is in fact in such skepticism as this that one finds the real power and meaning of most genuine modern Pessimism.   Not so much in the hopelessness of our efforts to reach our ideals once chosen as in our perpetual hesitation or unsteadiness in the choice of ideals, we most frequently find the deepest ground for pessimistic despair.   Choose an ideal, and you have at least your part to play in the world. The game may seem worth the trouble ; for far off as may be what you seek, there is the delight and the earnestness of free self-surrender to a great aim. But pessimism is almost inevitable if you have been long trying to find an ideal to which you can devote yourself, and if you have failed in your quest. Therefore those advocates of pessimism are most formidable who dwell less upon the ills of life, as bare facts, and more upon the aimlessness of life. Von Hartmann, therefore, to whom pessimism is more the supposed result of a process of summation, and thus is a belief that the sum of pains in life overbalances the sum of pleasures, produces little effect upon us by his balance-sheet.   But Schopenhauer, who dwelt not only upon the balance-sheet, but still more upon the fundamental fact that life is restless and aimless, — he is nearer to success in his pessimistic efforts.   It is here that one finds also the true strength of Schopenhauer's model, the Buddhistic despair of life.   Choose your aim in life, says in effect Buddhism, let it be wife or child, wealth or fame or power, and still your aim is only

one among many, lost in the eternal strife, at war
with all the rest, and never able to prove its right to
supremacy in the world. From life to life you pass,
now a Brahman, now a king, now a worm, now a
tiger, now a beggar, now in hell, now among the
demons of the air ; your aims alter everlastingly
with each new birth, and nowhere do you find life
anything but a succession of aims, no one of which
is intrinsically more significant than the others.
The world of aims is a world of strife, and no life
has any real significance. No desire is of any essential worth. Therefore, seeing all this, give up
desire. Have it as your one aim to have no aim.
Such is the outcome of the insight into the eternal
warfare of aims. The Buddhist parables try to
make plain this insignificance of life both by dwelling on the fact that men must finally fail to get their
aims, and by insisting that, if men temporarily succeed, their condition is no less insignificant than it is
when they fail. The failure is used to show a man
not so much the difficulty of getting his aim in this
bad world, as the worthlessness of his aim. The
success when it comes is embittered for the successful man by reminding him that all desire is transient, and that what he now loves will come to seem
hateful to him. In both cases the lesson, whether of
the success or of the failure, is, not that the order of
things is diabolical, and therefore an enemy of mankind, but that the desires themselves are hopelessly
confused and worthless. If Buddhism dwelt only
on the hopelessness of our efforts to get the good
things that we want, the doctrine would result in a

sort of Promethean defiance of the physical world, our powerful and cruel enemy. But Buddhism insists upon it that we know not what are the good things that we pretend to want. Our desires being ignorant, and endlessly changeable, we have no right to hope for success. The moral of their stories is not a protest against the physical evils about us, but a general condemnation of the vain aims that are in us.

The same aimlessness of life is the subject of lament in much of our modern romantic poetry. Here is, for the melancholy romantic poet, the great evil of existence, that we know not what is good. Here is the great disappointment of life, that we have no object in life. Here is the great failure, that we cannot make up our minds to undertake anything. Here is the great emptiness, that we have nothing to fill. And thus the ethical skepticism that has so far beset our path in the present investigation becomes, when we dwell upon it and fully realize its meaning, an ethical pessimism. We shall then illustrate afresh our problem if we consider how this difficulty of the choice of an ideal has affected the search of certain among our modern romantic poets for what they would call the ideal emotion.

II.

Of all the subjects of reflection in romantic poetry, none is more familiar than the question of the meaning and worth of human life as a whole. The first and natural answer of the modern poet to this question is well known. Human life means for him the emotional side of life. The highest good, when found, must be an emotional good. The romantic poet, criticising life, must aim to make clear what kind of emotional condition is the most satisfactory one. In this view we have no mere truism. Many forms of Hedonism would oppose the doctrine that in the intenser emotions can be found the ideal states of consciousness. The common sense of men of the world sees in the more moderate pleasures of polite leisure, in the attainment of practical knowledge, in a successful professional or business career, the sources of permanent satisfaction. Several schools of ancient philosophy regarded tranquillity as constituting the essence of a blessed life. But to all this the spirit of modern poetry was from the outset violently opposed. Tranquillity, once exchanged for storm and stress, is not again regarded as the goal. Active emotion, intense in quality, unlimited in quantity, is what the poets of the revolution desire. One need only mention "Werther," "The Robbers," "The Revolt of Islam," "Manfred," "Faust," to suggest what is meant by this spirit of the revolutionary poetry.

Life, then, can be of worth only in so far as it is full of the desirable forms of poetic emotion. But is such fullness of life possible? Is the view that makes it the ideal a tenable view? Must not the consistent following of this view lead ultimately to pessimism? The answer to this problem is the history of the whole romantic movement. Here must suffice a sketch of some of the principal results of the movement.

The stir of modern life, then, has awakened sensibility, quickened desire, aroused the passion for freedom, disturbed old traditions. Above all, the theological ideals of life have been, for the romantic poet, disturbed, perhaps shattered. His highest good must be sought in his own soul. What is the consequence? First, of course, a sense of splendid independence, a lofty spiritual pride. The joy of freed emotion is equaled by few delights on earth. The self-worship of poetic genius is surpassed by few forms of conceit. Shelley, rejoicing in his strength, writing " The Necessity of Atheism," and defending, in all innocence of evil, adultery and incest, is a good example of the expression of this spirit. Lavatar's account of the nature of genius is another instance : " As the apparitions of angels do not come, but are present, do not go away, but are gone, as they strike the innermost marrow, influence by their immortality the immortal in men, vanish and yet still influence, leave behind them sweet shuddering and tears of terror, and on the countenance pale joy, so the operation of genius. Describe genius as you will, — name it fruitfulness of soul, faith, hope, love, — the unlearned, the unlearnable, — the inimitable, the divine, — that is genius. 'T is inspiration, revelation, that may be felt, but not willed or desired ; 't is art above art, its way is the way of the lightning." [1] We cannot quote a tenth part of this rhapsody, wherein the self-admiration and the mutual admiration of the young men about Goethe, in the years just before and after 1780, receive a characteristic expression.

[1] See the passage at much greater length in Koberstein's *Gesch. der deutschen. Nationalliteratur,* bd. iv., p. 26, of the 5th edit.

This pride leads directly to the effort to build up a wholly new set of ideals. The patience of the statesman, of the student of science, of the business man, is unknown to these forceful young men. They must make a world of their own, and in a day too. At the same time they are without any definite faith. In fact, definite faith would endanger for them the freshness of their emotions. They fear any creed but one self-made. And they can more easily tear down than build up. One of the most interesting of the young geniuses of the age of the German romantic development [1] is the early lost Novalis (Friedrich von Hardenberg), a representative, like Shelley after him, of the emotional or romantic poetry in its pristine innocence. A truly noble soul, joined to a weak body, oppressed by many troubles, unable to grow to full manly spiritual stature, he shows us the beauty and imperfection of the emotional movement in close union. He writes pages of vague philosophy, which afterwards impressed the young Carlyle as an embodiment of a sense of the deep mystery of life. You find delight in wandering through the flowery labyrinths of such speculation; you learn much by the way, but you come nowhere. Only this is clear : the young poet persists that the world must in some way conform to the emotional needs of man. And he persists, too, that a harmonious scheme of life can be formed on a purely romantic plan, and only on such a plan. He actually

---

[1] The age in question extends from 1770 to 1830. No special effort is here made to follow chronological order. Our purpose is to cite illustrations, not to give a history.

8

explains no reality and completes no scheme of life. He hints, at length, that the Catholic church is the best expression of the needs of man. With this unsatisfactory suggestion, the little career of wandering ends in death. But in what could it have ended had life continued?

Perhaps in what was called by the close friend of Novalis, Friedrich Schlegel, the romantic irony. This is the next stage in the growth, or, if you like, in the decay of the romantic spirit. Emotion is our guide and our goal. But what is emotion? Something changeable and by nature inconsistent. Each emotion sets up a claim to fill the whole of life. For each new one, the earnest poetic soul feels willing to die. Yet each is driven away by its follower. The feet of them that shall bear it out are before the door even while the triumphant emotion is reigning over the heart within. Fullness of such life means fickleness. Novalis, upon the death of his betrothed, made a sort of divinity of the departed, and dated a new era from the day of her death. His diary was for a while full of spiritual exercises, suggested by his affliction. He resolved to follow her to the grave in one year. Within this year he was betrothed anew. If such is Novalis, what will be a lesser spirit? Conscious of this inevitable decay of each emotion, Friedrich Schlegel suggests that one should make a virtue of necessity, and declare that the higher life consists in a sort of enthusiastic fickleness. The genius must wander like a humming-bird in the garden of divine emotions. And he must be conscious and proud of his wanderings. Activity, or rather agility, is his highest perfection. The more numerous his emotions, the nobler the man. The fickler the man, the more numerous his emotions. This conscious union of nobility and fickleness is the romantic irony, which consists in receiving each new enthusiasm with a merry pride. 'T was not the first, and will not be the last. We see through it, even while we submit to it. We are more than it is, and will survive it. Long live King Experience, who showers upon us new feelings!

So much for an ingenious and thoroughly detestable view of life, in which there is for an earnest man no rest. This irony, what is it but the laughter of demons over the miserable weakness of human character? The emotion was to be our god. It turns out to be a wretched fetich, and we know it as such. 'T was mine, 't is his, and has been slave to thousands. It is gone, though we trusted in it. It was our stay, and it has flowed away like water. This is not fullness, but hollowness, of life. And how shall the romantic irony supply the vacancy? This irony is but the word of Mephistopheles about the ruin of Gretchen: *Sie ist die erste nicht.* Not the first change of emotion is this present one; not the first breaking up of the fountains of the great deep within us; but what misery in that thought! Then there is nothing sure, nothing significant. In our own hearts were we to find life, and there is no true life there; only masks with nothing beneath them; only endless and meaningless change.

The consciousness of this result is present in another form of the romantic spirit. The consequence is what Hegel, in the *Phänomenologie des Geistes*, described under the name of *Das Unglückliche Bewusstsein*, and what is more familiarly known to us as the Byronic frame of mind. The very strength of the previous emotion renders this consciousness of the hollowness of emotion the more insupportable: —

> " When the lamp is shattered
> The light in the dust lies dead."

The brighter the lamp, the deeper the darkness that follows its breaking.

The romantic despair thus described took many forms in the poetry of the early part of the century. To describe them all were to go far beyond our limits. A few forms suggest themselves. If we are condemned to fleeting emotions, we are still not deprived of the hope that some day we may by chance find an abiding emotion. Thus, then, we find many poets living in a wholly problematic state of mind, expecting the *god stronger than they, who, coming, shall rule over them.* Such a man is the dramatist and writer of tales, Heinrich von Kleist. " It can be," writes this poet to a friend, December, 1806, " it can be no evil spirit that rules the world, only a spirit not understood." In such a tone of restless search for the ideal of action, Kleist remains throughout his life. No poet of the romantic school had a keener love of life-problems purely as problems. Each of his works is the statement of a question. In so far Kleist resembles that more recent representative of the problematic school of poetry, Arthur Hugh Clough. Kleist answered his own questions at last by suicide. Others have other ways of fleeing misery. Ludwig Tieck, after running through the whole round of romantic questions, rids himself of his demons by turning his attention to other literary work, and lets most of the old romantic ideals alone, or playfully writes amusing stories about them. Friedrich Schlegel finally escapes from himself by means of a scholarly toil and Catholic faith. Hölderlin takes refuge in a mad-house. Shelley manages to endure his brief life, by dint of childlike submissiveness to his emotions, joined with earnest hope for yet better things. Schiller had joined with Goethe in a search for perfection in the ancient Greek world. There are many fashions of quieting the restlessness that belonged to the time, yet what one of them really answers the problems of the romantic spirit? There is still the great question: How may mankind live the harmonious emotional life, when men are driven for their ideals back upon themselves, when traditional faith is removed, when the age is full of wretchedness and of blind striving, when the very strength of poetic emotion implies that it is transient and changeable? The conscious failure to answer this question is more or less decided pessimism.

Could modern poetry free itself from that reflective tendency in which we have found its most prominent characteristic, the pessimism could disappear with the criticism of life. But this is impossible. Omit part of our lyric poetry, some of our comedy and of our satire, and the rest of our best nineteenth century poetic work is a more or less conscious struggle with pessimism. The grounds and the nature of this struggle have been set forth in the foregoing. The poet once for all accepts the emotional criterion of the worth of life. Determining to see in the harmonious emotional life the best life, feeling as the most certain of principles that " there is a lower and a higher," the poet seeks to picture the perfect existence thus defined. Failure means for him pessimism; not von Hartmann's really quite harmless " *eudämonologischer Pessimismus*," but the true pessimism of the broken will, that has tried all and failed. The life that ought to be, cannot be; the life that is, is hollow and futile : such will be the result of disappointed idealism. In our time, the idealistic poets that are not pessimists have all fought more or less consciously the same battle with pessimism. Think only of the " Excursion," or of the " In Memoriam," or again of "Faust," that epitome of the thought of our century.

But before we allow ourselves a word on the relation of " Faust " to our problem, let us look a little more closely at Byron. " Faust " is the crown of modern poetic effort. If that fails as a solution, all in this field has thus far been lost. But in Byron there is a confessed, one may add a professed, moral imperfection, whose nature throws light, not so much on the solution of the problem of pessimism, as on the problem itself.

The development of Byron's poetry has two very marked periods, the sentimental and the critical. The sentimental Byron of the years before 1816 is not of very great present interest. The Byron of

" Manfred," " Cain," and " Don Juan," represents an independent phase of the romantic movement, whose faults are as instructive as its beauties. This period of Byron's poetry is of course but very roughly described by the word critical, yet that word is at any rate suggestive. A sensitive man, and yet heroic, strong in spirit, but without fixed ideals of life, a rebel by nature who yet finds no greater soul to lead him, no faithful band to follow him in any definite effort for mankind, Byron is a modern likeness of him that in the legend afterwards became St. Christopher. Only Byron seeks the strongest without finding him, learns to despise the devil, and never meets the devil's master. Worn out with the search, the poet flings himself down in the woods of doubt and dreams " Don Juan." We look in vain for the right adjective with which to qualify this poem : it is so full of strength, so lavish of splendid resources, and yet in sum so disappointing. It has no true ending, and never could have had one. It is a mountain stream, plunging down dreadful chasms, singing through grand forests, and losing itself in a lifeless gray alkali desert. Here is romantic self-criticism pushed to its farthest consequences. Here is the self-confession of an heroic soul that has made too high demands on life, and that has found in its own experience and in the world nothing worthy of true heroism. We feel the magnitude of the blunder, we despise (with the author, as must be noticed, not in opposition to him) the miserable petty round of detestable experiences — intrigues, amours, dinners — in brief, the vulgarity to which human life is reduced ; but the tragedy is everywhere to be read between the lines, not in what is said. The romantic spirit has sought in vain for the satisfactory emotional state, and for the worthy deed to perform, and now rests, scornful and yet terrified, in dizzy contemplation of the confused and meaningless maze of sensations into which the world has resolved itself. "There is nothing there to fear or hope," this spirit seems to say.

> "When Bishop Berkeley said there was no matter,
> And proved it, 't was no matter what he said."

Or again : —

> "'To be or not to be?' Ere I decide
> I should be glad to know that which is being ;
> 'T is true we speculate both far and wide,
> And deem, because we *see*, we are *all-seeing*.
> For my part, I 'll enlist on neither side,
> Until I see both sides for once agreeing.
> For me, I sometimes think that life is death,
> Rather than life, a mere affair of breath."

In " Manfred " the same spirit seeks another, and not quite so successful, a form of expression. The only peace that can come to this world-weary spirit, Manfred expresses at the sight of a quiet sunset. The only freedom from eternal self-examination is found in an occasional glance at peaceful nature.

> " It will not last,
> But it is well to have known it though but once ;
> It hath enlarged my thoughts with a new sense,
> And I within my tablets would note down
> That there is such a feeling."

The famous last words of Manfred, —

> " Old man, 't is not so difficult to die," —

coming as they do after all Manfred's vacillation upon just this point, indicate the final resolution of despair to brave all possible wretchedness from without for the sake of feeling within, in all its strength, though but for a moment, the fierce defiance of the rebellious Titan. Hungry for deeds, finding nothing to do, fearing the possible future life, and hating the present, the hero at last resorts to an untrue but stirring assertion of absolute personal independence of all the hateful universe here and hereafter : —

> " Thou didst not tempt me, and thou couldst not tempt me.
> I have not been thy dupe, nor am thy prey —
> But was my own destroyer, and will be
> My own hereafter."

This is pessimism that overleaps itself. The outcome of self-analyzing romanticism is the determination to build afresh a world that shall be nobler than this poor world of decaying passive emotions. Feeling will not do. Manfred attains something by action, even though he first acts in the moment of death. Doing work of some kind is, then, that to which we are necessarily driven. But if the action of defiance can make death tolerable, why might not some kind of activity make life tolerable ? Is not the worthy life then to be found, not in emotion, but in work ? Is not the ideal state the ideal activity, not the ideal feeling ? This suggestion had been at the foundation of the prototype of Manfred, the Faust of Goethe.

Praise of the first part of Goethe's " Faust " is nowadays superfluous. Doubtless the work is a torso,[1] but so is the life of man. Extravagant en comium of "Faust," such as that wherewith Hermann Grimm has marred, as with a showman's harangue, the conclusion of his otherwise most instructive "Lectures on Goethe," seems as out of place as applause in a cathedral. The poem is grand and profound, because the life problems it so truthfully portrays are grand and profound; in form, if you except digressions, it is sublimely simple and unassuming. Its imperfections are as open to view as is its grandeur. The doctrine of the poem may be thus briefly suggested. Here is a world wherein nature, the expression of divine intelligence, is perfect; wherein man, by the same divine wisdom, is left in darkness and confusion. The angels, who simply contemplate nature's perfection, are the "true sons of God." But they do nothing. They only see and think. Man is to act. By his action he is freely to create such perfection as already passively exists in nature. That is, his life is to become an harmonious whole. The postulate of the Lord is that this is possible. Mephistopheles holds the opposite opinion. The question is to be solved by the case of Faust.

Faust is a man in whom are combined all the strength and weakness of the romantic spirit. No excellence he deems of worth so long as any excellence is beyond his grasp. Therefore his despair at the sight of the great world of life. So small a part of it is his. He knows that he can

[1] Cf. the opinion of M. Edm. Scherer as quoted in Mr. Matthew Arnold's essay, *A French Critic on Goethe*, in the *Mixed Essays*, p. 291.

never grow great enough to grasp the whole, or any finite part of the whole. Yet there remains the hopeless desire for this wholeness. Nothing but the infinite can be satisfying. Hence the despair of the early scenes of the first part. Like Byron's Manfred, Faust seeks death; but Faust is kept from it by no fear of worse things beyond, only by an accidental reawakening of old childish emotions. He thereafter feels that he has no business with life, and is a creature of accident. He is clearly conscious only of a longing for a full experience. But this experience he conceives as mainly a passive one. He does not wish as yet to do anything, only to get everything.[1] But at the same time with this desire for a tempest of new feelings, Faust has the consciousness that there never can be a satisfactory feeling. Mephistopheles, stating the case of the contented man of the world, assures him that the time will come for enjoying good things in peace. Faust indignantly replies that pleasure can never deceive him, the tolerable moment never come. In making this very assertion, however, and in concluding his pact with Mephistopheles upon the basis of this assertion, Faust rises above his first position, and assumes a new one. The satisfactory pleasure can never be given to him, and why? Because he will always remain active. Satisfaction would mean repose, repose would mean death. Life is activity. The meaning of the pact is of course that, for good or

[1] Cf. the lengthy discussion of this point in Friedrich Vischer, *Goethe's Faust, Neue Beiträge zur Kritik des Gedichts*, especially p. 291 and p. 304. " *Er* (Faust) *weiss also für jetzt nur von der Lust.*"

for evil, all the existence of a man is work, and that no one is ever wholly lost so long as the power of accomplishment remains his. But if work is the essence of life, then satisfaction must be found not in feelings but in deeds. The world is good if we can make it so, not otherwise. The problem of Faust is therefore the discovery of the perfect kind of activity.

With this insight the romantic spirit has risen beyond itself. The essence of romanticism is the desire for fullness of personal experience. The essence of this new spirit is the eagerness to accomplish something. The difference is vast. Faust, following this new tendency, might be led to an obscure toiling life of endless self-sacrifice. His pessimism (for in the early scenes he is a pessimist) might give way before unquestioning heroic devotion to some great end. Does this take place? We know too well the answer. The whole poem is indeed a conflict between the two tendencies in Faust, but the first, the desire for manifold passive experiences, is until the last scenes of the second part predominant. Faust is active, but his activity is mainly a continual pursuit of new experiences. Even at the end he is not active as other men are active; his work is done by magic; and the accomplishment for whose sake he is at last willing to say, *This is the highest moment*, is an anticipation, not a reality. In the real world the satisfactory work is never found. And thus the solution of the problem is not fully given, though the poet, while suggesting it, has done more than any other modern poet. The revolution had furnished as life-ideals grand emotion and heroic action. The two cannot wholly be harmonized. The highest forms of activity imply self-sacrifice, drudgery, routine, cool-headed calculation. The highest forms of emotion, pursued by themselves, intoxicate and enervate. It is the purpose of Goethe to lead his hero through the various stages of emotional life, for the sake of making him prefer in the end a mode of action to all forms of simple emotion. The result is to be a man above the deadness of ordinary work-a-day realism, yet as devoted to toil as the stupidest realist. There is to be a free surrender of a full self to the service of some high end. Nothing is lacking to the conquest over pessimism, except the clear statement of that for which the converted Faust is to work. The goal of activity once found, the problem will be solved, and the devil's wager lost. But the dim allegorical suggestions of the second part will not suffice to give us the account of what is wanted. Faust is to work for human progress, and progress means the existence of a whole nation of hard-laboring, fearless men who fight forever for their freedom. To have been the father of such a people is the highest blessedness. Good, indeed, we say; but to have wrought by the devil's aid, through magic and oppression, is this the highest? Is this the type of the best activity? And is the great problem after all really solved? For what is the ultimate good of the eternal warfare with nature in which mankind are thus left? Faust leaves behind him a nation of toilers, whose business it will be to build dikes to keep the sea out. A worthy end of romantic hopes, truly! That Goethe him self is not wholly content therewith is proven by the epilogue in heaven, which means, if it means anything, that the highest end of human activity is something very fine, but altogether inexpressible, invisible, inconceivable, indefinite, a thing of ether and dreams. One longs in this last scene for the presence of Mephistopheles, who surely has as much right there as in the prologue, and who would be sure to say, in his terse and sinewy fashion, just the right and the last word about the whole business.

The incompleteness of " Faust " is the incomplete. ness of modern thought. The poet is silent about the final problem, because modern thought is still toiling away on the definition of the highest human activity.

Thus we have found that our moral problem is shared by others than the moral philosophers. Almost at random we have taken a few suggestive illustrations of this same moral problem as it appears to the poets. Had we made use of the poets of the present day, we could have illustrated still other aspects of the question. The restless dramatic genius of Browning, for instance, always giving us glimpses of new ideals that men of strange fashions have or may have, unweariedly warns us not to pretend to narrow the possible objects of life down to one, however sacred we may think that one to be. Life, thus viewed, seems a grand everlasting warfare of ideals, among which peace is impossible. And with this insight into the actual and seemingly irreconcilable warfare of human aims, ethical doctrine must begin. The outlook is gloomy, but the problem must be faced.

III.

Such are some of the motives that give genuine meaning to modern pessimism. This instability of all ideals is the greatest danger to which idealism can be subject. And the problem is not one of mere theory, nor yet even of poetic emotion alone. The problem is one of daily life. We choose some fashion of life in the morning, and we reject it before night. Our devotional moments demand that all life shall be devotional; our merry moments that all life shall be merry; our heroic moments that all life shall be lived in defiance of some chosen enemy. But we are false to all these our ideals, even while we pretend to have them. And the most disheartening aspect of the whole matter lies in the fact that we cannot prove even our faithlessness to be unworthy, unless we can bring ourselves steadfastly to accept some ideal by which our faithlessness itself can be judged. And this would imply that we were no longer faithless.

We have thus reached the root of moral skepticism. The worst that moral skeptics can say is that all choice of ideals is an accidental caprice, that ideals have no basis but this caprice, and that a moral code depends for its successful propagation wholly on the persuasive personal force of the man that happens to have it and to teach it.

For the first, then, we provisionally accept this skeptical view. We shall regard the moral ideals in this light. We shall seek no impossible proof for any of them. But we shall try to see whither the skeptical view itself leads us.

If we look now for a final and perfectly cold-blooded statement of this moral skepticism, a statement that shall let us see once for all its meaning, its foundation, and its scope, the present author knows of no better expression of it than the one that is contained in the appendix to Mr. Arthur Balfour's "Defense of Philosophic Doubt," [1] under the title "The Idea of a Philosophy of Ethics." Mr. Balfour has shown us by the book in question that he has a very useful office in philosophic discussion, and we can only thank him for having made positive advance in ethics easier, by his clear statement of the difficulties that in the past have barred the way.

"Scientific judgments and ethical judgments deal," says Mr. Balfour, " with essentially different subject-matters." Scientific propositions state "facts or events, real or hypothetical." Ethical propositions do not " announce an event," nor yet do they tell any " fact of the external or internal world." Ethical writers too often consider the " psychology of the individual holding the moral law." But this is no matter for ethics, but only for psychological science. In fact, " if a proposition announcing obligation require proof at all, one term of that proof must always be a proposition announcing obligation, which itself requires no proof." " There is no artifice by which an ethical proposition can be evolved from a scientific or metaphysical proposition, or any combination of such." " The origin of an ultimate ethical belief can never supply a reason for believing

1 London, MacMillan & Company, 1879.

it, since the origin of this belief, as of any other mental phenomenon, is a matter to be dealt with by science ; and my thesis is that (negatively speaking) scientific truth alone cannot serve as a foundation for a moral system ; or (to put it positively), if we have a moral system at all, there must be contained in it, explicitly or implicitly, at least one ethical proposition, of which no proof can be given or required."

The reader may ask : Is all this the loftiest idealism, or is it simply philosophic skepticism about the basis of ethics ? We may leave the reader to examine for himself Mr. Balfour's very ingenious discussion, but one or two very obvious and simple consequences may be quoted from the rest of the essay, and these will serve well enough to show here the drift of the discussion.

" An ethical proposition is one that prescribes an action with reference to an end." Every such proposition " belongs to a system." " The fundamental proposition of every such system states an end, which the person who receives that system regards as final — as chosen for itself alone." " When two such systems conflict, their rival claims can only be decided by a judgment or proposition not contained in either of them, which shall assert which of these respective fundamental ' ends ' shall have precedence." " If revenge against a particular individual is for me an end-in-itself, a proposition which prescribes shooting him from behind a hedge may be one of the dependent propositions belonging to that particular system." " Though under the name ethical are in-

9

cluded not only moral, but also non-moral and immoral systems, the distinctions regarded from the outside between these subdivisions are not essential, and have no philosophic import." Such then is the skeptical outcome of this very idealistic position from which we ourselves started. Thus viewed, the moral world seems essentially chaotic. Each end, if chosen, has its own way of marshaling acts as good and bad. But one end cannot establish itself theoretically over against another. The warfare among them is practical, but is not rationally to be judged or ended. Each says, " In me is the truth about right and wrong. I am the Way." But for one another they have, not arguments, but anathemas. They give no proof, only assertion and condemnation. It is the contemplation of this chaos that has suggested to us that plausible and yet dreadful pessimism of which modern thought has had so much to say, and of which this chapter has tried to give some notion.

CHAPTER VI.

THE MORAL INSIGHT.

> Love is like understanding, that grows bright,
> Gazing on many truths.
>
> SHELLEY, *Epipsychidion.*

WE have needed to dwell on our ethical skepticism, to experience the real strength of its doubts, in order that we should be able to get new and better methods of construction for our own doctrine. Deep as is the truth that lies at the basis of many ethical doctrines now either doubted or abandoned, one thing always seems defective about their fashion of building. This one defect has made us question their worth as theories. And our theoretical doubt, as we dwelt upon it, has become practical. We have seen how this ethical skepticism leads to the gloomiest pessimism. Both the skepticism and the pessimism we must meet fairly and fearlessly. And we must ask them how even they themselves are possible.

I.

Our skeptical criticism of ethical theories has been so far either internal or external. We have criticised each doctrine in itself, questioning either its consistency or its inner completeness; or else we have criticised it with reference to other doctrines. In the first case our criticism led to no general skepticism, and had importance only in the special case. But the other kind of criticism was of more importance, and took another turn. We said to the doctrine : " Perfect as your system may be in itself, your assumption of your highest end always finds over against itself an equally stubborn assumption of an exactly opposing end. And you have no proof to offer for your rejection of that end. You simply insist upon calling it a diabolical end; you hurl at it your anathema. Now we, who have wanted proof, not mere enthusiasm, we, who stand critically before your doctrine, and view it from without, and desire to know why we are to accept it, we feel a skeptical indifference about your end, as soon as we compare it with the opposing end, and as soon as comparing, we find the difference between them to be one that rests, not on demonstrable truth, but on a mere kind of caprice. Practically we may agree with you in choosing, as men of action, your aim. Our personal caprice may agree with yours. But theoretically we cannot justify this aim. We find, in all that you say, no objective moral truth, but only somebody's capricious resolution. And even if we chance to accept your resolution, who knows when we shall change our minds, and begin acting in some new way, so that what we now call good shall be called evil? In brief, if there is to be possible anything more than moral preaching, if there is to be anything worthy of the name of demonstrated moral doctrine, then all your discussion must lead to something not dependent on the bare choice of individual moral agents. But in truth what you give us is just the fact of your choice. And hence it is that we are skeptics."

What does this our skepticism mean? Unreflective, self-satisfied skepticism always means mental death; but in self-critical skepticism, observant of itself as of everything else, moves the very life-blood of philosophy. And of this the whole of the present book will try to be an illustration. Just here, therefore, we want to be as watchful of our skepticism as we were of the systems whose theoretical weakness led us hither. What is the sense of this theoretical skepticism of our present attitude? On our reply all else turns. And our reply is: This skepticism expresses an indifference that we feel when we contemplate two opposing aims in such a way as momentarily to share them both. For the moment we realize equally these warring aims. They are ours. The conflict is in us. The two wills here represented are our will. And for this reason, and for this only, can we feel the skeptical indecision. Had we the will to choose the one end alone, we should unhesitatingly choose it, and should not see enough of the opposing will to be skeptics. Had we only the will that chooses the opposing end, we should feel equally indifferent to the first. Had we neither will at all in mind, did we realize neither one of the opposing ends, we should be feeling no hesitation between them. Our doubt arises from the fact that momentarily and provisionally we are in the attitude of assuming both. Our indifference is not the indifference of ignorance, but of knowledge; not of failure to understand either end, but of readiness to realize both ends. Hence it follows that moral skepticism is itself the result of an act, namely, of the act by which we seek to realize in ourselves opposing aims at the same time. This observation is of the greatest importance to us, and we must dwell upon it. It shows us that above all our skepticism is the supreme End that makes the skepticism itself possible.

The ethical aims themselves are all of them the expression of somebody's will. Their conflict is the conflict of wills. Doubt about them depends upon the realization of their existence and of their opposition. Therefore this doubt depends for its very existence on the conditions of this realization. We have tried to state what the conditions are. To realize opposing ends so completely that one feels a genuine doubt which of them to accept, implies, we say, the simultaneous provisional acceptance of both. And this may be shown in a more popular psychological way, as well as in a more general philosophical way. We take the psychological way first.

How can I know that there is anywhere a will, W, that chooses for itself some end, E ? Really to know this implies something more than mere outer observation of the facts. One must repeat in one's own mind more or less rapidly or imperfectly this will, W, that one conceives to exist in somebody else. And this need of repetition is a well-known psychological truth, very easily illustrated by all sorts of commonplace facts. Let us refer to some of these.

To think of a bodily act is to perform the act, or at least mentally to initiate the performance of the act. According to Professor Bain's now generally accepted principle, the memory or the conception of an act is physiologically connected with the fainter excitation of just the same nerve-tracts as would be more intensely excited in the real performance of the act. Therefore it is true that to think of yawning is to initiate a yawn, to think of walking is to initiate steps ; and, in case of any excitable person, or in case of any momentary predisposition to perform the act, the conception may immediately become the act, because the nascent excitation involved in the conception of the act may at once pass over into the completer excitation, and the ideal deed may become a visible fact. Thus the excited man, if not checked by company, may at once talk aloud to himself, his thoughts becoming words. If very much excited, he may mutter to himself even in the presence of company. He is much more apt to do this if he thinks not only of the words themselves, but of the act of speaking them, namely, if he imagines himself talking to somebody, and emphatically bringing his thoughts home to that other. In a weak state of body, this tendency to repeat an act whenever one conceives it may become quite distressing. To think of vomiting may mean to vomit. Or again, to think of laughter or of tears may in such a case make one laugh or cry. Hence the weak man may dislike to begin laughing, because he knows that, other exciting causes apart, the mere memory that he has laughed may keep him laughing afresh long after the sense of the ridiculous has passed away, so that to begin laughing may mean total exhaustion before he can stop.

Imitation rests at least in part upon this tendency. An act is performed, we witness it, we see or know how it is done, we conceive the effort that would lead to the performance of it, and forthwith this conception becomes the performance. We imitate the gesture of the actor or of the story-teller before us, and we feel an inner imitation of many acts, even though we suppress the outward signs. In general, for us to realize an act means that we shall do it, either in outward fact, or through a nascent performance that is not outwardly visible. Much of the recently so-called "mind-reading," more accurately named by some psychologists "muscle - reading," rests upon this foundation. For the conception of acts that are not outwardly performed is often indicated by slight motions or tensions of arm or of fingers, or of the whole body, and the muscle-reader, getting some close contact with his subject, amuses a company by interpreting these unseen, but readily felt signs of the thoughts of his subject. Very deeply do such facts enter into the structure of our mental life. Mr. Galton, investigating word-associations, found in many cases that the idea immediately aroused by a word was a sort of dramatic reproduction of the act expressed by the word. This dramatic reproduction consisted, at least in part, in the feeling of effort in those muscles that would be concerned in performing the act itself. If the momentary association first aroused by the sudden and unexpected sight of the

word involves this dramatic imitation of the act
named, how much more would the thought involve
the dramatic repetition of the act, if one were to dwell
upon the nature of this act, and were fully to realize
its nature in his own mind. So much then for psychological illustration of the view that we are here
advancing. If two opposing fashions of action are
present to our minds, and if mentally we are trying
to realize them both, then mentally we are seeking
to reproduce them both. Our skeptical hesitation
between them expresses our effort to attain mentally
both these ends at once. For what we have said
about bodily acts will apply equally well to what we
usually call mental acts, and even to general resolutions, all of which have a physical side, and are apt
to be symbolized by some bodily gesture that we
mentally or outwardly repeat when we think of the
act or of the resolution in question.

But all this is not a bare accident of the psychological structure of our minds ; it is a philosophical necessity. What represents a Will but a Will ? Who
would know what it is to have an end unless he actually had ends himself ? Who can realize a given
aim save by somehow repeating it in himself ? And
so it is rationally and universally necessary that one
shall realize the end of a moral system by reproduc-
ing in himself the will that accepts this end. But,
on the other hand, in so far forth as he reproduces
this will alone, he cannot refrain from accepting the
end. In so far forth as he reproduces this will, it is
his will. And the end is his end. Therefore our
skepticism itself was a hesitation, resulting from the

realization of several opposing ends, and from a simultaneous reproduction of the wills that aimed at them. Therefore, as we see, absolute ethical skepticism would not really be total absence of moral aim, but would rather be the neutrality that would result from a provisional acceptance of all the conflicting aims in the world of action. Absolute ethical skepticism, if it were actually possible without self-destruction, would still presuppose an end, namely, the effort to harmonize in one moment all the conflicting aims in the world of life. It would not be what it had supposed itself to be. Absolute skepticism would thus be founded on absolute benevolence. *Its own aim would be harmony and unity of conduct.* But just for that reason is absolute skepticism self-destructive.

Possibly this result may be somewhat unexpected. But did not the very pessimism of our last chapter illustrate it? Why this pessimism? This despair of life, what was it but the sense of the hopelessness of our task? What made the task seem hopeless? And what was the task? The task was the formation of an harmonious ideal of life. This task seemed hopeless, because we felt that the actual ideals of life among men are in deadly conflict. Our pessimism was after all not what it seemed to us to be. It was not the bare renunciation of all aims; it was the effort to satisfy them all, embittered by the sense that they were in seemingly hopeless conflict. Even our pessimism had its ideal. Without its ideal it would have experienced no despair. The conflict of aims would have meant no evil. The pessimistic despair was the natural outcome of our skepticism, solely because our skepticism was itself a realization of the aims with which men live, and of the warfare of these aims.

From the world of dead facts, we had said, you can get no ethical doctrine. Physical truth never gives moral doctrine. Therefore the world of facts seemed to stand on one side, and the world of moral aims seemed to stand on the other, no logical connection being discoverable between them. This was our theoretical objection to the ethical doctrines that we examined. Separate as they were from the world of facts, they seemed to dwell alone, ungrounded and conflicting acts of caprice. Yet for them to pass over to the world of facts was to lose their ethical character. But now we seek to overcome our difficulty by considering, not the world of physical facts themselves, but the world of ends. And this world we consider, not now in detail, but as a whole. What highest end is suggested, we ask, to him who realizes for himself this whole world of ends? The very end, we answer, that, as first dimly seen, forced upon us our skeptical pessimism. Whoso realizes an end, his, for the time being, is that end. And since it is his end, he mentally wills to realize it in ideal perfection. But whoso realizes the various conflicting aims in the world, his are all these aims at the moment of insight, when, so far as in him lies, he realizes them, and mentally desires their success. In proportion as his realization is or can be catholic and genuine, his will becomes, for the time, these conflicting wills. In him is now the warfare. He feels in his own person the bitterness of the universal strife. And therefore it is that, in the first moment of his new insight, the pessimism comes to him. "This warfare cannot be ended," he despairingly says. But has he thus uttered the final word? For he has not yet added the reflection that we are here insisting upon. Let him say: "Then I too have an end, far-off and unattainable though it seems, and so my will is not aimless. I desire to realize these aims all at once. Therefore I desire their harmony. This is the one good that comes up before my fancy as above all the various conflicting individual goods of the various separate aims. This Higher Good would be attained in a world where the conflict ceased. That would be the Ideal World, where all possible aims were pursued in absolute harmony."

Barren at first sight this reflection may appear. It may have been unexpected, but we shall certainly be disposed at first to call it fruitless. For here are the aims, and they do conflict. In the actual world there is ceaseless warfare. Only the wager of battle can decide among the opposing ethical faiths. But now, if some idealist comes who says that his insight gives him the higher ideal of Harmony, then one may reply that his ideal is, in its confessed nature, a mere fantasy of his benevolent imagination. Such harmony never can be realized, unless indeed some day, by the aid of bigger battalions, some one of the ideals overcomes all the rest. Yet is our idealist so lightly to be answered? Can he not at once reply: "My Ideal is thus defined, and fantastic though it be, far-off though it seems, it is still an ideal towards which I can direct my efforts. For behold, made practical, brought down from its lonesome height, my Ideal very simply means the Will to direct my acts *towards* the attainment of universal Harmony. It requires me to act with this my insight always before me. It requires me to consider all the conflicting aims that will be affected by each one of my acts, and to dispose my act with reference to them all. It sets up this new moral principle before me, a principle perfectly catholic, and above all that skepticism which we have felt with regard to the special moral aims. This Principle is: *So act as thou wouldst will to act if all the consequences of thy act for all the aims that are anywhere to be affected by this act, could be realized by thee now and in this one indivisible moment.* Or more briefly put: *Act always in the light of the completest insight into all the aims that thy act is to affect.* This rule is no capricious one, chosen for some individual reason, but an universal maxim, since its choice depends on the general realization of all the conflicting aims of the world of life. And thus we have after all found, in the very heart of our skepticism itself, a moral doctrine. In the midst of the warfare of individual wills, we have caught sight of an Universal Will.

II.

"But no," some one will say: "All this is still mere caprice. Has it not in fact fallen already a prey to the same skepticism that pursued other moral aims? For first, you have tried to found it on a physical fact, namely, on the fact that only by a given effort of will one thinking being can realize the will of another. But does this tell me that I ought thus to realize the conflicting wills that are in the world? And if I do not, what significance has this physical fact for me? But, on the other hand, physical facts aside, is not your doctrine just your capricious determination to respect the conflicting aims that exist in the world?"

This objection, if made, would be founded on a misunderstanding of what we have discovered. We have discovered something that has a value for us quite independently of its importance as a mere physical fact. We set out to find a distinction between right and wrong. Our difficulty always was that, since this distinction involves the acceptance of a highest aim as the standard of judgment, and since there are numerous aims possible, we always were confused by the fact that among these manifold aims there was found no ground of choice. For to show any reason why we have chosen in a given way between two of these aims, is to have a third aim that includes one and excludes the other. And the choice of this third aim seemed again just as accidental as the first choice would have been without this third aim to justify it. Thus our original thought of an aim, as the foundation of an ethical doctrine, had been shattered before our eyes into a spray of separate possible or actual aims, and we saw no way of collecting this spray again into unity. If that was the reason for our skepticism, then of course anything more that we may say about ethics must presuppose a hearer who can feel such skepticism, at least provisionally. The physical fact that he can understand the nature of our doubt is indeed presupposed ere we can go further, but that is no objection to our progress. The physical fact that we have an intelligent hearer must always be presupposed by us. If one cannot feel the doubt, then he cannot undertake any ethical inquiry. We only say to him : " If you doubt about the acceptance of a moral aim, this that we have pointed out to you is the real reason for your doubt. If now you understand your doubt, then you are actually in the state that we have described above. Your doubt has in fact a general character. It means a provisional moral skepticism, founded on an insight into the conflict of aims. This insight means skepticism because, and only because, you are at the moment of insight yourself possessed of the conflicting aims, yourself at war with yourself, and therefore undecided. This spray of aims into which your first pure idea of a moral aim as such has been scattered, this confused and blinding cloud of purposes, represents for you your own moral position. Divided in yourself, disunited, confused, you float cloud-like and inactive, seeking unity of aim and finding none. But if you reflect on all this, you see that in truth you occupy the position that we have above described. You really have still a highest aim. You seek unity. You desire the warfare to cease. You have an ideal. All this is, to be sure, a physical fact, dependent on your nature as voluntary being; but it is not valuable just for that reason alone, but for the reason that, in discovering this fact, you have discovered what you were seeking for. You have found that you are in possession of an ideal. You cannot get away from that ideal save by repeating the very process that has brought you to it. Your moral insight is attained, and the foundation of your doctrine is no longer a particular aim that is accepted by a mere caprice of one individual, but it is the necessary aim that arises in the mind of any one who actually realizes the warfare of the particular aims. It is the ideal of ideals. It is the absolute ideal that arises for you out of the consideration of the separate ideals. Each of them was relative to the mood of the man who happened to choose it; this Ideal is relative only to the insight that comprehends the whole moral world. Unable as we men are fully to realize just the actual nature of every single aim in the world of life, still we are able fully to realize certain conflicting aims; and, realizing this conflict, we can form for ourselves the notion of that absolute realization that means, as we have seen, first the skeptical despair of our last chapter, and then, by a deeper reflection, the ideal that we have just set forth above. Thus we no longer are capriciously deciding upon the worth of physical facts as such. We are passing a necessary judgment upon ideals as ideals.

And we have tried to show that this our resulting ideal is not a barren one. At first sight it seems so. At first sight one says: "This harmony is a self-contradictory dream." But no, not self-contradictory is the dream; for, if we cannot perfectly realize this new ideal, if absolute harmony is unattainable, one

can still walk in the light of the ideal. One can say :
" I will act as if all these conflicting aims were mine.
I will respect them all. I will act in the light that
has brought me my moral insight. And to that end
I will act at each moment as one would act who
saw himself about to suffer in his own person and
at one time all the consequences of his act for all
the aims that are to be affected by what he does."
But now the ideal becomes practical, now it ceases
to be barren. It is no longer the mere wish that
was at the heart of our skepticism, a wish gloomy, inactive, terrified at the warfare that is in the world.
It is a cool determination. It says: "This disease
of conflicting aims cannot now be cured, but it shall
be dealt with. These aims are as my own. I will
deal with them as such. I will work for their harmony." If one doubts this ideal, then he doubts
the very foundation of ethical doubt itself. But this
is not all that our absolute ideal accomplishes. Not
merely for the moment of insight does this ideal give
an aim ; but it extends itself to the other moments
of life. It says: " The highest good would be realiz-
able only in case not merely the aim of this moment
of insight itself, but the aims of all the conflicting
wills in the world, were brought into conformity to
this insight. The highest good would be attainable
if all the conflicting wills realized fully one another.
For then, not abandoning each its own aim, each
would have added thereto, through insight, the aims
of the others. And all the world of individuals
would act as one Being, having a single Universal
Will. Harmony would in fact be attained." There-

fore our ideal has another precept to give us. It
says: "Act in such wise as to extend this moral insight to others." Here is a definite practical aim,
and it justifies us in saying to all the conflicting
wills: "You should respect one another." For so in
fact they all would do if they had the moral insight.
And to have it, as we now see, is the prerequisite
to the attainment of the highest good, namely, this
ideal Harmony that we seek at the moment of moral
insight.

III.

We fear that such general discussion of what we
have called the moral insight may seem, at first sight,
too abstract to be real. We hasten to a more concrete study of this insight. Leaving those more abstract aims that have been used as the foundation of
moral systems, let us study our moral insight as it
applies to the special aims that come into conflict
when a man is dealing with his neighbor. Let us
see how just the considerations that we have applied
to the conflict of ethical aims in general apply directly to the conflict between selfishness and unselfishness, which we so long and so vainly considered
in the last chapter. This warfare of selfishness and
unselfishness is indeed not the deepest of moral
problems, and to solve the problem here involved is
not, as some have supposed, to define forthwith the
Highest Good. Yet we shall do well to fix our minds
for the time on this special problem.

Why is selfishness easier to me than unselfishness?
Because it is easier for me to realize my own future,

and my own desire about it, than to realize the desires
of my neighbor. My will is the *datum ;* his the dimly-
conceived, remote fact. Hence it seems to me obvious
that his will must be to me less significant than my
own. Therefore he and I are often in deadly warfare, just because I realize his will not in its inner
nature, but as a foreign power, and because he deals
even so with me. We stand over against each
other like two moral systems, condemning and fighting each the other. Now, however, there often appear disinterested moralists, who try to patch up our
differences. We have seen how and why they have
so often failed. They tell me that my neighbor and
I shall give each other much more selfish delight if
we stop fighting and begin coöperating. But that
wise advice in no way touches the root of the difficulty between us. If we did coöperate for this reason, we should still be two foreign powers, virtually
discordant. And whenever it happened that either
of us could do better by oppressing or by crushing
the other than by continuing to coöperate with him,
he not only would do so, but, so far as we have seen,
must do so. Another moralist hopes that if we
keep on coöperating long enough, we may evolve
into purely unselfish beings some day. The hope is
a pious one, but gives us no sufficient reason why we
ought to coöperate unselfishly now, when in fact we
are selfish. Yet another moralist asks us to reflect
on the nature of our emotions of pity and sympathy
for each other. We reply that these feelings are in-
determinate in character, and may lead us to do anything or nothing for each other. So all these mor-

alists leave my neighbor and me just where we were.
If it is to our personal advantage to fight, we shall
do so; otherwise we may by chance remain for a
while in practical harmony; but, throughout, our
moral aims will remain what they were, selfish and
conflicting.

Forsaking these unsatisfactory attempts to found
a moral doctrine concerning one's duty to one's
neighbor, let us try to do what Schopenhauer so
haltingly suggested, namely, to see what moral insight as moral insight, and not as pity or as far-
sighted egoism, tells us about the moral relations of
selfishness and unselfishness. If a man not merely
pities but knows his neighbor's will, what moral
ideal does he get? We affirm that insight into the
reality of the neighbor's will, insight that considers
his will as it is in itself, and that accordingly repeats
it in us, gives us a position above the struggle of
self and neighbor, and lets us see the higher ideal of
Harmony, whose precept is: *Act as a being would act
who included thy will and thy neighbor's will in the
unity of one life, and who had therefore to suffer
the consequences for the aims of both that will follow from the act of either.* This insight is not the
mere emotion of pity nor yet sympathy, but something different from these, namely, something that
involves the realization, and therefore the reproduction in us, of the opposing will of the neighbor. This
insight therefore deprives each will in its separateness of its absolute significance, and commands that
we should act with an equal reference to both. It
says not merely, "Love thy neighbor as thyself,"

but, "*In so far as in thee lies, act as if thou wert at once thy neighbor and thyself.*" "*Treat these two lives as one life.*"

We must try to show how this insight leads to this result. We must try so to bring home the insight to the reader that he shall in his person accomplish the act of which we speak, and so come to accept the ideal upon which we are insisting. It is in himself that he is to experience this ideal, or else he will not be able or willing to accept it. We can only suggest the way. And so we shall try forthwith to suggest what is the nature of that common imperfect realization of our neighbor's life which does not lead to the moral insight, and then to dwell upon this insight itself.

IV.

The common sense, imperfect recognition of our neighbor implies rather realization of the external aspect of his being, as that part of him which affects us, than realization of his inner and peculiar world of personal experience. Let us show this by example. First, take my realization of the people whom I commonly meet but do not personally very well know, *e. g.* the conductor on the railway train when I travel. He is for me just the being who takes my ticket, the official to whom I can appeal for certain advice or help if I need it. That this conductor has an inner life, like mine, this I am apt never to realize at all. He has to excite my pity or some other special human interest in me ere I shall even begin to try to think of him as really like me. On the whole,

he is for me realized as an automaton. But still frequently I do realize him in another way, but how?
I note very likely that he is courteous or surly, and
I like or dislike him accordingly. Now courtesy and
discourtesy are qualities that belong not to automata
at all. Hence I must somehow recognize him in this
case as conscious. But what aspect of his consciousness do I consider? Not the inner aspect of it as
such, but still the outer aspect of his conscious life,
as a power affecting me; that is what I consider. He
treats me so and so, and he does this deliberately;
therefore I judge him. But what I realize is his deliberate act, as something important to me. It seldom occurs to me to realize fully how he feels; but
I can much more easily come to note how he is disposed. The disposition is his state viewed as a power
affecting me.

Now let one look over the range of his bare ac-
quaintanceship, let him leave out his friends, and the
people in whom he takes a special personal interest;
let him regard for the first the rest of his world of
fellow-men : his butcher, his grocer, the policeman
that patrols his street, the newsboy, the servant in
his kitchen, his business rivals whom he occasionally
talks to, the men whose political speeches he has
heard or read, and for whom he has voted, with some
notion of their personal characters, — and then all
the rest of the outside world, the Turks or the In-
dians, the men of historic fame, Napoleon, Cicero,
Cæsar, the imaginary people in fictions that have
excited little of his stronger emotional interest : how
does he conceive of all these people? Are they not

one and all to him ideal or real *ways of behavior*
towards himself or other people, outwardly effective
beings, rather than realized masses of genuine inner
life, of sentiment, of love, or of felt desire? Does he
not naturally think of each of them rather as a way
of outward action than as a way of inner volition?
His butcher, his newsboy, his servant, — are they not
for him industrious or lazy, honest or deceitful, polite
or uncivil, useful or useless people, rather than self-
conscious people? Is any one of these alive for him
in the full sense, — sentient, emotional, and otherwise like himself; as perhaps his own son, or his
own mother or wife seems to him to be? Is it not
rather the kind of behavior of these beings towards
him which he realizes? Is it not rather in general
their being for him, not for themselves, that he considers in all his ordinary life, even when he calls
them conscious? And this being for him is what he
calls their dispositions. They are all good fellows
or bad fellows, good-humored or surly, hateful or admirable. They may appear even sublime or ideal
beings, as a Cæsar might to a student of history.
Yet their inner life need not therefore be realized.
They remain powers, ways of acting, dispositions,
wonderful examples of energy. They are still seen
from without. Not their inner, volitional nature is
realized, but their manner of outward activity; not
what they are for themselves, but what they are for
others.

Such then is our natural realization of our fellows
even when we call them conscious. The imperfect
realization in question extends even to the case of

closer affection. Lear realizes in his daughters, or
thinks that he realizes, only the dispositions that they
express. Real effort to enter into the inner life of
their emotions is foreign to his simple and imperious
mind. Even when I delight in another's love, I am
still apt to realize rather the disposition than the
inner and more personal emotional life that is the
cause of this way of behavior. The act is what I
want,[1] the voice, the look, the gift, or the other assurance of an energy in harmony with my will. The
ordinary emotion of gratitude is another very good
illustration of the imperfect realization of our neighbors that accompanies even the plainest verbal recognition of their conscious existence. As I write
these words, my heart is just now going out in admiration and respect, not to say affection, to a man
whom I but imperfectly know. I feel a desire to
do him a favor, if it were possible. Why? Do I
reflect on his true nature and needs as a being like
myself? Do I feel our common weakness, our common longings? Have I dispelled the illusion of selfishness that separates us? No, — I grieve and am
ashamed to confess it, — this being is to me almost
as wholly external as my plumber, not much better
realized than my walking-stick. I am dwelling not
on his own inner life at all. In my mind's eye I
see just his outer form. Yet he has written me a
graceful and pleasing letter, expressing his interest
in some of my plans, and his desire to help me. I
am selfishly delighted to find such help. I have an

---

[1] "I'd give all my income from dreamland
For a touch of her hand on my cheek."

instinctive feeling that it demands compensation. I
feel an animal delight in being in friendly company.
My gratitude is here no moral emotion at all.

The emotion of sympathy does indeed often tend
to make me realize the other and more completely
internal aspect of my neighbor's reality ; but sympathy does this in the halting and uncertain way described in a previous chapter. And at all events,
whatever sympathy leads to, it is not by itself the
insight. And so, to sum up our present way of
studying the illusions of selfishness, we find by these
examples that by nature our neighbor's conscious
life is realized for us rather as an active agency that
affects our fortunes, than as an inner experience, or
as it is in itself, namely, as a Will; and hence it is
that we are disposed to treat it with coldness, rather
than to respect its true nature. Resistance, conquest, employment of this agency, seem to us axi-
omatic aims of prudence ; unselfish respect for its
inner accompanying experiences seems to us a hard
if not a meaningless task. Such is the nature and
ground of the illusion of selfishness.

If now our activity of realization were confined to
the range of common-sense emotions, there would be
no escape from all this. It is our critical reflection
that appears on the scene, saying: " O common
sense, what thou hast realized cannot be all. We
must resolve to recognize more, else will our resolutions never lose their inconsistency and darkness.
Be honest, O common sense. Is not thy neighbor
after all just a dead fact of nature, an automaton
with certain peculiar energies ? " And common

sense answers: " No, for is he not most assuredly a conscious agent, whose action I realize?" "Dost thou then know that he wills, and *not* realize what this will means for him, namely, that he experiences it?" "No," answers common sense, " if he wills as I do, he must experience as I do." "Realize it then, and see what thou then wilt do with him." And common sense must, we affirm, so realizing, simply reply, "As he is real, he is as much an object for my effort as I myself am, in case I can affect him. Ours is one life." This common sense must see, if it fully realizes the neighbor. And if it realizes his activity, as it always in some fashion does, then it must come to realize his experience, and so to realize him fully, so soon as it undertakes to complete the incomplete act by which it has begun to realize his will. This completion may be hastened by pity, or may be hindered by the weakness that pity often involves; but when it comes, it must be an act of clear insight, made possible by the rational nature of our mental life. Whatever in our thought is done in part, we are ready either to abandon wholly, or to finish altogether, so soon as we realize that we have been doing it in part. Our resolution to recognize an existence cannot remain confused or self-contradictory when we come to realize where the confusion and self-contradiction lie. And as we simply cannot give up recognizing our neighbor, we must of necessity resolve, when we see this inconsistency of our natural realization, to realize him wholly.

Such is our reflective account of the process that, in

some form, must come to every one under the proper conditions. In this process we see the beginning of the real knowledge of duty to others. The process is one that any child can and does, under proper guidance, occasionally accomplish. It is the process by which we all are accustomed to try to teach humane behavior in concrete cases. We try to get people to realize what they are doing when they injure others. But to distinguish this process from the more tender emotion of sympathy, with all its illusions, is what moralists have not carefully enough done. Our exposition has tried to take this universally recognized process, to distinguish it from sympathy as such, and to set it up before the gates of ethical doctrine as the great producer of insight.

But when we say that to this insight common sense must come, under the given conditions, we do not mean to say: "So the man, once having attained insight, must act thenceforth." The realization of one's neighbor, in the full sense of the word realization, is indeed the resolution to treat him as if he were real, that is, to treat him unselfishly. But this resolution expresses and belongs to the moment of insight. Passion may cloud the insight in the very next moment. It always does cloud the insight after no very long time. It is as impossible for us to avoid the illusion of selfishness in our daily lives, as to escape seeing through the illusion at the moment of insight. We see the reality of our neighbor, that is, we determine to treat him as we do ourselves. But then we go back to daily action, and we feel the heat of hereditary passions, and we straightway forget what we have seen. Our neighbor becomes obscured. He is once more a foreign power. He is unreal. We are again deluded and selfish. This conflict goes on and will go on as long as we live after the manner of men. Moments of insight, with their accompanying resolutions; long stretches of delusion and selfishness : That is our life.

V.

To bring home this view in yet another way to the reader, we ask him to consider very carefully just what experience he has when he tries to realize his neighbor in the full sense that we have insisted upon. Not pity as such is what we desire him to feel. For whether or no pity happens to work in him as selfishly and blindly as we have found that it often does work, still not the emotion, but its consequences, must in the most favorable case give us what we seek. All the forms of sympathy are mere impulses. It is the insight to which they bring us that has moral value. And again, the realization of our neighbor's existence is not at all the discovery that he is more or less useful to us personally. All that would contribute to selfishness. In an entirely different way we must realize his existence, if we are to be really altruistic. What then is our neighbor?

We find that out by treating him in thought just as we do ourselves. What art thou? Thou art now just a present state, with its experiences, thoughts, and desires. But what is thy future Self? Simply future states, future experiences, future thoughts and desires, that, although not now existing for thee, are postulated by thee as certain to come, and as in some real relation to thy present Self. What then is thy neighbor? He too is a mass of states, of experiences, thoughts, and desires, just as real as thou art, no more but yet no less present to thy experience now than is thy future Self. He is not that face that frowns or smiles at thee, although often thou thinkest of him as only that. He is not the arm that strikes or defends thee, not the voice that speaks to thee, not that machine that gives thee what thou desirest when thou movest it with the offer of money. To be sure, thou dost often think of him as if he were that automaton yonder, that answers thee when thou speakest to it. But no, thy neighbor is as actual, as concrete, as thou art. Just as thy future is real, though not now thine, so thy neighbor is real, though his thoughts never are thy thoughts. Dost thou believe this? Art thou sure what it means? This is for thee the turning-point of thy whole conduct towards him. What we now ask of thee is no sentiment, no gush of pity, no tremulous weakness of sympathy, but a calm, clear insight.

But one says: "All this have I done from my youth up. Surely I hold and always have held my neighbor to be real and no automaton. Surely I have feared his reproof, have been angry at his ill-will, have rejoiced in his sympathy, have been influenced by his opinions, all my life. And yet I have remained selfish." Nay, but just at the moment when thou hadst to act towards him so or so, thou

wert no longer quick to realize him. Then it was
that thy passion made him for thee a shadow. Thou
couldst not love him, because thou didst forget who
he was. Thou didst believe in him enough to fear
him, to hate him, to fight with him, to revenge thyself upon him, to use his wit as thy tool, but not
enough to treat him as real, even as thou thyself art
real. He seems to thee a little less living than thou.
His life is dim, it is cold, it is a pale fire beside thy
own burning desires. He is a symbol of passion to
thee, and imperfectly, coldly, with dull assent, without full meaning to thy words, thou dost indeed say,
when asked, that the symbol stands for something
real, as real as thyself. But what those words mean,
— hast thou realized it, as, through selfish feeling,
thou dost realize thy equally external future Self?

If he is real like thee, then is his life as bright a
light, as warm a fire, to him, as thine to thee; his
will is as full of struggling desires, of hard problems,
of fateful decisions; his pains are as hateful, his
joys as dear. Take whatever thou knowest of desire
and of striving, of burning love and of fierce hatred,
realize as fully as thou canst what that means, and
then with clear certainty add : *Such as that is for
me, so is it for him, nothing less.* If thou dost that,
can he remain to thee what he has been, a picture, a
plaything, a comedy, or a tragedy, in brief a mere
Show? Behind all that show thou hast indeed
dimly felt that there is something. Know that
truth thoroughly. Thou hast regarded his thought,
his feeling, as somehow different in sort from thine.
Thou hast said: " A pain in him is not like a pain

in me, but something far easier to bear." Thou hast
made of him a ghost, as the imprudent man makes
of his future self a ghost. Even when thou hast
feared his scorn, his hate, his contempt, thou hast
not fully made him for thee as real as thyself. His
laughter at thee has made thy face feel hot, his
frowns and clenched fists have cowed thee, his sneers
have made thy throat feel choked. But that was
only the social instinct in thee. It was not a full
sense of his reality. Even so the little baby smiles
back at one that smiles at it, but not because it
realizes the approving joy of the other, only because
it by instinct enjoys a smiling face; and even so the
baby is frightened at harsh speech, but not because
it realizes the other's anger. So, dimly and by instinct, thou has lived with thy neighbor, and hast
known him not, being blind. Thou hast even desired his pain, but thou hast not fully realized the
pain that thou gavest. It has been to thee, not
pain in itself, but the sight of his submission, of his
tears, or of his pale terror. Of thy neighbor thou
hast made a thing, no Self at all.

When thou hast loved, hast pitied, or hast rever-
enced thy neighbor, then thy feeling has possibly
raised for a moment the veil of illusion. Then thou
hast known what he truly is, a Self like thy present
Self. But thy selfish feeling is too strong for thee.
Thou hast forgotten soon again what thou hadst seen,
and hast made even of thy beloved one only the instrument of thy own pleasure. Even out of thy power
to pity thou hast made an object of thy vainglory.
Thy reverence has turned again to pride. Thou hast

accepted the illusion once more.   No wonder that in this darkness thou findest selfishness the only rule of any meaning for thy conduct.   Thou forgottest that without realization of thy future and as yet unreal self, even selfishness means nothing.   Thou forgottest that if thou gavest thy present thought even so to the task of realizing thy neighbor's life, selfishness would seem no more plain to thee than the love of thy neighbor.

Have done then with this illusion that thy Self is all in all.   Intuition tells thee no more about thy future Self than it tells thee about thy neighbors. Desire, bred in thee by generations of struggle for existence, emphasizes the expectation of thy own bodily future, the love for thy own bodily welfare, and makes thy body's life seem alone real.   But sim-ply try to know the truth.   The truth is that all this world of life about thee is as real as thou art.   All conscious life is conscious in its own measure.   Pain is pain, joy is joy, everywhere even as in thee.   The result of thy insight will be inevitable.   The illusion vanishing, the glorious prospect opens before thy vision.   Seeing the oneness of this life everywhere, the equal reality of all its moments, thou wilt be ready to treat it all with the reverence that prudence would have thee show to thy own little bit of future life.   What prudence in its narrow respectability counseled, thou wilt be ready to do universally.   As the prudent man, seeing the reality of his future self, inevitably works for it; so the enlightened man, seeing the reality of all conscious life, realizing that it is no shadow, but fact, at once and inevitably deires, if only for that one moment of insight, to enter into the service of the whole of it.

So the illusion of selfishness vanishes for thy present thought (alas! not for thy future conduct, O child of passion!), when thou lookest at what selfishness has so long hidden from thee. Thou seest now the universal life as a whole, just as real as thou art, identical in joy and sorrow. The conflict of selfishness and unselfishness vanishes. Selfishness is but a half realization of the truth expressed in unselfishness. Selfishness says: *I shall exist.* Unselfishness says: *The Other Life is as My Life.* To realize another's pain as pain is to cease to desire it in itself. Hatred is illusion. Cowardly sympathy, that hides its head for fear of realizing the neighbor's pain, is illusion. But unselfishness is the realization of life. Unselfishness leads thee out of the mists of blind self-adoration, and shows thee, in all the life of nature about thee, the one omnipresent, conscious struggle for the getting of the desired. In all the songs of the forest birds ; in all the cries of the wounded and dying, struggling in the captor's power ; in the boundless sea, where the myriads of water-creatures strive and die ; amid all the countless hordes of savage men ; in the hearts of all the good and loving ; in the dull, throbbing hearts of all prisoners and captives ; in all sickness and sorrow ; in all exultation and hope ; in all our devotion ; in all our knowledge, — everywhere from the lowest to the noblest creatures and experiences on our earth, the same conscious, burning, willful life is found, endlessly manifold as the forms of the living creatures, unquenchable as the fires of the sun, real as these impulses that even now throb in thy own little selfish heart. Lift up thy eyes, behold that life, and then turn away and forget it as thou canst; but if thou hast known that, thou hast begun to know thy duty.

VI.

But this unity that the moral insight has found for us in life must not be falsely interpreted. Rightly interpreted, the moral insight will solve for us many very difficult problems; but we must not imagine that it shows us all this individual life as in any mystical sense already actually in the harmony that we seek. Not because these aims are already in themselves one, but because we, as moral seers, unite in one moment of insight the realization of all these aims, for that reason alone is this life one for us. It is in this sense alone that the moral insight gives us a solution of the problem of egoism and altruism, as well as a foundation for a general doctrine of the Highest Good. The moral insight does not enable us to say : These beings have always actually but blindly sought what was in itself the Highest Good. We can only say : Each one has sought in his blindness only what was to him desirable. And not, save by the realization of the conflict of desire, can the truly highest good be conceived. The moral insight discovers harmony not as already implied in the nature of these blind, conflicting wills, but as an ideal to be attained by hard work.

We point this out in order to show that we do not fall into the hackneyed error of those moralists who insist that they merely tell men what one thing it is that men have all been blindly seeking. Such moralists often say: " Our system is but an expression of the tendency that was always there, latent in men. It tells them in plain words what they always wanted, and then it tells them how to get this end." This specious pretense of so many moral systems we have implicitly condemned in the previous part of our discourse. It constitutes in many cases that appeal to the physical facts which we have set aside as always useless and often ungrounded. If one looks the pretense fairly in the face, how flat and stale it seems! Yonder vast wealth of conflicting aims among men, base and noble, devilish and divine, — what moralist has been able to sum all of them up in any formula, save in the wholly abstract formula that we have above referred to, namely, that all these beings seek what seems to them desirable. How presumptuous to say to them: " In fact you all desire this that I formulate in my text-book of morals." In fact they do not. And it is absurd to watch the turnings and twistings of language by which a moralist tries to make out that they do. For instance, let the moralist be J. S. Mill, and let him declare, as he does, that happiness is the one goal of all men. If happiness includes the attainment of any possible object of anybody's desire, then indeed the theory is a truism. But with this truism, of course, no sort of progress would have been made in ethics. Mill must tell us something about what

sorts of happiness there are, and about what sorts
ought to be sought most of all. He says, as we
know, that there are "higher" and "lower" pleasures, and that higher pleasures ought to be sought
in preference to the others, the pleasure of the intel-
lect, of generosity, etc., instead of the sensual pleasures. What can be the proof? That happiness
was the goal we were to learn, because all men actually seek it. But that the "higher" happiness is
the goal, rather than a lower form, how do we learn
that? Because men always choose it? In fact they
do not. So Mill has to shift the ground a little
They do not all of them actually seek it. but they
would seek it if they knew it. Most of them are ignorant of what they would prize most, namely, of
these "higher" pleasures. But here again Mill
meets a disheartening fact. Most men, if they ever
love "higher" pleasures at all, are found loving
them more for a while in the ideal enthusiasm of
youth than later in the prosaic dullness of middle
life. Men who have known the "higher" happiness do then deliberately turn away from it. This
is a regular fact of life, well known, and often lamented. How does this agree with Mill's doctrine?
Alas! it does not agree, and only by worthless devices can he conceal from himself the fact. The
people who enjoy the higher know the lower and reject it. The people who enjoy the lower do not
know of the higher, or, if they ever knew it, they
have forgotten it, or if they have not quite forgotten
the higher, they have "lost capacity for it." As if
all this could not just as plausibly be said from the

side of the "lower" pleasures. Just as if it were not constantly said from that side in every good drinking-song, with a result precisely opposed to Mill's. In fact Mill is driven in this controversy with imaginary opponents to the worst subterfuge possible for so skilled a thinker, when he at last says that the pleasure which seems the higher of two pleasures to the "most of those who have experienced both" is actually the higher. For thus, to keep up the show of merely interpreting to men their actual will, Mill has to appeal to the opinion of the majority, has to use a purely practical habit of deliberative assemblies for the purpose of deciding a question of theory, and then has most absurdly to declare that a man's experience about his own pleasure is worth nothing as a test of its value unless the majority of his fellows agree with him in his judgment.

In fact all this is benevolent trifling. Men declare at one time one pleasure to be "highest," that is, most desirable, and at another time they declare another pleasure to be the only desirable one. Different men persist in having different aims. To define their duty by telling them that they all have one aim is wrong. From the point of view of the moral insight all this struggling life becomes one; but that is not because it as yet ceases to struggle, but because the being possessed of the moral insight comes to realize it all at once. For him it is one, because he identifies himself with the struggling aims. He seeks their harmony, and must do so if he have the insight. But they are not in harmony as yet at all ; else would he have no work to do. Let him then not deceive himself. The conflict itself is real and not illusory. The illusion lies in the fact that no one of the fighters realizes the inner life of the others. But to overcome that illusion in any soul is not to show that all the fighters have been desiring the same thing.

J. S. Mill is by no means our only case of the effort to convince people that they always have had one object of search, which the moralist has but to name in order to bring peace on the earth. Bentham undertook the same task, and showed in his blunt way as much skill in subterfuge as he ever accused his opponents of showing, while he tried to make out that all men always have been Benthamites, to whom pleasure was the only good. Mr. Spencer in his turn tries to define the Good so that it shall agree not only with the popular usage of the word good, but also with the Spencerian notion of what constitutes the Good. If anywhere a usage of the word appears that does not agree with the Spencerian usage, Mr. Spencer insists, sometimes, that, if cross-questioned, the man who so uses it would have to come over to the Spencerian usage, and sometimes that the usage in question is a survival in culture of a savage notion, or that it is in some other way insignificant. Thus the proof of Mr. Spencer's view about the nature of the ideal becomes so simple and easy that when, a little further on, it is necessary to recognize the existence of pessimists, Mr. Spencer finds no difficulty in regarding it as perfectly plain that a man can become a pessimist only in case he believes that the Spencerian ideal of the Good is unattainable. Thus axioms are manufactured whenever we need them.

All this is mere neglect of whatever ideals do not at once fit into one's own ideal. Such neglect is unworthy of an ethical inquirer. Yet it has been frequently committed in recent times, and it is committed whenever a man endeavors or pretends, as Professor Clifford also very skillfully endeavored and pretended, to found ethical science wholly upon the basis and by the methods of natural science. Such attempts are like the efforts of a man trying to build a steamboat, who should first drop the steam-engine into the water, and then seek to build the boat up about the engine so as to float it and be driven by it. For natural science will indeed give us the engine of our applied ethics, as indispensable as the steam-engine to the boat. But first we must lay the keel, and we must get the boat ready for the engine, the ideal ready for the science that is to apply it. All such attempts as those that put the "scientific basis" first, lamely strive to conceal their helplessness behind a show of appealing to the "facts of human nature and of the social structure, as science discovers them." But these facts reveal a confused warfare of aims among men, no one aim being actually chosen by the whole of men. And then the "scientific moralist" tries to show by all sorts of devices that all men really have the same aim. But he cannot show that, because it is not true. What aim is common to the whole life of any one of us? Much less then is any aim common to all men.

But this mistake is not specially modern. Not only the modern scientific moralists have been guilty of it, but moral preachers of all schools since Socrates have been prone to insist on occasion, for purposes of persuasion, that somehow or other all evil conduct arises from mere ignorance of what one wants. This view is a mistake. One may want anything, and may know it very well. There is no known limit to the caprice and to the instability of the human will. If you find anybody desiring anything, the only tolerably sure and fairly universal comment is, that he will stop desiring it by and by. You can seldom get any ultimate analysis of the motive of such a desire.

But we do not found our moral system on any such analysis. We do not say even that it is physically possible for any of us to get and to keep the moral insight long together. What we affirm can once more briefly be summed up as follows : —

1. Moral insight, whenever, however, to whomsoever it comes, consists in the realization of the true inner nature of certain conflicting wills that are actual in the world.

2. An absolute moral insight, which we can conceive, but which we never fully attain ourselves, would realize the true inner nature of all the conflicting wills in the world.

3. The moral insight involves from its very nature, for those who have it, the will to harmonize, so far as may be possible, the conflicting wills that there are in the world, and that are realized at the moment of insight.

4. If the moral insight be concerned directly with two conflicting wills, my neighbor's and my own, then this insight involves the will to act as if my neighbor and myself were one being that possessed at once the aims of both of us.

5. If the moral insight be concerned with conflicting general aims, such as could express themselves in systems of conduct, then the moral insight involves the will to act, so far as may be, as if one included in one's own being the life of all those whose conflicting aims one realizes.

6. Absolute moral insight would involve the will to act henceforth with strict regard to the total of the consequences of one's act for all the moments and aims that are to be affected by this act.

7. The moral insight stands in all its forms opposed to ethical dogmatism, which accepts one separate end only. The insight arises from the consciousness that this one aim is not the only one that is actual. Imperfectly and blindly ethical dogmatism also realizes this truth, and so hates or even anathematizes the opposing aims. But the hatred is imperfect realization. The moral insight therefore says to those who possess the dogmatic spirit : "In so far as you seek a reason for the faith that is in you, you can find none short of the assumption of my position." The moral insight says to itself, " I ought not to return to the dogmatic point of view." So the moral insight insists upon giving itself the rule, " Dogmatism is wrong."

8. The only alternatives to the moral insight are : (a) ethical dogmatism, which once for all gives up

the effort to get any basis for ethics save its own irrational caprice ; and (*b*) ethical skepticism, which,
as we have seen, is only a preliminary form of the
moral insight, and passes over into the latter upon
reflection.

9. There is no other distinction between right and
wrong save what the dogmatic systems on the one
hand give as their capricious determinations, and
what the moral insight on the other hand shows as
the expression of what it involves.

Our conclusion so far is therefore this : Remain
blind if you will ; we have no means of preventing
you.   But if you want to know the whole ethical
truth, you can find it only in the moral insight.   All
else is caprice.   To get the moral insight, you must
indeed have the will to get the truth as between the
conflicting claims of two or more doctrines.   This
will being given, the moral insight is the necessary
outcome even of skepticism itself.

Yet now, after all our argument and enthusiasm,
the reader must know that what we have so far portrayed is only the most elementary aspect of the
moral insight.   The unity that we have insisted upon
is so far an empty unity, a negative freedom from
conflict.   To show the real worth of this whole view,
we must pass from the beggarly elements of duty to
more advanced conceptions.   The moral insight must
be so developed as to tell us about the Organization
of Life.   The empty unity must be filled with content.   We must discuss more *in concreto* what men
possessed of the moral insight will do.

CHAPTER VII.

THE ORGANIZATION OF LIFE.

Die wahre Freiheit ist als Sittlichkeit dies, dass der Wille nicht sub-
jektive, d. i. eigensüchtige, sondern allgemeinen Inhalt zu seinen
Zwecken hat. — HEGEL, *Encyclopädie*.

UNEXPECTEDLY we have been saved from our ethical skepticism even in and through the very act of
thinking it out. Here, as elsewhere in philosophy,
the truth is to be reached, neither by dreading nor by
discountenancing the doubt, but by accepting, experiencing, and absorbing the doubt, until, as an element in our thought, it becomes also an element in
an higher truth. We do not say, therefore, to com-
mend our moral principle, as it has just been propounded, that it is immediately acceptable to all
healthy consciences, or that it is a pious, or a respectable, or a popularly recognized principle. We say
only this : Doubt rationally about moral doctrines,
and your doubt itself, if real, thorough-going, all-embracing, merciless, will involve this very principle of
ours. We find the principle by means of the universal doubt, and it is this method of procedure that
distinguishes the foregoing discussion of the basis of
morals from many of those that have previously been
concerned with this problem. To point out that the
average man, or the reputed saint, or the inspired

prophet, or the great poet, or the reader himself, whenever he is enthusiastic has or has had a given ideal, is not to justify this ideal. Yet of such a nature are the justifications that most moralists have given for their ideals. If we have gained our result by any better method, that was because we were free to doubt all those pretended defenses of the good. We have found the nature of the absolute and universal will, by rigidly questioning the significance of all the individual wills.

But our ideal must be made to do work in the world. It must accomplish something, by solving for us a few concrete moral problems, such as actually trouble men. Even the present discussion must consider some of these consequences of our general principle; for religious philosophy, in seeking an ideal for life, does not want a barren abstraction, but such an ideal as can also be our guide. What does our principle tell a man to do?

The principle, as is plain, may be viewed in two ways. If by moral insight we mean what the last chapter defined, namely, insight into the fact of the existence of other conscious wills besides our own, coupled with full rational appreciation of this truth, then our principle may be viewed as saying to each of us: *Get and keep the moral insight as an experience, and do all that thou canst to extend among men this experience.* On the other hand, the principle may be equally well viewed as saying: *Act out in each case what the moral insight bids thee do;* that is, as before explained, *Having made thyself, in so far as thou art able, one with all the con*

flicting wills before thee, act out the resulting uni-
versal will as it then arises in thee. Two classes of
human duties are thus defined, one formal and provisional, the other permanent. We must explain in
some measure each of them, in order that we may
show the practical applications of our moral principle.

I.

The first class of duties comprises those that have
most especially to do with the moral education of our
race. We are, and must long remain, exceedingly
imperfect and blind creatures. If there is possible
any state of humanity in which all shall be ready to
act in accordance with the moral insight, that state
must be, morally speaking, better than any other.
Therefore the first demand that the moral insight
makes of us so soon as we get it is: *So act as to
increase the number of those who possess the insight.*
Here, of course, is a precept of a very formal character, and plainly provisional in its nature. It is as
if one were to be among blind men, himself blind,
and were by some magical act, say by accidentally
washing in a miraculous fountain, to get at one stroke
and for the first time the power of sight, in all its
maturity and perfection. Such an one would perhaps say: "How noble is this new sense! But to
what end shall I use it? For the first I must use
it to bring these other men to the fountain, to wash
their eyes, that they may miraculously learn in one
instant to see this glorious world." But some one
might object: "In this way, if the only use to be

made of a man's sight is to extend the power of sight to others, of what use is the power itself? The sole aim of seeing cannot be to cause others to see. Else what good would result to any one, if all followed your precept?" The answer would be plain: " When all or the most of us get the power, then indeed we can use it for other ends. But because it is the best of powers for all these other ends, therefore the best provisional use to make of it is, not to spend much time upon these ends, but to spend time upon extending the possession of the power. When this is done, then first will begin the real use of the power for its own sake." As in this case of the supposed miraculous acquirement of a new sense in all its maturity of power at one stroke, so it is in case of the much more gradual acquirement of the moral insight. To be sure, the ultimate aim of life cannot be merely the extension of the power to realize the wills that are active about us, but must at last be found by defining the course of action that best harmonizes these wills. But, provisionally, we have a task before us that is easily defined, because elementary. Harmony cannot be even partially attained, the best human activity cannot be even imperfectly developed, until a very great number of men have this, the very first, most elementary requisite of conscious morality, namely, the power to see the facts of human life as they are. So long as a man is bound up in his individual will, he may be instinctively upright, he cannot be consciously and with clear intent righteous. So long therefore as this is true of him, he will be dependent on traditions that are often pernicious, on conscience that is often brutal prejudice, on faith that is often bigotry, on emotion that is the blindest of all guides ; and if he does good or if he does evil, the power responsible for his deeds will not be a truly moral impulse. To gain the moral ends of humanity, the indispensable prerequisite is therefore the moral insight in its merely formal aspect, as an human power and as an experience of life. When a good many more men have reached the possession of this power, then more of life will be taken up with concrete duties. Until that time comes, the great aim must be this formal and provisional one : *to produce in men the moral mood*, and so to prepare the way for the further knowledge of the highest good. If we put the matter otherwise we may say : The moral insight, insisting upon the need of the harmony of all human wills, shows us that, *whatever the highest human good may be, we can only attain it together, for it involves harmony*. The highest good then is not to be got by any one of us or by any clique of us separately. Either the highest good is for humanity unattainable, or the humanity of the future must get it *in common*. Therefore the sense of community, the power to work together, with clear insight into our reasons for so working, is the *first* need of humanity. Not what good thing men may hereafter come to see, but how they shall attain the only sense whereby they can ever get to see the good, is the great present human concern.

Starting with this duty, we can now examine what rule of life this duty will give us. *Extend the moral insight among men, and in thy own life:*

this is the first commandment. The direct consequence is that, so regarded, the first duty of man in
the present day cannot be either to get happiness
himself, or, in view of this present state of human
life, to make other people happy. All that he may
indeed be in some measure required to do, but not,
in the present state of the world, as an end, but solely
as a means to an end. This at all events is not the
day for contentment, but for work ; and joy is now
a proper part of human life chiefly in so far as it
tends to preserve, to increase, or to foster the moral
insight. Here we have the present practical solution suggested for all the questions about the right
and wrong of so-called hedonism. Hedonism is the
product of an imperfect understanding of the moral
insight. Benevolent hedonism springs from the insight that men like to be happy. Realizing this, the
believer in universal hedonism says : *Make men
happy so far as thou canst*. But this principle of
hedonism is surely not the immediate truth for this
present time, whatever may or may not turn out to
be the case in future. For to labor to increase happiness may for the present mean to increase the moral
blindness of men. Some sorts of happiness tend to
make us blind, as has in fact been shown in a former chapter. Unless a man experiences very bitterly the reality of the conflict of wills in this world,
the moral insight is apt to forsake him. But until
the moral insight becomes practically universal, the
highest good for humanity cannot be got. Therefore all forms of happiness that hinder rather than
help the moral insight are evil, and we ought to do

what we can to get rid of them out of the world. And all experiences, however painful, that certainly tend to the increase of the power of moral insight, are good for men ; and if we see no other experiences more suitable for this purpose, we ought to do what we can to increase among men the number and the definiteness of these pains.

Yet of course it will at once appear, when we examine human emotional experiences in the light of what we know of men, that there is a decided limit to the morally educative power of painful experiences, and that, on the other hand, very many pleasant experiences are useful to the moral insight, either by directly aiding it, or by preparing a man to attain it. In considering this branch of the subject, we at last reach the point where a scientific psychology can give us a great deal of help. We rejected the so-called "scientific basis" for morals because it founds the *ought to be* upon brutal physical facts. Now, however, we can turn to science to help us in our present task, because, having defined our *ought to be*, we are dealing with applied ethics, and are asking how this moral insight is to be attained. Psychology must tell us what it can as to this matter. And here such suggestions as those in Mr. Spencer's "Data of Ethics" are indeed a useful aid to applied moral doctrine. We reject wholly the notion that Mr. Spencer or any like teacher has even caught a glimpse of the fundamental ethical problem. Mr. Spencer seems to be in the most childlike ignorance that there is any such problem at all. But we are glad to find that Mr. Spencer once having very

12

illogically accepted a partially correct fundamental notion about the ideal of life, does suggest a good deal about this problem of applied ethics with which we are now dealing. He does tell us some very sensible things about the attainment of this ideal.

Among these sensible suggestions is the insistence upon the value of pleasure as an indication of the increase of healthy life in the man who has the pleasure ; and the further insistence upon the thought that, since pleasure thus indicates in some wise health and efficiency, and since efficiency is an indispensable prerequisite to sound practical morality, there must always be a certain moral presumption in favor of happiness, and in favor of whatever tends to increase happiness. Properly understood and limited, this doctrine of Mr. Spencer's is an obvious and useful consequence from what we know of psychology. Mr. Spencer dwells on it at tedious and wholly unnecessary length, but he is surely justified when he protests, against the ascetics, that their ideal man must be in general a puny, inefficient, and perhaps wholly burdensome man, whose ill-health may make him, at last, hopelessly selfish. This we know on good scientific grounds, and it is well to have said the thing plainly in an ethical treatise.

But what is the result ? Is happiness the only aim of life because the permanently unhappy man is apt to be a poor diseased creature, useless, or even dangerous ? No ; the consequence of all this is that the first moral aim must be to make a man efficient in possessing and extending the moral insight. Efficiency for moral ends is still our proximate goal.

Happiness is, at least for the present, only a subordinate means. Therefore we say: By all means make men happy, so far as their happiness tends to give them and to preserve in them moral insight. True it is, as scientific psychology shows us, that a man, in order to be as good as possible, must generally be possessed of respectable health, of what he thinks a good place in the world, of friends, and of numerous pleasures. He must digest well, he must enjoy the esteem of his fellows, he must be strong, and he must be frequently amused. All this is true, and is in fact a commonplace. When an ascetic denies this, he maintains a pernicious heresy, that tends to destroy moral insight by depriving men of the physical power to get it. But these facts must not be misinterpreted. Whatever might be true of a society in which moral insight had been attained, nothing is plainer than that happiness at the present time cannot be regarded from our point of view as more than a means to the present great end. If we try to amuse our neighbors, to relieve their woes, to improve their worldly estate, we must do so not as if this were the end of the present life, but as workers in a very vast drama of human life, whose far-off purpose must govern every detail. The good Samaritan must say to himself, as he helps the poor wretch by the wayside: " In so far as I realize only this man's need, my purpose is indeed simply to relieve him. But my purpose must be higher than that. This man is not alone, but one of a multitude. My highest aim in helping him is not to make him individually happy, but to increase by this, as by all my acts, the harmony of mankind. Not alone that he may by and by go away and enjoy himself do I help him now, but because by so doing I hope through him to increase among men moral insight." There-fore, notwithstanding Schopenhauer's ridicule, Fichte was right in saying that we ought to treat the indi-vidual man not chiefly as an individual, but as an instrument for extending and serving the moral law. Because a certain kind of happiness means efficiency, and efficiency morality, therefore and therefore alone have we the right and duty, in this present genera-tion, to labor for this kind of happiness.

Equally, therefore, it becomes our duty to labor to increase pain, whenever pain is the best means of fostering the moral insight. Therefore, in this pres-ent day, it cannot be our duty to labor to diminish pain in the world, simply as pain. Again we must appeal to psychology to guide us aright. The pains that foster moral insight, although limited in num-ber and intensity, are numerous, and still imper-fectly defined. It would be a useful task to study more in detail than psychologists have yet done, the moralizing power of pain. This is a task for the psychology of the future. In general, of course, we can say that the range of such pains has been much exaggerated by ascetics. Bodily pain, if severe, is generally brutalizing, at least for most people, and the moral insight is in it only in so far as the past experience of bodily pain helps us to know the sig-nificance of the suffering of others, not by giving us that blind emotion of sympathy before criticised, but by giving us the means to form a cool abstract

estimate of the value of this evil of physical pain.
For thus we can realize the strength of the will that
seeks to escape it, and can act with due respect to
this will. But nature generally gives us enough experience of pain to furnish excellent material for the
calculations needed. Therefore, bodily pains, save
as punishments, are seldom useful instruments for
our great purpose. Not thus can self be duly mor-
tified.

It is different with certain mental pains. All
those that tend to make the individual feel his own
necessary limitations, and thereby to approach the
realization of the great world of life about him, are
necessary evils. His will must be overwhelmed, that
the Universal Will may have place to establish it
self in him. Therefore, without considering whether
we are thereby increasing or diminishing the sum
of human misery, we all of us unhesitatingly set
about the work of contending with blind self-confidence and self-absorption wherever it may appear.
Therefore it is right that we ridicule all pretentious
mediocrity that is unconscious of its stupidities.
Therefore, in fact, it is right that we should criticise
unsparingly all pretenders, however much they may
be pained by our criticism. Therefore it is well that
we should feel not a selfish but a righteous joy whenever pride has a fall, whenever the man who thinks
that he is something discovers of a truth that he is
nothing. Therefore, also, do we put down excessive
forwardness and vanity in growing children, although
so to do hurts their sensitive young selfishness very
keenly. In all such ways we must ask and we must

show no mercy, save when these keen pains of
wounded vanity are so given as to inflame and increase this vanity itself. All healthy, truthful criticism of individual limitations is a duty, even if it is a
present torture to the individual criticised. For this
individual is blind to other life because he is wrapped
up in himself. If by showing him his insignificance
you can open his eyes, you are bound to do so, even
though you make him writhe to see his worthlessness. For what we here defend is not that ill-natured
criticism whose only aim is to gratify the miserable
self of the critic, but the criticism whose edge is
turned in earnest against every form of self-satisfaction that hinders insight. Let a man be self-satisfied when he is at rest, after dinner, or in merry
company. It is a harmless and even a useful amusement. But when he is at work doing good he ought
to hate self-satisfaction, which hinders the moral insight, which exalts his will above the universal will,
which takes the half-done task for the whole task,
and altogether glorifies the vanity of vanities. If
now my critic rids me of such self-satisfaction, he
may hurt me keenly, but he is my best friend. My
life may often be miserable in consequence, but then
I am an instrument, whose purpose it is to attain, to
foster, to extend, and to employ the moral insight.
My misery is a drop, evil no doubt in itself (since
my poor little will must writhe and struggle when it
sees its own vanity and the hopelessness of its separate satisfactions), but a relative good, since through
it I may attain to the moral insight. All such pains
must be dealt with in the same way. Hence the

ntilitarian principle of benevolent hedonism, even if right in its application to the far-off future, has but little direct practical application to a life that must to-day be judged by such standards as these.

II.

But has the principle óf hedonism any truth even in its application to a world where all had attained the moral insight as an experience? If we consider the higher human activities, whose worth is not merely provisional, but permanent, the activities that men will carry on when they have freed themselves from selfish strife, is the aggregate happiness as such the goal of the action of this unselfish society?

There are existent already among men activities that belong to spheres where selfish strife is, relatively speaking, suppressed. These activities are foreshadowings of the life of the possible future humanity that may come to possess the moral insight. Art, science, philosophy, are the types of such life. These activities form still but a small part of the aggregate work of men, and so it must long be; yet, though subordinated in extent to the pressing moral needs of an imperfect state, these activities are already among the highest in our lives. But now, are they valuable because of the aggregate happiness that they cause, or for some other reason? To judge of this we must study the definition of the second, more permanent class of human duties.

Suppose then that the first and provisional aim of human conduct had been attained, and that all men possessed the moral insight, what would this insight then lead them to do? Here the hedonist will expect to have his revenge for our previous neglect of his advice. " My precepts have been set aside so far," he may say, " as having no immediate application to the moral needs of the moment. To get this merely formal condition of harmony among men, the moral man has been advised to subordinate all direct efforts towards making people happy, to the end of making them first possess what you have called the moral mood. But now at last, in the supposed case, the great end has been attained, and men are formally moral. Now surely they have nothing to do but to be as happy as possible. So at last my plan will be vindicated, and the ideal man will come to be a seeker of ideal pleasures."

The hedonist is too sanguine. His ideas of the highest state may have their value, but they are indefinite in at least one respect. When he says that he wants all his ideal men, in the ideal state, to be happy together, he never tells us what he means by the individual man at all, nor what inner relation that individual's happiness is to have to the happiness of other men. All men, in the ideal state, are to be harmonious and happy together: this the hedonist tells us; but he does not see how many difficulties are involved in the definition of this ideal state. He plainly means and says that in this ideal state the good of the whole society is to be an aggregate of a great number of individual happy states, which the various men of the blessed society are to feel. He assumes then that in the ideal state each

man would be able to say : " I, separately regarded,
am happy, and so are all my fellows." Now possibly the very notion of an ideal state, in which the
separate selves are as such happy, and in which
the blessedness of the whole is an aggregate of the
blessedness of the separate individuals, is a contradictory notion.   At all events it is a notion whose
meaning and validity every hedonist coolly and unquestioningly assumes.   Yet it is an assumption that
we must examine with care.

If a man sets before himself and his fellows the
goal of individual happiness, as the hedonist wants
him to do in the supposed ideal state, can he conceivably attain that goal ?   The hedonist supposes
that the only moral limitation to the pursuit of personal happiness is the moral requirement of altruism, according to which no one ought to seek his
own pleasure at the cost of a greater misery to another.   In the ideal state, as all would be in the
moral mood, and all disposed to help one another,
and to get happiness only together, this one limitation would be removed.   Then, thinks the hedonist,
the highest law would be : *Get the most happiness,
all of you.*   This happiness the hedonist conceives as
an aggregate of states that would exist in the various
separate individuals.   So each individual will strive
after his own joy, but in such wise as to hinder the
joy of nobody else.   But we oppose to this the question : Is there not some other limitation than this to
individual search for happiness ?   Is not the ideal
of individual happiness as such an impossible ideal,
not because the individuals in the imperfect state

lack harmony, but because, even in the supposed harmonious state, there would be an inner hindrance to
the pursuit of this ideal by any individual? Would
not the moral insight detect the hindrance, and so reject this ideal? There are at least some very familiar reasons for thinking this to be the case. These
reasons do not of themselves prove, but they certainly
suggest, that the notion of a progressive individual
happiness has in it some strange contradiction.

First, then, we have the old empirical truth that
individual happiness is never very nearly approached
by any one, so long as he is thinking about it. The
happy man ought to be able to say, " I am happy."
He can much more easily say, " I was happy; " for
present reflection upon happiness interferes in most
cases with happiness. So here is an inner difficulty,
very well known, in the way of making individual
happiness the goal of life. We have no desire to
dwell here upon this difficulty, which has so often
been discussed. We do not exaggerate its importance. We consider it only the first suggestion that
the hedonistic ideal of life has some inner contradiction in its very nature, so that there is some deeper
conflict here going on than that between selfishness
and altruism.

In the second place, we notice that, if anybody
tries to sketch for us the ideal state of human life
as the hedonist conceives it, we are struck with a
sense of the tameness and insignificance of the whole
picture. The result is strange. Here we have been
making peace and harmony among men the proximate goal of life, yet when this harmony has to be

conceived in hedonistic fashion, when the hedonist
gives us his picture of a peaceful society, where, in
the midst of universal good humor, his ideal, the happiness of everybody concerned, is steadfastly pursued,
we find ourselves disappointed and contemptuous.
That harmless company of jolly good fellows is unspeakably dull. One listens to the account of their
happiness as one might listen to the laughter and
merry voices of some evening club of jovial strangers,
who had been dining at the hotel in which one happened himself to be eating a late and frugal supper,
in sobriety and weariness. Those unknown creatures whose chatter in the next room the traveler
dimly hears at such a time, — a confused babble of
stupid noises ; how insignificant their joys seem to
him ! Who cares whether that really wretched set
of animals yonder, with their full stomachs and their
misty brains, think themselves happy or not ? To be
sure, among them the harmony seems in some sort
to have been momentarily realized. One would no
doubt seem to enjoy it all just as well as they, if he
were one of them. But one is viewing it at a distance, from outside ; and so looking at it he possibly
sees that a mass of individual happiness is not just
the ideal of ideals after all.

Just such, however, is the feeling that comes to one
in considering Mr. Spencer's description of his ideal
society. And similar feelings have been awakened
in many reflective people when they have considered
traditional notions of heaven, and have tried to estimate the value of the life of individual bliss therein
pictured. Professor William James has recently so

well stated these objections in a few brilliant sentences, that we cannot do better than to quote from
his recent article on " The Dilemma of Determin-
ism " : [1] —

" Every one must at some time have wondered at that
strange paradox of our moral nature, that, though the
pursuit of outward good is the breath of its nostrils, the
attainment of outward good would seem to be its suffoca-
tion and death.   Why does the painting of any paradise
or Utopia, in heaven or on earth, awaken such yawnings
for Nirvana and escape ?   The white-robed, harp-playing
heaven of our Sabbath-schools, and the ladylike tea-table
elysium represented in Mr. Spencer's ' Data of Ethics,' as
the final consummation of progress, are exactly on a par
in this respect, — lubberlands, pure and simple, one and
all.   We look upon them from this delicious mess of in-
sanities and realities, strivings and deadnesses, hopes and
fears, and agonies and exultations, which form our present state ; and *tedium vitæ* is the only sentiment they
awaken in our breasts.   To our crepuscular natures, born
for the conflict, the Rembrandtesque moral chiaroscuro,
the shifting struggle of the sunbeam *in* the gloom, such
pictures of light upon light are vacuous and expression-
less, and neither to be enjoyed nor understood.   If *this*
be the whole fruit of the victory, we say ; if the generations of mankind suffered and laid down their lives ; if
prophets confessed and martyrs sang in the fire, and all
the sacred tears were shed for no other end than that a
race of creatures of such unexampled insipidity should succeed, and protract *in sæcula sæculorum* their contented
and inoffensive lives, — why, at such a rate, better lose
than win the battle, or at all events better ring down the
curtain before the last act of the play, so that a business

[1] *Unitarian Review* for September, 1884.

that began so importantly may be saved from so singularly flat a winding-up."

Now not only does all this seem true in such cases, but we have similar feelings about even so ideal a picture of happy future life as is Shelley's, in the last act of the "Prometheus." There are indeed many deeper elements in that noble ideal of Shelley's, for he distinctly says that his true ideal is "Man — Oh! not men"; or, as he again expresses it : —

> "One undivided soul of many a soul
> Whose nature is its own divine control,
> Where all things flow to all, as rivers to the sea."

And when he says this, he gets far beyond mere hedonism. But yet there are other elements in his account that are not so satisfactory, and that are decidedly hedonistic. Their expression is indeed perfect. Surely if the noblest hedonism could ever succeed with us through the noblest of statements, such an advocate as Shelley would convince us. But when the poet glorifies mere individual pleasure, as he does in part of his picture, our clearest reflection is that, after all, the end of the tragedy is petty when compared with the beginning.

For consider what a world it is in which we begin the poem. At first glance it is a gloomy and terrible world of brutal wrong. But soon the picture grows brighter, even while the wrong is depicted. There is the glorious figure of the suffering Titan, there is the sweetness of the tender love that watches him ; and above the tyrant himself one feels that there is somehow a heavenly might, that does not suffer him to do his worst. The world in which

these things live is not intolerable. But then come
the spirits that sing to Prometheus, in his anguish,
of immortal deeds done on the earth, of great
thoughts and lofty passions. All these are born of
the conflict, and have their being in the midst of the
terrors of the tyrant's dominion. It is indeed no
perfect world, this ; and one needs some higher
light, such as Prometheus has, to prophesy that the
good will ever triumph ; but one sees forthwith that
from the perfect world, if it ever comes, these great
strivings for good, this sublime devotion and love
and heroism, must not wholly vanish. These things
must not be laid aside like old garments whenever
Prometheus wins and is free ; their spirit must be
preserved as an element in the higher life of the
future. If they are worth anything, their true nature must be eternal.

And as for the real worth of this world in which
the evil is so far triumphant — we learn something
of that from Demogorgon. This mysterious being
has indeed no very definite religious philosophy to
offer. He meets plain questions with vague answers, when Asia and Panthea catechise him ; and
one feels it to be well for his reputation as a profound teacher that his questioners are neither men
nor Socratic inquirers. But still what he tells of the
deep truth that is " imageless," is enough to make
us feel that even this world of horrors is not without
a divine significance. Jove reigns, but, whatever the
visible world may be, the truth of things is a world of
hope and love, where the real God is somehow above
all and through all, a Spirit of Eternal Goodness.

To have found this out in the midst of all the evil is surely not to have found life wholly vain.

But then what happens? By the accident that, according to Shelley, rules the world, the revolution is accomplished, and Zeus is hurled headlong into the abyss. What glorious life shall now begin? When the deep and magnificent truth that was felt to be beneath all the horror of the tyrant's reign, comes out into full light, what tongue shall be able to sing the glories of that beatific vision? We listen eagerly — and we are disappointed. Prometheus arises grandly from his bed of torture, and then — he forthwith bethinks himself of a very pretty cave, where one might be content to rest a long time in the refined company of agreeable women. There one will lie, and wreathe flowers, and tell tales, and sing songs, and laugh and weep; and the hours will fly swiftly by. And then what will become of the rest of the world? Oh, this world simply becomes a theatre of like individual enjoyments. Everybody to his cave and his flowers and his agreeable companions. And that will then be all. No organization; just good fellowship and fragmentary amusements.

No, that cannot be all. Shelley felt as much, and added the last act of the play. There we are to have depicted grandly and vaguely the life of organized love. The world shall be all alive, and the universal life shall join in the hymn of praise. All the powers of reality shall feel the new impulse of perfect harmony, and what shall spring from their union shall be some higher kind of existence, in which there is no longer to be any talk of thine and

mine; but the " one undivided soul of many a soul,"
" where all things flow to all, as rivers to the sea,"
shall enter upon a life of transcendent significance,
upon a task of eternal duration, and of a meaning
too high for us poor mortals of this present world
well to comprehend. But this is no longer pure
hedonism, although the verses hereabouts are so full
of the joyous outbursts and of the anticipations of
rapture. In fine, the outcome is no perfect and harmonious conception at all. We find the joy of the
freed and loving, yet still separate selves, and the
higher life of the all-pervading universal spirit, both
alike glorified; and we never get from the poet any
clearness about their actual relation. Is the world
blessed just because the tyrant no longer interferes
with each man's flower-wreathing and other amusements? Or is the sole source of bliss the disposition of everybody to give everybody else everything?
Or is the real source of the perfection this: that
these souls, no longer oppressed by hatred, have at
last come to feel not only their freedom, but also
some higher aim of universal life? Shelley hints,
but does not consistently make us feel, what his real
result is. There was in fact always about Shelley
that childish innocence of benevolent hope, to which
the only evil seemed to be the hatred of men for one
another, and the highest good the outburst of universal kindliness. Now that is the beginning of
moral insight, but cannot be all of it. As if the benevolence would not turn out to be utter emptiness,
unless there is something beyond it! As if there
could be any value in this unity of life, unless there

is something to be done by the one life after it is
united! As if the moral insight must not reveal
some deeper truth than can be seen in its first moments!

One expects what we are coming to. In discussing this problem of Shelley's we are reaching the
sense that the moral insight must be yet further
completed, or else it will be all in vain. The moral
insight says to us all : *Act as one being.* We must
come to that point; but we must also go beyond.
We must ask : What is this one being to do, after
the insight has made all the individuals of one will?
And we already begin to see, in opposition to hedonism, that it cannot be the end of this universal will
simply to make of us so and so many new separate
individuals once more. The mass of tediously happy
selves seems insipid to our common sense, just because we all dimly feel the truth that we must now
come to understand better, namely, that *the universal will of the moral insight must aim at the destruction of all which separates us into a heap of
different selves, and at the attainment of some higher
positive organic aim.* The " one undivided soul "
we are bound to make our ideal. And the ideal of
that soul cannot be the separate happiness of you
and of me, nor the negative fact of our freedom
from hatred, but must be something above us all,
and yet very positive.

Had we deduced our principle in any other way
than the one we chose, we should be unable to take
this, our present necessary step forwards. The feeling of sympathy, for instance, is concerned with the

13

individual object of our sympathy. To sympathize
with all men is to wish everybody happy, each after
his own fashion. But we rejected that emotional
sympathy as such. We said : The facts of life show
us a conflict of wills. To realize this conflict is to
see that no will is more justified in its separateness
than is any other. This realization is ethical skepticism, a necessary stage on the way to the true
moral insight. The ethical doubt means and is the
realization of the conflict. But this realization
means, as we see on reflection, a real will in us that
unites these realized wills in one, and demands the
end of their conflict. This is our realization of an
Universal Will. The rest of our doctrine must be
the development of the nature of the universal will.
This will first says to each of the individual wills :
" Submit thyself to me." Or otherwise put, let
each will be so acted out as if by One Being who
combined in himself all the other wills. Hence the
universal will must demand, not the indefinitely conceived or dimly and sentimentally desired separate
satisfaction of everybody, but an organic union of
life ; such an union as this our world would try to
make of itself if it were already in empirical fact
what the universal will demands it to be, namely,
one Self. This one Self, however, could no longer
will to cut itself up again into the separate empirical selves, any more than it could in any narrow,
priggish fashion set itself up for a new specimen of
a lofty individual, to be obeyed as an arbitrary law-
giver. It would demand all the wealth of life that
the separate selves now have ; and all the unity that

any one individual now seeks for himself. It would
aim at the fullest and most organized life conceivable. And this its aim would become no longer
merely a negative seeking for harmony, but a positive aim, demanding the perfect Organization of
Life.

III.

But the postulate of all hedonism, utilitarian or
other, this postulate of the absolute worth of individual satisfaction, finds its practical refutation for
every growing character in yet another form. Everybody has tried to realize the ideal of individualism,
this ideal of a happy or satisfied self, either for himself or for some loved one ; and everybody finds, if
he tries the thing long enough, what a hollow and
worthless business it all is. If there is, or is possible
anywhere, a really satisfied self, it certainly has no
place in any fleshly body ; and the reason is not
alone what disappointed people call the " disagreeable order of things in this wicked world," but the
inner contradictions of this notion of a perfected human self. Let us remind ourselves of some of these
contradictions.

Hedonism has no meaning, unless the satisfied human self is logically possible. The ideal of hedonism, with all its vagueness, has at least one essential
element, in that it demands the satisfaction of human selves by the free supply of all that they desire
for themselves. Hedonism therefore must and does
assert that what a man desires is his own contentment ; so that, if you could, physically speaking,

give him all that he asks for himself, you would have reached the goal for him. But now, if all this is a delusion, if in fact a man does not really want his own satisfaction alone, but does actually want something more, that is not his individual satisfaction, and that is not to be attained through his satisfaction, then the hedonistic ideal does not express the truth of life. And this paradoxical experience we all get, sooner or later. We find that our little self does desire something that, if gained, would be not its own satisfaction at all, but its own destruction in its separate life as this self. So the aim of life cannot be ultimately hedonistic. For, if possessed of the moral insight, we cannot will that each self should get the greatest possible aggregate of separate satisfactions, when in truth no one of the selves seeks merely an aggregate of self-satisfactions as such, but when each does seek something else that is unattainable in the form of separate self-satisfaction.

But possibly a reader may incredulously demand where the proof is of this self-contradictory desire that all the selves are declared to have. The proof lies in the general fact that to be fully conscious of one's own individual life as such is to be conscious of a distressing limitation. This limitation every one very shrewdly notices for the first in other people. The knowledge of it expresses itself in personal criticism. One first puts the matter very naïvely thus, that, whereas the rule of life for one's own person is simply to get all the satisfaction that one can, the appearance of anybody else who pretends to be content with *him*self must be the signal not for admira-

tion at the sight of his success, but for a good deal
of contempt. One sees at once that he is a person
of serious limitations. One sees and feels perfections
that the other has not. One despises then the other
man's complacency, because it is so plainly founded
in illusion. " If he could only see himself as others
see him," one says, " he could not be self-satisfied."
Criticism thus seems to indicate why he ought to be
discontented, and why he would, if he knew more,
feel a contempt for himself. All such criticism is
really an abandonment of the hedonistic principle.
If an individual ought to be dissatisfied, although he
is actually satisfied, and if he ought to be dissatisfied
merely because he has not some perfection that exists in somebody else, then the doctrine that a self
reaches its goal in so far as it reaches inner contentment is given up. No benevolent hedonist has any
business to criticise a happy man who is harming
nobody by his happiness. He is at the goal, or ap-
proximately so. Let him alone. To do otherwise,
by criticising him, is a crime.

But no ; every one feels that the true goal is not
attained for this man. And this feeling, though in
itself as feeling it proves nothing, is the first suggestion to many of some deeper truth. This truth,
however, enters like iron into his soul, when somebody else ably and justly and severely criticises him
in his turn. Here, for example, I have been for a
time content with myself, and have been saying to
my soul : " Soul, take thy ease," and here comes one
who says to me, very justly, " Thou fool," and points
out some great lack in my conduct, or in my charac

ter, or in my knowledge. And now I have a strange experience of conflicting passions. This critic has caused me a sharp pang. Perhaps I hate him for it; but then, when I go away and think the matter over, I see that as to the fact, he is right. This great limitation does actually exist for me, and perhaps I cannot remove it; so I can but suffer from the sense of it. I was innocent and ignorant before, and therefore happy. If the critic had not showed me to myself, I should have kept this bliss. But it is in vain now to think of returning to that innocence. I am indeed a wretch and a fool; and how shall I escape myself? Alas for my lost pleasure in contemplating my fancied perfection!

But no: cannot I in fact return to that ignorance, and to the blissful illusion of my own worth once more? Surely I can if I but try awhile. To flatter myself, to curse the critic, to talk of his jealousy and of his blindness: surely this will bring me back to my ignorance again in time. He will be forgotten, and I contented. But once more, my enlightened self revolts from this lie. The defect is real, and I know it. Would my ignorance make it less real? To have this defect and to suffer from it is bad enough; but with horror do I now contemplate the state of going on forever with this defect, but still ignorant of it and so not suffering from it. My old innocence seems really pitiful. It actually adds much to my present pang of chagrin, that I previously ought to have felt the chagrin, and yet had it not. I tremble when I reflect how, amid all that selfish complacency, I really was a fool the whole time, and appeared so to discerning people, and yet knew it not. And therefore now, through all the pang of the discovery, runs the feeling that I would not if I could, no, not for any delight of complacency, return to that state of hollow, delicious, detestable ignorance. It was a fool's paradise; but I have escaped from it. I know my nakedness, and I prefer the fruit of the tree of knowledge, with bitter exile, to the whole of the delights of that wretched place. It is a contradictory state, this. My knowledge is torture to my foolish, sensitive self; yet while I writhe with the vainest of pangs, I despise utterly the thought of escaping it by illusion, or by forgetfulness, or by any means save the actual removal or conquest of the defect. And this I feel even when the defect is seen to be utterly irremovable without the destruction of myself. Better go on despising myself, and feeling the contempt of others, than return to the delights of foolishness; or, if the pain of knowing what I am is insupportable, then it were better to die, than to live in despicable ignorance. Oh, wretched man that I am! Who shall deliver me?

Is all this mere emotion? or is it insight? In fact it is a growing, though still imperfect insight, a form of the moral insight. The pangs of this wounded self-love are themselves in truth also vanity, like the complacent self-love that they mourn; but only through the gateway of this pain can most people get beyond these vanities of individualism. For this wounded self-love, that refuses to be comforted by any deliberate return to its old illusions, is, as Adam Smith long since pointed out, an emotional expression of the result of putting ourselves at the point of view of our critics. We see our limitations as they see them. Our will conforms itself, therefore, to their contemptuous will concerning us, because we realize the existence of that will. In recognizing and sharing their contempt, we therefore realize in part the universal will that must condemn all individual limitations as such. We practically experience the truth that a perfectly fair judge of us all would not be satisfied merely with our individual contentments as such, but would also demand the destruction of all our individual limitations. We thus get practically far beyond hedonism. We see that as we are weak and wretched in the eyes of one another, we should all be far more so in the eyes of a god Our ideal of life must then be the notion of a life where no one being could fairly criticise any other at all. But such a life would be no longer a life of separate individuals, each limited to his petty sphere of work. It would be a life in which self was lost in a higher unity of all the conscious selves.

Singular may appear this conception even now, after all that we have said; but it is a practical conception in our every-day human life. That we criticise the limitations of others, and desire them to sacrifice their pleasures for the sake of removing these limitations, may be regarded at first as our cruel caprice, if you will so regard it. But when the edge of the sword is turned against us, when we, feeling the bitterness of criticism and seeing our limitations, long to be beyond them, hate ourselves for them, and yet refuse to escape from the pain of all this by forgetfulness of the defect, we pass from capricious criticism to something higher. We accept with agony the point of view of the one who stands outside of us. And, so doing, we pass in effect to the acceptance of the demands of the universal will. If there were a will that included in one consciousness all our separate wills, it could not will our individual defects as such. It would be absolute critic, as well as absolute harmonizer, of all of us. It would tear down these individual barriers of our petty lives, as the corporation of a great city may tear down wretched old rookeries. It would demand that we be one in spirit, and that our oneness be perfect. But if we experience this universal will, we experience that hedonism, whose life-blood is the insistence upon individual states as such, cannot be upheld by the moral insight, either now, or at any future stage of our human life on this earth. We perceive too that we all have a deep desire for self-destruction, in so far as we recognize that our self-love means absence of perfection.

IV.

We have seen in general the moral outcome of individualism. Let us study some of its forms and fortunes more in detail. Individualism, viewed as the tendency to hold that the ideal of life is the separate happy man, is itself very naturally the normal tendency of unreflecting strong natures, to whom happiness has been in a fair human measure already given. Children and child-like men, full of vigor, are innocently selfish ; or, when they act unselfishly, their

whole ideal is the making of others like themselves.
They fall into a notion about life that the author
not long since heard well-expressed by a cheerful
young friend, a former fellow-student, who, having
early plunged into a busy life, has already won both
influence and property. This man, full of the enthusiasm of first success, was talking over his life with
the writer, and fell to defining his opinions on various subjects, such as young men like to discuss. At
last he was asked about the view of life that he had
already formed in his little experience. He was
quick, honest, and definite in his answer, as he always has been. " My notion of a good life is," he
said, " that you ought to help your friends and whack
your enemies." The notion was older than the
speaker remembered; for Socratic dialogues on the
Just, with their ingenious Sophists making bold assertions, form no part of his present stock of subjects for contemplation. But what was interesting
in the fresh and frank manner of the speech was
the clearness of the conviction that a world of successful and friendly selves, whose enemies chanced
to be all recently " whacked," would be at the goal
of bliss. Such indeed is and must be the individualism of the successful and unreflecting man, by
whom all the world is classified as being either his
or not his, as to a cow all is either cow feed or not
cow feed. A man in this position has never yet
known the burden of Faust's soul when he says,
Cursed be what as possession charms us. If such
a man gets any moral insight, it will be on this stage
imperfect. He will seek only to multiply himself

in the forms of other men. These he will call his friends. That in which he does not recognize himself, he will " whack."

But most men cannot keep this form of the illusion of individualism. They pass most of their lives in the midst of disappointment. The self cannot get its objects. The ideal independence is hampered. The stubborn world asserts itself against us. We feel the littleness of our powers and of our plans. The broken and despairing self has to seek refuge elsewhere. And so individualism most commonly assumes another shape. In inner self-development we seek what the world refuses us in outer self-realization. Thoughts at least are free. Our emotions are our own. The world does not understand them ; but the world is cold and unappreciative. Let us be within ourselves what we cannot get in the outer world. Let us be inwardly complete, even if we are outwardly failures. Then we shall outwit the cruel world, and produce the successful self, in spite of misfortunes.

The reader need not be reminded of what vast development individualism has undergone in this direction. Literature is full of accounts of struggles for inward self-realization, made by men whose outer growth is impeded. The Hamlets and the Fausts of poetry, the saints and the self-conscious martyrs of great religious movements, are familiar examples. We have already in a former chapter studied the outcome of this romantic individualism in a few cases. There is no time to dwell here afresh at any length on so familiar a theme, but for the present we may point out that all illustrations of the tendency fall into two classes, representing respectively the sentimental and the heroic individualism. These are the forms of that Nobler Selfishness which benevolent hedonism defends. They are efforts to find the contented and perfected self. Their failure is the failure of individualism, and therewith of hedonism.

As for the sentimental individualism, we have seen already how unstable are its criteria of perfection, how full of fickleness is its life. The sentimental self admits that the world cannot understand it, and will not receive it ; but it insists that this neglect comes because the world does not appreciate the strength and beauty of the inner emotional life. The ideal, then, is devotion to a culture of the beautiful soul, and to a separation of this soul from all other life. Let other souls be saved in like fashion. One does not object to their salvation ; but one insists that each saved soul dwells apart in its own sensitive feelings, in the world of higher artistic pleasures. Now in fact such lives may be not uninteresting to the moralist ; but no moralist can be really content with their ideal. Its best direct refutation is after all a sense of humor strong enough to let the sensitive and beautiful soul see once in a while how comical is its demure pursuit of these subjective phantoms. This miserable life of deep inward excitements and longings, how absurd it seems to any critic who, standing outside, sees that there is nothing more than froth and illusion and hypocrisy in it. Heine's anecdote of the monkey boiling his own tail so as to get an inward sense of the nature and worth of the art of cookery, is what first comes to mind when we see such a man as this subjective idealist of the emotions. You have only to get him to laugh heartily once or twice, and his Philistine narrowness can no longer content him. "Why is just my feeling worth so much?" he will say. And then he will wake up to observe that his ideal was all a bad dream; and that an experience has no more or less worth because it happens in connection with the decomposition of his particular brain-stuff. Faust discovered that, as we have seen; and so in time will any other sensible man. The real reason after all why Mephistopheles could not get Faust's soul was that Faust could understand the Mephistophelean wit, which was throughout destructive of individualism. The sentimentalist who has no humor is once for all given over to the devil, and need sign no contract. He stares into every mirror that he passes, and, cursing the luck that makes him move so fast in this world, he murmurs incessantly, *Verweile doch, du bist so schön*. And so in the presence of the moral insight he is forthwith and eternally damned, unless some miracle of grace shall save him. It is noteworthy that one or two of our recent and youngest novelists in this country have gained a certain reputation by sentimental stories of collegiate and post-graduate life that precisely illustrate this simple-minded but abominable spirit. May these young authors repent while there is time, if indeed they can repent.

Less dangerous to genuine morality, and far higher in the scale of worth, is the Titanic form of individualism, the form that has given birth to such expressions as the Everlasting No of "Sartor Resartus." The name of Prometheus at once springs to our lips when we think of this view of life. Prometheus is so fully the representative of Titanism, that there is no better way of characterizing its whole spirit than to call it the Heresy of Prometheus, the finest of all moral heresies, and the last.

The world will not grant you outward freedom, and you see the hollowness of that inward life of blessed emotions. You despise it in others; you see that the moral insight cannot approve such a form of selfish separation in you or in them. But there is another form of self - development. You must be something. Why not be heroic? Possibly the ideal is a world of courageous selves, that find their perfection in their independence of action. Prometheus gave this ideal a peculiar emphasis by reason of the fact that he had a Zeus to defy. But the same ideal, in a more moderate expression, is the ideal of many a quiet, matter of fact man, who has little happiness, but much spirit and energy, who is too busy and too healthy to be sentimental, who knows little of poetry, who has never heard the name of Prometheus, but who knows what it is to hold his own in the fight with the world. This man you cannot put down; he cares little for the opinions of others. There is no judge above him save God or his conscience. He is no saint; but he is at least an admirable fellow. He belongs to the race of Achilles; he believes in the gospel of eternal warfare against whatever seems to him evil. He respects others; he wants to do good in his way. But he thinks that the best good that he could do would be to make other men brave like himself. This lonely, active, indomitable self he thinks the ideal type of perfection. For him the moral insight does not go beyond the approval of such life as this, indefinitely multiplied.

It is always a delight to follow this Titanism in its various shapes. Buddhism, as we know, is a religion wholly founded on self-denial, and it counsels austere self-extinction. And yet, by a strange freak of moral dialectics, it is Buddhism that has given us some of the best expressions of the Titanic individualism. In a Buddhist homily in the Sutta Nipâta[1] one may find such an outburst as the following, — one of the finest of the confessions of the Titans : —

" Having laid aside the rod against all beings, and not hurting any of them, let no one wish for a son, much less for a companion; let him wander alone like a rhinoceros.

" In him who has intercourse with others, affections arise, and then the pain which follows affection ; considering the misery that originates in affection, let one wander alone like a rhinoceros.

" He who has compassion on his friends and confidential companions loses his own advantage, having a fettered mind; seeing this danger in friendship, let one wander alone like a rhinoceros.

" Just as a large bamboo-tree, with its branches entangled in each other, such is the care one has with children and wife; but like the shoot of the bamboo not clinging to anything, let one wander alone like a rhinoceros.

" As a beast unbound in the forest goes feeding at pleas

[1] Max Müller's *Sacred Books of the East*, vol. x., part ii., p. ₰ qq.

ure, so let the wise man, considering only his own will, wander alone like a rhinoceros. . . .

. . . " Discontented are some ascetics, also some householders, dwelling in houses; let one, caring little about other people's children, wander alone like a rhinoceros.

" If one acquires a clever companion, an associate righteous and wise, let him, overcoming all dangers, wander about with him glad and thoughtful.

" If one does not acquire a clever companion, an associate righteous and wise, then as a king abandoning his conquered kingdom, let him wander alone like a rhinoceros. . . .

. . . " Seeing bright golden bracelets, well-wrought by the goldsmith, striking against each other when there are two on one arm, let one wander alone like a rhinoceros.

" Thus, if I join myself with another, I shall swear or scold; considering this danger in future, let one wander alone like a rhinoceros. . . .

. . . " Both cold and heat, hunger and thirst, wind and a burning sun, and gadflies and snakes, — having overcome all these things, let one wander alone like a rhinoceros.

" As the elephant, the strong, the spotted, the large, after leaving the herd walks at pleasure in the forest, even so let one wander alone like a rhinoceros. . . .

" Not adorning himself, not looking out for sport, amusement, and the delight of the pleasure in the world; on the contrary, being loath of a life of dressing, speaking the truth, let one wander alone like a rhinoceros. . . .

. . . " This is a tie, in this there is little happiness, little enjoyment, but more of pain, this is a fishhook, so having understood, let a thoughtful man wander alone like a rhinoceros.

" Having torn the ties, having broken the net as a fish in the water, being like a fire not returning to the burnt place, let one wander alone like a rhinoceros. . . .

. . . " Not abandoning seclusion and meditation, always wandering in accordance with the Dhammas, seeing misery in the existences, let one wander alone like the rhinoc eros.

" Wishing for the destruction of desire, being careful, no fool, learned, strenuous, considerate, restrained, energetic, let one wander alone like a rhinoceros.

" Like a lion not trembling at noises, like the wind not caught in a net, like a lotus not stained by water, let one wander alone like a rhinoceros.

" As a lion strong by his teeth, after overcoming all animals, wanders victorious as the king of the animals, and haunts distant dwelling-places, even so let one wander alone like a rhinoceros."

. . . " They cultivate the society of others, and serve them for the sake of advantage ; friends without a motive are now difficult to get, men know their own profit and are impure ; therefore let one wander alone like a rhinoceros."

When one contemplates the ideal of the heroic individualism in this its purest form, rugged, empty of sensuous comforts, yet noble and inspiring in all but the highest degree, one feels how hard the decision as to its worth will be, unless the moral insight gives very definitely and authoritatively its ruling in the matter. But fortunately, in trying to judge of even so splendid a caprice as this, we are not left to our individual opinion. The will of the Titan as to the world of life is simply, by hypothesis, not the universal will. The one being that included in his life all

14

our petty lives, how must he regard this self-seeking
loneliness of disposition? What is this heroic life
but an overflow from the great stream of universal
life, a pool, that, left to itself by some subsiding
flood, slowly dries away in its shallow stagnancy,
until it becomes a mud-puddle? And as for the
proof of this, what becomes of your hero if you take
him at his word, and leave him to himself like a rhinoceros? Then indeed he soon sinks to the level of
a peevish animal. His admirable character is what
it is by reason of his conflicts with his fellows, and
by reason of the respect that he excites in others.
Stop talking about him, cease admiring him, do not
even fight with him, ignore him utterly; and with
these external supports see his inner heroism vanish.
He exists as hero, in fact, only because he is in organic relation to the world about him. His boasted
loneliness is an illusion. Could not Mephistopheles
have his laugh here too?

But the Titan is often properly the hero not only
of a comedy, but also of a tragedy; and a tragedy,
as we know, always discovers to us the gloomy worthlessness of this individual life as such. Mortal man,
once brought to possess the moral insight, finds his
destiny not in himself, but in the life about him, or
in the ideal life of God. And the tragedy expresses
one way of getting this insight.

In short, just what the Heresy of Prometheus asserts to be the perfect, namely, the complete and all-
sided development of life, just that can belong only
to the general, not to the individual life. Hence
Titanism always contradicts itself. It says that I,

the narrow, limited self, who am dependent for every quality of my life on constant living intercourse with other people, must become perfect, independent, practically infinite. But to ask this is to ask that I destroy myself, and my Titanism with me. Unquiet is and must be the life that seeks perfection in any group of selves. And so the ideal cannot here be found.

V.

Somewhat hastily, as our limits have required, we have pursued the definition of our ideal through the imperfect forms of individualism. And now what must it be that the moral insight, with its Universal Will, demands of the possible future moral humanity, not as the negative task of preparing the way for goodness, but as the positive ideal task of the community in which the moral insight is attained? This demand is: *Organize all Life*. And this means: Find work for the life of the coming moral humanity which shall be so comprehensive and definite that each moment of every man's life in that perfect state, however rich and manifold men's lives may then be, can be and will be spent in the accomplishment of that one highest impersonal work. If such work is found and accepted, the goal of human progress will be in so far reached. There will then be harmony, the negative expression of the moral insight ; and there will be work, and organization of work. And this work will be no more the work of so and so many separate men, but it will be the work of man as man. And the separate men will not know or care whether they separately are happy; for they shall have no longer individual wills, but the Universal Will shall work in and through them, as the one will of two lovers finds itself in the united life of these twain, so that neither of them asks, as lover, whether this is his perfection or the other's that he experiences. For their love makes them one. In such wise we must figure to ourselves the ideal state of humanity. And anything short of that we are required by the moral insight to alter in the direction of that end.

The reader may ask, What work can be found that can thus realize the universal will? It is not for us to know the whole nature of that work. We set before us the ideal task to discover such forms of activity as shall tend to organize life. The complete organization we cannot now foresee. But we can foresee in what general direction that human activity will tend, if it is ever discovered. For we have certain human activities that do now already tend to the impersonal organization of the life of those engaged in them. Such activities are found in the work of art, in the pursuit of truth, and in a genuine public spirit. Beauty, Knowledge, and the State, are three ideal objects that do actually claim from those who serve them harmony, freedom from selfishness, and a wholly impersonal devotion. Both in art and in the service of the state, the weakness of human nature makes men too often put personal ambition before the true service of their chosen ideal. The faultiness of all such individualism is, however, generally recognized. The dignity and se-

verely impersonal relationships and language of official life are intended to express the sense that no individual has as such the right to recognition at the
moment when he exercises an official function. He
lives at the time wholly in his office. The state is
just then everything. Even so all higher criticism
professes to disregard the personal pleasure of the
artist, and the personal whim of the critic. The
production and the criticism of Art are no amusements of two individuals. They are work done
in the service of the one mistress, the divine art itself. But still, notwithstanding the recognition of
this ideal devotion to one's country or to one's art,
our typical politician and our typical ambitious artist show us that these activities still but imperfectly
overcome individualism, or lead men to the higher
plane of moral life. Better success in organizing life
one finds, when one passes to the activity of truth-
seeking, especially in fields where human thought
is best master of itself, and best conscious of its
powers. When one considers the work of a company
of scientific specialists, — how each one lives for his
science, and how, when the specialty is advanced
and well organized, no one in official expressions
of his purely scientific purposes dares either to give
himself airs of importance as an individual, or to
show any benevolence or favoritism or fear in considering and testing the work of anybody else; when
one sees how impersonal is this idea of the scientific
life, how no self of them all is supposed to have a
thought about his science because it pleases him,
but solely because it is true, — when one consid-

ers all this, one sees faintly what the ideal relation of mankind would be, if the ideal work for all men were found. This devoted scientific spirit is itself only an ideal even to-day; and all sorts of personal motives still interfere to disturb its purity. But here, at all events, one sees dimly in a concrete instance what the organization of life may yet become.

Now suppose a world in which men had some one end of activity that united somehow all the different strivings of our nature, — æsthetic, social, theoretical. Suppose that in the pursuit of this end all the petty, selfish aims of individuals had been forgotten. Suppose that men said no longer: "I have won this good thing for myself and my friends," but only, "This good is attained," no matter by whom. Suppose that thus all life was organized in and through this activity, so that a man rose up and lay down to rest, ate and drank, exercised and amused his senses, met his fellows, talked with them, lived and planned with them, built his cities, wandered over the oceans, searched the heavens with his telescopes, toiled in his laboratories, sang his songs, wrote his poems, loved and died, all for the service of this one great work, and knew his life only as the means to serve that one end, then would the ideal of the moral insight be attained. The world of life would be as one will, working through all and in all, seeking the ends of no one individual, caring not for any stupid and meaningless "aggregate" of individual states, but getting what as insight it demands, the absolute Unity of Life. Then

indeed we should have reached the ideal; and this being the ideal, all is good that helps us in the direction thereof, and all is evil that drives us in the opposing direction.

The imperfection and the relative justification in its place of benevolent hedonism are thus indicated. The moral insight being attained by all men as an experience, this insight could not will for individuals such painful experiences as would degrade the sufferers below the level of the insight itself, back to the struggles and the illusions of individualism. It would be the business of men then as now, to remove useless pain out of the world, not however for any other reason than that pain implies separation of the sufferer from the consciousness of universal life, and consequent disharmony of his will in its relation to other wills. Pain that springs from selfish disappointments we must often temporarily increase, that we may lead a man out of himself. But for the rest, the moral insight rejects pain, though only because it means disharmony of the wills that are in the world.

Thus we have completed the expression of our general ideal. We must add a few concrete precepts that this ideal has to give us concerning the conduct of our daily life. Plainly, if such a goal as this is what we aim at from afar, the acts of our lives must be influenced by it. What relation between me and my neighbor to-day does this moral law establish?

Thou and I, neighbor, have in this world no rights as individuals. We are instruments. The insight that begins in me when I find thee, must go further

I find not only thee, but also Life Universal. Inasmuch as I do anything for thee, I do it also to
the life universal; but, even so, it is only because
I serve the life universal that I dare serve thee.
Thy happiness, however near and dear thou art to
me, is but a drop in this vast ocean of life. And
we must be ready to sacrifice ourselves to the Whole.
But while we live together, and while we may without sin enjoy each other's presence, how shall we treat
each other? As mere masses of happy or miserable
states? As selves to be made separately perfect!
No, that cannot be. We must live united with each
other and the world. Therefore must we do our
part to find work vast enough to bring us all in so
far as may be into unity, without cramping the tal-
ent of any of us. Each then is to do his work, but
so as to unite with the work of others. How may
we accomplish this? By seeking to develop every
form of life that does bring men into such oneness.
Our vocation, whatever it be, must not end simply
in increasing what people call the aggregate happiness of mankind, but in giving human life more
interconnection, closer relationship. Therefore we
must serve as we can art, science, truth, the state,
not as if these were machines for giving people pleasant feelings, but because they make men more united.
When we urge or seek independence of character,
we must do so only because such independence is a
temporary means, whose ultimate aim is harmony and
unity of all men on a higher plane. In all this we
must keep before us very often the high ideal that
we are trying to approach. And when we judge of

a good action we must say, not that this was good because it made some one happy, but that it was good because it tended directly or remotely to realize the Universal Will.

And so, however much mere harmony may be our aim, we must be ready very often temporarily to fight with disorganizing and separating tendencies, forces, or men. When we fight we must do so for the sake of conquering a peace in the name of the Highest. And so we must fight resolutely, fearlessly, mercilessly. For we care not how many stubbornly disorganizing spirits are crushed on the way. The One Will must conquer. But on the other side we must be very careful of every soul, and of every tendency that may, without destruction, be moulded into the service of the Universal Will. The moral insight desires that no hair fall from the head of any living creature unnecessarily. The one aim is stern to its steadfast enemies, but it is infinitely regardful of all the single aims, however they may seem wayward, that can at last find themselves subdued and yet realized in its presence, and so conformed to its will. All these rivulets of purpose, however tiny, all these strong floods of passion, however angry, it desires to gather into the surging tides of its infinite ocean, that nothing may be lost that consents to enter. Its unity is no abstraction. The One Will is not a one-sided will. It desires the realization of all possible life, however rich, strong, ardent, courageous, manifold such life may be, if only this life can enter into that highest unity. All that has will is sacred to it, save in so far as any will refuses to join with the

others in the song and shout of the Sons of God.
Its warfare is never intolerance, its demand for submission is never tyranny, its sense of the excellence
of its own unity is never arrogance; for its warfare
is aimed at the intolerance of the separate selves,
its yoke is the yoke of complete organic freedom,
its pride is in the perfect development of all life.
When we serve it, we must sternly cut off all that
life in ourselves or in others that cannot ultimately
conform to the universal will; but we have nothing
but love for every form of sentient existence that can
in any measure express this Will.

VI.

We have done for the present with the ideal, and
must turn to reality. Our religious consciousness
wants support for us in our poor efforts to do right.
Is this real world that we have so naïvely assumed
thus far, in any wise concerned to help us in realizing
ideals, or to support us by any form of approval in
our search for the right? We must face this problem coolly and skeptically, if we want any result.
We must not fear the thunders of any angry dogmatic thinker, nor the pain that such researches must
cause us if they are unsuccessful. It is something
very precious that we seek, and we must run great
risks, if need be, to get it.

Let us begin to define a little better what this is
that we seek. By a support for moral acts in outer
reality, we do not mean merely or mainly a power
that will reward goodness. The moral insight cares

not for individual rewards. Only the good intention is truly moral. Good acts done for pay are selfish acts. So the outer support that we want in our morality is not reward as such. We want to know that, when we try to do right, we are not alone; that there is something outside of us that harmonizes with our own moral efforts by being itself in some way moral. This something may be a person or a tendency. Let us exemplify what we mean by some familiar cases. Job seeks, in his consciousness of moral integrity, for outer support in the midst of his sufferings. Now whatever he may think about rewards, they are not only rewards that he seeks. He wants a vindicator, a righteous, all-knowing judge, to arise, that can bear witness how upright he has been; such a vindicator he wants to see face to face, that he may call upon him as a beholder of what has actually happened. "Oh that I knew where I might find him, that I might come even to his seat. I would order my cause before him, and fill my mouth with arguments. I would know the words which he would answer me, and understand what he would say unto me. . . . There the righteous might dispute with him; so should I be delivered forever from my judge. Behold I go forward, but he is not there; and backward, but I cannot perceive him: On the left hand, where he doth work, but I cannot behold him: he hideth himself on the right hand, that I cannot see him: But he knoweth the way that I take: when he hath tried me I shall come forth as gold."

So again in the great parable of the judgment day,

in the twenty-fifth chapter of Matthew, the moral force of the story is not expressed by the rewards and punishments described, any more than in Elijah's vision on Horeb, — the Lord was in the thunder and in the fire. But the moral force of the scene lies in the concluding words that the judge is made to speak to the multitudes of just and unjust. "Inasmuch as ye did it unto the least of these, ye did it unto me." That is, if we may paraphrase the words of the judge: "I," he says, "represent all beings. Their good is mine. If they are hungry or naked or sick or imprisoned, so am I. We are brethren ; ours is all one universal life. That I sit in this seat, arbiter of heaven and hell, makes me no other than the representative of universal life. Such reverence as ye now bear to me is due, and always was due, to the least of these my brethren." The infinite sacredness of all conscious life, that is the sense of the story ; the rest is the scenic accompaniment, which, whether literally or symbolically true, has no direct moral significance. Now the knowledge such as Job sought, the knowledge that there is in the universe some consciousness that sees and knows all reality, including ourselves, for which therefore all the good and evil of our lives is plain fact, — this knowledge would be a religious support to the moral consciousness. The knowledge that there is a being that is no respecter of persons, that considers all lives as equal, and that estimates our acts according to their true value, — this would be a genuine support to the religious need in us, quite apart from all notions about reward and punishment. A thinking being, a seer of all good and evil, is thus desired. This thinking being would still have religious significance, even if it had no other attributes than these. Should we find it necessary to regard this being as without affection, sympathy, or even power to act, as without willingness to avenge wrong-doing, if we had to deprive it of everything else that is human save knowledge; let this be a passionless and perfect knowledge, an absolutely fair judgment of our moral actions, and there would still be in the world something of religious value. It is not affirmed that we ought to rest content with such a conception as this, but at all events this conception would not be valueless. Even so again, the conception of some natural tendency in the world that, being "a power not ourselves," "makes for righteousness," this conception, as Mr. Matthew Arnold has so well shown us, would have a religious value. Something of this kind then, more or less definite and full of life, is what we seek. What indication is there that such search is not hopeless? For the author's part, he professes to be quite willing to accept any result of research, however gloomy or skeptical, to which he is led by genuine devotion to the interests of human thought as thought. But he insists that as moral beings we should make clear to ourselves what are the interests of thought, and that we should see whether they do lead us to results that are not wholly skeptical, nor altogether gloomy. There is no reason for clipping our own wings for fear lest we should escape from our own coops and fly over the palings into our own garden. Let us get all the satisfaction from philosophy that we can. In truth we shall never get too much.

But, for the rest, the reader must be reminded of one thing that was said in the opening chapter about the magnitude and boldness of the demands that religious philosophy makes in coming to the study of the world. We said that we will be satisfied only with the very best that we can get. We want to find some reality that our ideal aims can lead us to regard as of Infinite Worth. If we cannot find that, then the best possible aspect of reality must be chosen instead. We will not be satisfied with little, if we can get much. Our religious demands are boundless. We will not falsify the truth ; nor yet will we dread any disaster to our ideal aims, however great the disappointment that would result from failure. But, while pursuing the truth with reverence, we will not withdraw our demands until we see that we can get no certain success in them.

We insist, therefore, that the religiously valuable reality in the world shall be, if so we can find it, a Supreme Reality, no mere chance outcome of special circumstances, but an ultimate aspect of things.

Furthermore, the special form that our ideal has taken demands another character in our object of religious satisfaction. It must be such as to support the realization of our particular ideal. If a power, it must aim at the unity of our lives ; if in some other way approved as the deepest truth of things, it must show us how our ideal either can be realized by us, or else is already realized at the heart of this truth.

Such is the work of our second book. We approach it not as if we expected any mystical revelation, but solely as having for our one desire to find out what a sensible man ought reasonably to think of the world wherein he finds himself.

BOOK II.

THE SEARCH FOR A RELIGIOUS TRUTH.

CHAPTER VIII.

THE WORLD OF DOUBT.

WHEN we turn from our world of ideals to the world actually about us, our position is not at once a happy position. These ideals that we have agreed upon, in so far as they are our own, do not make the world, and people differ endlessly about what the world is and means. Very naturally, then, we also must ourselves begin with difficulties and doubts. For if we want a religious doctrine that in these days can stand us in good stead, we must fear nothing, and must run the risk of all the disasters of thought. The warfare of faiths is so angry and ancient, that we must be content if, with our best efforts, we get anything out of it at all. As millions of brains must toil, doubtless, for centuries before any amount of ideal agreement among men is attained or even approximated, we must be content if we do very little and work very hard. We can be tolerably certain that in a world where nearly all is dark very much of our labor will be wasted. But this is natural. There is the delight of activity in truth-seeking; but when, at the outset, you compare your hopes and claims with the shadowy and doubtful results that you may reach, the comparison cannot seem otherwise than melancholy. Through the failures of millions of devoted servants, the humanity of the future may possibly (we do not, at least at this point in our study, know that it will certainly) be led to a grand success. This far-off divine event to which, for all we know, our fragment of creation may be moving, but which at any rate we regard with longing and delight, constitutes the moral aim of our philosophic studies. It is good to strive.

In the present chapter, therefore, we shall devote ourselves for the most part to negative criticism of certain views that are or may be held about the real world.

I.

That skepticism in studying reality is to some extent useful, most people will admit. But not every one will follow us at once into the thorough-going and uncompromising skepticism that we shall have to present in the following as the very basis of our positive doctrine. It is surprising how easily the philosophic need is satisfied in the minds of most persons, even in the minds of many professed philosophic students. A few very complacent questions, readily if unintelligibly answered, put to rest the whole desire that such people feel to cross-examine reason. In fact they seem to hold that a certain disrespect would be shown by questioning reason any more sharply; and so their philosophy is like a Congressional investigation of the doings of a politician, conducted by his fellow-partisans. But we feel, in writing this book, that such a philosophy, whose only business it is to " whitewash " reason, is an in-

sult to reason. Reason's investigations of its own nature are not partisan affairs conducted for the sake
of effect; nor does reason seek, like a demagogue, to
get a popular "vindication," but solely to reach the
deepest possible insight into its own absolute truth.
Hence we refuse utterly to have the following regarded as in any narrower sense an "apology" for
any religious truth, since the defensive or apologetic
attitude in presence of religious problems is once for
all an insult to genuine religion. If there is truth
absolute, we desire to know the same, and if we ever
get a glimpse of it, doubtless it will need very little
apology from us. But meanwhile we propose to
doubt fearlessly and thoroughly. If our limits prevent here the proper exhaustive search for all the
actual difficulties of the views that we present, still
we want to have, and as far as may be to show, the
spirit of honest, determined, conscientious skepticism. A clerical friend of the author's impressed
him very much in early youth by the words: "God
likes to have us doubt his existence, if we do so sincerely and earnestly." These words are almost a
truism; they surely ought to be a truism. Yet they
have been forgotten in many a controversy. Surely
if God exists, he knows at least as much about philosophy as any of us do; he has at least as much appreciation for a philosophic problem as we can have.
And if his own existence presents a fine philosophic
problem, he delights therein at least as much as we
do. And he then does not like to see that problem
half-heartedly handled by timid, whining, trembling
men, who constantly apologize to God because the

existence of certain fools called atheists forces them to present in very pious language certain traditional proofs of his existence. No, surely not in this spirit would a rational God, if he exists, have us approach the question. But with at least as much coolness and clearness of head as we try to have when we toil over a problem in mathematics; with at least as merciless an analysis of all that is obscure and doubtful and contradictory in our own confused ideas as we should use in studying science; with at least as much eagerness in finding out the weakness and the uncertainty of men's wavering and ill-trained judgments as we should bring to the examination of an important commercial investment, — with at least so much of caution, of diligence, and of doubt we should approach the rational study of the Highest. For what can insult God more than careless blundering? It is shameful that men should ever have treated this matter as if it were the aim of religious philosophy to have a store-house of formulated traditional answers ready wherewith to silence certain troublesome people called doubters. In these matters the truly philosophic doubt is no external opinion of this or that wayward person; this truly philosophic doubt is of the very essence of our thought. It is not to be "answered" or "silenced" by so and so much apologetic pleading. The doubt is inherent in the subject-matter as we must in the beginning regard the same. This doubt is to be accepted as it comes, and then to be developed in all its fullness and in all its intensity. *For the truth of the matter is concealed in that doubt,* as the fire is concealed in the stony coal. You can no more reject the doubt and keep the innermost truth, than you can toss away the coal and hope to retain its fire. *This doubt is the insight partially attained.*

Such must be our spirit. And now, to apply it at once to the problems before us, where shall we begin our search for a religious truth? We are to find, if possible, some element in Reality that shall have religious significance. But how shall we do this unless we have made clear to ourselves in what sense we know Reality at all? It would seem that our religious philosophy must begin with the problem of all theoretical philosophy: What can be our knowledge of this world, and whereon can this knowledge be founded?

A dark and dismal topic, one may say. But remember, here and here only can our beloved treasure be found buried. Either there is no religious philosophy possible, or it is here; and here we must delve for it. Nor let one be too much terrified at once by the forbidding aspect of the question. It is indeed no easy one; yet to answer it is but to know the real meaning of our own thoughts. This truth that we seek is not in the heavens, nor in the depths; it is nigh us, even in our hearts. Only inattention can be hiding it from us. Let us look closer.

This real world that popular thought declares to exist outside of us — we have so far taken it on trust. But now, what right have we so to take it? What do we mean by it? When we say that we can know it, do we not mean that it is in some way bound to conform to some of our thoughts? Or, if you will put the matter in the reverse order, and will say, with seeming modesty, that our thought is so constituted as to have a certain likeness to reality, do you really make the matter clearer? The mysterious conformity between our thought and what is no thought of ours remains, and we have to make clear our assurance of that. This assurance itself, if we got it, would seem to be in just the same position as is the conformity of which it is to assure us. Itself again would be outside of the external real world, and in our thought. Yet this assurance is to tell us something about that external world, namely, its conformity to certain of our thoughts. What can we thus know about any external object at all?

The difficulty is an old one. Our solution of it, if we get any, must determine the whole of our religious thought. Let us see at all events where the difficulty arises, and why. Whether or no there is possible any solution, the difficulty plainly lies in a certain conceived relation between us and the world. All the common metaphysical and religious doctrines begin by setting a thinker over against an external world, which is declared independent of his thought, and which his thought is then required to grasp and know. This supposed relation of subject and object gives metaphysics its seemingly insoluble problems. This thinker, whose thought is one fact, while that world out there is another fact, how can he learn by what takes place in his thought, that is, in the one of these two supposed entities, what goes on in the other of these entities, namely, in the world? Once for all, this marvelous relation of preëstablished har-

mony between these supposed separate entities demands philosophic deduction. The relation, to be
sure, may be itself a metaphysical figment. We
hold that it is. We shall try to show hereafter the
baselessness of this notion of a world of external
fact on one side, in the barren isolation of its transcendental reality, with an equally lonesome thinker
on the other side, somehow magically bound to follow after the facts of that world. We hold, to put
it in plain language, that neither the external world
nor the individual thinker has any *such* reality as
traditional popular beliefs, together with most metaphysical schools, have desired us to assume. But,
for the first, we cannot yet undertake to trouble the
reader with this our philosophic speculation. That
will come in its good time, we hope not too unintelligibly, and it will have its place in our religious
doctrine.

We begin, however, with the popular metaphysical concept, of a separate external world, and of a
thinker bound somehow to repeat the facts of it in
his thought. We ask, with popular metaphysics:
How can we be sure that he does this? And from
metaphysical systems, both popular and unpopular,
we get an amazing jargon of answers.

The most popular answer, after all, is a threat, a
threat repeated endlessly in all sorts of apologetic
books, but still a mere base, abject, wholly unphilo-
sophical threat. It is said to us that we must believe our human thinker to be capable of thinking
correctly the facts of this supposed external world,
because, if he does not, the result will be disastrous

to the whole common sense conception of the world.
If this thinker does not somehow magically reproduce external facts in his private mind, then is our
faith vain, and we are all very miserable. It is as-
tonishing how this, the most helpless abandonment
of all philosophic thought, is constantly reiterated
by certain of those who pretend to be philosophers.
Can a threat scare us from philosophy? To get a
sure foundation for our religion, we begin by asking
how a man can really know the external world at
all. We get as reply the threat that, unless we admit the knowledge of the external world, we must
be in eternal doubt, and therefore wretched. To
doubt this knowledge, we are told, would be to
doubt all that makes life worth living. But it is
just because we want to find a sure basis for what
makes life worth living that we begin with this
doubt. We are determined to get at the root of
this matter, however bitter may be the evil that will
befall us if our skepticism does not succeed in getting past this guarded gateway of philosophy. We
persist in asking, all threats to the contrary notwithstanding, just how and why and in what sense the
external world can be known to us, if indeed this
conception itself of an external world is justly
formed at all.

Yet we grant that the full force and need and
bitterness of our problem may not be plain to the
reader, unless he has first undertaken to examine
with us at some length the philosophic character
and consequences of this popular metaphysical conception of the external world. To get him to share

well our doubt, we must first provisionally accept
this notion of popular metaphysics itself. We must
waive for the moment our difficulty, that it may recur to us with greater importance by and by. Let
the reader once come to see that this popular notion
of an external world is an utterly vague conception,
capable of numberless forms, and religiously unsatisfactory in all of them, and then we shall expect
him to feel the force of the deeper philosophic problems involved. This present chapter will therefore
proceed directly to an examination of the popular
notions about the external world. We shall examine them, namely, to find whether they offer any
religious aspect. We shall find that they do not
offer any such aspect in any satisfactory sense.
That the good is supreme in the external world as
popularly conceived, nobody can establish. This
supposed external world is once for all a World of
Doubt, and in it there is no abiding place. When
the reader has come to feel with us this truth, then
he will be ready to look deeper into the matter.
Then some other more genuinely philosophic conception of Reality will have its place. Hence in
the rest of this chapter we shall be accepting provisionally notions that we are hereafter to reject,
and assuming much on trust that is at best very
doubtful. We shall show that, even so aided, the
popular notions about the religious aspect of this
world cannot bear criticism. This visible world of
popular faith will lose its worth for us. We shall
have to look elsewhere.

The religious significance once removed from the

popular realistic philosophy, with its crudely meta‑
physical notion of things, we shall be ready to listen
to skepticism about the foundations of this notion ;
and we shall be ready for some new conception.
This new conception will indeed not falsify the true
moral meaning of that innocent faith in a real world
upon which we have so far depended in our research.
The popular notion of an external world, practically
useful for many purposes, and sufficient for many
scientific ends, will be refuted and rejected in its
contradictions and in its absurdities, but the soul of
truth that is in it will be absorbed into a higher
conception both of the eternal Reality and of our
relation thereto. Our seeming loss will become our
gain. That bad dream, the dead and worthless
World of Doubt in which most of our modern teach‑
ers remain stuck fast, will be transformed for us.
We shall see that the truth of it is a higher World,
of glorious religious significance.

So for the first we turn to that supposed world of
popular metaphysics, to test its religious value. It is
conceived as a world existent in space and time, and
as a world of real things which act and interact. For
convenience sake, we shall in the following use the
word Power to mean any one of these things, or any
group of them, that in this external world may be
supposed to produce effects upon any other thing or
group of things. However these Powers get their ef‑
ficiency, the religious significance of the supposed ex‑
ternal world, if it has any, must lie in the supremacy
of the Good in this world of the Powers. One must
then view this external world historically as a mass

of Powers, which work together in harmony or in discord, and which give you Products. The religious ideals must find satisfaction here, if at all, in contemplating the goodness of these powers and of their works. If the religious ideals here fail, there will be the other aspect open. Regarded in a truly philosophical way, and in its eternal nature, the world, as we shall hereafter come to see, cannot be supposed to be either a power or a heap of powers. For powers have their being only in time, and only in relation to one another. If then all fails when we consider this external world of powers, this figment of popular metaphysics, the eternal nature of reality in some deeper view of that nature may still be found of infinite value to us. In fact we *shall* find the search for a religious truth, among the powers of this popularly conceived external world, very disheartening. The jargon of their contending voices will not unite into any religious harmony. We shall find these powers like the thunder and the fire. The still small voice is not in them. We shall be driven to some other aspect of the world. We shall approach that aspect in ways that imply no disrespect to those who have been so long scientifically studying the history and forces of the assumed external world. Their results, with the practical consequences in daily life, and with all that Agnosticism about the nature and purposes of the powers of this visible world which such men nowadays feel bound to proclaim, we shall on the whole accept. We too shall be Agtics, namely, as to the powers that rule the visible world. But we shall find a very different way, untrodden by scientific research, and yet, we hope, not a way of mere dreams, not a way into a world of fancy, but a way that leads us to a point whence we get a glimpse into that other aspect of things. This way Modern Idealism since Kant has been busy in finding and clearing. How wearisome some of the exploring expeditions have been, we well know. Our search also may end in a wilderness; but we fancy ourselves to have found an open path that to some readers will seem at least in part new. And some of the prospects on that road may not be wholly disheartening, even to the most exacting religious seeker. But all this is anticipation. First then: The World as a theatre for the display of power, physical or metaphysical. This is the World of Doubt.

II.

Let us begin our study of the powers that work together in the supposed external reality, by accepting for a moment, without criticism, the notion of this supposed external world from which *scientific experience* sets out. Let us say: there it is, an objective world of moving matter, subject to certain laws. All the powers are but manifestations or forms of matter in motion. Planets revolve, comets come and go, tides swell and fall, clouds rise and rivers flow to the sea, lightning flashes, volcanoes are active, living beings are born, live, and die, all exemplifying certain universal principles, that are discoverable by experience, that are capable of being used to predict the future, and that are related to one another in such a way as to show us a vast connected whole, the natural universe. This matter however is dead; these laws are ultimate given truths. We did not make them, cannot see why just they and none other were from the beginning; we must accept them as they are. The whole world is a vast machine. A mind powerful enough might be possessed of the knowledge that La Place, and, in our own generation, Prof. Du Bois Reymond, have so finely described as the scientific ideal. Such a mind might have an universal formula, in its possession, a key to the mysteries of the succession of phenomena. Such a being could then, using this formula, calculate all events, as astronomers now predict eclipses. At every instant multitudes of air pulsations quiver about us. These, in all their forms, our mind possessed of this universal formula, would have been able to predict ages ago, just as certainly as you now can predict that the sun will rise to-morrow morning. All is predetermined: the glitter of every ice crystal on your frozen window-panes on a winter morning, the quiver of every muscle in the death agony of the fish that you pull out of a mountain-stream, the falling of every yellow leaf in the autumn woods, — each of these events could have been foreseen, mathematically calculated, and fully described, by one able to use the universal formula, and possessed, myriads of æons ago, of an exact knowledge of the positions of the atoms of the original nebula from which our great stellar system condensed. Such is the natural world.

What religious aspect can this vast machine possess? What room is there for a higher element to be introduced into this mass of dead mathematical facts? The answer of some representatives of science in our day is well known to us. Whatever else is doubtful, say such men, there stands fast the great law of progress. Evolution in the physical world becomes actual progress in the world of human life. The world, under the influence of all these far-reaching laws, is actually growing forever better. Thus natural law agrees with morality. Thus there is a religious aspect to the mechanical laws of the universe.

Let us consider once more the law of progress. We spoke of it in a previous chapter. There it did not help us. For we wanted to agree upon the nature of morality. We were not helped towards such agreement by the knowledge that there is in the world a physical evolution. For we could not tell what ought to be, merely by considering what is. We had first to agree upon a moral law, before we could decide whether evolution is actually progress. But now, perhaps, we can make use of the law of evolution to aid our inquiry into the religious aspect of reality. For now, having defined what the good is, we may estimate whether the world is growing toward the good. And if the world is morally progressing, then one great demand of the religious consciousness is fulfilled. Then there is a power not ourselves that works for righteousness. Or is this really the consequence of the law of evolution?

The first answer is that if there is any tendency at work in the world that as time goes on more and more helps men in their struggle towards morality, this tendency is indeed, as far as it goes, what we want to find. And if such a tendency is found, as we are told, in evolution, the result is in just so far encouraging. Although the external world still often hinders moral growth, yet, we are told, as evolution reaches higher and higher stages, the world comes to harmonize more and more with man's moral growth. This also seems to be what we seek. In time morality will become a natural product of early childhood. Men will be born with characters that we now seek in vain to develop by a life-time of labor. Natural evolution, then, does help moral progress, and the world is more moral to-day than ever before. This then is to be the religious aspect of the outer world. Does it contain enough of the truth of things to content us?

We are far from doubting the scientific worth of the natural laws that have been discovered of late years, and that have made so clear to us the great truth of far-reaching physical evolution. But let us reflect before we accept these facts as furnishing any deeply important contribution to our present problem. We thoroughly believe in evolution; but we must take, in these matters, a very high position. If the world of powers apart from man is to have a religious aspect, then this aspect must belong to this world as a whole. A minor power for good is not enough. It will not suffice to find that one bit of reality fights for our moral needs while another bit of reality fights against them, unless we can in some way harmonize these conflicting aspects, or unless we can show that they that be with us are not only more important or significant than they that be

16

against us, but are really the deepest truth of things.
Else we shall be left face to face with a gloomy world
of conflict, where the good and bad are mingled in
hopeless confusion. If such a world is the fact, we
must accept that fact; but we cannot then say that
we have made sure of an answer to our religious
needs. Now suppose that in examining the world
we found two tendencies at work, equally fundamental, equally active, fairly balanced in power, producing in the long run equally permanent, equally transient results, but always in deadly antagonism to each
other, the one making for moral goodness, the other
for moral evil. Suppose that the world appeared as
the theatre and the result of this struggle of the good
and of the evil principles, could we say that we had
found in these facts a religious aspect of reality?
We should hardly answer in the affirmative. So
long as we must fix our minds on this struggle of
equally balanced powers, we could not find the world
a religiously encouraging vision. We should either
have to regard the world in some other and higher
aspect, or we should have to give up regarding it as
religiously interesting. An answer to our moral
needs that is drowned by a hubbub of opposing
noises can be no harmonious song. Now we affirm
that so long as you look upon the world as a growth
in time, as a product of natural forces, as an historical development, you can never make it certain, or
even probable, that this world is not such a scene of
endless warfare. Hence the progress that you may
observe can never overbalance the probability that
this progress is a transient and insignificant fact, in

the midst of a chaos of confused tendencies. Therefore progress on this planet for a few thousands or
millions of years indicates nothing about any true
harmony between nature and morality.

Let us call attention to one aspect, well-known,
yet often neglected in recent discussions of a few
familiar facts. Modern science is justly sure of
physical evolution, but is no less sure that evolution on this planet is a process that began at a
period distant by a finite and in fact by a not very
great time from the present moment. That our
planet was a nebulous mass at a date at most somewhere between twenty millions and one hundred millions of years ago, we have all heard, and we have
also had explained to us some of the proofs of this
fact. Our planet is still imperfectly cooled. At a
comparatively recent period in the history of this
stellar universe, this little point of it was a spheroid
of glowing vapor, from which the moon had not yet
been separated. The present heat of the earth is an
indication of its youth. Furthermore, what our
planet is to become in time, the moon itself tells us,
having cooled, by reason of its small size, more rapidly than we have done. Cold and dead, waterless,
vaporless, that little furrowed mass of rock deso-
lately rolls through its slow days, looking with passionless stare at our stormy, ardent earth, full of motion and of suffering. What that mass is, our earth
shall become. And progress here will cease with
the tides. All these are the commonplaces of popular science. Progress then, as we know it here, is
a fact of transient significance. Physical nature

permits progress rather than renders it necessary. Progress is an incident of a certain thermal process, a kind of episode in the history of the dissipation of the energy of our particular mass of matter, and thus, in so far as we yet know, a present occurrence just in our neighborhood, a local item in the news of the universe. Now these are the familiar facts whose meaning we want to enforce in an often neglected aspect.

But, one says, all this has been anticipated hundreds of times. It is really unfair to insist upon such things. For at least here, at least now, the world does realize our moral needs by showing us progress. Is not this all that we need? May we not be content with the few millions of years of growth that remain to our race before the earth grows cold? Is it not foolish to look into futurity so curiously? What matters it whether chaos comes again in far-off ages?

But we still insist. We desire, vainly or justly, yet ardently, that the world shall answer to our moral needs not by accident, not by the way, not for a time, but from its own nature and forever. If we can see that present progress is an indication of the nature of the universe, that the present is a symbol or a specimen of eternity, we shall be content. But if this is not so, if present progress is seen to be a mere accident, an eddy in the stream of atoms, then present progress is a pleasant fact to contemplate, but not a fact of any deep significance. Still we shall be crying in the darkness for support and finding none. For nature will say to each of us: "I

give support to thy moral needs so long as the temperature of thy earth crust is high enough to prevent
thy oceans from being absorbed, so long as the ra-
diant heat of the sun is given out in sufficient quantities to keep thee warm.   When the next stage is
reached, I propose to freeze and to dry thy fair
home and all thy moral needs, until there shall be
nothing found on thy planet lovelier than the ruined
crags of thy hills as they glimmer in the last red
rays of a torpid sun.   What is thy progress to me?"
Notice then where our real difficulty lies.   The aspect of the facts that we now mean is this.   It is
not because progress is to endure on this planet for
a short or for a long time, but *because the world in
which this progress is so to end seems, thus regarded, wholly indifferent to progress,* — this is the
gloomy aspect.   To-day, even while progress is so
swift and sure, at this moment, we are living in a
world for which, as science displays it to us, this
progress is as indifferent and unessential as the
fleeting hues of an evaporating soap-bubble.   Is the
physical fact of progress, thus regarded, a moral
help to us?

Yet men turn away from these plain and often-
mentioned facts to all sorts of fantastic dreams of a
coming golden age.   They make of future humanity
a saintly people, living in devotion, or a merry people, always dancing to waltzes yet undreamt of, or a
scientific people, calculating by some higher algebra
the relative positions and motions of the molecules
in the rocks on the other side of the moon.   Every
dream of progress is to be realized in that blessed

time, and we are invited to praise a nature that could produce all this blessedness by pure physical law. Now we must indeed wish well for the men of the year A. D. 1,000,000, but we can receive no religious support from the knowledge that if all goes right and if the sun keeps well at work, the men of that time will be better than we are. For still the world as a whole gives no support to our real moral needs, for only by a happy accident will this blessedness be possible. Or, in short, two tendencies are seen before us in the world, one working for evolution, for concentration of energy in living beings, for increase of their powers, for progress ; the other for dissipation of energy, for death, for the destruction of all that is valuable on our earth. We learn that the latter tendency has triumphed quite near us, on the moon. We hear that it is certain in time to triumph on the earth, and that the other tendency is to be only of transient superiority. We know that its present predominance here is, physically speaking, a happy accident, which a cosmical catastrophe might at any moment bring to an end. And now we are asked to see in this combination of facts a religious aspect. For the writer's part, he refuses to regard it as anything but an interesting study in physics. He delights in it as science, but it has nothing to do with religion. Yet some people talk of a Religion of Evolution.

But no doubt believers in universal progress are ready with hypotheses that shall show how significant a fact progress really is. A world that has progressed so many millions of years doubtless has

resources of which we know nothing. There are all
the stars with their vast stores of energy. Possibly
they are infinite in number. Progress ceasing just
here may flash out in renewed brilliancy elsewhere.
Who knows what is in store for the future, when
the present seemingly chaotic arrangement of the
stars gives way to vastly higher organized systems
of interacting bodies, in whose light life shall flour-
ish eternally?

Well, all this we can all fancy as well as our
scientific neighbors. Nobody would call such dreams
scientific, but they are logically possible dreams,
and they are very beautiful. But they have one
terrible negative consideration against them. This
progress is either conceived as having gone on
through infinite past time, or else it has no genuine
significance for the true nature of the universe. A
world that has now grown, now decayed, that has
sometimes progressed, sometimes become worse, is a
world in which progress is an accident, not an essential feature. But now, if progress has gone on
through infinite time, it has so gone on as to make
possible, after all this infinite time, just the misery
and imperfection that we see about us. Let us remember that fact. This poor life of ours is in the
supposed case the outcome of infinite ages of growth.
That must be our hypothesis, if we are to cling to
progress as an essential truth about the world. Very
well then, all our temptations, all our weakness, our
misery, our ignorance — the infinite past ages have
ended in fashioning them. Our diseases, our fears,
and our sins — are they perfect? If not, then what

is the meaning of endless progress toward perfection? For we are an outcome of this infinite progress. Another infinity of progress is not certain then to remove such imperfections. Here is progress put to the simple test. Is it the removal of evil? Then can infinite progress, as facts show us, pass by with evil yet unremoved. And if progress is not the removal of evil, then what means progress? Is not the temporary removal of evil more probably a mere occasional event in the history of the world?

It is surprising that we ever think of talking about universal progress as an essential fact of the popularly conceived external world. If nothing certain can be made out about it, still the world as a whole seems, as far as we can judge by the above considerations, so indifferent to progress, that it is marvelous to behold the religious comfort that, in their shallow optimistic faith, so many amiable people take, while they wax fervent over the thought of progress. Let us have clear ideas about the matter. What is in the true nature of reality is as eternal as reality itself. Then progress is either an unessential, insignificant aspect of reality, or it is eternal. If progress has been eternal, then either the world was in the beginning infinitely bad, or else infinite progress has been unable to remove from the world the finite quantity of evil that was always in it. For here in the empirical world is evil now — if indeed there is any empirical world at all — plenty of evil unremoved.

If you found a man shoveling sand on the sea-

shore, and wheeling it away to make an embank-
ment, and if you began to admire his industry, seeing how considerable a mass of sand he had wheeled
away, and how little remained in the sand-hill on
which he was working, you might still check yourself to ask him : " How long, O friend, hast thou
been at work? " And if he answered that he had
been wheeling away there from all eternity, and
was in fact an essential feature of the universe, you
would not only inwardly marvel at his mendacity,
but you would be moved to say : " So be it, O friend,
but thou must then have been from all eternity an infinitely lazy fellow." Might we not venture to suspect
the same of our law of universal physical progress?

But let us already hint by anticipation one further thought. Why is not any purely historical view
of the world open to the same objection ? If the history began by some arbitrary act of will at some
time not very long since, then this history, viewed
by itself apart from the creative act, may be intelligible enough in its inner unity and significance, although an arbitrary act of will can be no true explanation. But the whole physical world cannot be
regarded at once as a complete, self-existent whole,
with an eternity of past life, and as, in its deepest
truth, an historical process of any sort. For it is of
the essence of an intelligible historical process to
have, like a tragedy in Aristotle's famous account of
tragedy, a beginning, a middle, and an end. An infinite series of successive acts cannot be one organic
historical process. Either this everlasting series of
facts has no significance at all, or else it must have

had essentially the same significance all the way
along. So, if the world is infinite in time, it cannot as a whole have, strictly speaking, any history.
The longest continued story in the most thrilling of
the cheap weeklies reaches, as we are given to understand, a conclusion at some time. Imagine an
infinite continued story, with the poor lovers eternally weeping and quarreling, and you will see what
an infinite historical process in the world would
mean. It would of course be an eternal repetition
of the same thing, no story at all. If the world, regarded in time, cannot as a whole have any genuine
history at all, it is then hopeless to look in the
world's history, as distinct from the world's nature,
for anything of fundamental religious significance.

And so we are thrown back to our starting-point.
This splendid conception of science, this world of
unalterable mechanical law, in which all things that
happen are predetermined from all eternity, this
mathematical machine, has a real history no more
than the ebbing and flowing sea-tides would have
from day to day any history, apart from the fact
that they once did not so ebb and flow at all. Eternally repeated rhythms, or ceaseless new combinations of elements, clash of atoms, quiver of ether
waves, mechanical changes forever ; but no eternal
progress, no historical sense to the whole, — that
seems the conception of the physical world as a
whole to which we are driven. It is a strictly mathematical, a physically intelligible, conception, but
what religious significance has it ? Yet such is the
conception that we must have of any eternal physical process.

We have gone through this thorny path of problems, because we want already to indicate one thing as the result of it all, namely, that not what the present world has come from, not what it is becoming, not what it will be by and by, but what it eternally is, must furnish us with the deepest religious aspect of reality. All else is subordinate. We do not care so much to know what story anybody has to tell us about what has happened in the world, as to know what of moral worth always is in the world, so that whatever has happened or will happen may possess a religious significance dependent on its relation to this reality. That which changes not, wherein is no variableness, neither shadow of turning, that must give us the real religious truth upon which all else will depend. A particular event in the world may have a religious significance, but that significance will depend on the relation of this event to eternal truth. And the eternal truth is what we want to know.

Therefore our search will become somewhat narrowed, whenever at least we grow fully convinced of this truth. The " power that makes for righteousness " will become a conception of doubtful religious value. An eternal power, that with all its past eternity of work cannot yet quite vindicate righteousness ? Perhaps we shall have to find the religious aspect of things elsewhere. But let us leave, at all events, the world of pure science.

As we do so some objector may interpose the assertion that we have generalized too hastily in speaking of the insignificance of the historical aspect of things; for, after all, we have been talking of natural science. Let us turn then to the more philosophical theories of the powers that are at work in this supposed external world of metaphysics. There are philosophical theories that try to show us of what hidden reality this mechanical world of ours is the mere appearance, or phenomenal symbol. Let us see if any of them can give a religious interpretation to the powers that rule the world.

III.

We pass, then, from the scientific to the more metaphysical view of the world. What can we hope from realistic metaphysics? Let us first consider the value of that philosophic view nowadays most frequently held, namely, what in general is called Monism. We hear nowadays, with almost wearisome repetition, of Matter and Spirit, of Force and Intelligence, of Motion and Sensation, as being opposite aspects, or faces, or manifestations, of one ultimate Reality, until we wonder whether clear thinking is not in danger of losing itself altogether in the contemplation of a mere empty form of words. From whispers and low mutterings with bated breath about the inscrutable mystery of the ultimate unity of Being, one turns with satisfaction to efforts towards some intelligible account of the sense in which all things can be regarded as manifestations of one Power or actual Existent. Yet in truth even these efforts, in so far as they consider the world of the Powers, have thus far failed to satisfy the demands of criticism. Where they are clearly stated they are inadequate. Where they resort to figures of speech and tell us about the two sides of the shield, or the convexity and concavity of the same curve, as illustrations of the ultimate oneness of nature amid the various manifestations of experience, there these efforts merely sink back into the primitive incoherency so dear to all pre-Kantian metaphysics. The same curve is, indeed, convex and concave; but matter and spirit are simply not the two faces of a curve, and the relevant circumstance on which this metaphor turns will never be clear to us until we learn, quite literally, wholly apart from fables about shields, just how, in what sense, and by what evidence, matter and mind are known to be of like substance. And that we must do, ere this hypothesis can have for us a religious value. The failure of dogmatic Monism, if it should take place, ought, indeed, not to throw us over into the arms of an equally dogmatic Dualism; but we must refuse to accept the monistic hypothesis until it has been freed from all trace of mysticism. We shall here follow the plan announced at the outset of the chapter, and confine our attention to the realistic Monism, that regards the events in the external world as the results of the action of the one Power. A very different form of monism we shall ourselves hereafter maintain. But just now we deal in negations.

Let us begin with the attempts that have been made to interpret the results of modern physical science in a monistic sense, by regarding the ultimate physical or chemical units as endowed with some

form of actual or potential consciousness. Organ
isms of the highest sort are combinations of atoms.
The whole is the sum of its parts. Why may not
the mental possessions of these highest organisms
be the sum of the indefinitely small mental powers
of the atoms? An atom in motion may be a thought,
or, if that be saying far too much of so simple a
thing, an atom in motion may be, or may be endowed
with, an infinitesimal consciousness. Billions of
atoms in interaction may have as their resultant quite
a respectable little consciousness. Sufficiently complex groups of these atoms of Mind-Stuff (to use
Professor Clifford's ingenious terminology) might
produce a great man. One shudders to think of the
base uses to which the noble mind-stuff of Shakespeare might return; but the theory tries to be an
expression of natural phenomena, not merely an æsthetic creation, and must not pause before such consequences. And, if it be the truth, might it not
somehow, no matter in what way, be made of religious value? Or otherwise, if true, might it not end
our vain search for a religion?

Such is an outline that will suggest to the initiated
thoughts common to several modern theories of being. Are these theories in a fair way to satisfy critical needs? The writer is not satisfied that they
are. Time does not permit any lengthy discussion
of the matter here, but let us remind ourselves of the
considerations that will most readily occur to any
one that is disposed for a moment to accept one of
these modern forms of monism. Even if they prom-
ised us the religious aspect that we seek, we could
not accept them. As it is, we need not fear them.

Can our consciousness be regarded as an aggregate of elementary facts, such as sensations or as atoms of pleasure and pain? If so, what aggregate of sensations forms a judgment, such as, " This man is my father?" Evidently here is indeed an aggregate of sensations represented, but also something more. What is this more? A product, it may be said, formed through association from innumerable past experiences. Granted for the moment; but the question is not as to the origin of this consciousness, but as to its analysis. This judgment, whereby a present sensation is regarded as in definite relation to real past experiences, as a symbol, not merely of actual sensations now remembered, not merely of future sensations not yet experienced, but of a reality wholly outside of the individual consciousness, this fact of acknowledging something not directly presented as nevertheless real — is this act possibly to be regarded as a mere aggregate of elementary mental states? Surely, at best, the act can be so regarded only in the sense in which a word is an aggregate of letters. For and in the one simple momentary consciousness, all these elements exist as an aggregate, but as an aggregate formed into one whole, as the matter of a single act. But in themselves, without the very act of unity in which they are one, these elements would be merely an aggregate, or, in Mr. Gurney's apt words,[1] "a rope of sand." Our mental life then, as a union of innumerable elements into the one Self of any moment, is more than an aggregate, and can never be explained as an aggregate of elementary atoms of sensation.

[1] *Mind* for April, 1881, article, "Monism."

Nor may we say that the ultimate atomic states of consciousness may be, as it were, chemically united into a whole that is more than an aggregate. Physical atoms in space, if endowed with sufficiently numerous affinities, may unite into what wholes you will; but a mental fact is a mental fact, and no more. An ultimate independent unit of consciousness, conceived after the analogy of a sensation, can have to another like unit only one of three relations: it may coexist with this other unit, or it may precede or follow it in time. There is no other relation possible. Affinity, or attraction, or approach of one pain or pleasure, of one sensation of pressure or of motion to another, is a meaningless jingle of words, unless, indeed, such an expression is used to name figuratively the relations that in and for a comparing, contrasting, uniting, and separating active consciousness, two ideas are made to bear. Thus, then, this atomic monism brings us no nearer than before to the relation between the data of consciousness and the facts of physical nature. For the rest, how mechanical science can be satisfied to regard its material points as nothing but independently existing fragments of mind, whose whole being is intensive; how, out of these intensive units, space-relations are to be constructed at all — these questions we may for the present neglect. Atomic monism, a synthesis, or, rather, a jumble of physiological psychology with doctrines that are incompatible with any science whatever, has never answered these questions, and doubtless never will.

But let us not be over-hasty. There are other

orms of monism now extant. The purely material-
.stic monism, for which the hard and extended atoms
of naïve realism are already and in themselves po-
tentially mind, the old-fashioned materialism of days
when Mind-Stuff and physiological psychology were
alike undreamed of, may indeed be neglected.
That doctrine needed not critical philosophy, of more
than a very undeveloped sort, to do away with it
once for all. Modern monism knows of supposed
atoms that are in their ultimate nature psychical;
and of supposed psychical forces or agents that, when
seen from without, behave much like extended atoms.
But the old fragment of matter that, being no more
than what every blacksmith knows as matter, was
yet to be with all its impenetrability and its inertia
a piece of the soul, has been banished from the talk
of serious philosophers. There remain, then, the
numerous efforts that see in the world the expression
of psychical powers as such, not mere mind-stuff
atoms, but organized wholes, related in nature to
what we know by internal experience as mind, yet
higher or lower, subtler or mightier, wiser or more
foolish, than the human intelligence. These views
may be divided into two classes : those that see in
nature the manifestations of a logical or intelligent
power, and those that see in it the manifestations of
an alogical or blind, though still psychical power.
Each of these classes again may be subdivided according as the power is conceived as conscious or as
unconscious in its working. How do these ontological efforts stand related to critical thought ?

First let us consider logical monism. Since hu-

17

man intelligence is itself an activity, a working towards an end, and since the logical monist thinks
the external universe after the analogy of the human
reason, the constant tendency is for him to conceive
the world as a process whereby his World Spirit
makes actual what was potential. Modern science,
in fact, when viewed speculatively, though it does not
confirm, yet lends itself easily to such efforts, and
we can always, if we choose, imagine the evolution
of the organic kingdom as possibly the process of
self - manifestation of one eternal rational Power.
Only in this way we are very far from a satisfactory
ontology. A world, the work or the child of the universal reason, developing in time, how can any reflective mind be content with this account of things?
The universal reason surely means something by its
process, surely lacks something when it seeks for
higher forms. Now, on a lower stage the universal
reason has not yet what it seeks, on the higher stage
it attains what it had not. Whence or how does it
obtain this something? What hindered the possible
from being forthwith actual at the outset? If there
was any hindrance, was this of the same nature with
the universal reason, or was it other? If other,
then we are plunged into a Dualism, and the good
and evil principles appear once more. But if there
was no external hindrance, no illogical evil principle
in existence, then the universal reason has irrationally gone without the possible perfection that it
might possess, until, after great labor, it has made
actual what it never ought to have lacked. The infinite Logos thus becomes no more than the " child

playing with bubbles" of the old philosopher.
Everything about the process of evolution becomes
intelligible and full of purpose — except the fact
that there should be any process at all where all was
in, and of, and for the universal reason at the outset.
The infinite power has been playing with perfection
as a cat with a mouse, letting it run away a few
æons in time, that it might be caught once more in a
little chase, involving the history of some millions of
worlds of life. Is this a worthy conception ? Nay,
is it not a self-contradictory one ? Evolution and
creative Reason — are they compatible? Yes, indeed, when the evolution is ended, the hurly-burly
done, the battle lost and won ; but meanwhile — ?
In short, either evolution is a necessity, one of the
twelve labors of this Hercules-Absolute, or else it is
irrational. In the one case the Absolute must be
conceived as in bonds, in the other case the Logos
must be conceived as blundering. Both conceptions
are rank nonsense. This kind of Monism will not
satisfy critical demands.

And then there is the objection, stated by Schopenhauer, and by we know not how many before
him, and that we have already insisted upon, namely,
that every historical conception of the world as a
whole, every attempt to look upon Being as a rational process in time, as a perpetual evolution from
a lower to a higher, is beset by the difficulty that
after an infinite time the infinite process is still in
a very early stage. Infinitely progressing, always
growing better, and yet reaching after all this eternity of work only the incoherent, troublous, blind

imperfection that we feel in ourselves, and that we see in every dung-heap and sick-room and government on the earth, in every scattered mass of nebulous matter, in every train of meteor-fragments in the heavens — what is this but progress without a goal, blind toil? The world would be, one might think, after an infinity of growth, intensively infinite at every point of its extent. We mortals see no one point in the physical universe where one viewing things as we in this chapter have chosen to do, namely, from outside, might lay his hand and say : *Here the ideal is attained.*

Yet we should be very far from dreaming of accepting the opposing dogmatic theorem, the antithesis of this sublime Antinomy, namely, " The world is the product of an irrational force. The One is blind." Schopenhauer undertook the defense of this antithesis, and, in bad logic, as we all know, he somewhat surpassed even that arch blunderer, the universal Will of his own system. This Will, after all, desired a good deal of trouble, and got his wish. But Schopenhauer desired a consistent statement, and, with all his admirable ingenuity and learning, he produced a statement whose inconsistencies have been exposed too often to need much more discussion. No ; to the defenders of the alogical hypothesis, as a dogmatic doctrine, it has not yet been given to make out more than the purely negative case that we have stated above. Dogmatic panlogism can be assaulted, with much show of success. The opposite doctrine has not yet been dogmatically maintained without even worse confusion.

Panlogism and Alogism are difficult enough in themselves, but how much worse becomes their condition when, as in the " Philosophy of the Unconscious," of Von Hartmann, either one of them, or a hybrid of the two, is burdened with yet another hypothesis, namely, that the One Being is unconscious, and yet in nature psychical. Founding himself on certain physiological facts, very doubtfully interpreted, on a monstrous perversion of the mathematical theory of probabilities, on an ingenious view of the history of philosophy, on a like ingenious criticism of Kant, Von Hartmann has expounded an ontological doctrine of which, after all, serious thought can make nothing. This unconscious being, existent not for itself, for it is conscious of nothing, nor for others, because all else is a part of it (and, for the rest, nobody ever thought of it before Von Hartmann), shall be the maker and upholder of the universe. Surely all this is a philosophy of round squares, and is not to be taken very seriously.

Of course the previous criticism is absurdly inadequate to the magnitude of the problems involved, and is intended only as the merest sketch, dogmatically stated, of critical objections to certain ontologies. Seeming irreverence, in this hasty style of doing battle, must be pardoned. Only against imperfect metaphysic as such do we war. Critical philosophy holds no theoretical opinion sacred, just as it regards no earnest practical faith as other than sacred. The question is here not yet what we are to believe, but what we can in argument maintain, and what our method of search ought to be. Abso-

lute and Infinite, Logos and not Logos, Mind-Stuff
and Spirit — what are they all for critical philosophy, but, in the first place, mere ideas, conceptions
of reason, to be mercilessly analyzed without regard
for consequences?

One way remains whereby this realistic monism
can still hope to reach a satisfactory statement of the
world-problem. Suppose that, once for all, the historical form of statement is abandoned, while the notion of the Reason as a power is retained. This may
be done in either of two ways. The universal reason
may be conceived as manifesting itself in time, but
not in a series of events that are united as the parts
of a single process. The world-life may be conceived
not as a single history, but as an eternally repeated
product of the One reason, a process ever renewed
as soon as finished, an infinite series of growing and
decaying worlds — worlds that are like the leaves
of the forest, that spring and wither through an eternity of changing seasons. The rationality of the
world-process is thus saved for our thought by the
hypothesis that reason is not like a belated traveler,
wandering through the night of time, seeking for
a self-realization that is never reached, but, rather,
like the sun that each day begins afresh his old
task, rejoicing as a giant in the fullness of his attained power. Whoever regards the world as it now
is as plainly a sufficient expression of infinite rational power, is at liberty to accept this hypothesis;
but he must prepare to answer those of his objectors to whom reason means perfection, and to whom
the world of sense will not appear as just at present
more perfect than the world of *Candide's* experi-

ences. For every one but the blind optimist there
is difficulty in regarding this wind-swept battle-field
of human action as obviously and altogether a drama
of unhindered infinite reason, to be repeated with
unwearying tautology through an unending future.
Thus, then, we are tossed back and forth between
the possibilities suggested by our hypothesis. " *The
world is the manifestation of infinite reason;* "
good, then, but how? " *The world is a rational
growth from lower to higher.*" How, then, is this
possible if the infinite reason rules all and desires
the higher? Was it not always at the goal? So,
then : " *The world is not one process merely, but
an eternal repetition of the drama of infinite reason,
which, as infinite, is thus always active and always
at the goal.*" But this hypothesis is seemingly over-
thrown by the appearance of the least imperfection
or irrationality in nature. The first starving family, or singed moth, or broken troth, or wasted effort, or wounded bird, is an indictment of the universal reason, that, always at the goal, has wrought
this irrational wrong. The other possible hypothesis leaves us, after all, in the same quandary. Time
may be a mere "mirage." For the eternal One
there is, then, no process; only fact. This notion
of a timeless Being is, no doubt, very well worth
study. But, then, the eternal One is thus always at
the goal, just as in the other case. The One, we
should think, cannot be infinite and rational and yet
productive of the least trace of wrong, absurdity,
error, falsehood. Again our Monism fails. For,
after all, the world has been viewed by us only from
without; and so remains dark.

IV.

Our monism fails, namely, to establish itself on any ground of experience. Absolute refutation is indeed not yet thus attained, for the defender of the hypothesis of an infinite reason always has at his disposal the suggestions of the ancient theodicy, modified to suit his needs. He can say: "The partial evil is, somehow, we cannot see how, universal good." Or, again, "Evil results from the free-will of moral agents, who have to suffer for their own chosen sins." The latter answer, a very plausible one in its own sphere, is for the general problem insignificant. That there is free-will we do not dispute, and that free-will, if it exists, is a cause of much mischief is undoubted. Yet if the universe is so made that the free-will of the slave-driver, or of the murderer, or of the seducer, or of the conqueror, works untold ill to innocent victims, then the fault of the suffering of the victims rests not wholly with the evil-doer, but partly with the order of the world, which has given him so much power, such a wide freedom to do the mischief that he desires. The world in which such things happen must justify its religiously inspiring nature in some other way.

The other answer, that *partial evil is universal good*, we have to regard as a much deeper answer, shallow as have been the uses often made of it in the past. But if it is to be a valid answer, it must take a particular form. The words are usually spoken too glibly. Their meaning, if they are to have any, we must very carefully consider, ere we can dare to accept them. Only from a higher point of view shall we in fact be able to apply them. In the world of the Powers they find no resting-place.

How can a partial evil be an universal good? Only in certain cases. The notion plainly is that the evil in the external world of popular thought is, as known to us, only a part of the whole, and the whole, it is said, may be in character opposed to the part. This must indeed be the case, if the world as a whole is to be the work of an Infinite Reason. For if so, the evil must be, not merely a bad lesser part that is overbalanced by the goodness of the larger half of the world, but non-existent, save as a separate aspect of reality, so that it would vanish if we knew more about the truth. This is what the saying asserts : not that evil is overbalanced by good (for that would leave the irrational still real), but that evil is only a deceitful appearance, whose true nature, if seen in its entirety, would turn out to be good. One could not say of a rotting apple, however small the rotten spot as yet is, that the partial rottenness is the universal soundness of the apple. If I have but one slight disorder in but one of my organs, still you cannot say that my partial disorder must be universal health. The old optimists did not mean anything so contradictory as that. They meant that there is no real evil at all ; that what seems to me to be evil, say toothaches, and broken households, and pestilences, and treasons, and wars, all that together is but a grand illusion of my partial view. As one looking over the surface of a statue with a microscope, and finding nothing but a stony surface, might say, *how ugly!* but on seeing the whole at a glance would know its beauty; even so one seeing the world by bits fancies it evil, but would know it to be good if he saw it as a whole. And the seeming but unreal evil of the parts may be necessary in order that the real whole should be good. Such is the position of our optimists. This is the Platonic-Augustinian doctrine of the unreality of evil.

The logical possibility of all this we do not for the first either dispute or affirm. But we are dealing with a world of difficulties, and we can only point out the antecedent difficulty of this theory. If the world of experience simply lacked here and there interest, or positive signs of rational perfection, then one might well compare it to the statue, that seen only piecemeal, and through a microscope applied to its surface, would wholly lack the beauty that appears when all is viewed at once. Then one might say, with great plausibility, that if perceptible harmony is simply lacking to our partial view, the great whole may still be a grand harmony. But the trouble lies in the seemingly positive character of evil. Not simple lack of harmony, but horrible discord, is here. How the tortures of the wounded on a field of battle can anyhow enter into a whole in which, as seen by an absolute judge, there is actually no trace of evil at all, this is what we cannot understand. It seems very improbable. Only absolute proof will satisfy us. And of course, as has been indicated, by some of our examples above, it is not the quantity of any evil (if an evil be a quantity at all), but the quality of it, that makes us urge it in

opposition to the claims of reason to be the ruler of
all things. Any evil will do, if it seems to be a real
and positive evil. For then it seems positively at
war with reason.

Actually, however, theodicies and kindred efforts,
whether monistic or not, in trying to vindicate the
rational in the world have seldom consistently maintained this high and slippery ground of the theory
of Plato and of St. Augustine. Far from declaring
that all physical evil is and must be apparent, the
popular theodicies have often consented to accept
the reality of this positive evil, and to minimize its
significance by certain well-worn, and, for the purposes of this argument, contemptible devices. They
have pointed out that the evil in the world, though
a reality separate from the good, exists as a means to
good. Or, again, they have said that evil is necessary as something outside of the good, setting it off
by way of contrast. Both devices, if applied to a
world in which good and evil are conceived as separate entities, are unworthy of philosophic thinkers.

For consider the first device. " Evil is a reality,
not an illusion, but it is a means to good. Therefore in the world as a whole, good triumphs. Therefore reason, which desires the good, is the One
Ruler." But first, to mention a lesser objection,
the basis in experience for this view is surely very
narrow. Much evil exists whose use as a means we
cannot even faintly conceive. But grant this point.
Then the real evil is a means to a separate and external good end. But if the end was good, why was
it not got without the evil means? Only two answers

are possible to this, in case the evil is separate from the good. Either the One Reason was driven to take just this way, and could take no less expensive one; or the One Reason, not being bound to this road, still arbitrarily chose to take it instead of a better. But either answer is fatal. Was the One Reason unable to do better? Then it is not the only power at work. The Monism fails. The Reason was bound. But he who binds the strong man is stronger than he. If, however, the One chose this way rather than a better, then the One chose evil for its own sake. The dilemma is inevitable.

To exemplify: If pain is an evil, and if the evil of the pain caused you by a burn, or cut, or bruise is justified by saying that all-wise nature makes your skin sensitive to the end that you may be helped in keeping it whole; then the obvious answer is, that if nature is all-wise and all-powerful and benevolent towards you, it was her business to find a way of keeping your skin in general whole, without entailing upon you the tortures of this present injury. If a machine that we make runs poorly, we are not disposed to blame ourselves, in case we are sure that we have done our very best with it. But the machines of all-wise nature must not run with destructive friction, unless all-wise nature intends destructive friction. The same remark applies to all the eloquent speeches about the educative value of our sufferings. If nature could make us perfect without suffering, and if suffering is not itself an organic part of our perfection, but only an external means thereto, then it was nature's rational business to de-

velop us differently. But if nature could not perfect
our characters save through this imperfect means,
then nature's means were limited. Nature was not
all-powerful. Reason had some irrational power beyond it that it could not conquer. Even so we cannot yet run certain engines without smoke. When
we are more civilized, we shall abolish smoke, because we shall get more power over the processes of
combustion. At present, by this hypothesis, nature
can only make characters perfect through suffering,
this smoke of the engine of life. So much the worse
for nature, unless indeed, in some unknown way,
suffering is really no true evil at all, but itself a
perfection that, if seen from above, would become
plainly universal good. And does that as yet look
probable ?

Even worse is the other device often suggested
for explaining evil. " Evil is a reality, but it is useful as a foil to good. The two separate facts, good
and evil, set each other off. By its contrast, evil
increases the importance of good." When this remark is made about us personally with our limitations of body and circumstance, with our relativity
of feeling and of attention, the remark has some
psychological interest. Made to justify the supposed
universal reason, the remark is childish. Always,
indeed, it is possible that evil as a separate entity
may be made out to be an illusion; and that good
and evil have some higher unity that involves the
perfection of the world. But if evil is real, and separate from goodness, then the talk about explaining
it as a useful contrast is of no worth in the present

argument. For we ask: Could not the One create a perfect good save by making good more attractive as set off against the foil evil? Shall we say that Reason could do better than to depend upon this contrast? Then why the evil? If, however, the One Reason could not do better, but had to use the contrast, then the One was less powerful in its devices than is the maker of a concert - programme, who has no need to introduce into his concert any saw-filing or tin-trumpeting or pot-scraping to set off the beauty of his songs and symphonies. But as a fact of experience, is most evil seemingly even thus useful? Are the sick needed to make the healthy joyous? Was Judas necessary in order that Jesus should show himself wholly good? Tradition, in this latter case, says yes, and adds the mystical speech about the need that the offense should come. But what enlightened man nowadays will have it that, supposing good and evil to be separate facts, there can be logically possible nothing thoroughly good, in case some of this evil were removed? Could not Jesus have been what he was without Judas? One doubts here the fact of the necessity of the evil, even in our own little lives; and one is indignant at the trifling that supposes so weak a device as mere external contrast to be the sole device at the disposal of the One Reason. Yet this weak hypothesis of good and evil as externally contrasting separate entities is, after all, provokingly near in form to what we shall hold to be the true solution of the great problem. But that solution is still far away from us and from this world of sense.

Thus far, then, monism seems, if not an impossible, still a decidedly doubtful, view of the world. Its value as furnishing religious support seems small. We cannot yet by experience prove that the rational power is supreme in the world ; and we fail to make clear to ourselves *a priori* how it should be supreme. So far we remain agnostics. Our only escape would seem to be through the still doubtful doctrine of the unreality of Evil. And that way seems very dark.

V.

Dualistic Theism here confronts us, the doctrine in which the wise of so many ages have found so much support, the doctrine of a Father, separate from the world of created finite beings, who directs all things, pities and loves his children, and judges with supreme truthfulness all human acts. The religious value of this doctrine, on one side at least, nobody can possibly question. The Father, as Jesus conceives him, has in a very high sense the character that we desire to find in reality. To be sure, there is the other side. This God of the dualistic view is seemingly limited. As a Father pitieth his children, so this God pitieth. But this pity seems to be the love of one who yet cannot or will not save us from all our evil. And if the evil is a reality, and is meant to work for our good, still there is the unanswerable objection that if the Father is not bound by an irrational power beyond him, he need not have put us into so evil a state, but might have wrought us our good in some less painful and dan

gerous way. In fact, the only plausible explanation
of real evil, in case there is separate evil in the
world, an explanation which shall yet be consistent
with the Father's power and goodness, is the previously mentioned explanation, that, if beings were
created, as we are, free, they must needs be also
free to choose the evil. But this explanation only
serves to explain the evil that has directly resulted
from free choice, that directly affects those who
made the choice, and that was distinctly foreseen
by them when they chose it. No other evil is justi-
fiable as a result of free-will; all other evil seems
absolutely mysterious, when viewed with reference
to God's goodness; and very little of the evil that
we experience in this world is the direct result of
the deliberate choice of those who suffer it. It is
hardly necessary to illustrate these facts, which, like
the most of the present chapter, belong to the best-
known and most frequently misrepresented of the
matters of human controversy. The poor of great
cities, the men who inherit loathsome diseases, the
naturally weak of will, the insane, the sufferers in
accidents, the soldiers led to slaughter, the slaves,
the down-trodden peasants and laborers of the world :
all these, whose ills are simply inconceivable in
might, have no more brought all this on themselves
of their own free-will, than have the healthy and
happy, the heirs of wealth, the ever-joyous, earned
for themselves the good fortune to which they are
born. A man can do much with and for himself ;
but the best part of him, and commonly of his environment, is determined by birth. And for most of

that " with which the face of man is blackened," the power is thus responsible which no free-will of man has made. This evil must either be an organic element in a real higher perfect unity of the world, or else free-will is no explanation or justification for its existence.

But really, the intelligent reader needs, when we get to this most familiar part of our discussion, no very lengthy repetition of the old story. His mind is doubtless made up already, and he will desire only a brief reminder of the chief points that have to do with this question and with those questions most nearly related thereto.

If, then, the doctrine of God's Fatherhood is to be religiously useful to us, we must make up our minds whether the Father that we seek is to be the omnipotent Ruler of things, or only a limited Power, or again, something else that is not power. In the last mentioned case, he belongs to that aspect of the world which we just now purposely exclude from consideration. If the Father is a Power, then we all know the old but eternally fresh dilemma about his nature. He is either infinite or limited. If he is infinite, we find arising all the difficulties just suggested in our consideration of the hypothesis of an Infinite Reason, and one other difficulty, worse, if anything, than they all. That difficulty we shall mention soon again. But if, on the other hand, the Father is to be conceived as a limited power, if we are to accept some sort of modern Manicheanism, then no *a priori* disproof of the possibility of the hypothesis can be offered; since, *a priori*, any finite

18

power you please is a possibility; but our great trouble will then lie in the fact that only experience can establish such an hypothesis, which by its very nature needs *a posteriori* proof. And experience, as summed up in science, has in fact simply no need of that hypothesis. Hence we shall be left altogether in doubt, at least while we study the World as Power.

Such is the argument in its most general statement. Now as to the points in greater detail. The great difficulty mentioned above as lying in the way of the hypothesis of an infinite creative power is a difficulty in the conception of creation itself. Creation, for the popular conception, certainly involves producing a thing of some kind by a creative act, the thing produced existing forthwith outside of the creator. To give up this separation of creator and product is to become pantheistic. And with monism we are not here concerned. But now the idea of an infinite creative Power outside of his products involves more than one difficulty. We shall not dwell on the old difficulty that this infinite Power would become finite as soon as there was in existence something outside of it. We shall proceed at once to a more fruitful and serious difficulty, which we find in the fact that the concept of producing an external thing *involves, of necessity, a relation to a Law, above both producer and product, which determines the conditions under which there can be a product at all.* The creative power must then work under conditions, however magical and mysterious its acts may be. And working under condi-

tions, it must be finite. No device for minimizing
the meaning of this separation of creative power and
created thing will really escape the difficulty resulting. And this difficulty will appear in all cases
of supposed creation. It may be summed up once
more in the statement that any creative power in act,
just as much needs explanation in some higher law
and power as does the thing created itself, so that
whatever creates a product external to itself becomes
thereby as truly dependent a power as we ourselves
are. Let us exemplify.

" *Let there be light*," shall represent a creative
act. If the light that results is simply a fact in God,
then our difficulty is avoided, but the very conception of a power creating anything external to itself
is abandoned. Then one becomes frankly pantheistic, and identifies all things with the creative power.
But if the light is not the creative act, but separate from it, then you have an insurmountable difficulty in the conception. For the power that makes
the *fiat* is not itself the created thing, but, as it were,
this power *finds* the product as a result of the *fiat*.
God saying, *Fiat lux*, finds that this act, this word,
or whatever process it symbolizes as actually happening in the divine mind, is followed by the external
appearance of something, namely, light. Now as
creator of light, God is not yet conceived as the
creator of those conditions under which just this
fiat could be followed by just these consequences.
But the external success of the *fiat* presupposes external conditions under which the *fiat* can succeed.
Just as when I say, " let there be light," and pro-

duce it by my own *fiat* plus the necessary physical
acts, even so the conceived Deity in the conceived
case, though needing no other means save his *fiat*,
has yet needed that, and has found his *fiat* a sufficient cause of this external change from darkness to
light. But just as my success in making light needs
explanation by the laws of an external world, so
God's success in making it also needs explanation, in
the case thus conceived, although his means are supposed to have been less complex than mine have to
be. He too is put by this conception in a world of
law external to himself, the laws of this world being
such as require that, in order to produce light as an
external fact he shall perform a certain act, the *fiat*.
These laws secure him success, in the supposed case,
under just these conditions. The *fiat* may itself be
whatever process you will.

But how then did these conditions arise? How
is it that God is able to make light as an existence
external to himself? The external conditions on
which his present success depends may indeed have
been again created by himself. Even so a man could
now possibly make some ingenious mechanism, com-
pounded of telephones and what else you will, so as
to be able to light a whole building by the impulse
produced by some very simple act, *e. g.*, by speaking
the words, " Let there be light," against some prepared membrane. But then we are involved in just
the same difficulties. As the man's mechanical skill
would imply a conformity to laws of nature preceding his present power to make light by the word of
his mouth, even so, if God's creative power has pre-

viously created the conditions of the success of this his present *fiat*, the same questions would arise about those conditions, and so on *ad infinitum*. Always even the infinite series of acts would imply, at every step of the regress, God working upon a nature external to himself, and so God as a finite power, subject to the laws that let him work.

But then may we not hereupon accept the doctrine of God's infinity, and say that this infinite power is identical with its products? Shall we not be pantheists of the old-fashioned sort, and yet keep the doctrine of God's Fatherhood? The attempt is hopeless. And the difficulties in the way of the religious use of the pantheistic hypotheses have already been considered. Furthermore, many theistic thinkers have felt the force of an old set of arguments that, in this country and recently, Professor Bowne, in his " Metaphysics," has more than once set forth at length, namely, the thought that, if God can be as Creator identical with his other creations, he cannot as a Power well be identical with us, who feel ourselves to be also creative powers, and not mere forms or acts in any other power. But if we are separate from God, then in this class of cases his creation of us involves all the difficulties before pointed out. When he made us, his *fiat* was successful beyond himself. The success needs a preëxistent law, or, if you will, a preëxistent power outside of him, to explain it ; just exactly as my power to move my hand or to wink my eye implies a whole universe of being outside of me in order to give my will just this position of authority. Merely assume in your thought these conceptions, namely, a power that acts and an external product resulting from its acts; and at once you need a higher power and a higher law, external to the first power, to explain how the first power, acting in just this way, could achieve just this external result. Hence either God creates nothing external to himself, or else, in creating, he works under the laws that presuppose a power higher than himself, and external to himself. In the briefest form: Acts that produce external changes imply adjustment of means to ends. The creation of external things is such an act. Unless an actor is identical with the product itself, he must therefore be subject to the external conditions of adjustment, *i. e.*, he must be finite.

Certain thinkers are accustomed to suppose that they honor God by having obscure and self-contradictory ideas about him. Hence they avoid all of the foregoing difficulties by calling the creative act a mystery. Now there are mysteries and mysteries. We do not know how trees grow, nor why the planets obey the law of gravitation. But we are sure that they do. On the other hand, we do not know how squares can be round; but we happen in this case to perceive that squares cannot be round. Now if somebody tells me that God is a round square, and appeals to me to consider reverently whether piety allows me to assert, in view of the mystery of God's being, that God is not a round square, my answer is very plain. I say at once that it must be as irreverent to call God absurd and self-contradictory in his nature as to call him anything else discreditable;

and that I, for my part, hesitate not to declare very frankly that though I know very little about God, I am sure that he is no round square. Now even so, an absurd and self-contradictory account of the act of creation must not be allowed to escape us by pleading that creation is a mystery, and that nobody can see *how* God makes things. For, mysterious as creation may be, we can be sure that if creation is of such a nature as to involve an external power and an external law, outside of God's creative power itself, then God is himself not infinite. And we can be equally sure that unless God as creator is identical with his products, the idea of a creative act does involve just such a power preceding the act and outside of God himself. The device then by which so many thinkers seek to escape from this well-known and ancient net of dialectics, seems for us necessarily unsuccessful. There are mysteries that we have reverently to accept, and before long we ourselves shall find such, and we shall be glad to bow before them. But if creation is indeed such a mystery, at all events a self-contradiction about creation is not such a mystery.

VI.

We have dwelt at length on one of the alternatives of Theism. Disheartened, and without any enthusiasm, we turn to the other. Must we after all remain content in our religion without any assurance of the supremacy of the good? Must we be content with this halting half Theism of the empirical Design-Argument? If we must be, we must be. But what if that too should fail us? Let us at least try it. This unsatisfactory view says: " What powers there may be in the world we can never wholly know. But we think that there is evidence that they that be for the moral law are more than they that be against it. And this evidence is given us by the empirically discerned marks of benevolent design about us in the world." This view, whatever its religious worth, is at all events capable only of empirical proof, and pretends only to such a rank. And it is in discussing this hypothesis, in the dim light of the weary centuries of dispute about it, that one comes at last fully to feel the bitterness of the doubt that, like a tormenting disease, assails and eternally must assail one who tries to be content with this dreary visible world in which we have been so far vainly seeking for comfort. Wrangle upon wrangle, ceaseless balancing of probabilities this way and that, opinions and ridicule and abuse forever, and no result: such is this empirical teleology that seeks a world-manufacturer, and cannot discover him. Let us take up the miserable business just where we happen to find it.

There is no doubt about this, that the doctrine of evolution has rendered the popular empirical proof of a special designing power much harder than we used to suppose. And when we pass to this aspect of our question, we must confess at once that we have nothing to say which can be new to any reader of modern discussion. This empirical teleology will always remain a doubtful subject for human inquiry. Any dogmatic disproof of intelligent finite powers or daemons above us must be regarded as impossible. The only question to be here solved is the possibility of purely inductive proof of the existence of such higher intelligent agencies. And here, as we hold, just the ancient difficulties as to the proof of any empirical teleological theory survive, and are, in spite of all that recent writers have done, rather increased by our knowledge of the facts of evolution. Especially does evolution make the empirical hypothesis of the existence of any finite and good daemonic power, intelligently and morally working in the world, continually more and more obscure. For first, as to the intelligence of the higher powers, what the theory of evolution has done for us in this respect is simply to make us feel that we know not, and cannot yet even guess, how much what we empirically call bare mechanism can do to simulate the effects of what, in an equally empirical and blind way, men call intelligence. Therefore no empirical design-argument has longer anywhere nearly the same amount of persuasive power that it once seemed to have. The matter stands thus: An empirical design-argument might very plausibly reason that, if I find a child's blocks arranged to make a house or to spell words, I can assume that some designing human hand has so placed them. But the inductive force of the argument rests on my previous knowledge that nothing is so apt to put blocks in that order, in this present visible world, as just a designing human hand. But if I discovered certain physical conditions that did very frequently work, and that did often so arrange blocks, then I should no longer consider the given arrangement good proof of human design. Even so, until I see that natural selection can simulate the designing power of human beings, I may be disposed to regard a given case of apparent design in nature as a fair inductive proof of some great carpenter or watch-maker working there. But the induction, never overwhelming, becomes very weak when I learn that there are so-called physical conditions such as we or chance can produce, which, however, do nevertheless result in things that my eye would have called full of design. For then I am led to feel as if I could pass no judgment at all upon concrete cases. Yet only by concrete cases can an empirical hypothesis be proved. Therefore unless a pebble proves design an eye does not prove design.

But design, we hear, is not incompatible with evolution. Of course not. And if there is a designer, who works through evolution, then indeed he shows wonderful foresight and mastery. But the question is, not what is compatible with evolution, but what can be proven from bare experience. And what the modern man has very justly come to see is that mere experience must leave him in utter doubt about what powers, intelligent or not intelligent, are the sources of all our experience. We can find laws; but they take us only a short way. And the more we know about nature, the less inclined we feel to dogmatize on the basis of mere experience about what powers are behind the scenes. They may be intelligent, and they may be what we call in this world of sense mechanical. But as finite powers, given in experience, we men know them solely by

their effects. And their effects are very remote
hints of their real nature. It is really painful to
read the elaborate wastes of effort made in our day
to prove that some theological dogma about some
power beyond experience is not refuted by experience. As if such proof made anybody's creed
either more or less doubtful. A really well-founded
Theism would not be, in this tedious way, eternally
on the defensive.

But there is the other aspect of the matter. An
intelligent power, were it admitted, would not need to
be moral. If there is design, is the designer demon-
strably good? Let us pass over to that question.

VII.

If evolution has done anything for us, it has
tended to increase our sense of the mystery of the
world of experience, and therefore the philosophically minded religious student is in truth, for yet
this other reason, weary of all this empirical Theism,
namely, because he despairs of finding out, by such
an empirical process, anything about the actual purposes of any designer, even if there be a designer.
To study English literature in the rubbish heaps of
a book-binder's work-shop, would seem to a wise man
a much more hopeful undertaking than to seek any
one notion of the real plan on which this world is
made from a merely empirical study of our little
fragment of nature. Science is right in abandoning
such undertakings wholly and for all its now probable future work. Religion must find the religious

aspect of reality in a totally different direction. The higher the realities that we study, the harder the task. The heavens declare very many things not wholly clear to us; but the earth and man declare, as natural facts, very many more and more confusing things. Only a poetical abstraction can show us any one plan of religious value in the world of sense, any one declaration of anybody's glory therein. An equally strong opposing interest would find just as good evidence for what it sought if it should hold another view of what is designed. Nature is, so regarded, a confused hum of voices. "Nature," says one voice, "is meant to provide bountifully for the wants of sentient life." "Therefore," says another voice, "all the weak, the sick, the old, must starve, and all the carnivorous destroy their neighbors." "Nature aims at the evolution of the highest type of life," says the first voice. "Therefore," it is replied, "she bountifully provides swarms of parasites of all sorts to feed on higher life." "Nature desires order and unity," says the voice from the heavens. "Therefore she makes meteors and comets," replies the echoing voice. — And if now the Fiend appears, and suggests, as the only satisfactory design-hypothesis, something of this sort, how could experience answer him? — "Nature," he says, "is designed by a being who delights in manifold activity of all sorts, in variety of organization throughout the world, in the fine contrasts of the numberless forms of sentient life, and in whatever means vigor. He likes to see many living creatures, and he likes to see them fight. He likes the sight of suffering, as well as of joy;

because both mean variety of action. He delights in
the triumphs of the victors, in the groans of the conquered, in the sportiveness of young animals, in the
writhing of a poor beast that dies in torture, in the
insidious struggle for existence that the *Entozoa*
carry on, in the hopeless sighs that men send up to
him in their woe, and in the ideal raptures and
agonies of saints, artists, and lovers. All these things
he likes, because they are just so many forms of existence. He wants plenty of life and vigor to contemplate, as a boy wants stiff soap-suds to make
pretty bubbles for his pleasure as he lies idle. This
being is doubtless finite (like his brother, the Setebos of the inimitable monologue that Browning has
put into Caliban's mouth). But just now he reigns
hereabouts, even as Caliban's Setebos reigned in the
island. And his designs are so obviously shown in
nature, that anybody ought to believe in him who
simply looks at the facts of experience."

Of this horrible doctrine we apprehend that experience as such offers no disproof. For all that
science can say, we might be in the hands of just
such a demon. Hence it behooves religious students
to cease looking for the living God among the dead
facts of physical science, and to betake themselves
to their own proper field. Science simply leaves all
such hypotheses utterly doubtful. Our little corner
of the world may have become what it is in any one
of numberless physically definable ways. And, if
designed, its immediate purpose may be any one of
numberless purposes. It is not probable that experience can tell us much about that matter. Science

is very right in appealing to experience with wholly
different aims, namely, for the sake of understanding
the laws of the sequence of phenomena, to the end
that we may be able to know what the world-plan,
however it may be formed, does actually render us
capable of accomplishing just now and here in our
concrete dealings with things. And if science, in
doing all this, has to make certain postulates, and to
accept them on faith, then such faith, though it needs
indeed a deeper foundation, is at least not identical
with the presumption that, undertaking not simply
to postulate, but to prove beyond doubt, pretends to
discover with certainty, from bare experience, that
the world-maker's plans do agree with our plans.
After all, such empirical Theism is assuming its
safest and most characteristic form when it appears
no longer as a genuine investigator, but poses as the
defendant's attorney, takes prudent refuge behind the
rules of debate, and demands that other people shall
assume the burden of proof, and either show it to be
certainly false, or else accept it for the sake of propriety.

VIII.

We turned to the supposed external World of
Powers, and we have found it either dumb, or else
given to dark and doubtful speeches. The Powers
may indeed be somehow of the highest worth. But
to us, even if we accept unquestioningly the supposed
external world, the worth of it all seems doubtful,
and more so the longer we study the matter. The
partial evil may be universal good; but we could not

in this external world see how, nor could we find proof of the fact. What a Power causes, that the power seems responsible for. And so the Powers that cause the inestimable might of evil in the world seem of very doubtful religious worth.

We have already suggested in outline why this doubtful result was to be expected. These Powers were *assumed* to exist apart from our thought, in time and space, and to work in time. They have, as workers in time, no certain and eternal significance. A single Infinite Power is, properly speaking, a misnomer. If a power produces something that is external to itself, then the very idea of such an occurrence implies another power, separate from the first, and therefore limiting it. If however the power is identical with its own products, then the name power no longer properly belongs to it. For, as we shall see when we come to speak of the world in its other aspect, namely, as eternal, the conceptions of power and product, of cause and effect, and of all like existences, are found to be only subordinate to the highest conception of the world as Thought. For the Eternal Thought are all these powers; but in themselves they belong to the flux of things. Each one of them says, *Not in me*, when you ask it for the significance of the world as a whole. Each power says: " I work here along with the others. I fight, I strive, I conquer, I obey, I seek my ends as I can. But beyond me are the conditions that limit me. " And these conditions are the other powers. The world of powers is the world of the children of the dragon's teeth. Their struggles are endless. The only religion that they can teach is the religion of endurance and of courage. Or one may compare them to the warriors in king Atli's house. Only the all-seeing Eternal Thought can possibly discover their significance. Of themselves they are just the fighters in the blood and dust of the banqueting hall.

All this we just now affirm without full proof. But our previous discussion has been one long illustration of it. You find or think you find in the world a religiously valuable power or tendency at work. But at once there stands beside it its sworn foe. Is it Evolution that you have found? There stands beside it Dissolution. Is it the tender care of a fatherly nature for the very sparrows? Then appears beside it the cruelty and deceit of nature. Is it the beauty of the world that suggests a power-loving beauty? Nay, but the rottenness and the horror of natural disease and decay assert as boldly the workings of a power that hates beauty. Are all these seeming powers just mere phantoms, whose truth is in the laws of physics? Then the world is a vast wreck of colliding molecules. Are these powers real tendencies? Then their fight is seemingly endless. The world of the powers is indeed full of physical law, because and only because its facts are found, by means of thought that has a deeper foundation, to be cases of certain general rules. But for our religious purpose, this world of the powers seems a chaos.

"But," says some one, "all this is no disproof of the existence of a real but to us not perfectly clear

harmony of all the powers.   This is simply absence
of proof."   Yes; but if proof is what we want, and
if every single power sends us beyond itself for the
interpretation of the meaning of the whole, we cannot hope to grasp that meaning so long as we avoid
studying the world in its eternal aspect.   The powers themselves make and unmake.   We understand
them not.   They remind us of the night-scene of
Faust : —

Faust. Was weben die dort um den Rabenstein ?
Mephistopheles. Weiss nicht was sie kochen und schaffen.
Faust. Schweben auf, schweben ab, neigen sich, beugen sich.
Mephistopheles. Eine Hexenkunst.
Faust. Sie streuen und weihen.
Mephistopheles. Vorbei ! Vorbei !

And if we will hear the wisdom of Mephistopheles
about all this, he has elsewhere given his view, which,
as an opinion about the world of powers by one of
the more authoritative powers in it, is worthy of
as much respect as any other suggestion from an
equally limited being : —

" Was soll uns dann das ewige Schaffen !
Geschaffenes zu nichts hinwegzuraffen !
' Da ist's vorbei ! ' Was ist daran zu lesen ?
Es ist so gut als wär'es nicht gewesen.
Und treibt sich doch im Kreis, als wenn es wäre.
Ich liebte mir dafür das Ewig-Leere."

And possibly it would be hard for us to be sure of
much more meaning in this world of powers as such,
than Mephistopheles has found.

For us, we turn, not with despair, but with hope,
elsewhere.   We go to seek the Eternal, not in experience, but in the thought that thinks experience.
19

Our hope is not less because we have found in the temporal a world of doubt. Our song is simply the "*Good-by proud world, I'm going home*," of the religious minds of all ages. The truly religious elements of theism are not hurt by the destruction of traditions about theistic arguments. It is only an example of shallow thought when either the destructive or the constructive thinkers imagine that the battle is decided if the world of the powers is judged in one way or in another. Religion is as independent of all that as Sirius is independent of the north wind.

CHAPTER IX.

THE WORLD OF THE POSTULATES.

Das beständige Wetzen der Messer ist langweilig, wenn man Nichts
zu schneiden vorhat. — LOTZE, *Metaphysik*.

> What's so false as truth is
> False to thee?
>
> BROWNING.

IF the reader has become thoroughly weary of the
world of doubt, we are only glad of the fact. Armed
with a genuine philosophy, a man may indeed go
back to that world, and find in it an expression of
ideal truth in empirical form. We hope to have
such a right ourselves in time; but, without a well
thought out philosophy, a man venturing into the
world of empirical facts to find there any religious
significance actually discovers himself to be in a nest
of hornets; and he deserves as much. We desired
to bring the reader to feel this with us; else our
own prudent flight from that world to another might
seem to him unnecessary. Now we are ready to
come nearer to our former question. What right
has any one to assume that empirical external world
at all as having any absolute truth? " O thou that
hast troubled us," we may say, " what art thou at
bottom more than our own assumption?" What
right has that external world to be the sole region

where we could seek the religious truth, when perchance the external world, as we assumed it, is not
a truth at all? Let us consider once more our steps.
Perchance the religiously inspiring reality is in some
higher world. If we are only skeptical enough, perchance we shall find that Reality. Then, indeed,
the old assumption of an external world of empirical facts may remain a part of our future thought,
but it will get a new sense, and occupy a new place.

The first answer that occurs to this our question
about the meaning of the external world that has
so far troubled us, is this: The assumed world is
no fixed *datum*, to which we are bound to submit at
all hazards, but a *postulate*, which is made to satisfy certain familiar human needs. If this postulate
is found to have no religious significance, we may
supplement the doubt thus arising by remembering
that we who postulated once have the right to postulate again. Our religiously satisfactory truth may
be reached, not by hypotheses about powers in the
empirical world, but by a deeper faith in something
that is eternal, and behind or above the world of the
senses.

This view gives us a new world, the world of the
Postulates. We cannot be content to remain in this
world, but we must pass through it on our way up-
wards. Let us hear it described.

I.

The world of Doubt has passed before us, a huge
mass of inexplicable facts. Here and there we find

a connection ; we hope that we shall soon find more
connection ; but still the vast plan, if indeed there
be a plan, we search for in vain. But now, strangely
enough, all this doubt affects in no wise the willing
trustfulness of our devotion to the interests, not only
of common life, but also of science. The doubt confuses us only when we talk of religion. That the
world as a whole is dark, nobody admits more cheerfully than does the modern scientific man, even when
he looks to his science for all his religious consolation. For he seeks no consolation save what the
phenomena as such furnish. But his philosophical
doubt about the ultimate foundation of science is
no check to his scientific ambition. He believes in
science just as ardently as if he did not in the very
first breath of each new philosophical dispute declare that the real world is unknowable. His faith
in the methods of his specialty is as firm as his indifference to all extra - scientific speculation. His
work is in fact done with a kind of instinctive confidence in himself and his fellows. The instinct is
no doubt highly trained, but it remains an instinct,
and a delightful one it is to him. The untrained
instincts of the unscientific man must indeed be criticised and altered in many respects ere they can
serve the purposes of science ; but, after all the criticisms and alterations, the instinct remains with almost all men an instinct, — useful, pleasing, yes, indispensable ; but its philosophical justification few
people care to know, while its self-confidence every
scientific essay, or lecture, or instructor will attest.
Why now is it that, trusting as we all do this scien-

tific instinct, we all feel it hard to give a like trust to the religious instinct, whose most general tendency is to have some sort of faith in the goodness of things? Why is it that the doubtfulness and the contradictions of the real world seem to everybody to throw a cloud upon religion, even when it is not supernatural religion, but to have no significance whatever for the bases of science? This scientific notion of a world of law, all of whose facts could conceivably be predicted by one formula, why does that remain in our minds untouched by the doubts of the skeptical philosophers, while the same skepticism at once seems to remove from us that trust in the moral goodness of things which religion has tried to establish in our hearts? Shall the world be indifferent to one set of our ideals, and not to another? Shall the moral value of things be dark, and not also their value for the purposes of science? Why is the one doctrine so different from the other? You are placed in a world of confusion, and you assert that in its ultimate and eternal nature it answers your moral needs. That seems presumptuous. You did not make that world. How do you know whether it cares for your moral ideals? Very well then, be impartial. You are placed in a world of confusion, and you assert that it answers your intellectual needs, namely, that it is a world of order, whose facts could be reduced to some rational and intelligible unity. What business have you to do that? In both cases you transcend experience. Nature gives you in experience partial evil that you cannot in all cases perceive to be universal good. Nature also gives you in experience partial chaos that you cannot in all cases perceive to be universal order. But unwaveringly you insist that nature is orderly, that the chaos is an illusion; and still you do not feel ready to insist that the partial evil is universal good. Why is this so? Is the ethical side of reality less important than the other? Or is it the very importance of the religious aspect of things that makes us more ready to doubt the truth of this aspect?

Such questions occur to us as suggesting a possible way out of our difficulties. It is not exactly our desired way, but is it not possibly a good way? Science, namely, uses a certain kind of faith, whenever such faith is practically necessary. This scientific faith is indeed no faith in particular uninvestigated facts, but it is a faith in general methods and principles. The creed of science knows of no dogmas about unexperienced single facts, as such; but it does know of dogmas about the general form of the laws that must be assumed to govern all experience. Now why may not religion be reduced to certain essential general and fundamental moral demands, that we must make in the presence of reality? Why are not these a legitimate, yes, a morally necessary object of faith? Why, as the scientific man postulates a theoretical rationality in the world, may not we postulate a moral rationality in the world? These questions stand in our path. Might not the answer to them transform our barren doubts into something less disheartening?

We see what all this supposed religious faith would mean. It would not be a faith in any particular facts of experience that might have for us personally a selfish value, whether greater or less. It would be, like the scientific faith, wholly general. It would demand that the world in its entirety should be regarded as in some higher sense morally rational. It would say: The real world must be, whatever its true nature, at least as high in the moral scale as my highest ideals of goodness. Have we a right to such a faith? Let us cautiously consider this point.

But at once we must distinguish the proposed religious faith from what we should call mere blind faith. Blind faith in what we cannot establish is indeed inadmissible. But then, is there not another kind of faith, the kind that Kant used in his practical philosophy? To this may we not now turn? Perhaps the world of the powers, approached in the usual way, is dark, but the world for the practical reason may be opened in another way. Kant said, in effect: "Such and such supersensual realities, of religious significance, cannot be theoretically proven; but we can see why we ought to postulate their existence, that is, we can see *why we ought to act as if they existed.* Behind the veil of sense, we must postulate that there is an intelligible world, in which all is harmony, and in which the highest good is realized." May we not also try with Kant to do this?

We shall in any case find this effort, an effort that has been so often made since Kant, a subject well worth our study and careful examination. In truth it is not by itself satisfactory; but we shall see that it enters as one moment into the higher view that we shall hereafter reach. So, in our own way, we shall now try to answer the question suggested to us by Kant's method. Does not then the religious aspect of the world lie in the fact that, despite the contradictions of the world of sense, we may, and indeed, morally speaking, must postulate, that the Eternal, of which this world is the mere show, is in itself absolutely righteous? We shall not be able to answer this question with a simple affirmative; but still, postulates must enter in some wise into every moment of our lives, and must therefore have some value in religion.

II.

In the last chapter we sought for a demonstration of religious truth, and found none. But perhaps it was not demonstration that we should have sought. Possibly religion may be content to rest on postulates.

A postulate is a mental way of behavior. In so far it is like all other thought. In general, to believe that a thing exists is to act as if it existed. But the act may be forced upon one, or it may be freely chosen. One cannot fail to act upon the principle that $2 + 2 = 4$, so soon as he perceives it. But one may voluntarily determine to act in a given way, not being rationally forced so to do, and well knowing the risk. In such cases one voluntarily takes to himself the form of belief called a postulate. Thus, apart from any philosophic theory, we all postulate a certain kind of uniformity in nature. We do so, whenever we reflect upon the matter, voluntarily. For we then say that surprises are always possible, and that any law may have exceptions, but that we must act as if we knew certain laws to have no possible exceptions. Postulates, however, are not blind faith. Postulates are voluntary assumptions of a risk, for the sake of a higher end. Passive faith dares not face doubt. The postulate faces doubt, and says : " So long as thou canst not make thyself an absolute and certain negative, I propose to act as if thou wert worthless, although I do well see thy force." Blind faith is emotion, and often cowardly emotion. The postulate is deliberate and courageous volition. Blind faith says : " I dare not question." The postulate says : " I dare be responsible for assuming." Examples of both are very common. Blind faith the fond parent has, who says of his wicked son : " I know that he must be good, hence I will not suspect him, nor train him ; I will not watch him, nor warn others against him." A postulate the wise parent makes, who sends his fullgrown son boldly out into the world, with the best attainable safeguards, saying : " It is useless to keep him longer in leading-strings, or to protect him from the world. It is now his place to fight his own battles, since I have done what I could to get him ready. I postulate that he will win the fight ; I treat him, and must treat him, as if he were sure to win, although I well know the risks." The sea-captain beginning his voyage postulates that he can get through. The general postulates that he will be victorious. The Prime Minister of a country postulates that he can do his country better service than could the Opposition. We all postulate that our lives are worth the trouble. Yet we all know perfectly well that many just such postulates must in the nature of things be blunders. But they imply not blind faith, but active faith. With blind faith little good is done in the world; without active faith, expressed in postulates, very little practical good can be done from day to day. Blind faith is the ostrich behind the bush. The postulate stands out like the lion against the hunters. The wise shall live by postulates.

III.

But how is this postulating activity actually related to our knowledge of reality? Much more closely than one might suppose. Very much of our thought naturally rests upon a blind faith, or upon what many take to be a blind faith; but this, when we reflect upon it with due attention to the office it fills, is transformed before our eyes into practically unavoidable postulates. Such are the assumptions upon which our science rests in forming its ideal of an " universal formula." There may indeed be some deeper basis for these postulates of science. But most men know nothing of this basis. And so, when we accepted in our last chapter these postulates, we had to admit that they are a kind of faith. If we then nevertheless objected to certain religious doctrines that they rest on insufficient evidence, we did this because they set themselves up as dogmas.

With further consideration, we might come to accept some one of them again in the form, not of a demonstrable dogma, but of a practically unavoidable postulate, uncertain of course, but taken and to be taken on risk ; just as every one of us goes through the world taking all sorts of risks day by day.   Anything not contradictory may be a possible object of postulates ; although, again, every postulate is to be assumed only after careful criticism, and only because we cannot do better.

To do justice then to the proper office of postulates in our religious theory, we must sooner or later consider in what cases they naturally arise, what is the proper extent of their use, what is the basis upon which they can be made, in any special case, to rest ; and, finally, whether, in view of all this, we can give them any important place in our religious doctrine. We confess at once that we want something much better than a postulate as the basis of our religion, in case we can get it.   If postulates are to have any part in our religion, we want them to be justified by some ultimate religious certainty that is more than a postulate.   We shall investigate all that in time. We shall see what we shall see.   Meanwhile, what is the work of postulates in the actual daily life of human thought ?

Popular belief about an external world is for the first an active assumption or acknowledgment of something more than the data of consciousness. What is directly given in our minds is not external. All direct data are internal facts ; and in the strictest sense all data are direct.   Suppose a merely pas-

sive acceptance of what is in consciousness, and you
have no belief in an external world. An addition to
the data of consciousness, a more or less clearly voluntary reaction, is involved in your idea of external
reality. The truth of this principle appears when
your belief in any particular object is called in question. You hold that you see yonder a snowy mountain. Your companion insists that beyond the wide
misty valley there is to be seen only a gray cloud.
You reassert your belief, and in the reassertion feel
more definitely than at first the active addition of
your own belief to the meagre data of sense. The
addition existed, however, in your first assertion.
Or again, one man is trying, perchance in sport, to
make another doubt the existence of material objects. " There is no external matter," says the first.
" There are but these states of consciousness in our
minds. Nothing beyond them corresponds to them."
The second, maintaining the position of the man of
common sense, retorts sharply : " Doubtless I cannot
refute altogether your fine-spun arguments ; but they
are nevertheless nonsense. For I persist in believing
in this world of sense. I live in it, I work for it, my
fellows believe in it, our hearts are bound up in it,
our success depends upon our faith. Only dreamers
doubt it. I am not a dreamer. Here is a stone ;
I hit it. Here is a precipice ; I fear and shun it.
My strongest conviction is concerned with the existence of this world of sense. Do your worst ; I am
not afraid of talk." Thus then by every device of
the active spirit, by reminding himself of his most
cherished interests, of his affections and hatreds, by

arousing his social sentiments, by bodily acts, the practical man preserves himself from fantastical speculation. When better-trained thinkers call the belief in an external reality " a natural conviction, to be retained until we are compelled to abandon it," or " a convenient working hypothesis, to be received on the testimony of consciousness, testimony assumed to be trustworthy until the opposite is proven," what are these but similar practical considerations, appeals to the will ? Concerning data of immediate consciousness such remarks would be wholly out of place. That I see a certain color at this moment is not a " convenient working hypothesis." Is consciousness merely a " presumably trustworthy witness " when it testifies to the pangs of toothache? Nobody could balance evidence as to the reality of his sensation *quâ* sensation when consciousness is filled with the sound of a street-organ. Sound, color, pang, these are data, not merely things believed in. But the external world — that is actively accepted as being symbolized or indicated by the present consciousness, not as being given in the present consciousness.

In short, the popular assertion of an external world, being an assertion of something beyond the data of consciousness, must begin in an activity of judgment that does more than merely reduce present data to order. Such an assertion must be an active construction of non-data. We do not receive in our senses, but we posit through our judgment, whatever external world there may for us be. If there is really a deeper basis for this postulate of ours, still, at the outset, it is just a postulate.

All theories, all hypotheses as to the external world, ought to face this fact of thought. If the history of popular speculation on these topics could be written, how much of cowardice and shuffling would be found in the behavior of the natural mind before the question: "How dost thou know of an external reality?" Instead of simply and plainly answering: "I mean by the external world in the first place something that I accept or demand, that I posit, postulate, actively construct on the basis of sense-data," the natural man gives us all kinds of vague compromise answers: "I believe in the external reality with a reasonable degree of confidence; the experience of mankind renders the existence of external reality ever more and more probable; the Creator cannot have intended to deceive us; it is unnatural to doubt as to external reality; only young people and fantastic persons doubt the existence of the external world; no man in his senses doubts the external reality of the world; science would be impossible were there no external world; morality is undermined by doubts as to the external world; the immovable confidence that we all have in the principle of causality implies the fixity of our belief in an external cause of our sensations." Where shall these endless turnings and twistings have an end? The habits of the law-courts as condensed into "rules of evidence," the traditional rules of debate, the fashion of appealing to the "good sense" of honorable gentlemen opposite, the motives of shame and fear, the dread of being called "fantastical," Philistine desire to think with the majority, Philistine terror of all revolutionary suggestions, the fright or the anger of a man at finding some metaphysician trying to question what seem to be the foundations upon which one's bread winning depends, — all these lesser motives are appealed to, and the one ultimate motive is neglected. The ultimate motive with the man of every-day life is the will to have an external world. Whatever consciousness contains, reason will persist in spontaneously adding the thought: "But there shall be something beyond this." The external reality as such (*e. g.* the space beyond the farthest star, any space not accessible, even whatever is not at any moment given in so far as it is viewed from that moment, in particular every past event) is never a datum. We construct but do not receive the external reality. The "immovable certainty" is not such a dead passive certainty as that with which we receive a pain or an electric shock. The popular assurance of an external world is the fixed determination to make one, now and henceforth.

In the general popular conceptions of reality we find then the first use of postulates. We have as yet no justification for them. But even thus we get no adequate idea of their use and of their number. We must look at the facts of every-day mental life a little more closely. For there is a curious tendency of many to make these postulates appear something else than what they are. Often they are interpreted as if they were no postulates at all, but data of sense. Often, again, their active nature is disregarded in yet another way, and they appear as blind passive faith. Such in fact they must appear if we reflect upon their mere content, and not upon the processes by which we get them. But if we interpret them rightly, we shall see that they ought to be regarded as beliefs, taken for the first on risk, and because the risk is worth taking.

IV.

Sometimes we hear men asserting that their beliefs are independent of their will. Such a man will express himself in some such way as the following: —

"I try to conquer prejudice; but having done this, I can do no more. My belief, whatever it is, forms itself in me. I look on. My will has nothing to do with the matter. I can will to walk or eat; but I cannot will to believe. I might as well will that my blood should circulate."

But is this expression a fair one? Does such a man really remain passive in the struggle that goes on within him? We think not. These beliefs in such a man have resulted, we hold, from a sort of struggle between him and the surrounding world. The world has tried sometimes to check his thought, and to confine it to one channel; sometimes to confuse his thought, and to scatter it into spray before the quick, heavy blows of innumerable, disconnected sense apparitions. But the man, if he is a man of energy, has controlled the current of his thought. He has fought hard, now for freedom from oppressive narrowness of thought, now for wholeness and unity of thought; and perhaps he has in so far con-

20

quered as to be the master of a manly and many-sided system of doctrine. We think him responsible for this system; and we hold that any such man ought to admit the responsibility.

To study briefly the nature of the process involved in all such cases will be important for our whole doctrine. We shall see thereby how much our theory of the world must itself tend to fall under the head of the purely practical. We shall appreciate also the limitations of ordinary thought, and the need of some higher ideal standard to rescue us from the pure subjectivity of mere postulates. And we shall be contributing by the way to a question of applied ethics, the question of the morality of belief.

Every one recognizes that at least our more abstract knowledge depends largely upon our own mental activity. Knowing is not mere passive reception of facts or of truths. Learning is not solely an affair of the memory. The man that without reflection commits things to memory is justly compared to a parrot, and might yet more justly be compared to the sponge of Hamlet's figure: "It is but squeezing you, and, sponge, you shall be dry again." No knowledge, then, without active hospitality in the mind that receives the knowledge. But as soon as we recognize in mental life this our power to modify our knowledge by means of our own activity, just so soon do all the old comparisons of the mind to a wax tablet, to a sheet of paper, or to other like passive subjects of impression, lose for us their meaning. Mental life becomes for us, in view of these facts, a field of constant activity. The commonest processes of knowledge acquire a new significance.

Two kinds of activity are concerned in the attainment of knowledge. One kind consists in simply receiving impressions from without, such as sensations, or, on a higher plane, statements of truth; the other consists in modifying and in organizing these impressions. The receptive activity is partly a physical activity, since the one who receives information must use his eyes and ears, must keep awake, must at times move about; and this receptive activity is also partly made up of the mechanical processes of the memory. Association by contiguity, or learning by rote, is in the main a receptive process, though this process of reception requires some active effort on the part of the receiver. Committing words and sentences to memory is often hard labor, as we all of us learned when we first were tortured with ill-wrought geographies and grammars, or with merciless Latin declensions and conjugations. But of the whole of this receptive activity we shall make no further mention in this connection. Simply receiving, keeping your mind in a submissive attitude, turning your eyes in the proper direction, using your ears, writing down your notes, memorizing whatever needs memorizing — all this is essential to knowledge, but has no reactive effect, does not modify the form or the matter of your knowledge. Secondly, however, knowledge is determined for each of us by his own reaction upon what he receives ; and this second mentioned kind of mental activity, that which forms our topic at present, consists in a modification as well as in an organization of what we have received from without. All processes of reasoning, and so all original discoveries in science and in philosophy, all speculations, theories, dogmas, controversies, and not only these complex processes, but, as we shall see, even simple judgments, commonplace beliefs, momentary acts of attention, involve such independent reaction upon the material furnished to us from without. The nature of this reaction we are further to examine.

Let us consider simpler forms of knowledge. Sense-impressions constantly suggest to us thoughts; in fact, we have few thoughts that are not either immediately suggested by sense-impressions, or else sustained in their course by a continuous stream of suitable sense-impressions. To carry on even a train of abstract reasoning, sense-impressions either present or repeated seem necessary as supports. But when sense-impressions come to us, what transforms them into thought?

The answer is, First of all, attention, an active mental process. The sense-impression is itself not yet knowledge. A sense-impression to which we give no attention slips through consciousness as a man's hand through water. Nothing grasps and retains it. Little effect is produced by it. It is unknown. You cannot even tell what it is. For to know what such an unnoticed impression is would be to pay attention to it. But let us now consider some familiar examples of the working of attention. A simple instance will bring home to us how the boundaries of our consciousness are crowded with unknown impressions — unknown, because not attended to; but yet in some inexplicable way a part of our consciousness, since an effort of attention serves to bring them, any one of them, clearly into mental vision. At this instant you are looking at something. Now, without moving your eyes, try, by merely attending to your visual impressions, to say what is now in the field of vision, and where is the boundary line of the field of vision. The experiment is a little hard, because our eyes, condensed embodiments as they are of tireless curiosity, are always restless, and rebel when you try to hold them fast. But conquer them for an instant, and watch the result. As your attention roams about the artificially fixed visual field, you will at first, indeed, be confused by the vagueness of all but the centre; but soon you will find, to your surprise, that there are more different impressions in the field than you at first can distinguish. One after another, many various impressions will appear. But notice: you can keep your attention fixed on only a portion of the field at a time. The rest of the field is always lost in a dim haze. You must be receiving impressions all the time from all points of the field. But all of these, except the few to which you pay attention, nearly or quite disappear in the dim thickets that seem to surround the little forest-clearing made by our attentive consciousness. A like experiment can be tried with the sense of hearing, when you are in a large room full of people who are talking all around you in many independent groups. A mass of sound comes to your ear. Consciousness interferes to make you pick out one or another of the series of sounds, an act which is indeed made possible by the natural analytic tendency of the human auditory sense, but which does not take place without a noticeable effort of attention. When you are learning a foreign language, and are for a while much among those who speak it, there comes a time when your ear and mind are well enough trained to follow and understand ordinary speakers with only a little effort of attention; but yet, at this stage, you are able, by simply withdrawing your attention a mere trifle, to let very common phrases run through your sense without your understanding them one whit. You can thus, by a slight change of attention, convert the foreign language from a jargon into a familiar speech, and back again into a jargon, just as, in the fixed visual field, you can make yourself see an object pretty plainly, or lose it altogether, by ceasing to give attention.

All these instances, which could be indefinitely multiplied, prove, first, that what we call attention modifies the knowledge that we at any moment get; and secondly, that this modification, through attention, may take place without any change in the impressions that at any moment come from without. The first stage in getting knowledge from bare sense-impressions is therefore the modification of sense by attention — a process belonging wholly to the subjective side; *i. e.* to our own minds.

But what is attention? and how does it modify sensation? Apparently, attention in the previous instances has been merely a power to increase or to diminish the intensity of impressions. But is this all that attention does? No: there are many cases in which attention directly affects the quality, at least of our complex impressions. This direct modification is commonly attended by some alteration of our emotional state. It is a familiar fact, that in listening to a series of regular and even beats, such as the strokes of an engine, or of a pendulum, or the ticking of a watch, we have a tendency to modify the impressions by introducing into their series the more elaborate regularity of rhythm. In paying attention to them, we increase, at our pleasure, the intensity of every third or fourth beat as heard, and so make a rhythm, or series of measures, out of the actually monotonous impressions. Now attention, which here first acts by modifying the intensity of impressions, soon produces the effect of qualitatively modifying our total impression of the whole series. If I have taken the fancy to listen to the even strokes in quadruple time, intensifying by my own act every fourth stroke, the character of the series is changed for me. The impressions are less monotonous, and they arouse new associations. They seem to be caused by some force that rhythmically increases and decreases. Perhaps a melody, or some phrase of a few words, arises in my mind, and persists in associating itself with the strokes. Probably some vague feeling, as of rhythmic motion through the air, or of pleasure or of displeasure in the presence of some rhythmically moving living being, is awakened. Qualitatively, my consciousness is thus altered through my attention. I seem to be experiencing something that, as an objective reality, I do not experience. More striking becomes this qualitative alteration of experience through attention, in case you bring two watches of different beat, or a watch and a clock, and listen to both at once at the distance of a few inches, first, perhaps, stopping one ear to avoid confusion. Here, by attention, you make or try to make a compound rhythm, and this effort alters a good deal the total impression that you derive from the sound. If the two series are such that a simple small multiple of the interval of one gives you a simple small multiple of the other's interval, you can combine the two series into one rhythm, and then there is an immediate impression as if the two series were really but the complex ticking of one source of sound. But if the series will not agree, there is an odd sense of something wrong, a disappointed effort to combine, joined, perhaps, with a tendency to hasten one of the series, so as to make it agree with the other. Another case where attention alters the quality of total impressions, and not merely the intensity of any part, appears in certain psychological laboratory experiments, described by Wundt in his " Physiologische Psychologie." Here, for the sake of determining the actual time taken by an act of attention, an observer is to make an electric signal as soon as he becomes conscious of a certain impression, while the impression itself is produced by an assistant at a time exactly determined. The source of the impression is the ringing of a bell, the flash of an electric spark, or something of the kind agreed upon at the outset. To distinguish from one another the various causes of the delay of the signal, the conditions of experiment are variously modified. In one set of experiments, the observer does not know beforehand whether he is to experience a flash of light, or a sound, or some sensation of touch, nor how intense the sensation will be, nor when it will come; but he knows that he is to be on the lookout for one of the three kinds of sensation. He waits, with attention all aroused. In this case, it always takes him longer to signal than if he knew beforehand the kind and the strength of the coming sensation. Moreover, his attention now makes him uneasy; the coming sensation is expected, with signs of excitement, and is often received with a start. Here the feeling of effort that accompanies attention affects by its strength the character of the impression received. Moreover, in many of these experiments there appear phenomena that show that attention alters our perception of time, not merely as to length, but also as to sequence; so that under circumstances, an impression that really precedes another can appear in consciousness as succeeding it. Yet more: attention sometimes serves to combine two sets of simultaneous impressions, and to make them seem as if proceeding from one source.

So much for the influence of attention alone. But what is attention? We reply, evidently an active process. When impressions are modified by attention, they are actively modified. And if you ask about the nature of this active process, the reply is, attention, in its most elementary forms, is the same activity that in a more developed shape we commonly call will. We attend to one thing rather than to another, because we will to do so, and our will is here the elementary impulse to know. Our attention leads us at times into error. But this error is merely an accompaniment, the result of our will activity. We want to intensify an impression, to bring it within the sphere of knowledge. But in carrying out our impulse, we do more than we meant. We not only bring something into clearer consciousness that was before out of clear consciousness, but we qualitatively modify this thing in attending to it. I want to observe a series of beats, and in observing it, I make one beat in three or four seem heavier than the others, or I even alter the apparent length of one interval in three or four, by making it seem longer than the others. I observe a series of visual impressions, and at the same time a series of auditory impressions ; if there is a certain agreement between them, I irresistibly unite these two series by my act of attention into one series, and refer them to a common cause. And so in the other cases. Attention seems to defeat, in part, its own object. Bringing something into the field of knowledge seems to be a modifying, if not a transforming, process.

We all know how this same law works on a higher plane. Giving our whole attention for a time to a particular subject seems necessary for the growth of our knowledge. Yet such attention, if long kept up, always modifies our power to know, affects our whole mental condition, and thus injures our power to appreciate the relations between the subject of our

;tudy and the other things in the world. Constant attention to one thing narrows our minds, until we fail to see the very thing we are looking at. Our lives are thus really passed in a constant flitting from one more or less partial and distorted view of things to another, from this one-sided judgment to that. Change the book you are reading, and your whole notion of the universe suffers some momentary change also. Think this week in the fashion of Carlyle, attending to things as he brings them to your attention, and human life — in fact, the whole world of being as you thought of it last week, when you were following some other guide — becomes momentarily clouded. This truth seems out of relation to that. Your change of attention qualitatively alters your apprehension of truth. Attending now even to the same things, you view them in new lights. The alteration of mental attitude becomes confusing to yourself. But refuse to make any such changes, settle down steadfastly to some one way of regarding all things, and your world becomes yet more misty. You see only a few things, and those in such a bad light that you are in danger of utter darkness. Frequent change of mental view (we of course do not mean constant change of creed or of occupation, but only frequent alteration of the direction of our thought) is essential to mental health. Yet this alteration implies at least some temporary change in our knowing powers, and so some change in our appreciation of truth.

Before going on to speak of the effect of our own activity upon our knowledge, when attention is combined with active recognition of impressions, we want to formulate the law that governs the action of attention upon sense-impressions apart from recognition. This law seems pretty well established by experience, and is, at all events, quite simple. It is this : Any act of attention tends, first, to strengthen the particular set of impressions to which it is at the moment adapted; and secondly, to modify those impressions in such a way as shall make the total impression derived from them all as simple an impression as possible. These two statements could be reduced to one, thus: Attention constantly tends to make our consciousness more definite and less complex; that is, less confused and more united. More definite, less confused attention tends to make consciousness; since, out of many vague impressions, attention fixes upon one or a few, and helps them to crowd out the others. Less complex and more united or integrated attention makes the impressions attended to ; as when, for the indefinite multiplicity of the successive even beats of a watch or of an engine, attention substitutes the simpler form of a rising and falling rhythm of more and less emphatic beats, or as when two parallel series of impressions are reduced to one, by combination. If impressions are so complex and so imperative in their demands as to impede greatly the simplifying and clarifying efforts of attention, the result is a disagreeable feeling of confusion, that may increase to violent pain.

This law, that our consciousness constantly tends to the minimum of complexity and to the maximum of definiteness, is of great importance for all our knowledge. Here we have a limitation that cannot be overleaped. Whatever we come to know, whatever opinions we come to hold, our attention it is that makes all our knowing and all our believing possible; and the laws followed by this, our own activity of attention will thus determine what we are to know and what we are to believe. If things have more than a certain complexity, not only will our limited powers of attention forbid us to unravel this complexity, but we shall strongly desire to believe the things actually much simpler than they are. For our thoughts about them will have a constant tendency to become as simple and definite as possible. Put a man into a perfect chaos of phenomena, sights, sounds, feelings ; and if the man continued to exist, and to be rational at all, his attention would doubtless soon find for him a way to make up some kind of rhythmic regularity, which he would impute to the things about him, so as to imagine that he had discovered some law of sequence in this mad new world. And thus, in every case where we fancy ourselves sure of a simple law of Nature, we must remember that a good deal of the fancied simplicity may be due in the given case not to Nature, but to the ineradicable prejudice of our own minds in favor of regularity and simplicity. All our thought is determined, in great measure, by this law of least effort, as it is found exemplified in our activity of attention.

But attention is not the only influence that goes to transform sense-impressions into knowledge. Attention never works alone, but always in company with the active process of recognizing the present as in some way familiar, and of constructing in the present ideas of what is not present. At these two other active processes we must very briefly glance.

Recognition is involved in all knowledge. Recognition does not always mean a definite memory of a particular past experience that resembles a present one. On the contrary, recognition is frequently only a sense of familiarity with something now present, coupled with a more or less distinct applying of some predicate to this present thing. I recognize a horse, a landscape, a star, a friend, a piece of music, a book, when I feel more or less familiar with the impression of the object in question, and when, at the same time, I predicate more or less distinctly something of it. This, I say, is my friend, or the north star, or Webster's Dictionary, or Smith's horse. Or, perhaps, in recognizing, I recognize, not merely the whole object, but one of its qualities, or of its relation to other things. Then I say, this is large or small, good or bad, equal or unequal to another thing, and so on. In all these cases, recognition involves a lively reaction of my mind upon external impressions. Recognition is not found apart from attention, though attention may exist more or less completely without recognition. Recognition completes what attention begins. The attentive man wants to know, the recognizing man knows, or thinks that he knows. Recognition implies accompanying attention. Attention without recognition implies wonder, curiosity, perplexity, perhaps terror. But what is the law of this process of recognition? Does the process affect the impressions themselves

that are the basis of the recognition? The answer
is: Very distinctly, recognition does affect the impressions. The activity involved in recognition alters the data of sense, and that in almost every case.
Two of the ways in which this alteration occurs
are these: (1.) In recognizing, we complete present
data by remembered past data, and so seem to experience more than is actually given to our senses.
Thus, then, in reading, we read over misprints (even
against our own will), thinking that we see words
when we do not see them, or when we see only parts
of them. Again: in listening to an indistinct
speaker we often supply what is lacking in the sounds
he makes, and seem to hear whole words when we
really hear but fragments of words. Or, merely
whistling a few notes, we recall to ourselves, and
seem to have present, the complex instrumental harmony of some music that we have heard played.
Or, in dim twilight, we imagine the form of a man,
and seem to see it plainly in detail, when, in fact, a
mass of shrubbery, or a coat on a chair, is the one
source of our impressions. In all these cases, the
activity of recognition alters the data of sense, by
adding to them, by filling out the sketch made by
them. (2.) However, even the qualities of sense-impressions are altered according to the way in which
we recognize their objects. The colors of a landscape
are dimmer, and less significant as colors, so long
as we recognize the objects in the landscape. Look
under your arm, with head inverted, and the colors
flash out with unwonted brilliancy. For when you
so look, you lose sight of the objects as such, and

give your attention solely to the colors. Mistake a few brown leaves in some dark corner of a garden for some little animal, and the leaves take on for the moment the distinctive familiar color of the animal; and when you discover your blunder, you can catch the colors in the very act of fading into their dull, dry-leaf insignificance. Many facts of this sort are recorded by psychologists and by artists, and can be observed by any of us if we choose. To separate a sensation from its modifications that are produced by recognition is not a little difficult.

Now, in both these kinds of alteration a law is observed, very similar to the one previously noted. The alterations of the data of sense in the moment of recognition are alterations in the direction of simplicity and definiteness of consciousness. The present is assimilated to the past; the new is made to seem as familiar as possible. This reaction of the mind upon new impressions is easily seen in our thoughts and words in the first moment of great surprise or fright. When Macbeth turns from his door to the table, and sees the ghost of Banquo in his chair, his first words are not the "*Avaunt, and quit my sight!*" wherewith he greets the second appearance of the ghost, nor yet even the "*Which of you have done this?*" that he utters as soon as he recovers himself. No: his first conscious reaction, in presence of the horrible impression, is a quiet remark, "*The table's full.*" And when they tell him that there is a place reserved, he persists with a "*Where?*" In this scene, Shakespeare's instinct is perfectly accurate. Our effort always is to make the new as familiar as possible, even when this new is inconceivably strange. It takes us some time to realize, as we say, a great change of any sort. Recognition, however, is yet further modified by the interest with which we at any moment attend to things. But when we speak of interest, we are led to the third kind of active modification by which our minds determine for us what we know.

At every moment we are not merely receiving, attending, and recognizing, but we are constructing. Out of what from moment to moment comes to us, we are building up our ideas of past and future, and of the world of reality. Mere dead impressions are given. We turn them by our own act into symbols of a real universe. We thus constantly react upon what is given, and not only modify it, but even give it whatever significance it comes to possess. Now this reaction takes a multitude of forms, and cannot be fully discussed without far more than our present space. But we can name one or two prominent modes of reaction of mind upon sense-data in this province of mental life.

1. Definite memory is possible only through present active construction from the data of feeling. Nothing can come to us certifying for itself that it formed a part of our previous experience. When we know a thing as past, we actively project our idea of it into a conceived past time. Without this active interference of our own minds, everything would be but a present, and there would be no time for us, only fleeting life from moment to moment.

2. Definite belief in external reality is possible

21

only through this active addition of something of our own to the impressions that are actually given to us. No external reality is given to us in the mere sense-impressions. What is outside of us cannot be at the same time within us. But out of what is in us, we construct an idea of an external world. To be sure this belief needs higher justification, like all other beliefs. But at the outset it is just an activity of ours.

3. All abstract ideas, all general truths, all knowledge of necessary laws, all acceptance of doctrines, begin in like fashion, through an active process coming from within. Change the fashions of our mental activity, and nobody can tell how radically you would change our whole conception of the universe.

4. All this active construction from sense-impressions expresses certain fundamental interests that our human spirit takes in reality. We want to have a world of a particular character; and so, from sense-impressions, we are constantly trying to build up such a world. We are prejudiced in favor of regularity, necessity, and simplicity in the world; and so we continually manipulate the data of sense for the sake of building up a notion of a regular, necessary, and simple universe. And so, though it is true that our knowledge of the world is determined by what is given to our senses, it is equally true that our idea of the world is determined quite as much by our own active combination, completion, anticipation of sense experience. Thus all knowing is, in a very deep sense, acting; it is, in fact, reacting and creation. The most insignificant knowledge

is in some sense an original product of the man who knows. In it is expressed his disposition, his power of attention, his skill in recognition, his interest in reality, his creative might. Exact knowledge is, in fact, best illustrated by cases where we ourselves make what we know. So only is mathematical knowledge possible; mathematical ideas are all products of a constructive imagination. And so it is in all other thought-life. Mentally produce, and thou shalt know thy product. But we must remember, for what we produce we are in some sense morally responsible; and thus, in discussing the nature of knowledge, we are trespassing on the border-land of ethics.

To sum up all in a few words: Plainly, since active inner processes are forever modifying and building our ideas; since our interest in what we wish to find does so much to determine what we do find; since we could not if we would reduce ourselves to mere registering machines, but remain always builders of our own little worlds, — it becomes us to consider well, and to choose the spirit in which we shall examine our experience. Every one is certain to be prejudiced, simply because he does not merely receive experience, but himself acts, himself makes experience. One great question for every truth-seeker is: In what sense, to what degree, with what motive, for what end, may I and should I be prejudiced? Most of us get our prejudices wholly from the fashions of other men. This is cowardly. We are responsible for our own creed, and must make it by our own hard work. Therefore, the deepest and most important of all questions is the one, " *For what art thou at work?*" It is useless to reply, " *I am merely noting down what I find in the world. I am not responsible for the facts.*" The answer is, " A mere note-book thou art not, but a man. These are never simply notes; thy thoughts are always transformed reality, never mere copies of reality. For thy transforming activity, as well as for thy skill in copying, thou art answerable."

V.

It is not then that postulates occur here and there in our thoughts, but that, without postulates, both practical life and the commonest results of theory, from the simplest impressions to the most valuable beliefs, would be for most if not all of us utterly impossible ; this it is which makes active faith so prominent a subject for philosophical consideration. An imperfect reflection makes that appear as blind faith which ought to appear as postulate. Instead of saying that he takes all these things on risk, and because they are worth the risk, the natural man is persuaded by such imperfect reflection to say that he trusts very ardently that he is running no risk at all. Or again : the natural man is moved to fear any examination into the bases of his thought, because he does not wish to discover that there is any risk there. And so we live dishonestly with our thoughts. Where there is a deeper basis, that involves more than mere risk, let us find it if we can. But where we have nothing better than active faith, let us discover the fact, and see clearly just why it is worth while to act in this way.

To speak more particularly of the postulates of developed science. The ancient discussions about the basis of physical knowledge of all sorts have had at least this as outcome, that it is useless to pretend to make science of any sort do without assumptions, and equally useless to undertake the demonstration of these assumptions by experience alone. No one has ever succeeded in accomplishing such a thing, and the only difference among thinkers about these assumptions is that some think it worth while to seek a transcendental basis for them all, while others insist that a transcendental basis is as impossible as a purely experimental basis is inadequate, and that in consequence we can only use the form of threat and say : Unless you make these assumptions, the spirit of science is not in you. As for the exact form that in more elaborate scientific work ought to be taken by these postulates, opinion differs very much, but an approximation to their sense may be attempted very briefly as follows.

In addition to those postulates that, as we have seen, accompany and condition all thinking alike, science may be considered as making a more special assumption. This assumption has been well defined by Professor Avenarius, in his well-known essay on " Die Philosophie als Denken der Welt Gemäss dem Princip des kleinsten Kraftmasses." He regards it as an outcome of the general law of parsimony that governs all mental work. The world of phenomena is conceived at any stage in the simplest form, and the reality that we accept is for us at any time the simplest description of the phenomena as known to us. To put this view in our own way, we might say that the world is scientifically viewed as a perfectly united whole, which would, if fully known, fully satisfy our highest mental desire for continuity and perfect regularity of conception. Therefore it is that the "universal formula" of the last chapter is a conception that expresses the scientific ideal. With less perfection, harmony, and unity of thought about the world, science will never rest content so long as she continues to be science. But for this very reason science postulates that this perfect order must be already realized in the world. It is not merely that this order is the practically unattainable but still necessary ideal for our reason; but we must postulate that this order is already present in things, far off as our thought is from it. This postulate gives life to our scientific thought. Without it our search for an order that need not exist is meaningless play.

This postulated order, however, if found, would mean for us relative simplicity and economy of conception. The infinite mass of phenomena would be conceived as one whole. The maximum of wealth of facts would be grasped with the minimum of mental effort. We postulate after this fashion that the world loves parsimony, even as we do.

To illustrate by the case of one science. A great master of mechanical science has called it the science which gives the simplest possible description of the motions in the world. If we accept this account of mechanics, we are at once puzzled by the fact that most mechanical theories make assumptions about the forces at work in the world, and that all of them predict coming facts. But forces form no part of the experience or of the mere description of motion. And the future is not yet given to be described. How then does all this agree with the definition in question? Very well indeed. For those who assume forces to explain given motions, always assume just those forces that will directly explain, not any description at random of the motions given in experience, but the simplest possible description. Any motion being relative, never for our experience absolute, we can assume at pleasure any point in the world as the origin or point of reference that shall be regarded as at rest, and so we can get an infinite number of descriptions of any given motions. We can make any object in the world move at any desired speed or in any desired direction, simply by altering the origin to which we shall choose to refer its motion in our description thereof. But all these possible descriptions are not equally useful for the purposes of the science. Some one of them is the simplest for all the motions of the system in question; and this we regard as best expressing the actual natural truth in the matter. The assumption of just such forces as would explain this simplest system of motions as described, satisfies us. We say, these forces are the real ones at work. But still we know that the forces assumed only express in another form the fact that the description in question is the simplest. Is this, however, really all that the science does with the given motions? No, one thing more the science assumes, namely, that if the system of motions in question is not subject to any external influence, it will remain fundamentally and in deepest truth the same in future, that is: *The simplest description of the given motions in a system of bodies that is wholly independent of the action of bodies without the system, this description is permanent for all states of the system.* This assumption is needed before mechanical science can venture on any prediction, or beyond mere description of past and present motions. This is the postulate of the uniformity of nature in its mechanical shape.[1] The complete present description of the world would reveal the whole future of the world.

What, however, does this postulate of uniformity express for our thought? What is the philosophical outcome of it? It expresses for our thought the demand that nature shall answer our highest intellectual needs, namely, the need for simplicity and absolute unity of conception. Mechanical science can no more do without this assumption than can any other science.

The ground that we have here very briefly passed over is known to all readers of modern controversy. We can only add our conviction that, as far as it goes, the foregoing view is a perfectly fair one. Whether or no there be any deeper basis for this

[1] Professor Clifford, in his essay on *Theories of the Physical Forces*, in his *Lectures and Essays*, vol. i., p. 109 *sqq.*, has undertaken to reduce this postulate to the general one of Continuity. The philosophical outcome would be the same.

postulate, it is sure that science makes the postulate, and does not give any deeper basis for it. For natural science it is a faith.

Now this faith, not blind faith but postulate, not basely submitted to merely because we must submit to it, but boldly assumed because we think it worth the risk, wherein does it differ from what our fundamental religious faith would be if we made of that also no mere dogmatic creed, but a general assumption, no mere passive trust, but an active postulate? Beneath all the beliefs that we could not demonstrate in our last chapter, lay the determination not so much to prove one cast-iron system of dogmas, as to find some element of reality that should have an infinite worth. The world should be at least as high as our highest conception of goodness. And to this end the partial evil should be in deepest reality universal good, even though our imperfect eyes could never show to us how this could be, - could never see through the illusion to the "imageless truth" beneath. Therefore, although we vainly sought among the Powers of the world for proof of all this, may we not still hope to approach the Eternal Reality with these postulates, and to say: "Though thou revealest to us nothing, yet we believe thee good. And we do so because this faith of ours is a worthy one." Possibly then our Religion will be just the highest form of our conduct itself, our determination to make the world good for ourselves, whatever baseness experience shows us in it. Then we can say: Just as science is undaunted by the vision of the world of confusion, so shall our religious faith be undaunted by the vision of the evil of the world. We shall war against this evil in the trust that the highest reality is not against us, but with us, just as we try to comprehend the world with the faith that the highest reality is in conformity with our private reason. In both cases we take the risk, but we take the risk because it is worth taking, because to take it is the highest form of activity. As the faith of science helps to make life rational, so the religious faith helps to make life in the highest sense moral, by insisting that the ideal labors of our moral life are undertaken not alone, but in harmony with the world as known to the Infinite.

To make the parallel a little clearer, we may say that science postulates the truth of the description of the world that, among all the possible descriptions, at once includes the given phenomena and attains the greatest simplicity; while religion assumes the truth of the description of the world that, without falsifying the given facts, arouses the highest moral interest and satisfies the highest moral needs.

All this has often been said, but it has not always been clearly enough joined with the practical suggestion that if one gives up one of these two faiths, he ought consistently to give up the other. If one is weary of the religious postulates, let him by all means throw them aside. But if he does this, why does he not throw aside the scientific postulates, and give up insisting upon it that the world is and must be rational? Yea, let him be thorough-going, and, since the very perception of the walls of his room contains postulates, let him throw away all these

postulates too, and dwell in the chaos of sensations
unfriended.   There is no reason why he should not
do this unless he sees a deeper foundation for his
postulates.   We have no mere dogmas to urge here.
Let one abandon all mere postulates if he has not
the courage to make them, but then let one consistently give them all up.   The religious postulates
are not indeed particular creeds.   One may abandon
creeds of many sorts, and yet keep the fundamental
postulate.   But if he abandons the fundamental postulate of religion, namely, that universal goodness
is somehow at the heart of things, then he ought
consistently to cease from the fundamental postulate of science, namely, that universal, order-loving
reason is somehow the truth of things.   And to do
both is to lack the courage of rational and of moral
life.

Such is the way of the postulates.   And yet we
desire to find, if we can, a more excellent way.
These postulates must be confirmed if possible, and
then subordinated to higher results.   It was the
skeptical work of the last chapter to turn attention
away from false or inconclusive methods of establishing religious faith.   There we saw how much
must seem, according to all the ordinary apologetic
methods, theoretically doubtful.   In this chapter we
have seen how postulates, theoretically uncertain,
but practically worth the risk, are at the foundation
of our whole lives.   Hereafter we shall seek to dig
beneath these foundations to that other sort of theoretical certainty whereof we have made mention.   If
we get it, then all our work will have been worth

while. Our skepticism will have saved us from an-tiquated methods, and from worn-out dogmas. Our faith will have been purified by being reduced to certain simple postulates that are not identical with the traditional creeds, although those creeds tried to express them. And both our skepticism and our faith will then finally become elements of a broader Religious Insight.

The dead external reality, into whose darkness we had to peer in vain for light, has indeed transformed itself. It is no more merely dead, or merely exter-nal. It is ours and for us. It was a world of doubt in the last chapter, just because we made it dead and external. Now that we have seen how it was the expression of postulates, it seems to have become plastic and ideal. Yet what it has gained in plas-ticity, it has lost in authority. After all, is not this business of postulating into the void a dangerous one? Is it not a hollow and empty activity this, if we really reflect upon it? Courage indeed we must have; but is religion no more than courage? Nay; we must have if possible some eternal Truth, that is not our postulate, to rest upon. Can we not get some such comfort? And may there not be some higher relation of our lives to that truth, — such a relation that the truth shall be neither the arbitrary product of our subjective postulates, nor a dead ex-ternal reality such as was the world of doubt? We are bound still to search.

CHAPTER X.

IDEALISM.

Εἰς τὸν ὅλον οὐρανὸν ἀποβλέψας τὸ ἓν εἶναί φησι τὸν θεόν.
ARISTOTLE, *concerning the doctrine of Xenophanes.*

STILL we are seeking the Eternal. Postulates
about it we must indeed make, or else we shall do
nothing. But can we not go beyond the mere postulates? Is there no other road open to the heart of
things? In fact many other ways have been suggested. The religiously interesting efforts towards
a suggestion of such ways have been the special work
of philosophical Idealism in the past. Let us then
see to what results philosophical Idealism offers to
lead us.

I.

"The world of dead facts is an illusion. The
truth of it is a spiritual life." That is what philosophical idealism says. This spiritual life may be
defined in many ways. But the multitude of the
ways of defining it do not altogether obscure the
sense of the doctrine. Plato and St. Augustine and
Berkeley and Fichte and Hegel give us very various
accounts of the spiritual life that is to be at the
heart of things, but they agree about the general
thought. As to the proof of the doctrine, very many

writers have presented this idealism as a sort of product of poetical fantasy, and have thereby helped to
bring it into disrepute. We profess no such enthusiasm. If we are to give any foundation for our
postulates by means of an idealistic doctrine, then
this foundation must be no mere poetic fancy, but a
well-framed philosophic doctrine, able to stand criticism, and to satisfy very unemotional aims, as well
as the higher moral aims themselves. But if idealism is to receive rigid theoretical tests, we may still,
in view of our present discussion and its needs, be
helped on our way more directly if we first consider
very generally and briefly what idealism could do
for us if it were established, thereafter going on to
the theoretical consideration of its claims.

That the Eternal is a world of spiritual life is
what the idealists of the past have maintained, and
the religious force of their doctrine lay not so much
in the insight that was thus offered concerning the
nature of the powers that are in the world, as in another insight. Just here idealistic doctrine and its
outcome has been seldom comprehended, even by
the idealists themselves. The world, merely viewed
as a heap of warring Powers, cannot be a world of
spiritual life. If the real world is nevertheless a
world of such spiritual life, it must be so because,
beyond and above the Powers, there is this higher
spiritual Life that includes them and watches over
them as the spectator watches the tragedy, — a Life
in which they live and move and have their being.
The characters in a tragedy do not constitute as warring powers, in their separate existence, the signifi-

cance of the tragedy. The spectator, the overseeing thought, for which and in which these fancied powers contend, this it is that gives them unity and significance. Even so the highest spiritual life that the idealist finds in the world is not to be a power among other powers, but a thought for which exists all that is. Hence the deepest assertion of idealism is not that above all the evil powers in the world there is at work some good power mightier than they, but rather that through all the powers, good and evil, and in them all, dwells the higher spirit that does not so much create as constitute them what they are, and so include them all.

How all this is to be more fully explained, and how it is to be justified, if at all, by idealism, we shall see further on. But for the present we may suggest that such idealism as this has a peculiar advantage in dealing with the problems that we found insoluble in the discussion of the world of the Powers. There we found a world of contending elementary forces, A, B, C, etc. As contending powers they must needs appear finite. If one was good, another was or might be evil. And as we had to deal only with the warring elements, the thought that partial evil may, after all, be universal good seemed not very plausible, and quite indemonstrable. The world being the collection of the powers that are in it, the good and evil of the whole seemed to be the sum of the separate good and evil elements. But now we have a thought that may make possible the existence of universal goodness. If the tragedy as a whole is good, although its elements are evil, so like the trag-

edy may the world be universally good if the single
evils of reality, like the single parts of the tragedy,
are elements in a whole that exists for an all-seeing, all-inclusive Spirit, in whom are all things, and
whose nature as a whole is good. Thus, then, if we
cannot yet see just *how* the partial evil is universal
good in the all-inclusive mind, we can already, from
the outset at least, fancy that it may so be. The All-
Enfolding may be good even although of necessity
there are elements in his world of infinite experience
that, separately considered, may be evil. So idealism offers as its theodicy not that the world contains
a surplus of good powers, or that the creative power,
when it made the devilish powers, still meant well;
but the theodicy of idealism suggests a way in which
evil may be, after all, a partial view of an all-embracing goodness.

Hence the importance, for our present discussion,
of an effort to treat calmly and critically the main
doctrine of philosophic idealism. Here at least is
some suggestion of a chance that we may, in time,
come to rise above mere postulates, and may found
a positive religious theory. For the postulates are
indeed, in themselves, not enough. We want, if
possible, to get beyond them, though we are ready to
accept them as final if we can do no better. Yet
we are still forced to begin our account of idealistic
doctrine with nothing better than postulates.

II.

The imperfection of the author's private understanding of deeper truth has forced him to come to idealism in the first instance by a very straight and easy path, that most deeper idealists would deride. After he had by that road reached the definite conception of one form of idealism, he found a further thought by which this idealism seemed to be transformed into a doctrine of greater philosophical and religious significance. At the same time, the proof of the doctrine first seemed to him to become clear and all-embracing. Now a reader cares little for the contents of an author's note-book, or for a history of his opinions; but sometimes the exposition of a view is a little helped by presenting it in successive parts that follow in their order somewhat the line of the author's own development. Hence the present chapter shall suggest philosophic idealism as a mere hypothesis, that still only tries to express our fundamental postulates. Then we shall go on to see what deeper foundation for it we can find. And furthermore, our first suggestion of idealism shall be a purely theoretical conception, not assumed to satisfy directly an ethical postulate, but merely to express theoretical postulates about the world. Then we shall be able to see what religious doctrine can be built upon this foundation. This way commends itself as avoiding the greatest danger of idealism, namely, fantastic speculation with noble purposes, but with merely poetical methods. Our present method shall be coldly theoretical, how-

22

ever deeply our religious philosophy is concerned in the outcome.

For the first then we shall suppose our whole task to be the suggestion of a plausible, *i. e.* of a simple, adequate, and consistent hypothesis about the nature of external reality. Hereafter we shall consider more critically the foundation of such hypotheses. Provisionally, then, we shall suppose that, by a perfect theory of knowledge, the following result has been reached : Human beings are able to form ideas that correspond in some way with a real world, outside of themselves. That is, the sequence of human ideas corresponds to sequences of external events, or to relations of coexistence among external things. The necessary or uniform connections of human ideas correspond to regular or to universal connections among external things. Or, in the brief form of Mr. Herbert Spencer's phraseology, to each necessary relation $a : b$ in human consciousness there corresponds a relation $A : B$ in the external world. Suppose, then, that all this has been established. No one will admit more readily than the writer that this supposition is at this point merely tentative. Our theory of knowledge is yet to be completed, and between its conception and its realization there are still wide oceans of doubt. We shall, in fact, deal with the problems of this theory in the next chapter. But for the moment suppose admitted what scientific thought generally takes for granted, namely, the correspondence of inner and outer relations in such wise that the former are naturally copies of the latter. And, on this foundation, suppose that we intend to consider what hypothesis as to the nature of the related terms A and B in the external world is, on the whole, the most plausible.

For the sake of avoiding controversy we may for the moment leave out of account two old questions. We cannot really escape either, and both will sternly confront us before we get in at the door of the temple of certainty. But here at the outset we are playing with hypotheses, and may be absolved from the responsibility of securing ourselves beforehand from all possible attacks. The first is the question of the idealists: How can any reality be conceived unless as implying or including states of consciousness? For the moment we will waive this part of the Berkeleyan contention altogether; for we are not yet concerned to prove by metaphysical analysis the universal coincidence of consciousness and reality. We wish merely a plausible hypothesis to be advanced as to the nature of what more popular thought means by reality. The second question that at the outset we avoid is the one concerning the ground of the assumed agreement between the external and the internal orders of facts. Whether this ground lies in a causal determination of our consciousness by the external world, or in a preëstablished harmony of both, matters not. We first take our stand, then, upon the facts admitted by popular belief. Here are feelings, sequences of feelings, thoughts, trains of thought, systems of scientific belief: all internal facts. Beyond the consciousness of these internal facts stretches (so we now assume, and only assume) another world of facts, in which something corresponds to each one of these feelings, some order of facts to each sequence of feeling, some system of facts and of laws to each properly constituted system of beliefs. The external order of the world beyond corresponds to the order of this internal world of our consciousness, but is not this order. A plausible hypothesis is required as to the nature of this corresponding external order.

Let us examine Berkeley's familiar hypothesis, which, as a mere hypothesis, we can examine apart from any study of Berkeley's philosophical arguments for his idealism. According to Berkeley there exist conscious beings, more or less like ourselves, of whom the head and father is God. Now external to all beings besides God there is a real world. This real world is made up of the eternal system of God's thoughts.

" When I deny sensible things an existence out of the mind, I do not mean my mind in particular, but all minds. Now it is plain they have an existence exterior to my mind, since I find them by experience to be independent of it. There is some other mind wherein they exist, during the intervals between the times of my perceiving them ; as likewise they did before my birth, and would do after my supposed annihilation. And as the same is true with regard to all other finite created spirits, it necessarily follows, there is an *Omnipresent Eternal Mind*, which knows and comprehends all things, and exhibits them to our view in such a manner, and according to such rules as he himself hath ordained, and are by us termed the *laws of nature*." [1]

1 *Dialogues between Hylas and Philonous*, III.

This so familiar hypothesis of Berkeley is in part founded upon a thought that for the present we have agreed to neglect, *i. e.* upon the notion of the external world as the *cause* of our internal impressions. Not being caused by myself, my ideas, reasons Berkeley, must have an external cause. And the only intelligible cause is an active spirit. Yet for our present purpose this thought is not important. We are not asking about the cause of our conscious states, but about the way in which we can most plausibly conceive of an external world corresponding to these states. The correspondence is assumed. Into its ground, be it preëstablished harmony or physical influence, we do not just now inquire. Our only criteria of plausibility, if causal explanation is dropped, are therefore adequacy, simplicity, and consistency. Is Berkeley's hypothesis consistent with itself, and is it the simplest hypothesis possible? Stripped of non-essential features, the hypothesis is that there corresponds to our consciousness another higher and farther-reaching consciousness, containing all that is abiding in our consciousness, and much more besides. This consciousness is in form and matter a rational spirit, having definite purposes in the creation and education of the various finite spirits. These purposes require for their accomplishment that our conscious states should within certain limits agree with this higher consciousness, — should correspond to it in form and to a certain extent. This correspondence constitutes what we mean by truth. There is no external world but this other consciousness.

To Berkeley, as we know, the essential part of

this doctrine was the teleological part. That God's thoughts and our correspondence thereto result from and express God's purposes in creating the world, this was for Berkeley the main point to be proven. But if the teleological element of the doctrine be for this first left out of account, there is another part that we just now wish to hold fast. *Our thought is true by reason of its correspondence to the facts of an actual consciousness, external to our own:* this hypothesis has an interest apart from its origin and from its original use. Why in philosophy should we be afraid of doctrines because they have an association with some dreaded theological dogma, or with some enthusiastic and over-confident system of the past? About the nature of the external world we have at the outset nothing but hypotheses. Before we test them in any very exact way, we may with safety try to understand them. Perhaps what seemed the wildest of them all may turn out to be the very best. Because a certain hypothesis was put forward rather as a demonstrable and eternal truth than as a hypothesis, shall we reject it without further examination? Perhaps it may in fact turn out to be part of the eternal truth.

The hypothesis now before us is Berkeley's with the teleological element omitted, along with the causal. How this external consciousness comes to affect us, and why it takes just such forms as it does, we say not. This we ask: What is this supposed external consciousness? How does it correspond to our own? We shall not call the supposed consciousness by question-begging names. It is not for us just now either absolute or divine. It is simply consciousness, and external. The hypothesis is that truth consists in some kind of correspondence between our thought and this outer reality. What kind of correspondence?

Two conscious beings can have corresponding states of consciousness, without having like states. The notes of a melody could have corresponding to them the variations in intensity of some source of light. The light-flashes or beats would correspond to the notes of music by having the like rhythm; yet there would be no resemblance in the content. Correspondence may be yet more obscured. The dashes on a piece of paper that has passed under the point of a telegraphic pen, the series of characters printed from the press in a dozen languages, the sounds of the voice of a reader, the series of signals flashed from shore to a distant vessel, all these dissimilar series of events might correspond exactly and throughout, if it were their purpose to convey in various ways the same meaning. In order, then, that my consciousness should correspond to some other consciousness, external to mine, it is only necessary that for each event or fact in my consciousness there should exist some event or fact in the other consciousness, and that some relation existing among my conscious states should be like or parallel to the relation existing among the conscious states external to mine. The more numerous the points of resemblance between the two series of states, the closer the correspondence. But correspondence in the abstract implies only some one definite and permanent resemblance found throughout the two series.

Such being the nature of correspondence in general, let us consider our hypothesis more in detail. Suppose the clock yonder has some such reality as this hypothesis supposes. There is the clock, with its pendulum beating. For me now that clock is a combination of sensations, joined with a belief in certain possible sensations. For one in the same room with me, the clock has a like existence. But suppose that the clock has, apart from my consciousness, apart from the consciousness of any other human being or animal, an existence for some other, as yet undefined, consciousness. Suppose that for this consciousness the clock in its whole present condition exists, not at all as a " possibility of sensations," but solely and in all its parts as a present group of sensible facts, standing in definite relations. Suppose that the sensible facts that constitute this clock as it is given to this hypothetical consciousness are in quality unlike the sensations that for me constitute the clock; but that in their relations, in their number, in their grouping, in their differences from one another, these sensible facts as they are for the hypothetical consciousness agree with the sensations and with the "possibilities of sensation" that for me constitute the clock. Suppose that the clock as it is in the hypothetical consciousness endures for a considerable time, and is called the real clock. Then when I shut my eyes or go away or die, there exists still the real clock, *i. e.* the clock in the hypothetical consciousness. Though all my fellows die, there is still the real clock, independent of our consciousness. The clock may for a time go on running; that is, in the hypothetical consciousness there may be a rhythm of sensible events, corresponding to what for me, were I present, would be the rhythm of the pendulum-beats and the movement of the hands.

Now suppose this hypothetical consciousness extended, so that it contains facts corresponding to my ideas of the ether-vibrations that fall upon or that are reflected from the face of this clock. Suppose that it further contains facts corresponding to each of my ideas of the relative position of this clock and of other objects. Suppose at last that the hypothetical consciousness is extended to all the facts of what I call my universe of actual and of possible sensation. Suppose that each possible or actual experience of each moment in my life or in the life of any other animal is represented by some actual momentarily present fact in the hypothetical consciousness. Then consider the hypothetical consciousness at any moment, and see what it will contain. Every material atom, every wave of ether, every point of space, every configuration of material bodies, every possible geometrical relation, will be represented in the hypothetical consciousness by some definite fact. The relations of these facts will be in nature and in complexity similar to the relations among the facts of my actual or possible sensations. On the other hand, the limits of my possible consciousness at any moment will be determined by the actual consciousness of this supposed universal Knowing One. What it actually knows, I conceivably might now know. If it is conscious of a certain series of facts, then I might be conscious, were I now on the other side of the moon, of living creatures there. If the hypothetical consciousness contains another set of facts, then I might be unable to find such living beings were I there. And so with all facts of possible experience.

We can easily see how, under this supposition, conformity to the supposed universal consciousness will become on my part a goal of effort. Knowledge of possible experiences is useful to me. But all possible experiences are or will be actual in the hypothetical consciousness. If I am standing near a concealed pitfall, or am in danger of a blow, or in danger of death from poison, that fact, translated into ultimate terms, means, we may suppose, that in the universal consciousness there is now the knowledge of certain relative positions and motions of atoms. The sequence of states in the universal consciousness must be supposed to be a regular sequence, subject to fixed law. But sequence does not now especially concern us; since we speak only of the nature of this external consciousness. It is enough, therefore, to point out that this supposed universal knowing consciousness, this " Not-Ourselves," has, under the conditions stated, all the essential characteristics of a real world. It is beyond us; it is independent of us; its facts have a certain correspondence to our sensations. Under the supposition that by nature we tend to be in agreement with this consciousness, progress in the definiteness and extent of our agreement with it may be both possible and practically useful. This agreement would constitute truth.

No other real world need be supposed behind or above this consciousness. Rejection of an old theory and acceptance of a new, as when the Copernican doctrine replaces the Ptolemaic, will mean the growth of a belief that the new system of ideas corresponds more nearly than the old, not with dead matter, but with the sequence of states in the universal consciousness. The universal consciousness itself will be no illusory consciousness. It will not need a further consciousness to support it. It will need no dead matter outside of it. Our nature leads us to look up to it as to our model. Itself is the pattern, looking up to no other model. The purpose of thought will be conformity with this perfect, untrammeled thought. For us there is a little range of actual sensation, in the midst of a vast ocean of possible sensation. For the universal consciousness there are at any moment only actual data. We see the clock-face ; and for us the inside of the clock is possible sensation only. For the supposed consciousness the inside will be as much present as the outside. For us colors and odors suggest possible sensations, which science interprets as being in the last analysis the possible sensations known as atoms, motions, velocities, distances. For the universal consciousness, these atoms, motions, velocities, and distances, or the ultimate facts to which these notions correspond, are not possible but actual data. There need be then, in the last analysis, no dead unconscious atoms, nor yet unconscious little atom-souls, striving, fighting, loving, uniting ; there need be in the last analysis only a consciousness of facts corresponding to what we mean by motion, velocity, extension, distance, impenetrability. Corresponding to the relation $a : b$ in our consciousness there will then be the external fact $A : B$, whereof so much is supposed to be known : first, that the relation $a : b$ is somewhat like the relation $A : B$; secondly, that the terms A and B, whatever their particular character, are facts for a consciousness, and nothing but facts for a consciousness. And the hypothetical consciousness for which these facts are all present, together with their manifold relations, this we may call a World-Consciousness. An illusion in my consciousness will mean a failure to correspond with the world-consciousness. A truth for my consciousness will be a relation $a : b$ that corresponds with some relation $A : B$ in the world-consciousness. But for the world-consciousness itself there will be no question of its own truth or falsity. It will be for and in itself. It will not have to create a real world ; it will be a real world. It will not have a Nature as its own Otherness, over against itself. It will be in its own facts and in their sequence a nature. As to the individual intelligences, its relation to them is so far viewed as one of independence. Whether hereafter we shall be forced to modify our view or not, so far we treat the individual intelligences as separate from the world consciousness. They are neither its "emanations" nor its "modes." But their whole business and purpose will be to carry out and to make full and definite that correspondence with this universal consciousness upon which their existence and their peace depend. A certain lack of correspondence with the universal consciousness on the part of any animal's ideas will be followed by the cessation of that particular grouping of facts in the universal consciousness that is known to us as this animal's body. With the dissolution of this animal's body will cease his consciousness, his chance of disagreeing in his states with the states of the universal consciousness, and therefore his lack of correspondence. An ultimate law of sequence, with which, as with all causal connection, we have here nothing to do, thus binds the individual beings to the World-Consciousness. The whole universe exhibits the phenomenon, first, of one great consciousness, embracing an infinitude of geometrical, physical, chemical, physiological facts ; and, secondly, of a vast multitude of individual conscious beings, whose number and sorts we shall never be able to tell, whose destiny, however, demands of all of them a more or less imperfect likeness between their states and the relations thereof on the one hand, and the facts of the universal consciousness on the other hand. The universal consciousness, be it noted, is so called thus far as including in its ken all ultimate mathematical and physical facts. Of its nature beyond this we pretend to suppose nothing. And we have not supposed it to include the individual conscious beings. Our hypothesis is not yet pantheistic, nor theistic. We simply suppose a " Not - Ourselves " that includes all natural knowledge. This is the External Reality.

We have omitted, moreover, all reference to the teleological element that is generally introduced into ny theory of a World-Spirit. So far, in fact, our World-Consciousness is not what people mean by a World-Spirit. A Spirit, "weaving the living robe of Deity," our World-Consciousness is not; for as so far described it does nothing, it merely looks on. It looks at its own states, and these are supposed to be altogether its own, given from no higher source. But as to their succession or their worth, their beginning or their end, we have said nothing. This Consciousness has these states, but we have supposed them as yet to be attended by no emotion of pleasure or of pain, by no modifying reaction of will. This consciousness is not a Creator, it is a Seer. As for the individual conscious beings, it does not make or unmake them by an exercise of power. They, on the contrary, are made and unmade according as there arise or disappear in this universal consciousness certain groups of data that, as represented in our mortal thought, are called organic living bodies, with tissues, motions, structures, functions. These groups pass, and with them the individual consciousness that coexisted with each. This growth and decay is simply a law of experience, an ultimate and inexplicable sequence. But the universal consciousness of nature, for which each of these groups of physical facts existed, that remains. In other words : Each animal body is represented in the universal consciousness, and exists only in so far as it is represented therein, or is known to its possessor or to other animals. The individual mind that coexists with this body has thus far no representative in the universal consciousness, but seems to exist and be real for itself. With the group of facts in the universal consciousness to which, as we say, corresponds our idea of the body, the independent group of facts called the animal's mind lives and dies. The universal consciousness and the individual minds make up together the sum total of reality. So far and so far only do we as yet go. The sequel will show whether we can rest content with this.

Continuing to mention the consequences of our hypothesis, we see that the well-known questions so often asked of idealists are no longer puzzling when we accept such an idea as the foregoing. Such questions are : What existed before there was any conscious life on the planet? In what sense was there light or heat, matter or motion, before there were eyes to see, tactile organs to feel, animal intelligence to understand these external facts? The question of Kant too about the subjectivity of space would seem to have been answered. Before there were conscious beings on this planet, this planet existed only in and for the universal consciousness. In that consciousness were facts corresponding to all the phenomena, or possibilities of experience, that geological science may declare to have really existed at such a time. When the earth became filled with life, there appeared in the universal consciousness the data known as organisms. And at the same time, beside the universal consciousness, somehow related to it, there arose individual conscious beings, whose states were more or less imperfect copies of the universal consciousness in certain of its facts. Even so, empty space is now existent beyond the borders of finite observation only as a group of states in the world-consciousness. Space is subjective, belonging to the states of the universal consciousness; and yet to us objective, since in thinking it we merely conform ourselves to the universal consciousness. But the consequences of our hypothesis are numberless. Enough has been said of them for the present purpose.

Wild and airy indeed! But why so? The ordinary uncritical Atomism is a worse hypothesis, because we never get from it the least notion of how this eternally existent matter may look and feel when nobody sees or feels it. The mystical " one substance with two faces " is worse, because that is no hypothesis, only a heap of words. Schopenhauer's " Wille " is worse, because it is only a metaphor. The hypothesis that ascribes to the atoms independent life and volition is no more adequate than our hypothesis, and much less simple. The old-fashioned pantheistic " Welt-Geist " of Schelling, and of the romantic philosophy generally, is more poetical than our hypothesis, but that Welt-Geist is a Power; and no one ever comes to understand how this One Spirit, who after all is represented as a sort of big half-conscious Daemon, a gigantic worker, is related to the many individual minds. They are parts of him, or else apart from him. In the one case their confidence that they really exist as powers and are not " things in his dream," is unfounded; in the other case his all-embracing unity is destroyed. In our hypothesis nothing is as yet wonderful but the one miracle of the series of orderly conscious states, following through

all time according to fixed laws. Beyond that all
is clear. That there should be a consciousness containing ideas of all material relations, is no harder
to believe than it is to believe in the ordinary unintelligible world of atoms. That beside this consciousness, and in fixed relation to its facts, there
should exist a great number of different series of
conscious states, each series being called an individual, this is no harder to believe than are the ordinary facts of nervous physiology. In reality this
hypothesis gives us a simple expression, easily intelligible, for all the facts and laws of physics, of nervous physiology, and of consciousness. Take, as a
final case, Professor Clifford's well-known example of
the man looking at the candle. In the world-consciousness there is the group of states c, c', c''. . . .
That is the real candle. In the world-consciousness
there is also the group of states h, h', h''. . . . That
is the " cerebral image" of the candle, a physiological fact. Finally, according to the laws of reality,
the existence in the world-consciousness of the facts
h, h', h'', . . . grouped as they are, has coexistent
with it the group of ideas C in the man's mind.
This group C corresponds more or less completely to
the group c, c' c'', . . . as that group exists beyond
the man's mind, in the world-consciousness. The
group C is the man's idea of the candle. Such is
our hypothesis in a nut-shell. We urge for the moment only this in its favor : that it is simple, intelligible, plausible. After all, it is but an hypothesis.
We must now follow it until we shall find it, by virtue of one momentous consideration, suddenly trans-

23

formed from an hypothesis into a theory, and from a doctrine of an eternal normal thought into a doctrine of an all-embracing Spirit.

III.

In several respects our hypothesis needs explanation before it can well please a philosophic student. This explanation will next lead us into a decidedly technical discussion, and this a reader not specially accustomed to philosophic discussions, if such a reader we yet have, will do well to omit. We must in fact, in the present section, more particularly set forth the motives that have determined us to try just this hypothesis about Reality.

First, then, we are concerned to show why we have left out of view the causal element that popular thought makes so prominent in its conception of Reality. For popular thought, the world is a Power that causes our perceptions. But we, both here and in our subsequent religious discussion, shall consider the eternal not as Power, but as Thought. Why is this? We shall here try to explain, still regarding the real world merely as something postulated to meet the inner needs of our thought. Let us ask, without as yet going beyond this point of view, what is the deepest motive of our purely theoretic postulates about reality? Is it not to have something that *corresponds to our ideas*, and so gives them truth? Therefore is not the postulate that reality corresponds to our ideas, deeper than the postulate that a real world causes our ideas? And so is not the

causal postulate in fact but a subordinate form in
our theory of the world? To exemplify. When I
say that my thought demands some cause, C, for a
sensation, s, does not my thought even here actually
demand something prior to the principle of causation, and deeper than that? Does not my thought
here demand that my idea c of cause in general, and
my idea r of the causal relation R between C and s,
shall *a priori* somehow correspond to the truth of
things? Can I conceive of a real cause save by virtue of a postulate that my conception of a real cause
is like the real cause itself? Therefore, when men
say: "We know external Reality because we know
that our sensations need a cause, and that this cause
must be external to us," do they say more than this:
"We know (or postulate) that to one of our ideas,
namely, the idea of a necessary causal relation, there
corresponds a reality external to the idea?" For
surely I do not know the validity of my idea of a
causal relation merely on the ground that I know
that this idea of causal relation must itself have
been caused by the real existence of causal relations
in the world. Such an attempt to justify my idea
would mean endless regress. The deeper notion
that we have of the world is therefore founded on
the insight or on the postulate that there must be,
not merely a sufficient cause for our thought, but a
sufficient counterpart thereto.

We can easily illustrate this view by considering
the nature of our thought about past time. The
judgment or assertion that there has actually been
a series of past events, is not a judgment of causal-

ity.   I believe in a past as I believe in a future, not
to satisfy my faith in the principle of causality, but
to satisfy my tendency to postulate an indefinite
time-stream, like in nature to my present succession
of immediately given states.   I believe in a real
time, not primarily as the cause but as the counterpart of my notion of time.   How otherwise shall I
form the idea of a cause at all, unless I have already
assumed the reality of time?   A cause for my belief in the past is to be conceived, if at all, only as
already a past fact.   The conception that it is to create is a condition of its own existence, unless indeed
one has admitted what we wish admitted, that, however the case may be with the belief in any one past
fact, the belief in past reality as such is prior to our
belief that our present state has been caused by the
past.   But the same priority of the belief in some
agreement between my idea and the external reality,
is found in all departments of thought.   A material
cause of my experience is a cause in space.   But,
however I came by the idea of space, my present belief in the reality of space precedes any particular
belief in a material cause for a particular sensation,
and renders the latter belief possible.   The conception of reality furnished by the search for causes is
thus always subordinate to the conception of reality
furnished by our first postulate.   This first postulate is, that our ideas have something beyond them
and like them.   So at each moment of my life I
postulate a past and future of my own, like my present consciousness, but external thereto.   So my social consciousness, my original unreflective tendency

to work with and for other beings, implies the postulate of the external existence of my fellow-men, like myself and like my ideas of them. So to the present intuition of the space in the retinal field or at my finger tips I join the postulate of an infinitely extended not perceived space, like the perceived space, and like my space-ideas.

The external reality conceived by us is therefore, so far as we have yet seen, conceived through a spontaneous reaction of the receiving consciousness in presence of the senso-data received. The forms of this reaction it was the purpose of the Critical Philosophy to define. The task set by Kant has not yet been accomplished. But the fact of some reaction seems established. And the general law of the process seems to be that the external reality is conceived after the pattern of the present data, with such modification as is necessary to bring the conception into harmony with already established habits of thought, and with the conceived results of previous experience. The aim of the whole process seems to be to reach as complete and united a conception of reality as is possible, a conception wherein the greatest fullness of data shall be combined with the greatest simplicity of conception. The effort of consciousness seems to be to combine the greatest richness of content with the greatest definiteness of organization.

This character of our activity in forming our notion of reality implies the subordination of the causal postulate to other motives. In the scientific field the postulate of causality is predominant, because there the notion of a world of causal sequences in

time and in space has been already built up, and
what remains is to fill out the picture by discovering
the particular sequences. But if I try to banish altogether from my notion of external reality the idea
that it is an adequate counterpart of my subjective
states of consciousness, what will remain? Simply
the notion of an utterly unknowable external cause
of my sensations. Of this nothing will be said, but
that it is. Science, experience, serious reflection
about reality, will utterly cease. I shall have remaining a kind of Disfigured Realism, where the
real will be as unknowable, as unreal as possible.
But reintroduce the omitted postulate, admit that
reality is conceived as the counterpart of my consciousness, and then the principle of causality can
be fruitfully applied. Then indeed experience may
lead us to conceive the external reality as unlike
this or that suggestive sensation, unlike this or that
provisional idea. But we shall be led to new conceptions, and shall be able to make definite progress, so
long as we postulate some sort of likeness between
inner and outer.

In brief, as causality means uniform sequence, the
acceptance of any causal relation as real involves
a conception of the uniform sequence that is to be
accepted. When finally accepted, the sequence in
question is conceived as a real fact, wholly or partially external to present consciousness, but like our
present idea of itself. Causal sequence cannot therefore be placed first, as giving us a totally undefined
notion of an external reality; but second, as ena-
bling us to develop in detail the idea that reality is

like our own states of consciousness. Of course to
prove by sense experience that the external reality
is like our states of consciousness, this we can never
accomplish. But from the outset we have seen that
verification through experience is in this field impossible. The whole of this sensuous reality, past, present, future, all that is outside of what one now sees
and feels, all space, time, matter, motion, life beyond
this immediate experience, — all that is so far only
a postulated experience, and therefore never a datum, never in detail verifiable for sense. Since we
believe in this external reality, if experience suggests
with sufficient force the idea that some causal sequence is real, our postulate that such suggestions
have their counterpart in an external world leads us
to regard the conceived causal sequence as an externally real fact. Not however do we first conceive of
the external reality as cause, and then in the second
place only find it to be or not to be the counterpart
of present consciousness. All our thinking is based
on the postulate that the external reality is a counterpart and not merely a cause. If with time, we
drop mythological conceptions of external reality,
we do so only because, in the presence of a larger
and fuller experience, we no longer find old conceptions, founded largely on lower forms of emotion and
on narrower experience, adequate to our notion of
the external counterpart of consciousness. For demons and entities we substitute atoms and ethereal
media, not because we abandon the position that external reality resembles our ideas, but because wider
experience is found to be best reduced to unity by

the latter, not by the former ideas. The atoms and the media are themselves only provisional notions, since more experience may be better reduced to unity, for all we yet know, by some other ideas. But throughout remains the postulate : external reality is somewhat like our ideas of its nature.

We have been betrayed by the doctrine that we have combated into forms of speech that do not adequately express the Critical notion of reality. We hasten to complete our conception by adding the omitted elements. External reality is like our conceptions of it ; so much, we have seen, is universally postulated (postulated, be it noticed, not directly experienced, not forced upon us from without). But the kind of likeness still remains to be defined. Can the external reality be conceived as being, although in nature like our conscious states, yet in no necessary relation to consciousness, as being neither a consciousness nor for a consciousness? The answer is the whole struggle of idealistic thought, the whole progress of philosophical analysis in modern times. One cannot go over the field again and again forever. The state of the controversy can be roughly stated thus: When the notion of external reality is based solely upon the application of the notion of causality, all degrees of likeness or unlikeness between thought and things are assumed, according to the tastes of individual thinkers. External reality is once for all absolved from the condition of being intelligible, and becomes capable of being anything you please, a dead atom, an electric fluid, a ghost, a devil, an Unknowable. But if the subordinate character of this postulate of causality is once understood, the conception of reality is altered. What is real must be not only vaguely correspondent to an ill-defined postulate, but in a definite relation of likeness to my present consciousness. That this is the actual postulate of human thought is shown by those systems themselves that ignore the postulate of likeness, and has been illustrated in the foregoing. But what forms does this postulated likeness take? For the first, the postulated likeness between my idea and the external reality may be a likeness between my present conscious state and a past or future state of my own, or between this present state and the conscious state of another being. The whole social consciousness implies the postulate of a likeness between my ideas and an actual consciousness external to mine, fashioned in my own image. But the second generally recognized form in which the postulate of the likeness of internal and external appears is the form according to which I postulate that a present idea of my own is not like one of my own past or future states, not like any actual past or future state in another being of my own kind, but like a possible experience. That our ideas can adequately express possibilities of sensation that are actually never realized, either in ourselves or in any other known creature, this is a familiar postulate of natural science. The laws of nature are generally, as is admitted by all, what Lewes called "ideal constructions," expressing experiences for us never realized, but permanently possible. And so extended is the use of the concept of possible experience, that, as we know, Mill in one of his most interesting chapters gave "permanent possibility of sensation" as an adequate definition of matter.

Now the position of modern phenomenism is, that by these two postulates, or forms of the one postulate of Likeness, the whole notion of external reality is exhausted.

The external world means, according to this position, the possible and actual present, past, and future content of consciousness for all beings. And this result of modern phenomenism we regard, thus far, as the most acceptable postulate about the world. Either as postulate or as demonstrable theory the position is maintained by all the modern idealists. You can find it, for example, stated in Fichte's "Bestimmung des Menschen" and other shorter philosophic essays (less successfully, we think, though much more at length, in the two larger expositions of the "Wissenschaftslehre), in the Hegelian "Phänomenologie," in Schopenhauer's "Welt als Wille und Vorstellung," in Ferrier's "Institutes of Metaphysic," in J. S. Mill's "Examination of Hamilton," in Mr. Shadworth Hodgson's "Time and Space" and "Philosophy of Reflection," in M. Renouvier's "Logique Générale," in lesser books innumerable, for example, in Professor Baumann's "Philosophie als Orientirung über die Welt" (in the first chapter), in Professor Schuppe's "Erkenntnisstheoretische Logik," in Professor Bergmann's "Reine Logik." Not of course that all this multitude of thinkers, different in method, in ability, in aim, in everything but in the fact that they are post-Kantian idealists, would accept the foregoing statement as a fairly complete account of their doctrines. Some of them would laugh at the simplicity of our terms. But, we choose to mention so confused a list to show how, in the midst of the greatest variations, they all agree about one fundamental truth, namely, that thought, when it inquires into its own meaning, can never rest satisfied with any idea of external reality that makes such reality other than a datum of consciousness, and so material for thought. Sensualism and the most transcendent *a priori* speculation agree in coming at last to flee in ceaseless unrest from every support for an external reality that may seem to offer itself beyond the bounds of consciousness. This phenomenism of post-Kantian speculation we accept, as at all events the simplest and least contradictory postulate.

So much, then, for one motive of our hypothesis about the world-consciousness. Reality appears as the object either of an actual or of a possible consciousness. But there remains in this definition of the postulate still one obscure point. What is meant by possible consciousness? What can there be for consciousness beyond the grand total of all actual past and future states of consciousness in all beings? For what purpose and by what right shall we build a world of possibility above or beside the world of actual experience? This question seems too little appreciated and too much evaded by most thinkers. When Mill called matter a "permanent possibility of sensation," he left room open for the puzzling question: But what is this creature called a possibility? Is it an actual fact? Then what actual fact? If not actual, then in being a mere possibility matter is non-existent.

This scholastic character of the abstract noun "possibility" was remarked and criticised by Professor Max Müller in an article in "Mind," III.[1] We shall not find in most writers on this subject less scholastic or better defined terms for naming the same aspect of the postulate of external reality. In fact, if we suppose that one surveys the whole range of actual consciousness, past, present, and future, and postulates no facts that are not for and in consciousness, it is difficult to see what will be the meaning of any added "possible reality." Possible, for the first, is anything that one conceives, in so far as one conceives it at all. I could possibly have wings and a long tail, an hundred eyes, and a mountain of gold. All that is possible, but in what sense? In this sense, that I do actually imagine myself as possessing these things. "Empty possibilities," or "imaginations as one would," are facts of consciousness in so far forth as they are imagined ; and they have no other existence. The world of truth is not enriched by these possibilities, whose whole existence is in the actual conscious idea of them. But not in this

---

[1] P. 347. "If therefore Mill and his followers imagine that by defining Matter as the permanent possibility of sensation, and Mind as the permanent possibility of feeling, they have removed the difficulty of Kant's *Ding an sich*, they are mistaken. Their possibility of sensation, if properly analyzed, means things or substances which can become objects of sensation." Professor Müller's result is not one that we can wholly accept ; his criticism of the word possibility is important.

sense is matter to be a "permanent possibility of
sensation." The icebergs in the polar seas are to be
real, not in so far as I now imagine them, but in so
far as there exists or holds good the law, that were
I present I should see them, were I to touch them I
should feel them, and that both seeing and feeling
would be determined in certain ways beyond the
control of my will. The pages of that closed book,
the bones inside the body of that cat, my own brain,
the molecules of the oxygen that I am breathing, all
these, in so far as they are not now actually in my
consciousness, are to be still real as "possible experiences." But what kind of unreal reality is this
potential actuality?

If we inquire into the motive that leads us to
postulate these possible experiences, we shall find it
to be the familiar and universal wish to apply the
postulate of uniformity to our confused actual experience. Our actual experience is not always gov-
erned by obvious laws of regular sequence. But in
postulating consciousness beyond our own immediate
data, we are led, by our known prejudice in favor of
unity and simplicity, to postulate that the real suc-
cessions of facts are uniform, whatever may be the
case with the fragments of reality that fall within
our individual experience. I see an apple fall, and
no more than that. But I postulate that if I could
have had experience of all the facts, I should have
observed a series of material changes in the twig on
which the apple hung, that would have sufficed to
restore the broken uniformity and continuity of my
experiences. In this way it is that, as remarked

above, the conception of causal sequence does not create, but organizes and perfects, our notion of external reality. There is something beyond our experience, namely, another experience; that is the first postulate. Experiences form an uniform and regular whole of laws of sequence. That is the other postulate, subordinate to the first. This postulate helps to form for us our idea of the material world beyond individual consciousness; an idea that science accepts for its uniformity, without inquiring further into its nature, while a more critical reflection declares that the facts assumed as existent beyond the range of individual conscious beings are "possible experiences."

This assumption of " possible experiences," an assumption made to satisfy the postulate of uniformity, was expressed, in our hypothesis of a world-consciousness, by the supposition of an universal actual experience. Why? We answer, because the assumed "possible experiences" themselves, by ideally filling up the gaps of actual experience, are intended to lead us to the conception of one uniform absolute experience. This absolute experience, to which all facts would exhibit themselves in their connection as uniformly subject to fixed law, is conceived as "possible." But once again, what does that mean? Is the meaning only the empty tautology that if all the gaps and irregularities of individual experience were got rid of by means of connecting links and additional experiences, these gaps and irregularities would disappear? Is the meaning only this, that if there were an absolute experience of an absolutely regular series of facts, this experience would be absolute and uniform? Or again, is it enough to say that any possible experience, an iceberg in the polar sea, my brain, the inside of yonder book, exists for me only as " my representation " ? Of course, I know of it only what I conceive of it, yet I postulate that it has some reality beyond my representation. This postulate is for us in this preliminary discussion a fact, of which we want to know, not the justification (for we still seek none higher than the fact itself of the postulate), but the meaning. I know of my fellow only what I conceive of him. Yet I postulate that my conception of him is like him, whereas I do not postulate that my conception of a dragon is like any real animal. Just so I postulate that my conception of the " possible experience " called an atom, or the North Pole, is valid beyond my experience, and beyond the actual experience of any known animal. But I do not postulate that my conception of the possibility that future men might have wings and tails is like any future reality whatever, or in any way valid beyond my conception.

Here, then, is our dilemma. Matter as a mere possibility of experience is more than any animal's known actual experience. And yet this matter is to be real for consciousness. Nor is it to be real for consciousness simply in so far as the possible experience is represented or conceived. The reality consists not merely in the representation in present consciousness of a possible experience, but in the added postulate that this conception is valid beyond the present consciousness. How is this postulate to be satisfied unless by assuming an actual world-consciousness?

Let us sum up the conditions to which we have here subjected our theory of reality. External reality was to be postulated, not given; existent for us because we willed it to be. To a portion of our conscious states we ascribed a validity beyond the present. This ascription of validity was to constitute our whole knowledge of the external world; for example, our belief in our own past and future states, in our neighbor's existence, and in the existence of space, of matter, and of motion. Such an external reality was always conceived as more or less completely the counterpart of our idea of it, and hence, as in nature, like the facts of our consciousness. The idea that we at any moment form of the reality beyond ourselves was the expression of the effort to reduce to unity the present sense-data and the present conception of our own past experience. This reduction to unity took place in certain forms. Thus we conceived the external reality as in space and in time, and, in the second place, as in causal relation to ourselves. The conception of causal relations thus projected into the external reality becomes, when completed, the conception of a completely united and uniform whole of facts. We conceived the external reality as subject to fixed laws of sequence, certainly existent, even though, in our limited experience, they be undiscoverable. As subject to such laws the external reality was a whole, possessing organic unity. But the external reality was also conceived as being real for consciousness and real only for consciousness. The external reality, being an organic whole, must therefore be conceived as the object of an absolute experience, to which all facts are known, and for which all facts are subject to universal law. But there thus has arisen an obscurity in our theory of reality. The real is to be only for consciousness. Consciousness, however, is popularly thought as existent in our fellow-beings. And yet the postulated reality is to be an organic whole, containing series of facts that to these beings are known only as possible, not as actual, experiences.

We are then in this position. To complete our theory, we "want a hero." Not, to be sure, a Don Juan, but a hypothetical subject of the "possible experiences." This hypothetical subject we have postulated only as a hypothesis. That is, its existence is not yet seen to be a necessary result even of the postulate that there is an external reality. One can form other hypotheses. But this hypothesis has the advantage of being simple and adequate. Moreover, to assume a consciousness for which the "possible experiences" are present facts, is to do no more than our theory seems to need; whereas any other hypothesis (Berkeley's theological hypothesis, for example, in its original form) seems to assume more than is so far demanded by our theoretical conception of reality. For the sake then of expressing one aspect of our fundamental postulate, we suggest what of course we have not yet proven, that all the conceived "possible experiences" are actual in a Consciousness of which we so far suppose nothing but that it knows these experiences, or knows facts corresponding in number and in other relations to these experiences. Thus our idealistic doctrine in this its first form is explained and defended.

IV.

But all this hypothesis needs the deeper confirmation that we are here seeking for our philosophic doctrines. How is any such idealism to be established? And then, if established, how is this notion of a passionless eternal thought to be transformed into anything that can have a religious value? What we have advanced as hypothesis, expressing the postulates of popular thought, is to receive such additions and such foundation as shall fit it to rank as a reasonable philosophic theory of reality. So far it has been a wish of ours, and we have not even shown that it is a pious wish. Can we make of this All-Knower a religiously interesting Spirit? And what shall we do with his still vague relation to the single conscious lives that are to get truth by agreeing with him? If he is not in deepest truth a power that makes them, then so far there is a strange, dark, inexplicable necessity, determining somehow their harmony with him. Plainly, though we find it best to approach our doctrine by this road, we have not yet reached the heart of the mystery.

There is one haunting thought that now must be permitted to come for a time out of its hiding-place and to confront us. It says: " All this postulating how vain and worthless, this hope for a proof of your doctrine how absurd, when your very hypothesis shuts up your human thought as it were in a cage. As you state the relation of the Universal Consciousness in which exists the physical world, and the individual consciousness of the particular thinker, you make indeed the truth of this individual thought dependent on its agreement with that all-seeing thought, but as you so far utterly separate the individual thought from the all-seeing thought, you make impossible any sort of transition from one to the other. This individual can never go out of himself, to meet that Infinite thought, and to see if he agrees with it. You put the model all-embracing thought M in a relation to the poor human thought h, in which no transfer of thought really takes place, but still you give to h the command that it shall copy M. Then you postulate that which is by your hypothesis unknowable, namely, that this correspondence has been attained, and this empty postulate you call a philosophy. After all, say what you will of the beauty and nobility and courage of postulates, all this seems a rather wearisome business. For the postulates appear the vainest of all things when viewed in the light of the very theory that they are to establish."

This objection is a common-sense one, and formidable. But, like all philosophic skepticism, rightly understood it will be our best friend. Possibly, indeed, we shall have to complete somehow our notion of the relation of the individual minds to the all-embracing mind; but meanwhile let us take the objection in its worst form. What does it lead to when carried to its fullest extent? It leads to absolute skepticism. It says: "Perhaps then, after all, the relations of our individual thought are such that there is possible for us no foundation whatever for our postulates. They are all in the air. Everything is doubtful. We may be in error everywhere. Certainty about the real world beyond is unattainable." At this point then we are face to face with the uttermost theoretical skepticism. What shall we do with it? Why, just what we did with ethical skepticism in an earlier chapter. We must receive it in a friendly spirit, and must find out what it means and assumes. It will, in fact, transform this far-off external world of the postulates into a true world of Spiritual Life.

One thing this skepticism implies, — one thing so simple as generally to escape notice among the assumptions of our thought. *It implies that we can be in error about an external world.* Therefore even this extreme skepticism assumes that *there is a difference between true and false statements about nature.* But now what is involved in saying that a statement is either true or false? To affirm, to deny, to doubt, all imply a real distinction between truth and error; all three then involve in common the assumption that there is such a distinction. That which is involved alike both in the truth and in the falsity of a statement must itself be certainly true, and cannot be doubted. But what is this assumption implied in the very assertion that a statement about an external world is or may be false? This inquiry we must make if we are to understand our own skepticism.

If we begin this inquiry, we are met at once by a very vexatious paradox. There seems to be an aspect in which all sincere judgments are true. Let us remember the fable of the knights and the shield. Each accused the other of lying. To each the other's account seemed deliberate falsehood. Yet each spoke the truth. Only neither expressed himself fully. Each should have said, " The shield as it appears from my side is golden " or "is silver." But each left out the qualification. Each said *the shield*, simply. And hence the battle.

But this commonplace about the knights and the shield begins to worry us, when we reflect upon it, by becoming altogether too general in scope. Do we, in fact, ever make sincere assertions about things save as they appear to us? If I say, " Sugar is pleasant to the taste," and my neighbor says, "Sugar is hateful to the taste," is this a conflict of veracity? May we not both of us be sincere and truthful in what we say? And are color-blind men lying when they say that there is no difference in color between strawberries and the leaves of the strawberry plant when seen in certain lights? But why is it not just so with all the rest of the things that people say? If you are sincere in what you say, are you not always in your assertions simply relating how your ideas appear to you and are grouped? If you say that *nothing happens without a cause,* do you not mean that what you conceive by the word *cause* is conceived by you as in connection with every event that you now have in mind? If you say that a *straight line is the shortest distance between two points,* do you not mean that what you now conceive under the name *straight line* agrees with what you now mean by shortest distance? Very well then, how can there be any direct opposition between two sincere statements? Your neighbor says that *Darwinism is absurd.* You say that *Darwinism is true.* Where now is in fact the controversy? He says that he has two ideas in mind ; namely, an idea of what he chooses to call Darwinism, and an idea of what he chooses to call absurdity. He says that these two ideas agree, just as the knight said that *his* shield (*i. e.* the shield as seen by him) was silver. You say that your idea of Darwinism agrees with your idea of truth, as the other knight said that the shield as seen by him was golden. Why fight about it? Thus all statements appear to be narratives of what goes on in our own minds. If they are sincere, if we mean them, who shall doubt that they are all true? Can any of us make assertions that are more than clear accounts of how we put our own ideas together? Why may not the thief before the judge sincerely say : " O judge, my idea of what I call chicken-stealing agrees with my idea of what I call virtue " And the judge may truthfully reply : " O rascal, my idea of what I call your chicken-stealing agrees with my idea of what I call detestable petty larceny." Are these two opinions really opposed, so that one is true, the other erroneous? Are these not rather different aspects of the universe? What is truth, moral or physical? Is not every investigation, every argument, every story, every anticipation, every axiom, every delusion, every creed, every de-

nial, just a mere expression of a present union of
ideas in somebody? Where do two assertions meet
on common ground, so that one can be really true,
the other really false? Have different judgments,
in different minds or made at different times, any
real common object at all? If they have not, how
can there be any truth or falsity at all?

This paradox is wild enough if you look at it
fairly. And yet many thinkers actually have maintained it under various disguises as the doctrine of
what is called the Total Relativity of Truth. Having himself passed through and long tried to hold
and to rationalize this doctrine of Relativity, the
author has some right to say something in opposition
to it. What he has to say can be very briefly put.
In its paradoxical form as above stated, the doctrine
may be made plausible, and is a suggestive paradox,
but it is certainly meaningless. If there is no real
distinction between truth and error, then the statement that there is such a difference is not really false,
but only *seemingly* false. And then *in truth* there
is the distinction once more. Try as you will, you
come not beyond the fatal circle. If it is wrong to
say that there is Absolute Truth, then the statement
that there is absolute truth is itself false. Is it however false only relatively, or is it false absolutely?
If it is false only relatively, then it is *not* false absolutely. Hence the statement that it is false absolutely is itself false. But false absolutely, or false
relatively? And thus you must at last come to some
statement that is absolutely false or absolutely true,
or else the infinite regress into which you are driven

makes the very distinction between absolute and relative truth lose all its meaning, and your doctrine of total Relativity will also lose meaning. " No absolute truth exists," — can you say this if you want to ? At least you must add, " No absolute truth exists *save this truth itself, that no absolute truth exists.*" Otherwise your statement has no sense. But if you admit this truth, then there is in fact an absolute distinction between truth and error.

And when we here talk of an " absolute " distinction between truth and error, we mean merely a " real " distinction between truth and error. And this real distinction the fiercest partisan of relativity admits ; for does he not after all argue for relativity against " absolutists," holding that he is really right, and they really wrong.

Yet, sure though we feel of the distinction, the paradox and its plausibility remain. How have different judgments, made at different times, any real common object at all ? If they have none, then where is the postulated distinction of truth and error ? What shall we do with our paradox ? In what sense can a private opinion of one man be a genuine error ? There must be such a thing as real genuine error, or else even our very skepticism fails to have the least sense, and we fall back into the utterly irrational chaos of not being able with truth to say whether we doubt that we are doubting. But yet how shall we explain the possibility of error ? For here is an unique and fundamental postulate.

The next chapter shall be devoted to a more special and detailed study of this problem. But already

we shall venture to suggest our solution. It is one
that needs possibly some little consideration, and the
reader will pardon us if we already state it, although
we shall repeat it in another form hereafter. In
fact, it is a critical matter for our whole discussion.
Here, in fact, will be the point where we shall pass
from idealism as a bare hypothesis, expressing postulates, to idealism as a philosophic doctrine, rest-
ing upon the deepest possible foundation, namely,
on the very difference between truth and error itself.
Our logical problem will become for us a treasure-
house of ideal truth. But just now we make only a
suggestion, to which as yet we can compel no agreement.

When one says even the perfectly commonplace
thing that not all assertions are equally true, that is,
that not all of them agree with the objects with which
they mean to agree, he really makes an assumption
upon which all thinking, all controversy, all the
postulates that we previously studied, all science, all
morality depend; and, as we maintain, this assumption is: *That the agreement or the disagreement
of his judgments with their intended objects exists
and has meaning for an actual thought, a consciousness, to which both these related terms are
present, namely, both the judgment and the object
wherewith it is to agree.* So that, if my thought
has objects outside of it with which it can agree or
disagree, those objects and that agreement can have
meaning, can be possible, only if there is a thought
that includes both my thought and the object wherewith my thought is to agree. This inclusive thought

must be related to my thought and its objects, as
my thought is related to the various partial thoughts
that it includes and reduces to unity in any one of
my complex assertions. For only by some such
unity as this can this higher thought compare my
judgment with its object, and so constitute the
relation that is implied in the truth or in the error
of my thought. So, in the commonplace assumption that a statement of mine can agree or can fail
to agree with its real object, when this object is
wholly outside my thought, in this assumption, without which you can make no rational statement, is
contained implicitly the assumption that all reality,
spiritual and material, is present in its true nature
to an all-embracing, intelligent thought, of which
mine is simply one subordinate part or element.
In truth, as we shall come to see, regarded in itself,
my mind can be concerned only with its own ideas.
That is the view of all so-called subjective idealism.
But if my mind can be concerned only with its own
ideas, then sincerity and truth are identical, truth
and error will be alike impossible. What I talk
about will be my ideas ; their objects will be themselves other ideas of mine, and meaning only these
ideas when I make assertions, I cannot fail to make
correct assertions about these, the objects that I
mean. But thus controversy, progress towards
truth, failure to get truth, error, refutation, yes,
doubt itself, will all cease to have any meaning
whatsoever. But if my thought is related to a
higher thought, even as the parts of one of my
thoughts are related to the whole thought, then

truth and error, as objective truth and objective error, are possible, since my thought and its object, both as I think this object and as it is, are together in the universal thought, of which they form elements, and in which they live and move and have their being. As my thoughts have a unity more or less complete in themselves, so all thoughts and objects must be postulated as in unity in that thought for which is the whole universe. As I can say to myself with solely subjective truth, *This line that I mentally picture is in truth shorter for me than that, and to say otherwise is to speak falsely;* even so my statement, *All straight lines are in all cases shortest lines between their extremities,* is true objectively, and its contradictory false only in case both the world of possible straight lines and my thoughts about this world are known to a higher thought, are in fact members of a higher thought, which, comparing what I cannot compare, making a synthesis of what is to me separate, unifying what is for me diverse, finds my thought really true or false.

This is the barest outline of a proof by which, in the next chapter, we shall try to reach the position which some call absolute or objective idealism. We shall find this theory as just set forth a necessary assumption, which we shall make because we want to think clearly, and because we find nothing else that even suggests an answer to the critical questions that trouble us as to the nature of thought. We shall not substitute this conception of reality for the scientific conception. On the contrary, this conception will merely undertake, presupposing the scientific spirit, to include the scientific conception of the world in one that will, as a whole, better satisfy the needs of this scientific spirit itself. Our theory will give us no *a priori* account of facts of experience, but a theory of that which makes experience, as a whole, possible. This theory, which we offer as the one rational account of the nature of truth, is the doctrine that the world is in and for a thought, all-embracing, all-knowing, universal, for which are all relations and all truth, a thought that estimates perfectly our imperfect and halting thoughts, a thought in which and for which are we all. No other view, as we shall affirm, offers any chance of a philosophy, nor any hope of even a rational scientific notion of things.

The reader may be impatient to see, in detail, the argument by which we undertake to establish such a thesis as the foregoing. Of that argument he shall get enough in another chapter. But we ask him to wait yet a moment, while we hint to him the consequences, for our religious theory, that will flow from our hypothesis when we have got it more certainly in our minds.

The ambiguous relation of the conscious individuals to the universal thought in the foregoing first statement of our idealism, will be decided in the sense of their inclusion, as elements, in the universal thought. They will indeed not become "things in the dream" of any other person than themselves, but their whole reality, just exactly as it is in them, will be found to be but a fragment of a higher reality. This reality will be no Power, nor will it produce the individuals by dreaming of them, but it will complete the existence that in them, as separate beings, has no rational completeness. This will be our first result.

Then will follow other thoughts. In so far as there is any objective truth in moral conceptions, this truth is eternally known to this all-embracing thought. If there be moral or immoral acts, they are forever known and judged in and by this all-embracing conscious thought. And thus we shall have found Job's longed-for, perfect, all-knowing judge. "He knoweth the way that I take." Here is an absolute estimate, objectively present in the world, an estimate of all your good and evil deeds. You are a part of the universal life. Your thoughts are parts of the whole. Your acts form an element in the universe that the great Judge knows. All of you then is known and justly estimated by the absolute thought that embraces all possible truth, and for whom are all relations, present, past, and future of all possible beings, acts, and thoughts in all places. If there be any virtue, this virtue is known to the infinite thought of the universe. If there be any vice, that vice is estimated, in all its infinite baseness, by the infinite consciousness. Inasmuch as ye do good unto the least of these, ye do it with the universal consciousness as onlooker; your work is all accomplished in the presence of the Absolute.

With this truth before us, we shall be ready to leave unsolved our problems about this or that Power, about this or that future state, about the fallen angels, or about the historical justification of God's ways. The world of Divine Life will be in deepest truth not a Power at all, but the Infinite Knowing One, for whom are all the powers, but who is above them all, beyond them all, — no striving good principle that cannot get realized in a wicked world, but an absolute Judge that perfectly estimates the world. In the contemplation of this truth we may find a religious comfort.

And then, by all this, we shall make the postulates of our previous chapter appear in a new light. The postulates, we said, express the conditions under which we are determined to do our work. They are expressions of the spirit of courageous devotion to the highest. They find and can find no perfect verification in experience. They dwell in part on the unseen. But they do not resist verification, if any can be offered from a higher source. But this, our new doctrine, if we truly get to it, will offer them their higher verification. Their office will not thereby be vacated or abolished. They will forever remain the maxims of our work. But they will no longer be just leaps in the dark. We shall see that when science assumes rationality, and religion assumes goodness, as at the heart of things, they have neither of them acted vainly. We shall then have reason to go on assuming both, and to regulate our lives accordingly. Faith of some sort will continue to be our meat and drink; but it will be faith with a philosophical foundation.

The reader will pardon us for having detained him so long in the study of idealism as a bare postulate, when we have a more serious doctrine behind. The inveterate prejudices and misunderstandings to which idealistic theories fall prey, furnish our excuse for trying to reconcile ourselves to an imperfect form of idealism as a mere postulate, before going on to set forth an absolute idealism as a demonstrable theory.

CHAPTER XI.

THE POSSIBILITY OF ERROR.

On ne sert dignement la philosophie qu'avec le même feu qu'on sent pour une maîtresse. — ROUSSEAU, Nouvelle Helöise.

WE have before us our theorem, and an outline of its proof. We are here to expand this argument. We have some notion of the magnitude of the issues that are at stake. We had found ourselves baffled in our search for a certainty by numerous difficulties. We had found only one way remaining so far quite clear. That was the way of postulating what the moral consciousness seems to demand about the world beyond experience. For many thinkers since Kant, that way has seemed in fact the only one. They live in a world of action. "Doubt," they say, "clouds all theory. One must *act as if* the world were the supporter of our moral demands. One must have faith. One must make the grand effort, one must risk all for the sake of the great prize. If the world is against us, still we will not admit the fact until we are crushed. If the cold reality cares naught for our moral efforts, so be it when we come to know the fact, but meanwhile we will act as if legions of angels were ready to support our demand for whatever not our selfish interest, but the great interest of the Good, requires."

Such is the view of the men whose religion is founded upon a Postulate.

We, too, felt that such faith is religious. We were willing to accept it, if nothing better could be found. But we were not content with it. Life has its unheroic days, when mere postulates fail us. At such times we grow weary of toiling, evil seems actually triumphant, and, worse than all, the sense that there really is any perfect goodness yet unattained, that there is any worth or reason in our fight for goodness, seems to desert us. And then it will indeed be well if we can get for ourselves something more and better than mere postulates. If we cannot, we shall not seek to hide the fact. Better eternal despondency than a deliberate lie about our deepest thoughts and their meaning. If we are not honest, at least in our philosophy, then are we wholly base. To try once more is not dishonest.

So we did make the effort, and, in the last chapter, we sketched a result that seemed nearly within our reach. An unexpected result this, because it springs from the very heart of skepticism itself. We doubted to the last extremity. We let everything go, and then all of a sudden we seemed to find that we could not lose one priceless treasure, try as we would. Our wildest doubt assumed this, namely, that error is possible. And so our wildest doubt assumed the actual existence of those conditions that make error possible. *The conditions that determine the logical possibility of error must themselves be absolute truth*, that was the treasure that remained to us amid all our doubts. And how rich that treas-

25

ure is, we dimly saw in the last discussion. That
dim insight we must now try to make clearer. Perhaps our previous discussion has shown us that the
effort is worth making.

Yet of one thing the reader shall be warned. The
path that we travel is hereabouts very thorny and
stony. It is a path of difficult philosophical investigation. Nobody ought to follow it who does not
desire to. We hope that the reader will skip the
whole of this chapter unless he wants to find even
more of dullness than the rest of this sleepy book
has discovered to him. For us, too, the arid way
would seem hard, were it not for the precious prize
at the end of it.

I.

The story of the following investigation shall first
be very briefly told. The author had long sought, especially in the discussions of Kant's "Kritik," and
in the books of the post-Kantians, for help in seeing the ultimate principles that lie at the basis of
knowledge. He had found the old and well-known
troubles. Experience of itself can give no certainty
about general principles. We must therefore, said
Kant, bring our own principles with us to experience. We know then of causation, because causation is a fundamental principle of our thought,
whereby we set our experience to rights. And so
long as we think, we shall think into experience the
connection of cause and effect, which otherwise would
not be there. But hereupon the questions arose that
have so often been asked of Kant and the Kantians

Why just these principles and no others? "That is inexplicable," replies Kant. Very well, then, suppose we give up applying to experience those arbitrary principles of ours. Suppose we choose to stop thinking of experience as causally connected. What then? "But you cannot stop," says Kant, "Your thought, being what it is, must follow this one fashion forever." Nay, we reply, how knowest thou that, Master? Why may not our thought get a new fashion some day? And then what is now a necessary principle, for example, that every event has a cause, would become unnecessary or even nonsensical. Do we then know *a priori* that our *a priori* principles must always remain such? If so, how come we by this new knowledge?

So Kant leaves us still uncertain about any fundamental principles upon which a sure knowledge of the world can be founded.

Let us, then, examine a little deeper. Are there any certain judgments possible at all? If one is skeptical in a thorough-going way, as the author tried to be, he is apt to reach, through an effort to revise Kant's view, a position something like the following, — a provisional position of course, but one that results from the effort to accept nothing without criticism: " Kant's result is that our judgments about the real world are founded on an union of thought and sense, thought giving the appearance of necessity to our judgment, sense giving the material. The necessity of any judgment amounts then only to what may be summed up in the words : *So the present union of thought and sense makes things ap*

pear. If either thought or sense altered its character, truth would alter. Hence every sincere judgment is indeed true for the moment in which it is
made, but not necessarily true for other moments.
We only postulate that it is true for other moments."
"And so," to continue this view, "it is only by
means of postulates that our thought even seems to
have any unity from moment to moment. We live
in the present. If our thought has other truth or
falsity than this, we do not know it. Past and future exist not for this present. They are only postulated. Save as postulated, they have no present
meaning."

When he held and expressed this view, the author
is free to admit that he was not always clear whether
he ought to call it the doctrine of the relativity of
truth or not. It might have avoided the absurdities
of total relativity by taking form as a doctrine that
the present moment's judgment is really true or
false, for a real past and future, but that we, being
limited to present moments, can never compare our
judgments with reality to find whether our judgments are true or false. But although this interpretation is possible, this view often did express itself for the author as the doctrine of the total relativity of truth. The latter doctrine to be sure has
no real meaning, but the author used with many
others to fancy that it had.

To apply the view to the case of causal relations.
"We continually postulate," the author used to
point out, "we demand, without being able to prove
it, that nature in future shall be uniform." So,

carrying out this thought, the author used to say:
" In fact future nature is not given to us, just as the
past is not given to us. Sense-data and thought
unite at every instant afresh to form a new judgment
and a new postulate. Only in the present has any
judgment evident validity. And our postulate of
causal relation is just a way of looking at this world
of conceived past and future *data*. Such postulates
avoid being absurd efforts to regulate independent
facts of sense, because, and only because, we have in
experience no complete series of facts of sense at all,
only from moment to moment single facts, about
which we make single judgments. All the rest we
must postulate or else do without them." Thus one
reaches a skepticism as nearly complete as is possible to any one with earnest activity of thought in
him. From moment to moment one can be sure of
each moment. All else is postulate.

From the depths of this imperfectly defined skepticism, which seemed to him provisionally the only
view he could adopt, the author escaped only by asking the one question more : " If everything beyond
the present is doubtful, then how can even that doubt
be possible?" With this question that bare relativity of the present moment is given up. What are
the conditions that make doubt logically intelligible ?
These conditions really transcend the present moment. Plainly doubt implies that the statement
doubted may be false. So here we have at least one
supposed general truth, namely, " All but the immediate content of the present moment's judgment,
being doubtful, we may be in error about it." But

what then is an error? This becomes at once a problem of exciting interest. Attacking it, the author was led through the wilderness of the following argument.

II.

Yet before we undertake this special examination of the nature of error, the reader must pardon us for adding yet another explanatory word. The difficulty of the whole discussion will lie in the fact that we shall be studying the possibility of the plainest and most familiar of commonplaces. Common sense hates to do such things, because common sense thinks that the whole matter is sure from the outset. Common sense is willing to ask whether God exists, but unwilling to inquire how it is possible that there can exist an error about anything. But foreseeing that something is to follow from all this, we must beg common sense to be patient. We have not the shadow of doubt ourselves about the possibility of error. That is the steadfast rock on which we build. Our inquiry, ultra-skeptical as it may at moments seem, is into the question : *How* is the error possible? Or, in other words : *What is an error?* Now there can be little doubt that common sense is not ready with any general answer to such a question. Error is a word with many senses. By error we often mean just a statement that arouses our antipathy. Yet we all admit upon reflection, that our antipathy can neither make nor be used to define real error. Adam Smith declares, with common sense on his side, in his " Theory of the Moral Sentiments," [1]

1 Part I., sect. i., chap. iii., near the beginning.

that : " To approve or disapprove of the opinions of others is acknowledged, by everybody, to mean no more than to observe their agreement or disagreement with our own." Yet no one would accept as a definition of error the statement that : *Error is any opinion that I personally do not like.* Error has thus a very puzzling character. For common sense will readily admit that if a statement is erroneous, it must appear erroneous to every " right mind " that is in possession of the facts. Hence the personal taste of one man is not enough to define it. Else there might be as many sorts of error as there are minds. It is only the " right mind " whose personal taste shall decide what is an error in any particular case. But what then is a normal mind? Who is the right-minded judge? There seems to be danger that common sense shall run at this point into an infinite regress. I say : *That opinion is an error.* What do I mean? Do I mean that I do not like that opinion? Nay, I mean more. I mean that *I ought not to like or to accept it.* Why ought I not? *Because the ideally right-minded person would not,* seeing the given facts, hold that opinion about them. But who is the ideally right-minded person? Well, common sense may answer, *It is my ideal person, the right-minded man as I conceive him.* But why is my ideal the true ideal? *Because I like it?* — *Nay, because, to the ideal judge, that kind of mind would seem the ideal.* But who is the ideal judge? And so common sense is driven from point to point, unable to get to anything definite.

So much, then, to show in general that common

sense does not know what an error is, and needs more light upon the subject. Let common sense not disturb us, then, in our further search, by the constant and indignant protest that error must somehow exist, and that doubt on that subject is nonsense. Nobody has any doubts on that subject. We ask only *how* error exists and how it can exist.

For the rest, what follows is not any effort to demonstrate in fair and orderly array, from any one principle or axiom, what must be the nature of error, but to use every and any device that may offer itself, general analysis, special example, comparison and contrast of cases, — anything that shall lead us to the insight into what an error is and implies. For at last, immediate insight must decide.

We shall study our problem thus. We shall take either some accepted definition of error, or some special class of cases, and we shall ask : How is error in that case, or in accordance with that definition, possible ? Since error plainly is possible in some way, we shall have only to inquire : *What are the logical conditions* that make it possible ? We shall take up the ordinary suppositions that common sense seems to make about what here determines the possibility of error. We shall show that these suppositions are inadequate. Then the result will be that, on the ordinary suppositions, error would be impossible. But that result would be absurd, if these were the only possible suppositions. Hence the ordinary suppositions must somehow be supplemented. When, therefore, we seem to say in the following that error is impossible, we shall mean only, impossible under the ordinary suppositions of common sense. What supplement we need to these suppositions, our argument will show us. In sum we shall find the state of the case to be this : Common sense regards an assertion as true or as false apart from any other assertion or thought, and solely in reference to its own object. For common sense each judgment, as a separate creation, stands out alone, looking at its object, and trying to agree with it. If it succeeds, we have truth. If the judgment fails, we have error. But, as we shall find, this view of common sense is unintelligible. A judgment cannot have an object and fail to agree therewith, unless this judgment is part of an organism of thought. Alone, as a separate fact, a judgment has no intelligible object beyond itself. And therefore the presuppositions of common sense must be supplemented or else abandoned. Either then there is no error, or else judgments are true or false only in reference to a higher inclusive thought, which they presuppose, and which must, in the last analysis, be assumed as Infinite and all-inclusive. This result we shall reach by no mystical insight, by no revelation, nor yet by any mere postulate such as we used in former discussions, but by a simple, dry analysis of the meaning of our own thought.

The most formidable opponent of our argument will be, after all, however, not common sense, but that thought mentioned in the last chapter, — the thought that may try to content itself with somewhat plausible jargon, and to say that : " *There is no real difference between truth and error at all, only a kind of opinion or consensus of men about a conventional distinction between what they choose to call truth and what they choose to call error."* This view, as the author has confessed, he once tried to hold. Still this meaningless doctrine of relativity is not the same as the view that contents itself with the postulates before discussed. That view might take, and for the author at one time did take, the possible and intelligible form thus expressible: *" Truth and error, though really distinguishable, are for us distinguished only through our postulates, in so far as relates to past and future time."* Such views, while not denying that there is real truth, despair of the attainability for us of more than momentary truth. But the doctrine of Total Relativity, this view above expressed, differs from genuine skepticism. It tries to put even skepticism to rest, by declaring the opinion, *that there is error*, to be itself an error. This is not merely a moderate expression of human limitations, but jargon, and therefore formidable, because jargon is always unanswerable. When the famous Cretan declared all statements made by Cretans to be in all cases lies, his declaration was hard to refute, because it was such honest - seeming nonsense. Even so with the statement that declares the very existence of error to be an erroneously believed fancy. No *consensus* of men can make an error erroneous. We can only find or commit an error, not create it. When we commit an error, we say what was an error already. If our skeptical view in previous chapters seemed to regard truth and error as mere objects of our postu-

lates, that was only because, to our skepticism, the
real truth, the real error, about any real past and
future, seemed beyond our reach, so that we had
to content ourselves with postulates. But that real
error exists is absolutely indubitable.

This being the case, it is evident that even the
most thorough-going skepticism is full of assumptions. If I say, " There may be no money in that
purse yonder," I assume the existence of the purse
yonder in order to make just that particular doubt
possible. Of course, however, just that doubt may
be rendered meaningless by the discovery of the
actual non-existence of that particular purse. If
there is no purse yonder, then it is nonsensical either
to affirm or to deny that it contains money. And
so if the purse of which I speak is an hallucination
of mine, then the doubt about whether, as an actually existent purse, it has money in it, is deprived
of sense. My real error in that case would lie in
supposing the purse itself to exist. If, however, I
abandon the first doubt, and go on to doubt the real
existence of the purse, I equally assume a room, or
some other environment, or at all events the universe,
as existent, in order to give sense to my question
whether the purse has any being in this environment
or in this universe. But if I go yet further, and
doubt whether there is any universe at all outside of
my thought, what does my doubt yet mean? If it
is to be a doubt with any real sense, it must be a
doubt still with an object before it. It seems then
to imply an assumed order of being, in which there
are at least two elements, my lonely thought about

an universe, and an empty environment of this thought, in which there is, in fact, no universe. But this empty environment, whose nature is such that my thought does wrong to suppose it to be an universe, what is that? Surely if the doubt is to have meaning, this idea needs further examination. The absolute skepticism is thus full of assumptions.

The first European thinker who seems to have discussed our present problem was Plato, in a too-much-neglected passage of the "Theætetus," [1] where Socrates, replying to the second definition of knowledge given by Theætetus, namely, *knowledge is True Opinion*, answers that his great difficulty has often been to see how any opinion can possibly be false. The conclusion reached by Plato is no very definite one, but the discussion is deeply suggestive. And we cannot do better here than to pray that the shade of the mighty Greek may deign to save us now in our distress, and to show us the true nature of error.

III.

Logicians are agreed that single ideas, thoughts viewed apart from judgments, are neither true nor false. Only a judgment can be false. And if a reasoning process is said to be false, the real error lies still in an actual or suppressed assertion. A fallacy is a false assertion that a certain conclusion follows from certain premises. Error is therefore generally defined as a judgment that does not agree with its object. In the erroneous judgment, sub-

[1] Plato, *Th.*, p. 187 *sqq.*

ject and predicate are so combined as, in the object,
the corresponding elements are not combined. And
thus the judgment comes to be false. Now, in this
definition, nothing is doubtful or obscure save the
one thing, namely, the *assumed relation between the
judgment and its object*. The definition assumes as
quite clear that a judgment has an object, wherewith
it can agree or not agree. And what is meant by
the agreement would not be obscure, if we could see
what is meant by the object, and by the possession of
this object implied in the pronoun *its*. What then
is meant by *its object*? The difficulties involved in
this phrase begin to appear as soon as you look
closer. First then the object of the assertion is as
such supposed to be neither the subject nor the predicate thereof. It is external to the judgment. It
has a nature of its own. Furthermore, not all judgments have the same object, so that objects are very
numerous. But from the infinity of real or of possible objects the judgment somehow picks out its
own. Thus then for a judgment to have an object,
there must be something about the judgment that
shows what one of the external objects that are beyond itself this judgment does pick out as its own.
But this something that gives the judgment its object can only be the intention wherewith the judgment is accompanied. A judgment has as object
only what it intends to have as object. It has to
conform only to that to which it wants to conform.
But the essence of an intention is the knowledge of
what one intends. One can, for instance, intend a
deed or any of its consequences only in so far as he

foresees them. I cannot be said to intend the accidental or the remote or even the immediate consequences of anything that I do, unless I foresaw that
they would follow; and this is true however much
the lawyers and judges may find it practically necessary to hold me responsible for these consequences.
Even so we all find it practically useful to regard
one of our fellows as in error in case his assertions,
as we understand them, seem to us to lead to consequences that we do not approve. But our criticisms
of his opinions, just like legal judgments of his acts,
are not intended to be exact. Common sense will
admit that, unless a man is thinking of the object of
which I suppose him to be thinking, he makes no
real error by merely failing to agree with the object
that I have in mind. If the knights in the fable
judge each other to be wrong, that is because each
knight takes the other's shield to be identical with
the shield as he himself has it in mind. In fact
neither of them is in error, unless his assertion is
false for the shield as he intended to make it his
object.

So then judgments err only by disagreeing with
their intended objects, and they can intend an object
only in so far forth as this object is known to the
thought that makes the judgment. Such, it would
seem, is the consequence of the common-sense view.
But in this case a judgment can be in error only
if it is knowingly in error. That also, as it seems,
follows from the common-sense suppositions. Or, if
we will have it in syllogistic form : —

Everything intended is something known. The

object even of an erroneous judgment is intended.
∴ The object even of an error is something known.

Or: Only what is known can be erred about.
Nor can we yet be content with what common sense
will at once reply, namely, that our syllogism uses
known ambiguously, and that the object of an erroneous judgment is known enough to constitute it the
object, and not enough to prevent the error about it.
This must no doubt be the fact, but it is not of itself
clear; on the contrary, just here is the problem. As
common sense conceives the matter, the object of a
judgment is not as such the whole outside world of
common sense, with all its intimate interdependence
of facts, with all its unity in the midst of diversity.
On the contrary, the object of any judgment is just
that portion of the then conceived world, just that
fragment, that aspect, that element of a supposed
reality, which is seized upon for the purposes of just
this judgment. Only such a momentarily grasped
fragment of the truth can possibly be present in any
one moment of thought as the object of a single assertion. Now it is hard to say how within this arbitrarily chosen fragment itself there can still be room
for the partial knowledge that is sufficient to give to
the judgment its object, but insufficient to secure to
the judgment its accuracy. If I aim at a mark with
my gun, I can fail to hit it, because choosing and
hitting a mark are totally distinct acts. But, in the
judgment, choosing and knowing the object seem in-
separable. No doubt somehow our difficulty is solu-
ble, but we are here trying first to show that it is a
difficulty.

To illustrate here by a familiar case, when we speak of things that are solely matters of personal preference, such as the pleasure of a sleigh-ride, the taste of olives, or the comfort of a given room, and when we only try to tell how these things appear to us, then plainly our judgments, if sincere, cannot be in error. As these things are to us, so they are. We are their measure. To doubt our truthfulness in these cases is to doubt after the fashion of the student who wondered whether the star that the astronomers call Uranus may not be something else after all, and not really Uranus. Surely science does not progress very far or run into great danger of error so long as it employs itself in discovering such occult mysteries as the names of the stars. But our present question is, How do judgments that can be and that are erroneous differ in nature from these that cannot be erroneous? If astronomers would be equally right in case they should agree to call Uranus Humpty Dumpty, why are not all judgments equally favored? Since the judgment chooses its own object, and has it only in so far as it chooses it, how can it be in that partial relation to its object which is implied in the supposition of an erroneous assertion?

Yet again, to illustrate the difficulty in another aspect, we can note that not only is error impossible about the perfectly well-known, but that error is equally impossible, save in the form of direct self-contradiction, about what is absolutely unknown. Spite of the religious awe of some people in presence of the Unknowable, it is safe to say, somewhat

irreverently, that about a really Unknowable nobody
could make any sincere and self-consistent assertions
that could be errors. For self-consistent assertions
about the Unknowable would of necessity be meaningless. And being meaningless, they could not well
be false. For instance, one could indeed not say
that the Unknowable contemplates war with France,
or makes sunspots, or will be the next Presidential
candidate, because that would be contradicting one's
self. For if the Unknowable did any of these things,
it would no longer be the Unknowable, but would
become either the known or the discoverable. But
avoid such self - contradiction, and you cannot err
about the Unknowable. For the Unknowable is simply our old friend *Abracadabra*, a word that has no
meaning, and by hypothesis never can get any. So
if I say that the Unknowable dines *in vacuo* with
the chimera, or is Humpty Dumpty, I talk nonsense,
and am therefore unable to make a mistake. Nonsense is error only when it involves self-contradiction.
Avoid that, and nonsense cannot blunder, having no
object outside of itself with which it must agree.
But all this illustrates from the other side our difficulty. Is not the object of a judgment, in so far as
it is unknown to that judgment, like the Unknowa-
bles for that judgment? To be in error about the
application of a symbol, you must have a symbol that
symbolizes something. But in so far as the thing
symbolized is not known through the symbol, how
is it symbolized by that symbol? Is it not, like the
Unknowable, once for all out of the thought, so that
one cannot just then be thinking about it at all, and

26

so cannot, in this thought at least, be making blunders about it? But in so far as the thing symbolized is, through the symbol, in one's thought, why is it not known, and so correctly judged? All this involves that old question of the nature of symbols. They are to mean for us more than we know that they mean. How can that be? No doubt all that is really possible, but how?

IV.

We follow our difficulty into another department. Let us attempt a sort of provisional psychological description of a judgment as a state of mind. So regarded, a judgment is simply a fact that occurs in somebody's thought. If we try to describe it as an occurrence, without asking whence it came, we shall perhaps find in it three elements, — elements which are in some fashion described in Ueberweg's well-known definition of a judgment as the "Consciousness about the objective validity of a subjective union of ideas." Our interpretation of them shall be this: The elements are: The *Subject*, with the accompanying shade of curiosity about it; the *Predicate*, with the accompanying sense of its worth in satisfying a part of our curiosity about the subject; and the *Sense of Dependence*, whereby we feel the value of this act to lie, not in itself, but in its agreement with a vaguely felt Beyond, that stands out there as Object.

Now this analysis of the elements of a judgment is no explanation of our difficulties; and in fact for the moment only embarrasses us more. But the nature of the difficulty may come home to us somewhat more clearly, if we try to follow the thread of this analysis a little further. Even if it is a very imperfect account, it may serve to lead us up to the true insight that we seek into the nature of error. Let us make the analysis a little more detailed.

In its typical form then, the judgment as a mental state seems to us to begin with a relatively incomplete or unstable or disconnected mass of consciousness, which we have called the Subject, as it first begins to be present to us. This subject-idea is attended by some degree of effort, namely, of attention, whose tendency is to complete this incomplete subject by bringing it into closer connection with more familiar mental life. This more familiar life is represented by the predicate-idea. If the effort is successful, the subject has new elements united to it, assumes in consciousness a definiteness, a coherency with other states, a familiarity, which it lacked at the outset of the act of judgment; and this coherency it gets through its union with the predicate. All this is accompanied further by what one for short may call a sense of dependence. The judgment feels itself not alone, but looks to a somewhat indefinite object as the model after which the present union of ideas is to be fashioned. And in this way we explain how the judgment is, in those words of Ueberweg's definition, " the consciousness about the objective validity of a subjective union of ideas."

Now as a mere completion of subject-idea through the addition of a predicate-idea, the judgment is simply a mental phenomenon, having interest only to the person that experiences it, and to a psychologist. But as true or as false the judgment must be viewed in respect to the indefinite object of what we have called the sense of dependence, whereby the judgment is accompanied. Seldom in any ordinary judgment does this object become perfectly full and clear; for to make it so would often require many, perhaps an infinite, series of judgments. Yet, for the one judgment, the object, whether full and clear or not, exists as object only in so far forth as the sense of dependence has defined it. And the judgment is true or false only with reference to this undefined object. The intention to agree with the object is contained in the sense of dependence upon the object, and remains for this judgment incomplete, like the object itself. Somewhat vaguely this single act intends to agree with this vague object.

Such being the case, how can the judgment, as thus described, fairly be called false? As mere psychological combination of ideas it is neither true nor false. As accompanied by the sense of dependence upon an object, it would be false if it disagreed with its imperfectly defined object. But, as described, the only object that the judgment has is this imperfectly defined one. With this, in so far as it is for the moment defined, the judgment must needs agree. In so far as it is not defined, it is however not object for this judgment at all, but for some other one. What the imperfect sense of dependence would further imply if it existed in a complete instead of in an incomplete state, nobody can tell, any more than one can tell what towns would grow up by a given rain-pool, if it were no pool, but a great lake. The object of a single judgment, being what it is, namely, a vaguely defined object, present to this judgment, is just what it is for this judgment, and the judgment seems once for all to be true, in case it is sincere.

Some one may here at once answer that we neglect in this description the close interdependence of various judgments. Thought, some one may say, is an organic unity. Separated from all else but its own incompletely defined object, a single judgment cannot be erroneous. Only in the organic unity of a series of judgments, having a common object, is the error of one of them possible. We reply that all this will turn out to be just our result. But the usual supposition at the outset is that any judgment has by itself its own object, so that thereby alone, apart from other judgments, it stands or falls. And thus far we have tried to show that this natural supposition leads us into difficulty. We cannot see how a single sincere judgment should possibly fail to agree with its own chosen object. But enough of our problem in general. We must consider certain classes of errors more in detail. Let us see how, in these special classes of cases, we shall succeed in verifying the natural presupposition of common sense, which regards error as possible only when our object is not wholly present to mind, and which assumes that a judgment can have an object that is yet only partially present to mind. In choosing the classes of cases, we shall first follow common sense as to their definition. We shall take just the assumptions of

daily life, and shall show that they lead us into difficulty. We are not for the first bound to explain
why these assumptions are made. That common
sense makes them is enough.

But let the reader remember : The whole value of
our argument lies in its perfect generality. However much we dwell on particular classes of errors,
we care nothing for the proof that just those errors
are inexplicable, but only for the fact that they illustrate how, without some entirely new hypothesis,
absolutely all error becomes impossible. This or
that class of judgments may be one in which all the
judgments are relative, but the total relativity of
our thought implies an incomprehensible and contradictory state of things. Any hypothesis about error
that makes total relativity the only admissible view,
must therefore give place to some new hypothesis.
And our illustrations in the following are intended
to show that just what constitutes the difficulty in
respect of these illustrations, makes the existence of
any error inexplicable without some new hypothesis.

V.

The class of errors that we shall first take seems,
to common sense, common enough. It is the class
known as errors about our neighbor's states of mind.
Let us then, for argument's sake, assume without
proof that our neighbors do exist. For we are not
here concerned to answer Solipsism, but merely to
exemplify the difficulties about the nature of error.
If our neighbors did not exist, then the nature of

the error that would lie in saying that they do exist would present almost exactly the same difficulties. We prefer, however, to begin with the common-sense assumption about ourselves and our neighbors as separate individuals, and to ask how error can then arise in judging of our neighbors' minds.

In the first place then : Who is my neighbor ? Surely, on the assumptions that we all make, and that we made all through the ethical part of our discussion, he is no one of my thoughts, nor is any part of him ever any part of my thought. He is not my object, but, in Professor Clifford's phrase, an " eject," wholly outside of my ideas. He is no " thing in my dream," just as I am not in his dream.

Yet I make judgments about him, and he makes them about me. And when I make judgments about him, I do so by having in my thought some set of my own ideas that, although not himself, do yet, as I say, represent him. A kind of dummy, a symbol, a graven image of my own thought's creation, a phantom of mine, stands there in me as the representative of his mind ; and all I say about my neighbor's inner life refers directly to this representative. The Scottish philosophy has had much to say to the world about what it calls direct or presentative, as opposed to representative, knowledge of objects. But surely the most obstinate Scottish philosopher that ever ate oatmeal cannot hold so tenaciously by his national doctrine as to say that I have, according to common sense, anything but a representative knowledge of my neighbor's thoughts and feelings. That is the only sort of knowledge that common sense will regard as possible to me, if so much as that is possible. But how I can know about this outside being is not now our concern. We notice only that our difficulty about error comes back to us in a new form. For how can I err about my neighbor, since, for this common-sense view, he is not even partly in my thoughts? How can I intend that as the object of my thought which never can be object for me at all?

But not everybody will at once feel the force of this question. We must be more explicit. Let us take the now so familiar suggestion of our great humorist about the six people that take part in every conversation between two persons. If John and Thomas are talking together, then the real John and Thomas, their respective ideas of themselves, and their ideas of each other, are all parties to the conversation. Let us consider four of these persons, namely, the real John, the real Thomas, John as Thomas conceives him, and Thomas as John conceives him. When John judges, of whom does he think? Plainly of that which can be an object to his thoughts, namely, of *his* Thomas. About whom then can he err? About *his* Thomas? No, for he knows him too well. His conception of Thomas is his conception, and what he asserts it to be, that it is for him. About the real Thomas? No, for it should seem, according to common sense, that he has nothing to do with the real Thomas in his thought, since that Thomas never becomes any part of his thought at all. "But," says one, "there must be some fallacy here, since we are sure that John *can* err about the real Thomas." Indeed he can, say we ; but ours is not this fallacy. Common sense has made it. Common sense has said : " Thomas never is in John's thought, and yet John can blunder about Thomas." How shall we unravel the knot ?

One way suggests itself. Mayhap we have been too narrow in our definition of *object*. Common sense surely insists that objects are outside of our thought. If, then, I have a judgment, and another being sees both my judgment and some outside object that was not in my thought, and sees how that thought is unlike the object in some critical respect, this being could say that my assertion was an error. So then with John and Thomas. *If Thomas could know John's thoughts about him*, then Thomas could possibly see John's error. That is what is meant by the error in John's thought.

But mere disagreement of a thought with any random object does not make the thought erroneous. The judgment must disagree with *its chosen* object. If John never has Thomas in thought at all, how *can* John choose tne real Thomas as his object ? If I judge about a penholder that is in this room, and if the next room is in all respects like this, save for a penholder in it, with which my assertion does not agree, who, looking at that penholder in that other room, can say that my judgment is false ? For I meant not that penholder when I spoke, but this one. I knew perhaps nothing about that one, had it not in mind, and so could not err about it. Even so, suppose that outside of John there is a real Thomas, similar, as it happens, to John's ideal Thomas, but lacking some thought or affection that

John attributes to his ideal Thomas. Does that
make John's notion an error? No, for he spoke and
could speak only of his ideal Thomas. The real
Thomas was the other room, that he knew not of,
the other side of the shield, that he never could conceive. His Thomas was his phantom Thomas. This
phantom it is that he judges and thinks about, and
his thoughts may have their own consistency or inconsistency. But with the real other person they
have nothing to do. The real other is not his object, and how can he err about what is not object
for him?

Absurd, indeed, some one will reply to us. John
and Thomas have to deal with representative phantoms of each other, to be sure; but that only makes
each more apt to err about the real other. And the
test that they can err is a very simple one. Suppose
a spectator, a third person, to whom John and
Thomas were both somehow directly present, so that
he as it were included both of them. Then John's
judgment of his phantom Thomas would be by this
spectator at once compared with the real Thomas,
and even so would Thomas's judgment of John be
treated. If now John's phantom Thomas agreed
with the real Thomas, then John's ideas would be
declared in so far truthful; otherwise they would be
erroneous. And this explains what is meant by
John's power to err about Thomas.

The explanation is fair enough for its own purpose, and we shall need it again before long. But
just now we cannot be content with it. For what
we want to know is not what the judgment of a

third thinker would be in case these two were somehow not independent beings at all, but things in
this third being's thought.   For we have started out
with the supposition of common sense that John
and Thomas are not dreams or thoughts of some
higher third being, but that they are independent
beings by themselves.   Our supposition may have
to be given up hereafter, but for the present we
want to hold fast to it.   And so John's judgment,
which we had supposed to be about the independently existing Thomas, has now turned out to be
only a judgment about John's idea of Thomas.   But
judgments are false only in case they disagree with
their intended objects.   What, however, is the object of John's judgment when he thinks about
Thomas?   Not the real Thomas, who could not possibly be an object in another man's thoughts.   John's
real object being an ideal Thomas, he cannot, if sincere, and if fully conscious of what he means by
Thomas, fail to agree in his statements with his own
ideal.   In short, on this our original supposition,
John and Thomas are independent entities, each of
which cannot possibly enter in real person into the
thoughts of the other.   Each may be somehow represented in the other's thoughts by a phantom, and
only this phantom can be intended by the other
when he judges about the first.   For unless one talks
nonsense, it should seem as if one could mean only
what one has in mind.

Thus, like the characters in a certain Bab ballad,
real John, real Thomas, the people in this simple
tale, are total strangers to each other.   You might

as well ask a blind man to make true or false judgments about the real effects of certain combinations
of colors, as to ask either John or Thomas, defined
as common sense defines them, to make any judgments about each other. Common sense will assert
that a blind man can learn and repeat verbally correct statements about color, or verbally false statements about color, but, according to the common-
sense view, in no case can he err about color-ideas
as such, which are never present to him. You will
be quite ready to say that a dog can make mistakes
about the odors of the numberless tracks on the
highway. You will assure us, however, that you
cannot make mistakes about them because these
odors do not exist for you. According to the common-sense view, a mathematician can make blunders
in demonstrating the properties of equations. A
Bushman cannot, for he can have no ideas corresponding to equations. But how then can John or Thomas
make errors about each other, when neither is more
present to the other than is color to the blind man,
the odor of the tracks on the highway to the dog's
master, or the idea of an equation to a Bushman?
Here common sense forsakes us, assuring us that
there is such error, but refusing to define it.

The inconsistency involved in all this common-
sense view, and the consequences of the inconsistency,
will appear yet better with yet further illustration.
A dream is false in so far as it contains the judgment
that such and such things exist apart from us; but
at least in so far as we merely assert in our dreams
about the objects as we conceive them, we make true

assertions. But is not our actual life of assertions about actual fellow-beings much like a dream to which there should happen to correspond some real scene or event in the world? Such correspondence would not make the dream really " true," nor yet false. It would be a coincidence, remarkable for an outside observer, but none the less would the dreamer be thinking in his dream not about external objects, but about the things in his dream. But is not our supposed Thomas so and only so in the thought of John as he would be if John chanced to dream of a Thomas that was, to an external spectator, like the real one? Is not then the phantom Thomas, John's only direct object, actually a thing in John's thought? Is then the independent Thomas an object for John in any sense?

Yet again. Let us suppose that two men are shut up, each in a closed room by himself, and for his whole life; and let us suppose that by a lantern contrivance each of them is able at times to produce on the wall of the other's room a series of pictures. But neither of them can ever know what pictures he produces in the other's room, and neither can know anything of the other's room, as such, but only of the pictures. Let the two remain forever in this relation. One of them, A, sees on his wall pictures, which resemble more or less what he has seen in his own room at other times. Yet he perceives these to be only pictures, and he supposes them to represent what goes on in another room, which he conceives as like his own. He is interested, he examines the phenomena, he predicts their future changes, he passes

judgment upon them. He may, if you like to continue the hypothesis, find some way of affecting
them, by himself acting in a way mysterious to himself so as to produce changes in B's actual room,
which again affect the pictures that the real B produces in A's room. Thus A might hold what he
would call communication with his phantom room.
Even so, B lives with pictures before him that are
produced from A's room. Now one more supposition, namely, that A and B have absolutely no other
means of communication, that both are shut up altogether and always have been, that neither has any
objects before him but his own thoughts and the
changing pictures on the wall of his room. In this
case what difference does it make whether or no the
pictures in A's room are actually like the things
that could be seen in B's room? Will that make
A's judgments either true or false? Even if A,
acting by means that he himself cannot understand,
is able to control the pictures on his wall by some
alteration that he unconsciously produces in B's
room and its pictures, still A cannot be said to have
any knowledge of the real B and his room at all.
And, for the same reason, A cannot make mistakes
about the real room of B, for he will never even
think of that real room. He will, like a man in a
dream, think and be able to think only of the pictures on his wall. And when he refers them to an
outside cause, he does not mean by this cause the real
B and his real room, for he has never dreamed of the
real B, but only of the pictures and of his own interpretation of them. He can therefore make no false

judgments about B's room, any more than a Bushman can make false judgments about the integral calculus.

If to our present world there does correspond a second world somewhere off in space, a world exactly like this, where just the same events at every instant do actually take place, still the judgments that we make about our world are not actually true or false with reference to that world, for we *mean* this world, not that one, when we judge. Why are not John's Thomas and the real Thomas related like this world and that second world in distant space? Why are not both like the relation of A's conceived phantom room and B's real room? Nothing of either real room is ever present to the other. Each prisoner can make true or false judgments if at all, then, only about the pictures on his wall; but neither has even the suggestion that could lead him to make a blunder about the other's real room, of which he has and can have not the faintest idea.

One reason why we fail to see at once this fact lies in the constant tendency to regard the matter from the point of view of a third person, instead of from the point of view that we still implicitly attribute to A and B themselves. If A could get outside of his room once and see B's room, then he could say: " My picture was a good one," or the reverse. But, in the supposed case, he not only never sees B's room, but he never sees anything but his own pictures, never gets out of his room at all for any purpose. Hence, his sole objects of assertion being his pictures, he is innocent of any power to err about B's room as it is in itself, even as the man born blind

is innocent of any power to err about the relations
of colors.

Now this relation of A and B, as they were supposed to dwell in their perpetual imprisonment, is
essentially like the relation that we previously postulated between two independent subjects. If I cannot have you in my thought at all, but only a picture
produced by you, I am in respect to you like A confined to the pictures produced from B's room. However much I may fancy that I am talking of you, I
am really talking about my idea of you, which for
me can have no relation whatever to the real you.
And so John and Thomas remain shut up in their
prisons. Each thinks of his phantom of the other.
Only a third person, who included them both, who
in fact treated them as, in the Faust-Epilogue, the
Pater Seraphicus treats the *selige Knaben* (*Er
nimmt sie in sich*, says the stage direction) — only
such an inclusive thought could compare the phantoms with the real, and only in him, not in themselves, would John and Thomas have any ideas of
each other at all, true or false.

This result is foreign to our every-day thought, because this every-day thought really makes innocent
use of two contradictory views of the relations of
conscious beings. On the one hand we regard them
as utterly remote from one another, as what Professor Clifford called ejects; and then we speak of
them as if the thoughts of one could as such become
thoughts of the other, or even as if one of them
could as an independent being still become object
in the thought of the other. No wonder that, with

such contradictory assumptions as to the nature of our relations to our neighbors, we find it very easy to make absurd statements about the meaning of error. The contradiction of common sense has in fact just here much to do with the ethical illusion that we called the illusion of selfishness. To clear up this point will be useful to us, therefore, in more ways than one.

VI.

Disappointed once more in our efforts to understand how error is possible, we turn to another class of cases, which lie in a direction where, at least for this once, all will surely be plain. Errors about matters of fact or experience are certainly clear enough in nature. And as this class of errors is practically most important, the subtleties of our previous investigation may be dismissed with light heart so soon as we have gotten rid of the few little questions that will now beset us. It is to be noted that all errors about material objects, about the laws of nature, about history, and about the future, are alike errors about our actual or possible experiences. We expect or postulate an experience that at the given time, or under the given conditions, turns out to be other than it was postulated or expected to be. Now since our experiences not now present are objective facts, and capable of clear definition, it would seem clear that error concerning them is an easily comprehensible thing.

But alas! again we are disappointed. That errors in matters of experience are common enough is

indubitable, but equally evident becomes the difficulty of defining what they are and how they are
possible. Take the case of error about an expected
future. What do we mean by a future time? How
do we identify a particular time? Both these questions plunge us into the sea of problems about the
nature of time itself. When I say, *Thus and so
will it be at such and such a future moment,* I postulate certain realities not now given to my consciousness. And singular realities they are. For
they have now no existence at all. Yet I postulate
that I can err about them. This their non-existence
is a peculiar kind of non-existence, and requires me
to make just such and such affirmations about it.
If I fail to correspond to the true nature of this
non-existent reality, I make an error; and it is postulated not merely that my present statement will
in that case hereafter turn out false or become false,
but also that it is now false, is at this moment an
error, even though the reality with which it is to
agree is centuries off in the future. But this is not
all the difficulty. I postulate also that an error in
prediction can be discovered when the time comes
by the failure of the prediction to verify itself. I
postulate then that I can look back and say: Thus
and thus I predicted about this moment, and thus
and thus it has come to pass, and this event contradicts that expectation. But can I in fact ever
accomplish this comparison at all? And is the comparison very easily intelligible? For when the event
comes to pass, the expectation no longer exists. The
two thoughts, namely, expectation and actual expe-

rience, are separate thoughts, far apart in time. How can I bring them together to compare them, so as to see if they have the same object? It will not do to appeal to memory for the purpose; for the same question would recur about the memory in its relation to the original thought. How can a past thought, being past, be compared to a present thought to see whether they stand related? The past thought lived in itself, had its own ideas of what it then called future, and its own interpretation thereof. How can you show, or intelligently affirm, that the conception which the past expectation had of its future moment is so identical with the conception which this present thought has of this present moment, as to make these two conceived moments one and the same? Here in short we have supposed two different ideas, one of an expected future, the other of an experienced present, and we have supposed the two ideas to be widely separated in time, and by hypothesis they are not together in one consciousness at all. Now how can one say that in fact they relate to the same moment at all? How is it intelligible to say that they do? How, in fine, can a not-given future be a real object of any thought; and how, when it is once the object thereof, can any subsequent moment be identified with this object?

A present thought and a past thought are in fact separate, even as were John and Thomas. Each one means the object that it thinks. How can they have a common object? Are they not once for all different thoughts, each with its own intent? But in order to render intelligible the existence of error about matters of fact, we must make the unintelligible assumption, so it would seem, that these two different thoughts have the same intent, and are but one. And such is the difficulty that we find in our second great class of cases.

VII.

So much for the problem, both in general and in some particular instances. But now may not the reader insist, after all, that there can be in this wise no errors whatever? Contradictory as it seems, have we not, after all, put our judgments into a position whence escape for us is impossible? If every judgment is thus by its nature bound up in a closed circle of thought, with no outlook, can any one come afterwards and give it an external object? Perhaps, then, there is a way out of our difficulty by frankly saying that our thoughts may be neither truths nor errors beyond themselves, but just occurrences, with a meaning wholly subjective.

We desire the reader to try to realize this view of total relativity once more in the form in which, with all its inherent absurdities, it now comes back to us for the last time. It says, " Every judgment, *A is B*, in fact does agree and can agree only with its own object, which is present in mind when it is made. With no external object can it agree or fail to agree. It stands alone, with its own object. It has neither truth nor error beyond itself. It fulfills all its intentions, and is true, if it agrees with what was present to it when it was thought. Only in this sense is there any truth or falsity possible for our thought."

But once more, this inviting way out of the difficulty needs only to be tried to reveal its own contradictions. The thought that says, " No judgment is true beyond itself," is that thought true beyond itself or not? If it is true beyond itself, then we have the possibility of other truth than the merely subjective or relative truth. If it is false, then equally we have objective falsity. If it is neither true nor false, then the doctrine of relativity has not been affirmed at all as a truth. One sets up an idea of a world of separate, disorganized thoughts, and then says, " Each of them deals only with its own object, and they have no unity that could make them true or false." But still this world that one thus sets up must be the true world. Else is there no meaning in the doctrine of relativity. Twist as one will, one gets not out of the whirlpool of thought. Error must be real, and yet, as common sense arranges these judgments and their relations to one another, error cannot be real. There is so far no escape.

The perfectly general character of the argument must be understood. One might escape it if it applied to any one class of errors only. Then one would say : " In fact, the class of cases in question may be cases that exclude the possibility of both truth and error." But no, that cannot be urged against us, for our argument applies equally to all possible errors. In short, either no error at all is possible, or else there must be possible an infinite mass of error. For the possibilities of thought being infinite, either all thought is excluded once for all from the possibility of error, or else to every possi-

ble truth there can be opposed an infinite mass of
error. All this infinite mass is at stake upon the
issue of our investigation. Total relativity, or else
an infinite possibility of truth and error; that is
the alternative before us. And total relativity of
thought involves self-contradiction.

Every way but one has been tried to lead us out
of our difficulty. Shall we now give up the whole
matter, and say that error plainly exists, but baffles
definition? This way may please most people, but
the critical philosophy knows of no unanswerable
problem affecting the work of thought in itself considered. Here we need only patience and reflection,
and we are sure to be some day rewarded. And indeed our solution is not far off, but very nigh us.
We have indicated it all along. To explain how
one could be in error about his neighbor's thoughts,
we suggested the case where John and Thomas
should be present to a third thinker whose thought
should include them both. We objected to this suggestion that thus the natural presupposition that John
and Thomas are separate self-existent beings would
be contradicted. But on this natural presupposition
neither of these two subjects could become object to
the other at all, and error would here be impossible.
Suppose then that we drop the natural presupposition, and say that John and Thomas are both actually present to and included in a third and higher
thought. To explain the possibility of error about
matters of fact seemed hard, because of the natural
postulate that time is a pure succession of separate
moments, so that the future is now as future non-ex·

istent, and so that judgments about the future lack
real objects, capable of identification. Let us then
drop this natural postulate, and declare time once
for all present in all its moments to an universal
all-inclusive thought. And to sum up, let us overcome all our difficulties by declaring that all the
many Beyonds, which single significant judgments
seem vaguely and separately to postulate, are present as fully realized intended objects to the unity
of an all-inclusive, absolutely clear, universal, and
conscious thought, of which all judgments, true or
false, are but fragments, the whole being at once
Absolute Truth and Absolute Knowledge. Then all
our puzzles will disappear at a stroke, and error will
be possible, because any one finite thought, viewed
in relation to its own intent, may or may not be seen
by this higher thought as successful and adequate in
this intent.

How this absolute thought is to be related to individual thoughts, we can in general very simply define. When one says : "This color now before me
is red, and to say that it is blue would be to make a
blunder," one represents an including consciousness.
One includes in one's present thought three distinct
elements, and has them present in the unity of a single moment of insight. These elements are, first,
the perception of red ; secondly, the reflective judgment whose object is this perception, and whose
agreement with the object constitutes its own truth ;
and, thirdly, the erroneous reflection, *This is blue*,
which is in the same thought compared with the perception and rejected as error. Now, viewed as sep-

arate acts of thought, apart from the unity of an including thought, these three elements would give rise to the same puzzles that we have been considering. It is their presence in a higher and inclusive thought that makes their relations plain. Even so we must conceive the relation of John's thought to the united total of thought that includes him and Thomas. Real John and his phantom Thomas, real Thomas and his phantom John, are all present as elements in the including consciousness, which completes the incomplete intentions of both the individuals, constitutes their true relations, and gives the thought of each about the other whatever of truth or of error it possesses. In short, error becomes possible as one moment or element in a higher truth, that is, in a consciousness that makes the error a part of itself, while recognizing it as error.

So far then we propose this as a possible solution for our puzzles. But now we may insist upon it as the only possible solution. *Either there is no such thing as error, which statement is a flat self-contradiction, or else there is an infinite unity of conscious thought to which is present all possible truth.* For suppose that there is error. Then there must be an infinite mass of error possible. If error is possible at all, then as many errors are possible as you please, since, to every truth, an indefinite mass of error may be opposed. Nor is this mere possibility enough. An error is possible for us when we are able to make a false judgment. But in order that the judgment should be false when made, it must have been false before it was made. An error is possible only when the judgment in which the error is to be expressed always was false. Error, if possible, is then eternally actual. Each error so possible implies a judgment whose intended object is beyond itself, and is also the object of the corresponding true judgment. But two judgments cannot have the same object save as they are both present to one thought. For as separate thoughts they would have separate subjects, predicates, intentions, and objects, even as we have previously seen in detail. So that every error implies a thought that includes it and the corresponding truth in the unity of one thought with the object of both of them. Only as present to an including thought are they either true or false. Thus then we are driven to assume an infinite thought, judging truth and error. But that this infinite thought must also be a rational unity, not a mere aggregate of truths, is evident from the fact that error is possible not only as to objects, but as to the relations of objects, so that all the possible relations of all the objects in space, in time, or in the world of the barely possible, must also be present to the all-including thought. And to know all relations at once is to know them in absolute rational unity, as forming in their wholeness one single thought.

What, then, is an error? An error, we reply, is an incomplete thought, that to a higher thought, which includes it and its intended object, is known as having failed in the purpose that it more or less clearly had, and that is fully realized in this higher thought. And without such higher inclusive thought, an assertion has no external object, and is no error.

VIII.

If our argument were a Platonic dialogue, there would be hereabouts an interruption from some impatient Thrasymachus or Callicles or Polus, who would have been watching us, threatening and muttering, during all of the latter part of our discussion. At last, perhaps, συστρέψας ἑαυτὸν ὥσπερ θηρίον, he would spring upon us, and would say : " Why, you nonsense-mongers, have you not bethought you of the alternative that represents the reality in this question of yours ? Namely, an error is an error, neither to the thought that thinks it, nor of necessity to any higher inclusive thought, but only to a *possible* critical thought that should undertake afterwards to compare it with its object. An error is a thought such that *if* a critical thought *did* come and compare it with its object, it *would be* seen to be false. And it has an object for such a critical thought. This critical thought need not be real and actually include it, but may be only a *possible* judge of its truth. Hence your Infinite all-knower is no reality, only a logical possibility ; and your insight amounts to this, that if all *were* known to an all-knower, he *would judge* error to be mistaken. And so error is what he would perceive to be error. What does all that amount to but worthless tautology ? "

This argument of our Thrasymachus is the only outwardly plausible objection that we fear to the foregoing analysis, because it is the only objection that fully expresses the old-established view of common sense about such problems. Though common sense never formulates our present difficulty, common sense still dimly feels that to some possible (not actual) judge of truth, appeal is made when we say that a thing is false not merely for us, but in very truth. And this possible judge of common sense we have now unhesitatingly declared to be an Infinite Actuality, absolutely necessary to *constitute* the relation of truth and error. Without it there is for our view no truth or error conceivable. The words, *This is true*, or *This is false*, mean nothing, we declare, unless there is the inclusive thought for which the truth is true, the falsehood false. No barely possible judge, who *would* see the error *if* he were there, will do for us. He must be there, this judge, to constitute the error. Without him nothing but total subjectivity would be possible; and thought would then become purely a pathological phenomenon, an occurrence without truthfulness or falsity, an occurrence that would interest anybody if it could be observed; but that, unfortunately, being only a momentary phantom, could not be observed at all from without, but must be dimly felt from within. Our thought needs the Infinite Thought in order that it may get, through this Infinite judge, the privilege of being so much as even an error.

This, it will be said, is but reassertion. But how do we maintain this view against our Thrasymachus? Our answer is only a repetition of things that we have already had to say, in the argument for what we here reassert. If the judgment existed alone, without the inclusive thought to judge it, then, as it existed alone, it either had an object, or had none.

But if it had none, it was no error. If it had one, then either it knew what its object actually was, or it did not know what its object was, or it partially knew and partially did not know what its object actually was. In the first case the judgment must have been an identical one, like the judgment *A pain is a pain*. Such a judgment knows its own object, therefore cannot fail to agree with it, and cannot be an error. If the judgment knew not its own object at all, then it had no meaning, and so could not have failed to agree with the object that it had not. If, however, this separate judgment knew its object enough to intend just that object, but not enough to insure agreement with it, all our difficulties return. The possible judge cannot give the judgment its complete object until he becomes its actual judge. Yet as fair judge he must then give it the object that it already had without him. Meanwhile, however, the judgment remains in the unintelligible attitude previously studied at length. It is somehow possessed of just the object it intends, but yet does not know in reality what it does intend, else it would avoid error. Its object, in so far as unknown to it, is no object for it ; and yet only in so far as the object is thus unknown can it be erred about. What helps in all this the barely possible judge? The actual judge must be there; and for him the incomplete intention must be complete. He knows what is really this judgment's object, for he knows what is imperfectly meant in it. He knows the dream, and the interpretation thereof. He knows both the goal and the way thither. But all this is, to the separate judgment as such, a mystery.

In fact, the separate judgments, waiting for the possible judge to test them, are like a foolish man wandering in a wood, who is asked whether he has lost his way. " I may have lost it," he answers. " But whither are you going? " " That I cannot tell? " " Have you no goal? " " I may have, but I have no notion what it is." " What then do you mean by saying that you may have lost the way to this place that you are not seeking? For you seem to be seeking no place; how then can you have lost the way thither? " " I mean that some possible other man, who was wise enough to find whither I am trying to go, might possibly, in his wisdom, also perceive that I am not on the way to that place. So I may be going away from my chosen goal, although I am unaware what goal it is that I have chosen." Such a demented man as this would fairly represent the meaningless claim of the separate judgment, either to truthfulness, or to the chance of error.

In short, though the partial thought may be, as such, unconscious of its own aim, it can be so unconscious only in case it is contained in a total thought as one moment thereof.

It will be seen that wherever we have dealt in the previous argument with the possibility of error as a mere possibility, we have had to use the result of the previous chapter concerning the nature of possibility itself. The idea of the barely possible, in which there is no actuality, is an empty idea. If anything is possible, then, when we say so, we postulate something as actually existent in order to constitute this possibility. The conditions of possible error must be actual. Bare possibility is blank nothingness. If the nature of error necessarily and with perfect generality demands certain conditions, then these conditions are as eternal as the erroneousness of error itself is eternal. And thus the inclusive thought, which constitutes the error, must be postulated as existent.

So, finally, let one try to affirm that the infinite content of the all-including mind does not exist, and that the foregoing idealism is a mere illusion of ours. He will find that he is involved in a circle from which there is no escape. For let him return to the position of total relativity and so say: "The infinite thought is unreal for me, and hence you are wrong." But then also he admits that we are right, for in affirming this infinite we affirm, according to this doctrine of total relativity itself, something that is just as true as it seems to us to be true. The opposing argument is thus at each moment of its progress involved in a contradiction. Or again, let him insist that our doctrine is not only relatively, but really false. Then however he will fail to show us what this real falsity is. In fact he says what all our previous examination shows to mean, this, namely, that an infinite thought does exist, and does experience the truth, and compares our thought with the truth, and then observes this thought of ours to be false, that is, it discovers that itself is non-existent. Whoever likes this result may hold it if he can.

IX.

Now that our argument is completed as an investigation, let us review it in another way. We started from the fact of Error. That there is error is indubitable. What is, however, an error? The substance of our whole reasoning about the nature of error amounted to the result that in and of itself alone, no single judgment is or can be an error. Only as actually included in a higher thought, that gives to the first its completed object, and compares it therewith, is the first thought an error. It remains otherwise a mere mental fragment, a torso, a piece of drift-wood, neither true nor false, objectless, no complete act of thought at all. But the higher thought must include the opposed truth, to which the error is compared in that higher thought. The higher thought is the whole truth, of which the error is by itself an incomplete fragment.

Now, as we saw with this as a starting-point, there is no stopping-place short of an Infinite Thought. The possibilities of error are infinite. Infinite then must be the inclusive thought. Here is this stick, this brickbat, this snow-flake: there is an infinite mass of error possible about any one of them, and notice, not merely possible is it, but actual. All the infinite series of blunders that you could make about them not only would be blunders, but in very truth now are blunders, though you personally could never commit them all. You cannot in fact *make* a truth or a falsehood by your thought. You only *find* one. From all eternity that truth was true, that falsehood false. Very well then, that infinite thought must somehow have had all that in it from the beginning. If a man doubts it, let him answer our previous difficulties. Let him show us how he can make an error save through the presence of an actual inclusive thought for which the error always was error and never became such at all. If he can do that, let him try. We should willingly accept the result if he could show it to us. But he cannot. We have rambled over those barren hills already too long. Save for Thought there is no truth, no error. Save for inclusive Thought, there is no truth, no error, in separate thoughts. Separate thoughts as such cannot then know or have the distinction between their own truth and their own falsity in themselves, and apart from the inclusive thought. There is then nothing of truth or of error to be found in the world of separate thoughts as such. All the thoughts are therefore in the last analysis actually true or false, only for the all-including Thought, the Infinite.

We could have reached the same result had we set out from the problem, *What is Truth?* We chose not to do so because our skepticism had the placid answer ready : " No matter *what* truth is, for very likely there is little or no truth at all to be had. Why trouble one's mind to define what a fairy or a brownie is?" "Very well, then," we said to our skepticism, "if that is thy play, we know a move that thou thinkest not of. We will not ask thee of truth, if thou thinkest there is none. We will ask thee of error, wherein thou revelest." And our skepticism very cheerfully, if somewhat incoherently, answers, that, " if there be little or no truth here below, there is at least any amount of error, which as skeptics we have all been detecting ever since we first went to school." " We thank thee for that word, oh friend, but now, what is an error ? " Blessed be Socrates for that question. Upon that rock philosophy can, if it wants, build we know not yet how much.

It is enough for the moment to sum up the truth that we have found. It is this : " *All reality must be present to the Unity of the Infinite Thought.*" There is no chance of escape. For all reality is reality because true judgments can be made about it. And all reality, for the same reason, can be the object of false judgments. Therefore, since the false and the true judgments are all true or false as present to the infinite thought, along with their objects, no reality can escape. You and I and all of us, all good, all evil, all truth, all falsehood, all things actual and possible, exist as they exist, and are known for what they are, in and to the absolute thought ; are therefore all judged as to their real character at this everlasting throne of judgment.

This we have found to be true, because we tried to doubt everything. We shall try to expound in the coming chapter the religious value of the conception. We can however at once see this in it: The Infinite Thought must, knowing all truth, include also a knowledge of all wills, and of their conflict. For him all this conflict, and all the other facts of the moral world, take place. He then must know the outcome of the conflict, that Moral Insight of our

28

first book. In him then we have the Judge of our ideals, and the Judge of our conduct. He must know the exact value of the Good Will, which for him, like all other possible truth, must be an actually realized Fact. And so we cannot pause with a simply theoretical idealism. Our doctrine is practical too. We have found not only an infinite Seer of physical facts, but an infinite Seer of the Good as well as of the Evil. He knows what we have and what we lack. In looking for goodness we are in no wise looking for what the real world does not contain.

This, we say, we have found as a truth, because we tried to doubt everything. We have taken the wings of the morning, and we have fled; but behold, we are in the midst of the Spirit. Truly the words that some people have thought so fantastic ought henceforth to be put in the text-books as commonplaces of logical analysis : —

> " They reckon ill that leave me out ;
> When me they fly, I am the wings,
> I am the doubter and the doubt." —

Everything finite we can doubt, but not the Infinite. That eludes even our skepticism. The world-builders, and the theodicies that were to justify them, we could well doubt. The apologetic devices wearied us. All the ontologies of the realistic schools were just pictures, that we could accept or reject as we chose by means of postulates. We tried to escape them all. We forsook all those gods that were yet no gods; but here we have found something that abides, and waxes not old, something in which there is no variableness, neither shadow of turning. No power it is to be resisted, no plan-maker to be foiled by fallen angels, nothing finite, nothing striving, seeking, losing, altering, growing weary; the All-Enfolder it is, and we know its name. Not Heart, nor Love, though these also are in it and of it; Thought it is, and all things are for Thought, and in it we live and move.

CHAPTER XII.

THE RELIGIOUS INSIGHT.

If thou betake thyself to the ever-living and abiding Truth, the desertion or death of a friend shall not make thee sad. — Imitation of Christ.

Cum contra sapiens, quatenus ut talis consideratur, vix animo movetur, sed sui et Dei et rerum aeterna quadam necessitate conscius, nunquam esse desinit, sed semper vera animi acquiescentia potitur. — SPINOZA, *Ethica.*

WE are in a new world of Divine Life. The dark world of the powers has passed away from our thought. Here is the Eternal, for which all these powers exist, in which they dwell. Here we are in the presence of the Ideal Judge who knows all Good and Evil. From the other side the world as we approached it had seemed so restless, so disheartening, so deaf. The world of our postulates was a brighter one only because we determined to make it so. But there was something lonesome in the thought that the postulates got, as answer from the real world, only their own echo, and not always that. Their world was rather their own creation than an external something that gave them independent support. Sometimes there seemed to be nothing solid that could echo back anything at all. Now we seem to look upon a truth that satisfies indeed no selfish longings of ours, no whims of theological tradition, no demands of our personal narrow lives. We shall not learn in this way who is first in the kingdom of heaven, nor how the dead are raised, nor any answer to any other special demand of any set of men. We learn, however, this at least: *All truth is known to One Thought, and that Infinite.* What does that imply? Let us see.

I.

Our argument is somewhat near to the thought that partially satisfied St. Augustine when he found it in his Plato. That there should be a truth at all implies, we have seen, that there should be an Infinite Truth, known to an Infinite Thought; or, in other words, that all is for thought, and without thought is nothing that is. We also are a part of this infinite thought. We know not yet more of the nature of this thought, save that it must be eternal, all-embracing, and One. What then shall we be able further to say about it?

To answer would be to expound a system of philosophy. But we must limit ourselves here to the necessary. And so, for the first, we shall try to point out what this ideal and infinite life of thought that we have found as the eternal truth of things *cannot* be expected to accomplish for the purposes of our religion, and then to consider what we may nevertheless dare to hope from it.

It cannot be expected to furnish us an *a priori* knowledge of any fact of experience, of any particular law of nature, of the destiny of any one finite being. All that remains just as dark as it was before.

We neither rejoice in this result, nor lament it. Nobody who wanders into the ideal world may expect to find it ordered for his individual advantage ; nor need he try to find there good investments for his money. The Infinite does not wait for his individual approval ; although morally speaking he may do well to get the approval of the Infinite. The Infinite was not elected to office by his vote, and he may not impeach it for disregard of his humble petitions for good things, nor threaten it with want of confidence because it does not secure passage for his private bills. In so far as to say this is to condemn the Real, we unhesitatingly do so. But then, as we saw in our ethical discussion, the moral insight is not so much concerned with private bills, as with certain greater matters. If the moral insight wants religious support, possibly the failure of all these personal concerns of ours to find any hint of response from the Absolute, may not render impossible the ethical undertakings of the human spirit. If as individuals we must hear the dreadful words from the spirit of nature : *Du gleichst dem Geist den du begreifst, nicht mir ;* still it is possible that with a higher insight, looking upon this same spirit in its eternal and inmost nature, we may yet come with full reason at last to say : *Erhabner Geist, du gabst mir, gabst mir alles, warum ich bat.* For there are demands and demands. Man, as lover, demands success in love, and the course of the world may thwart him ; as toiler, he demands for himself personal immortality, and the course of the world may care naught for his individual life ; as bereaved, as

mourner over his dead, he may demand for his loved
ones also this immortality, and the course of the
world may leave the fate of all his loved ones mysterious forever; as lover of mankind, he may demand an infinite future of blessed progress for his
race, and the law of the dissipation of energy may
give him the only discoverable physical answer to
his demand; as just man, he may cry aloud that evil
shall cease from among men, and the wicked may
still laugh in triumph unpunished. And yet for all
this he may find some higher compensation. Agnostic as he will remain about all the powers of this
world, about the outcome of all finite processes, he
will take comfort in the assurance that an Infinite
Reason is above all and through all, embracing
everything, judging everything, infallible, perfect.
To this Thought he may look up, saying: " Thou
All-Knowing One seest us, what we are, and how we
strive. Thou knowest our frame, and rememberest
that we are as dust. In thy perfection is our Ideal.
That thou art, is enough for our moral comfort.
That thou knowest our evil and our good, that gives
us our support in our little striving for the good.
Not worthless would we be in thy sight; not of the
vile, the base, the devilish party in the warfare of
this world. Thou that judgest shalt say that we,
even in our poor individual lives, are better than
naught. Thou shalt know that in our weakness and
blindness, in our pain and sorrow, in our little days,
in our dark world, ignorant as to the future, confused with many doubts, beset with endless temptations, full of dread, of hesitation, of sloth, we yet

sought, such as we were, to be in our own fashion like thee; to know the truth as thou knowest it, to be full of higher life as thou art full, to be above strife as thou art above it, to be of one Spirit as thou art One, to be perfect as thou art perfect. This thou shalt see in us, and this record shall be eternal, like our knowledge. In thee what we vaguely aim to conceive is clear light. In thee the peace that we strive to find is experienced. And when we try to do right, we know that thou seest both our striving and our successes and our failures. And herein we have comfort. We perish, but thou endurest. Ours is not thy eternity. But in thy eternity we would be remembered, not as rebels against the good, but as doers of the good; not as blots on the face of this part of thy infinite reality, but as healthy leaves that flourished for a time on the branches of the eternal tree of life, and that have fallen, though not into forgetfulness. For to thee nothing is forgotten."

This thought, of the Judge that never ceases to think of us and of all things, never changes, never mistakes, and that knows the Good simply because that Good is an element of the Truth — perhaps this can sustain us when all else fails. Nothing but this may be certain; but this, if it be not all that some people have sought, may be a help to us. This Religion may have no such hot little fires on its altars as we at first longed for; but then it is a very old objection to the stars to say that they bake us no bread, and only glitter up there in the dark to be looked at. Yet even the stars are worth something to us.

II.

But if we leave these limitations of our view, and pass to its positive religious value, our first sense is one of joy and freedom to find that our long sought ideal of a perfect unity of life is here attained. Let us look away for a moment from our finite existence, with its doubts and its problems, to the conception of that infinite life. In that life is all truth, fully present in the unity of one eternal moment. The world is no mass of separate facts, stuck one to another in an external way, but, for the infinite, each fact is what it is only by reason of its place in the infinite unity. The world of life is then what we desired it to be, an organic total; and the individual selves are drops in this ocean of the absolute truth.

Thus then, seen in the light of this our result, the human tasks that we sketched in our ethical discussion find their place in the objective world. Now, and in fact for the first time, we can see what we were really trying to accomplish through our ideal. We were trying in a practical way to realize what we now perceive to be the fullness of the life of God. So that the one highest activity, in which all human activities were to join, is known to us now as the *progressive realization by men of the eternal life of an Infinite Spirit*. So whereas we formerly had to say to men: Devote yourselves to art, to science, to the state, or to any like work that does tend to organize your lives into one life, we may now substitute one absolute expression for all those accidental expressions, and may say : *Devote yourselves to losing your lives in the divine life.* For all these special aims that we have mentioned are but means of accomplishing the knowledge of the fullness of the truth. And Truth is God.

Now this precept is no barren abstraction. It means to take hold of every act of life, however humble and simple. " Where art thou, O man ? " our ideal says to us. " Art thou not in God ? To whom dost thou speak ? With whom dost thou walk ? What life is this in whose midst thou livest ? What are all these things that thou seemest to touch ? Whose is all this beauty that thou enjoyest in art, this unity that thou seekest to produce in thy state, this truth that thou pursuest in thy thought ? All this is in God and of God. Thou hast never seen, or heard, or touched, or handled, or loved anything but God. Know this truth, and thy life must be transformed to thee in all its significance. Serve the whole God, not the irrationally separate part that thy delusions have made thee suppose to be an independent thing. Live out thy life in its full meaning ; for behold, it is God's life."

So, as it seems, the best that we could have wished from the purely moral side is attained. The Divine Thought it is that actually accomplishes what we imperfectly sought to attain, when we defined for ourselves Duty. In the Divine Thought is perfectly and finally realized the Moral Insight and the Universal Will of our ethical discussion. And this insight and will are not realized as by some Power, that then should set about to accomplish their ful-

fillment externally. But in the infinite, where all is
eternally complete, the insight is both present and
fulfilled ; the universal will gets what it seeks.
There is no lack there, nor hesitation, nor striving,
nor doubt, nor weariness ; but all is eternally perfect triumph.

Now this, though it sounds mystical enough to
our untrained common sense, is no mere poetry of
thought. It is the direct philosophical outcome of
what we have found by a purely logical process.
The driest thought, the simplest fragment of rationality, involves this absolute, infinite, and perfect
thought. And this it involves because it involves
the possibility of error, and because, as separate from
the infinite, this possibility of error in a single thought
becomes unintelligible and contradictory. We did
all that we could to escape this conclusion. We
wandered in the thickets of confusion and contradiction, until there was no chance of finding there a
further pathway. And then we turned to see, and
behold, God was in this place, though we had known
it not. The genuine God that we thus found was no
incomplete, struggling God, whom we might pity in
his conflict with evil, but the all-embracing thought,
in which the truth is eternally finished. And this
God it is that we now see as the complete realization
of our own ideal, as of all worthy ideals.

For consider if you will this element in our conception of this Thought. Can this infinite know itself as imperfect, or as not possessing some object
that it knows to be good ? This is impossible, and
doubly so. Not only does the conception of an In-

finite, in which and for which are all things, wholly
exclude the possibility of any good thing beyond
the Infinite itself, but also in still another way does
the same truth appear. For if you suppose that this
infinite thought desires some perfection G, that it
has not, then either it is right in supposing this perfection to be truly desirable, or it is wrong. In
either case the previous argument of Chapter XI.
shows us that the truth or the falsity of this judgment of desire about G must exist as known truth
or falsity for a higher thought, which, including the
thought that desires, and itself actually having this
desired good thing, compares the desired object with
the conception of the thought that desires it, and
judges of them both. Above the desire, then, must
in every case exist the satisfaction of the desire in a
higher thought. So that for the Infinite there can
be no unsatisfied desire. Unsatisfied desire exists
only in the finite beings, not in the inclusive Infinite.

The world then, as a whole, is and must be absolutely good, since the infinite thought must know
what is desirable, and knowing it, must have present
in itself the true objects of desire. The existence
of any amount of pain or of other evil, of crime or
of baseness in the world as we see it, is, thus viewed,
no evidence against the absolute goodness of things,
rather a guaranty thereof. For all evil viewed externally is just an evidence to us finite beings that
there exists something desirable, which we have not,
and which we just now cannot get. However stubborn this evil is for us, that has naught to do with
the perfection of the Infinite. For the infinite did

not make this evil, but the evil, *together with the making of it*, which indeed was also in its separateness evil, — all this is a phenomenon for the infinite thought, which, in knowing this evil, merely knows the absolute desirableness of that which it also possesses, namely, the absolutely good.

We have used here an argument that could not be used in our study of the "World of Doubt." When we there thought evil to be possible for the world as a whole, we conceived that a being who knew all the world would yet desire something better. But what would this imply? It implies that this being would desire a state of things different from the existing one, and would do so believing that state to be better than the existing one. But would he truly know this desired state to be better, or would he only hope so? Who truly knows the value of a state save the one that possesses it? Knowledge is of the present. Therefore this being would not really know the better state, unless it were already actual for him. But in that case he would include not only the present world, but the perfect world, and his total state could not be one of discontent. So the other alternative remains. Our supposed being would only hope the desired state to be better than what was real already for him. But would his hope be a true one? If so, then it could only be true in case this perfection is already realized in a higher thought. For the Infinite then the question, "Is there anything better than what exists?" must be nonsense. For him the actual and the possible fall together in one truth; and this one truth cannot be evil.

On another side, our conception gives us religious support. The imperfection of the purely moral view lay in part in the fact that there was an inner incompleteness about the very definition of our ideal, as well as a doubt about its attainability. This inner incompleteness must however be removed in and for the Infinite Mind. In dealing with the work of life, we came to a point where we said, thus far we can see our way, but beyond that our ideal remains incomplete. We must have faith, so we implied, that if we attained so much of the ideal social condition, the way from that point onward would become clear. But now we see why the way would of necessity become clear to one whose knowledge of life were broad enough and deep enough. For in the Infinite that includes all life, that rests above all finite strife in the absolute attainment of the ideal, there can be no incompleteness, no torso of an ideal, but a perfect knowledge of what is most excellent. Those faint foreshadowings of a perfect life that art and science and social work show to us, must be for the Infinite no faint foreshadowings, but absolute certainty and perfect clearness. Hence by our religious doctrine we get not merely the assurance that such ideals as we have are realized for the Infinite ; but, better than this, we get our first full assurance that our incomplete ideals have an actual completion as ideals. For we thus get our first full assurance that there is in the highest sense any definite ideal at all. Pessimism, as we have seen, implies either doubt about what the ideal state is, or unavoidable lack of that state. And the Infinite can be no Pessimist in either sense.

The religious comfort that a man can get from contemplating all this truth is indeed very different from the consolation of the separate individual as such that many people want their religion to give them. And this very fact furnishes us a good test of moral sincerity. The religious comfort that we find is no comfort save to the truly religious spirit in us. It says to us : "You that have declared your willingness to serve moral ideals because they are such, does this help you to know, not of a goodly place where you personally and individually shall live without tears forever as a reward for your services, but of an eternal Judge that respects in no whit your person, before whom and in whom you are quite open and perfectly known, who now and for all eternity sees your good and your evil, and estimates you with absolute justice ? This blaze of infinite light in which you stand, does it cheer you ? If it does, then you are glad to learn that above all your struggles there is the eternal Victory, amid all your doubts there is the eternal Insight, and that your highest triumph, your highest conception, is just an atom of the infinite truth that all the time is there. But if all this is true of you, then you do love the ideal for its own sake. Then it is not your triumph that you seek, but the triumph of the Highest. And so it is that you rejoice to learn how this that is best in the world not only will triumph, but always has triumphed, since, as you now learn, for God the highest good is thus a matter of direct experience."

The writer remembers well, how some years since, while all this doctrine seemed to him shrouded in doubt, he heard a very thoughtful and pious friend maintain that the greatest comfort to be got from a belief in God is the sense that however much the world may misjudge us, however much even our best and closest friends may misunderstand us, there is one perfect all-knowing Thought that comprehends us far better than we comprehend ourselves. Goodness is, in that thought, estimated at its full worth. Nothing is hidden from the Judge. And what we are, He knoweth it altogether. The present view seems to the author to meet the conditions that his friend here had in mind. Theism as a doctrine that there is a big power that fights and beats down other powers in the service of the good, is open to all the objections before suggested. This warrior, why does he not win? This slayer of evil things, this binder of Satan, who boasts that all things will yet be put under his feet, — has he not had all eternity in which to put all things under his feet, and has he done it yet? He may be indeed good, but somehow disaster seems to pursue him. Religious comfort in contemplating him you can have if you believe in him, but always you feel that this comfort is shadowed by the old doubt; is he after all what we want him to be, the victorious ruler of the world? But if we leave the eternally doubtful contemplation of the world as a heap of powers, and come to the deeper truth of the world as Thought, then these doubts must disappear.

Yet to show that this is true, we must dwell upon doubts a little longer, and must compare our present view of the solution of the problem of evil with the views condemned in Chap. VIII.

III.

So far we have come in joyful contemplation of the Divine Truth. But now is there not a serpent in this Eden also? We have been talking of the infinite goodness; but after all, what shall we still say of that finite "partial evil" of life? We seem to have somehow proved *a priori* that it must be "universal good." For, as we have said, in the Infinite Life of our ideal there can be no imperfection. This, we have said, is the demonstration that we missed all through our study of the world of the Powers. Since we approached that world from without, and never felt the pulse of its heart's blood, we had nothing but doubt after doubt when we contemplated the evil that seemed to be in it. Our efforts to explain evil seemed hollow and worthless. There might be some deeper truth involved in these efforts; but we knew it not. Well, are we right in declaring that we have altogether overcome our difficulty now? Apparently we are as far as ever from seeing *how* the partial evil can be the universal good; we only show, from the conception of the infinite itself, *that* the partial evil must be the universal good. God must see how; and we know this because we know of God. More than this we seem to be unable to suggest.

But will this do? Have we not forgotten one terrible consequence of our doctrine? The partial evil is universal good, is it? There is no evil? All apparent imperfection is an illusion of our partial view? So then *where is the chance to be in a free*

29

*way and of our own choice better than we otherwise
in truth should be?* Is not the arm that is raised
to strike down wickedness paralyzed by the very
thought that was to give it divine strength? This
evil that I fight here in this finite world is a delusion. So then, why fight it? If I do good works,
the world is infinitely good and perfect. If I seem
to do evil works, the world is in truth no worse.
Seeming good is not better than seeming evil, for if
it were, then the seeming evil would be a real defect
in God, in whose life is everything. If I have never
loved aught but God, even so I have never hated
aught but God. It is all alike. God does not need
just me. Or rather I may say, in so far as he needs
me to complete his infinite truth, he already has me
from all eternity. I have nothing to do with the
business, save to contemplate in dizzy indolence the
whirling misty masses of seeming evil, and to say
with a sort of amused reverence that they look very
ill and opaque to me, but that of course God sees
through them clearly enough somehow. The mist is
in truth crystalline water, and he has so quick a
sense as to look beyond the drops as easily as if they
were in the calm unity of a mountain lake. And
so, my religion is simply a contemplation of God's
wisdom, but otherwise an idle amusement.

So says the man who sees only this superficial
view of our doctrine. In so far as, standing once
more outside of some evil thing, we say: "That
thing yonder looks bad, but God must see it to be
good," we do indeed remain indolent, and our religion simply means a sort of stoical indifference to the

apparent distinction of good and evil. This is in
fact the proper practical attitude of even the most
earnest man in the presence of evil that he cannot
understand and cannot affect. In such matters we
must indeed be content with the passive knowledge.
Death and the unavoidable pains of life, the down-
fall of cherished plans, all the cruelty of fate, we
must learn to look at as things to us opaque, but to
God, who knows them fully, somehow clear and rational. So regarding them, we must aim to get to
the stage of stoical indifference about them. They
are to us the accidents of existence. We have no
business to murmur about them, since we see that
God, experiencing them, somehow must experience
them as elements in an absolutely perfect life. For
God we regard not as the mysterious power who
made them, and who then may have been limited to
the use of imperfect means, but as the absolute
thought that knows them; so that, however inexplicable they must now be to us, they are in themselves
nothing that God vainly wishes to have otherwise,
but they are organically joined with the rest of the
glorious Whole.

Such is indeed the only present word for us finite
minds about many of the shadows of seeming evil
that we have to behold in the world of the apparently external facts. Such however is *not* the last
word for us about the only evil that has any immediate moral significance, namely, the evil that we see,
not as an external, shadowy mist, but as a present
fact, experienced in us. Here it is that the objector
just mentioned seems really formidable to us. But

just here it is that we find the answer to him. For in the world of our own acts we have a wondrous experience. We realize evil, we fight it, and, at the same time, we realize our fragment of the perfect divine life in the moment itself of struggling with the evil. And in this wondrous experience lies the whole solution of the ancient problem of the existence of moral evil. For instance, I find in myself a selfish impulse, trying to destroy the moral insight. Now of this evil impulse I do not say, looking at it objectively : " It is somehow a part of the universal good ; " but, in the moment of moral action I *make* it, even in the very moment of its sinfulness, a part of my good consciousness, *in overcoming it.* The moral insight condemns the evil that it experiences ; *and in condemning and conquering this evil it forms and is, together with the evil, the organic total that constitutes the good will.* Only through this inner victory over the evil that is experienced as a conquered tendency does the good will have its being. Now since the perfect life of God must have the absolutely good will, therefore it also must be conscious of such a victory. Thus the solution of our difficulty begins to appear. And thus we reap a new religious fruit from our ethical doctrine, to whose main principles we must once more here refer the reader.

When I experience the victory of the moral insight over the bad will, I experience in one indivisible moment both the partial evil of the selfish impulse (which in itself as a separate fact would be wholly bad) and the universal good of the moral victory, which has its existence only in the over-whelming of the evil. So, in the good act, I experi-ence the good as my evil lost in goodness, as a rebel-lion against the good conquered in the moment of its birth, as a peace that arises in the midst of this tri-umphant conflict, as a satisfaction that lives in this restless activity of inner warfare. This child of inner strife is the good, and the only moral good, we know.

What I here have present in me when I do a good act is an element of God's life. *I here directly ex-perience how the partial moral evil is universal good ;* for so it is a relatively universal good in me when, overcoming myself, I choose the universal will. The bad impulse is still in me, but is defeated. In the choice against evil is the very life of goodness, which would be a pale, stupid abstraction otherwise. Even so, to take another view, in the overcoming of our separateness as individuals lies, as we saw in the previous book, our sense of the worth of the univer-sal life. And what we here experience in the single moment of time, and in the narrowness of our finite lives, God must experience, and eternally. In our single good acts we have thus the specimen of the eternal realization of goodness.

But now how simple becomes the answer to that terrible suggestion of a moment since ! How simple also the solution of the problem of evil ! " If I want to do evil, I cannot," said the objector ; " for God the perfect one includes me with the rest, and so cannot in his perfection be hurt by me. Let me do what I will, my act can only seem bad, and cannot be bad. All evil is illusion, hence there is no moral difference in action possible."

" Right indeed," we answer, " but also wrong, because half the truth. The half kills, the whole gives
life. Why canst thou not do any absolute evil? Because thy evil intent, which, in its separateness,
would be unmixed evil, thy selfish will, thy struggle
against the moral insight, this evil will of thine is no
lonesome fact in the world, but is an element in the
organic life of God. *In him thy evil impulse forms
part of a total good will, as the evil impulse of the
good man forms an element in his realization of
goodness.* In God thy separateness is destroyed,
and with it thy sin as evil. For good will in the infinite is what the good man finds the good will to be
in himself, namely, the organic total whose truth is
the *discovery of the evil.* Therefore is God's life
perfect, because it includes not only the knowledge
of thy finite wicked will, but the insight into its truth
as a moment in the real universal will.

If then thou wert good, thou wouldst be good by
including the evil impulse in a realization of its
evil, and in an acceptance of the higher insight. If
thou art evil, then in thyself, as separate being, thou
art condemned, and just because thy separate evil
is condemned, therefore is the total life of God, that
includes thee with thy condemnation and with the
triumph over thee, good.

This is the ground for the solution of the problem.
To go more into detail: Evil is for us of two classes:
the external seeming evil, such as death, pain, or
weakness of character; and internal evil, namely the
bad will itself. Because we know so little, therefore we can never tell whether those externally seen

seeming evils are blessings in disguise, or expressions of some wicked diabolical will-power at work about us. Somehow then, we never know exactly how, these seeming great evils must be in God universal good. But with regard to the only evil that we know as an inward experience, and so as a certain reality, namely, the Evil Will, we know both the existence of that, and its true relation to universal goodness, because and only because we experience both of them first through the moral insight, and then in the good act. Goodness having its very life in the insight and in its exercise, has as its elements the evil impulse *and* its correction. The evil will as such may either be conquered in our personal experience, and then we are ourselves good; or it may be conquered not in our thought considered as a separate thought, but in the total thought to which ours is so related, as our single evil and good thoughts are related to the whole of us. The wicked man is no example of God's delight in wickedness, just as the evil impulse that is an element in the good man's goodness, and a very real element too, is no proof that the good man delights in evil. As the evil impulse is to the good man, so is the evil will of the wicked man to the life of God, in which he is an element. And just because the evil will is the only evil that we are sure of, this explanation is enough.

Thus the distinction between good and evil remains as clear as ever. Our difficulty about the matter is removed, not by any barren external theodicy, such as were the forms of guess-work that we criticised in a previous chapter, but by a plain reflection on the moral experience itself. Goodness as a moral experience is for us the overcoming of experienced evil; and in the eternal life of God the realization of goodness must have the same sort of organic relation to evil as it has in us. Goodness is not mere innocence, but realized insight. To the wicked man we say: God is good because in thinking thee he damns thy evil impulse and overwhelms it in a higher thought of which thou art a part. And in so far as thy will is truly evil, thou art in God just as the evil is in the good man; thou art known only to be condemned and overcome. That is thy blessed mission; and this mission of evil such as thine is indeed an eternal one. So that both things are true. The world is wholly good, and thou, such as thou individually art, mayest be damnably evil if so thou desirest.

We do not say then that evil must exist to set the good off by way of external contrast. That view we long since justly rejected. We say only that the evil will is a conquered element *in* the good will, and is as such necessary to goodness. Our conception of the absolute unity of God's life, and that conception alone, enables us to apply this thought here. No form of dualistic Theism has any chance to apply this, the only satisfactory theodicy. If God were conceived as external to his creatures, as a power that made them beyond himself, the hopeless problems and the unworthy subterfuges of the older theodicies would come back to torment us. As it is, the solution of the problem of evil is given us in the directest and yet in the most unexpected way.

Let us compare this solution with others. Evil, said one thought, before expounded, is an illusion of the partial view, as the shapelessness of the fragment of a statue is no disproof of the real beauty of the whole. We replied in a previous chapter to this notion, by saying that evil seems so positive an element in the world as to make very hard this conception of the partial evil as good universally in the æsthetic sense in which shapelessness of parts may coexist with a total beauty of the statue. For the fragment of the statue is merely an indifferent bit of stone without character. But the evil in the world seems in positive crying opposition to all goodness. Yet now, in the moral experience, we have found a wholly different relation of evil part to good whole. My good act is good just because of the evil that exists in it as conquered element. Without the evil moment *actual* in it, the total act could be at best innocent, not good. It is good by reason of its structure. That structure includes the evil will, but so includes it that the whole act is good. Even so, as we declare, God's life includes, in the organic total of one conscious eternal instant, all life, and so all goodness and evil. To say that God is nevertheless perfectly good is to say, not that God is innocent, knowing of no evil whatever, and including none; but that he so includes the evil will in the structure of his good will, as the good man, in one indivisible moment, includes his evil will in his good will; and that God is good only because he does so.

Again, to pass to another explanation, it has been

said that evil exists in the world as a means to goodness. We objected to this that it puts the evil and
the good first in separate beings, in separate acts or
moments, and then makes the attainment of the good
result dependent on the prior attainment of the separate and independently present evil. Now all that
explanation could only explain and justify the acts
of a finite Power, which, not yet possessing a given
good thing, seeks it through the mediation of some
evil. In no wise can this explanation apply to God
as infinite. He is no finite Power, nor does he make
or get things external to himself. Hence he cannot
be said to use means for the attainment of ends.
But our explanation does not make evil a means to
get the separate end, goodness. We say that the connection is one of organic part with organic whole;
that goodness has its life only in the instant of the
discovery and inner overcoming of the evil will; and
that therefore any life is good in which the evil will
is present only as overcome, and so as lost in the
good will. We appeal to the moral experience to illustrate how, when we do good, the evil will is present as a real fact in us, which yet does not make us
as a whole bad, but just because it is present as an
overcome element, is, even for that very reason, necessary to make us good. And we go on to say that
even so in God the evil will of all who sin is present, a real fact in the Divine Life, no illusion in so
far as one sees that it exists in God and nowhere
else, but for that very reason an element, and a necessary element, in the total goodness of the Universal Will, which, realized in God, is related to the

wills of the sinners as the wills of the good men are related to their evil impulses.

The explanation that evil is needed to contrast with goodness has already been mentioned.

Evil therefore, as a supposed real fact, *separate* from goodness, and a totally independent entity, is and must be an illusion. The objections to this view that we previously urged in Chapter VIII. were all applicable to the world of powers, which we viewed and had to view externally. God's life, viewed internally, as philosophy must view it, is not subject to these criticisms. And the moral experience has taught us how we are to explain the existence of the only partial evil that we clearly know to be even a partial evil, namely, the evil will. The explanation is that the good act has its existence and life *in the transcending of experienced present evil.* This evil must not be an external evil, beyond the good will, but must be experienced in the same indivisible moment in which it is transcended. That this wondrous union is possible, we simply find as fact in the moral experience. No genuine moral goodness is possible save in the midst of such inner warfare. The absence of the evil impulse leaves naught but innocence or instinct, morally insipid and colorless. Goodness is this organism of struggling elements. Now, as we declare, in the infinite and united thought of God this unity of goodness is eternally present. God's life is this infinite rest, *not apart from but in the endless strife,* as in substance Heraclitus so well and originally taught.

IV.

The problem of the existence of evil thus treated as our limits allow, we must return to a study of the visible world. That we formerly refused to find religious comfort in that world, depended upon our previous manner of approaching it. It was, so approached, the world of doubt; but now it may prove no longer disheartening, so that we may be able to get in it a concrete hold of useful truth. We must briefly sketch the process of return. Our Infinite, once known, is known not as an abstraction, but as an immediately actual object of knowledge. His then is this visible world; and, knowing the fact, we return cheerfully and courageously among the facts that before seemed dead externalities, to find his truth in them. For our general belief in the infinite rationality of things is useless to supersede any jot or tittle of careful scientific study of the common world of experience. Be this aspect of the matter well understood. Some older forms of idealism have looked coldly on experience. Ours does not. To us, if you want to realize your ideal you must know the means, you must study applied ethics as well as the ideal itself; and only from science, from hard, dry, careful collection and collaboration of facts, from cautious generalizations, from endless experiments, observations, calculations, can mankind hope to learn the means of realizing their ideals. Yet more, only from exact science can you get the best concrete examples of that unity of conception, that mastery of complex details, that exhaustive perfection of insight, that we must attribute in an infinitely complete form to our all - embracing Ideal Thought, now that we have got it before us as our Ideal. That all facts and relations of facts should appear in one moment of insight to the all-knowing thought is our postulate, and, as we have shown, it is no mere postulate, but a necessary and absolute principle of philosophy. We must go to exact science to find illustrations of how all this can be in particular cases realized. As the equation of a curve expresses in one thought all the properties of the curve, as the law of a physical process includes all the cases of that process under any of the supposed conditions, as a function of a variable may be the sum of a long series of quantities, each one of which is a derived function of the first multiplied by a particular coefficient, so that the one function is the united expression of the numerous separate functions: even in such wise must the Infinite thought comprehend in some supreme highest unity all the facts and relations of facts that are in the world of truth. For us then the highest achievements of science are the dim shadow of the perfection of the infinite thought. And to science, accordingly, we must go, not for the invention, but for the intellectual illustration of our ideal. And science we must treat as absolute mistress of her own domain. Of the world as a whole, of the eternal as such, of infinite past time, of the inner truth of things, science pretends to tell and can tell nothing. Nor does science invent, nor yet can she prove, her own postulates, as we previously defined them. But in the application of her postu-

lates to the facts, in the discovery of particular laws,
science is almighty.   To doubt her capacity as highest judge in this field is flagrant contempt of court.
Science is just the Infinite Thought as far as it is
yet by us realized in the facts of nature. *A priori*
we can realize nothing about finite facts, save that
they must be *capable* of rational comprehension.
We know that the Infinite thinks them, and this is
all that we know about them.   What they are, experience must tell us.

Such then are some of the restrictions imposed
upon our thought.   We must now consider more
carefully how we must treat the scientific postulates
that were our only comfort in studying reality before
we reached our present insight.

When we postulated that the world must in the
best sense satisfy our fundamental intellectual needs,
we assumed what is necessary for science, but what
science itself does not satisfactorily explain.   Have
we now reached any foundation for this theoretical
postulate?   We have in fact reached one.   The postulate of science amounts to this, that the real connections among facts must be such as would be rationally comprehensible if they were known.   But
we have found in fact that all facts not only must
be rationally comprehensible, but are rationally comprehended, in and by the one Divine Mind.   The
postulate of science expresses therefore in part and
as a mere assumption, what we now know as a whole,
and as a result of demonstration.   The unity of the
Divine Thought implies that all facts, if we knew
them well enough, would appear rationally interde-

pendent, reducible to unity, a total of realities expressible as one truth. Just as in the one concept of the nature of number is implied all the infinite series of properties that a complete Theory of Numbers would develop, so in the one concept of the universe, which constitutes the Divine Mind, all the facts of all possible experience are comprehended and are reduced to perfect unity. There must be then in fact a universal formula. What this formula is we do not see, and just because we do not see it, we have to look here and there in experience for any traces of the unity and rational connection of facts. Nor can we ever be sure that a connection surmised by us is the really rational connection of things. A law discovered by us is only our attempt to imitate the Divine Thought. Our attempt may in a given case fail; our induction may be mistaken. But the foundation of our inductive processes is the thought that, since the real world is a perfectly rational and united body of truth, that hypothesis which reduces to relatively rational unity the greatest number of facts is more apt to represent the truth of things than any hypothesis of less scope, and of less rational significance. Just because this natural dualism with which we set out is a blunder, just because in fact the world is not rent in twain by our arbitrary distinction of object and subject, but is in deepest truth one united world, a single thought; therefore it is that when we consider those facts which we have from moment to moment to regard as external, we can be assured that there is a certain and not an arbitrary basis for our views about them. The vis-

ible world becomes again hard reality, which we experience and try to comprehend, just because we
know that in itself this world is once for all comprehended.

Practically then, in dealing with the world of concrete facts, we must be realistic. It is our duty, for
humanity's sake, to study and to believe in this external world, to have faith in the great postulates of
common sense, to use all the things of the world.
But the basis of this faith common sense can never
find. And we have found it in the Absolute.

V.

Have we then discovered that something of infinite religious worth of which we went in quest? Or
can we say that our life is in vain in such a world?
Truly our religious longing has met with a genuine
response, but it was not such a response as we at
first expected, nor such as most systems appear to
desire. Personal needs and hopes apart, most men
who make systems to satisfy the impersonal religious
longing, seek to prove that the world as a whole
progresses towards goodness, so that, in the great
consummation of this progress, evil shall certainly
and finally disappear, leaving the world as innocent
and insipid as in the days of Eden. Now we have
found a thought that makes this concept of progress
not only wholly inapplicable to the world of the infinite life, but wholly superfluous. If, as we insisted
above, moral goodness is not the absence, but the organic subordination, of the evil will, its overthrow in

the good will, in which it is still actually present as subdued, then, whenever the world contains any moral goodness, it also, and for that very reason, contains, in its organic unity, moral evil. The world is morally good in spite of the evil will, and yet because of the evil will, since, as every moral experience shows us, the good will is just this triumphant rest in strife above the evil will. Therefore we have no sympathy with those who expect the future " salvation " of the world as a whole in time through any all-pervading process. The only destruction of moral evil that ever takes place or can take place is the transcendence of the evil will by the good will in the very moment of the life of the evil will. If moral evil were to be, as the older systems often expect, absolutely destroyed, and the world so freed therefrom that the evil will was totally forgotten, then what remained would be no moral good any more, only the laziness of an infinitely vacant life. Not indeed to set off the good by any external contrast, but to constitute a moment in the organic unity of the good act, is this evil in the world. And the whole vast trouble about understanding its presence arises because we usually separate it from the very unity with goodness in which we find it whenever we consciously do right ourselves. Then when so separated, as we separated it in a former chapter, moral evil, viewed as an external opaque fact, is inexplicable, disheartening, horrible. Only when we do right ourselves do we practically get the solution of the problem. Only the moral man knows how and why evil exists. For in him the evil will is an essential element of his goodness. The conflicts of morality are and must be eternal.

Our present explanation of evil in the world is, we have seen, the only one that can both give us the absolute religious comfort, and save us from the terrible moral paralysis involved in destroying, for the Infinite, the distinction between good and evil. The moral experience itself contains the miracle of this solution in the simplest and clearest shape. And it relieves us of any need to long for an absolute peace. For in it the distinction of good and evil is the sharpest, the significance of the strife is the most vivid, at the very instant when, in the strife, the evil will, present and real still, is yet conquered by the good will, and so lost in the universal goodness of the total good act. The distinction of good will and evil will becomes thus the greatest possible; and yet only through the reality of this distinction in the unity of the moral life is goodness present and triumphant. Progress in this world as a whole is therefore simply not needed. The good is eternally gained even in and through the evil. How far the actual process of evolution may in our part of the universe extend is a matter for empirical science.

But our own ideal of human life as a " progressive realization of the good," — what of that? The answer is obvious. The good will that is in us as a temporal fact, not being yet fully realized or triumphant in us *as we are in ourselves as mere finite beings*, must aim at complete expression of itself in time and in us, and through us in those whom we seem to influence. For only *in so seeking* to per-

fect us in whom it exists, is this good will in us good
at all. In so far as we, viewed abstractly, in our
separateness from God, are good, we then do indeed
try to realize that life of God in which we are all
the time an element. For us this is progress. This
progress is the form taken temporarily in us by the
good will. But for God this is no real progress.
Therefore is it indeed true that the moral insight in
us must lead us to aim at progress in goodness, just
as, on the other side, the rational element in us leads
us to aim at progress in knowledge. But, meanwhile,
our moral progress and our rational progress, mere
minor facts happening at a moment of time, are but
insignificant elements in the infinite life in which, as
a whole, there is and can be no progress, but only
an infinite variety of the forms of the good will and
of the higher knowledge.

And so consciousness has given us in concrete
form solutions of our two deepest philosophic problems. The possibility of error, necessitating an inclusive thought, is illustrated for us by our own conscious thought, which can include true and false elements in the unity of one clear and true thought at
any moment. And the possibility and necessity of
moral evil, demanding a real distinction between
good and evil, a hateful opposition that seems at first
sight fatal to our religious need for the supremacy
of goodness in the united world, is illustrated for us
in a way that solves this whole trouble, namely, in
the unity of the conscious moral act. There at the
one moment are good and evil, warring, implacable,
yet united in the present momentary triumph of the

good will.   A world in which this strife, this victory, this absolute rest above the real strife and in
the midst of the real strife, is the supreme fact, is
the perfect world that religion needs.   It is a world
of the true Life of God.

VI.

And our insight appeals not only to our general
religious needs.   It comes with its truth home to the
individual man.   It demands that we consider what
our individual life is really worth when it is lived in
the presence of this Infinite Judge.   O man, what
is this thy daily life !   Thou livest for the applause
or in fear of the blame of thy neighbors.   An unkind
word cuts thee to the quick.   A little public favor,
or the approving word of a friend, is worth half thy
soul to thee.   And all the while thou knowest not
that One infinitely greater than multitudes of neighbors is here, not above thee only, nor afar in the
heavens, but pervading thy every thought.   And that
all-pervading Thought judges thee as these neighbors never can.   Myriads of their blunders about
thee are as nothing to an atom of this infinite Truth.
That rain-drop yonder in the sunshine is not more
filled with the light, than are all the most hidden re-
cesses of thy heart filled with that Infinite Presence.
No one of us is more famous than his neighbor; for
no one is known save by God, and to him all alike
are known.   To be sure, to know this is the same
as understanding rightly, that thou art in truth what
thou art.   All truth is truth because it is known by

a conscious Thought : therefore whatsoever thou art, whether it is consciously or unconsciously existent in thee, is known to the all-seeing Universal Consciousness. But commonplace as this seems to the philosopher, is it not more than a mere commonplace to thee, if thou lovest genuine righteousness? For is it not something to feel that thy life is, all of it, in God and for God? No one else knows thee. Alone thou wanderest in a dead world, save for this Presence. These other men, how can they know thee? They love thee or scorn thee or hate thee, but none of them love or scorn or hate thee for what thou art. Whatever they hold of thee, it is an accident. If they know more of thee, doubtless they would think otherwise of thee. Do they love thee? Then they know thee not well enough, nor do they see thy meanness and thy vileness, thy selfishness and thy jealousy and thy malice. If they saw these, surely they would hate thee. But do they hate thee? Then thou callest them unjust. Doubtless they are so. Some chance word of thine, a careless look or gesture, an accident of fortune, a trifling fault, these they have remembered ; and therefore do they hate thee. If they knew better things of thee, perhaps they would love thee.

Thus contradictory is thy life with them. And yet thou must labor that the good may triumph near thee by thy effort. Now in all this work who shall be thy true friend? Whose approval shall encourage thee? Thy neighbor's? Nay, but it is thy duty always to suspect thy neighbor's opinion of thee. He is a corrupt judge, or at best an ignorant judge.

He sees not thy heart. He is a respecter of persons.
He is too often a bundle of whims. If he also professes to be trying to serve righteousness, it is thy
duty to have ready faith in his good intent, if that
be possible for thee; but by all means doubt his
wisdom about thee, and thine about him. If he
praises thee for thy righteousness, listen not willingly
to his praise. It will deceive thee. He will most
praise thee when thou inwardly art not righteous.
If he blames thee for evil, let it warn thee; for if
he is not right now, he doubtless soon will be. But
take it not too much to heart. He is ignorant of
thee. He talks of thee as he might talk of the other
side of the moon, unless indeed he talks of thee just
as man in general, and not as to thy particular acts.
Trust him not in all these things. Realize his needs
as thou canst, strive to aid him in being righteous,
use him as an instrument for the extension of goodness; but trust not his judgment of thee. Who
then is, as the true judge of thy worth, thy only perfect friend?

The Divine Thought. There is the opinion of
thee to which thou canst look up. To be sure it is
revealed to thee only in thy consciousness of what
righteousness is and of what truth is. Nowhere else
hast thou a guide that can do more for thee than to
help to quicken thy insight. But, then, thy religious comfort is to be, not that the moral law is thun-
dered down from mountain-tops as if some vast
town-crier were talking, but that when thou seekest
to do right, the Infinite all-seeing One knows and
approves thee. If thou lovest righteousness for its

own sake, then this will comfort thee. If not, if
thou seekest sugar-plums, seek them not in the home
of the Infinite. Go among thy fellow-men and be a
successful hypocrite and charlatan, and thou shalt
have gaping and wonderment and sugar - plums
enough.

Herein then lies the invitation of the Infinite to
us, that it is, and that it knows us. No deeper sanction is there for true righteousness than this knowledge that one is serving the Eternal. Yet when we
say all this, are we simply doing that which we spoke
of in the opening chapter of this work? Are we
but offering snow to appease the religious hunger?
Is this doctrine too cold, too abstract, too far-off?
Cold and abstract and far-off is indeed the proof of
it. But that was philosophy. That was not the religious aspect of our doctrine, but only the preparation for showing the religious aspect of philosophy.
Is the doctrine itself, however, once gained, so remote from the natural religious emotion? What
does a man want when he looks to the world for religious support? Does he want such applause as
blind crowds give men, such flattery as designing
people shower upon them, such sympathy as even the
cherished but prejudiced love of one's nearest friends
pours out for him? Nay, *if* he seeks merely this,
is he quite unselfishly righteous? Can he not get
all that if he wants it, wholly apart from religion?
And if he looks for reward, can he not get that also
otherwise? But what his true devotion to the moral
law ardently desires is *not to be alone*. Approval
for what really deserves approval he needs, approval

from one who truly knows him. Well, our doctrine says that he gets it. Just as deep, as full, as rich, as true approval as expresses the full worth of his act, — this he has for all eternity from the Infinite. To feed upon that truth is to eat something better than snow, but as pure as the driven snow. To love that truth is to love God.

We spoke in the former book of the boundless magnitude of human life as it impresses itself upon one who first gains the moral insight. To many this first devotion to human life seems itself enough for a religion. But then one goes beyond this point, and says that human life has, after all, very much that is base and petty in it. Here is not the ideal. " Would that there were a higher life ! To that we would devote ourselves. We will serve humanity, but how can we worship it ? " Such is the thought of many an ardent soul that seeks no personal re- wards in serving the good, but that does seek some great Reality that shall surely be worthy of service. To such, our religious insight points out this higher reality. You that have been willing to devote your- selves to humanity, here is a Life greater in infinite degree than humanity. And now is it not a help to know that truly to serve humanity is just the same as to serve this Infinite ? For whatever had seemed disheartening in the baseness and weakness of man loses its discouraging darkness now that all is trans- figured in this Infinite light.

Let us then be encouraged in our work by this great Truth. But let us not spend too much time in merely contemplating this Truth. We, whose lives are to be lived in toil, — it is not good that we should brood over even an infinite Thought. For in our finite minds it will soon become petty, unless we realize it chiefly through our acts. Let us then go about our business. For every man has business and desire, such as they are.

As we turn away then for the time from our contemplation, we have one last word yet as to these practical consequences of our view. If the reader follows us at all in our argument, we want him also to follow us into the practical application of it to life. To work for the extension of the moral insight is, we have said, the chief present duty of man in society. All else is preparation for this work, or else is an anticipation of the higher stage when, if we ever grow up to that level, we shall have our further work to do in the light of the insight itself. But this chief present work of ours, this extension of the moral insight, is best furthered by devotion to our individual vocations, coupled with strict loyalty to the relations upon which society is founded. The work thus set before us demands the sacrifice of many ideal emotional experiences to the service of the Highest. Our comfort however in it all must be that the Highest is there above us, forget it as we may. If the reader accepts all this, then with us he has the assurance that, whatever becomes of the old creeds in the present religious crisis, the foundations of genuinely religious faith are sure.

Whenever we must pause again in our work for religious support, and whenever we are worn out with the jargon of the schools, we can rest once more for a time in this contemplation of the Eternal Truth. *Hic breve plangitur.* But not so is it in God's life. Our problems may be hard, but there all is solved. Our lives may be poor and contemptible, but there all is wealth and fullness of worth. Our efforts may often prove vain, but there naught exists that is vanity. For the imperfection of the finite is but the fragment of the Infinite Whole where there is no true imperfection. Is it not a Religion to feel this? And we shall then turn from such a contemplation once again as we do now, to look with fresher courage at this boundless, tossing sea of human life about us. This is not itself the Divine, but over it all God's winds are blowing. And to our eyes it is boundless. Let us go down into this great sea and toil, fearing no storm, but seeking to find there treasures that shall be copies, however faint, of that which is Eternal.

EPILOGUE.

YET some reader, to whom, as to the author, philosophic questions are directly matters of vocation, may possibly linger. To him are due one or two statements more, to set at rest certain of his doubts about our meaning. Perhaps he will ask the very natural, yet, after all, not very fruitful, question, " Is the foregoing theory of things Theism or Pantheism? Has it been your purpose to defend the essential portions of the older Theistic doctrines, or to alter them in favor of some newer faith?" This question expresses a difficulty that some plain people must feel when they read, not merely this book, but also many recent discussions. There are writers who have undertaken to defend Theism, and who have actually in all sincerity argued for the necessity of the Universal Thought. The plain people have reason to suspect such of trying to substitute for the " God of our Fathers " something else, to be called by the same name, and so to be passed off for the same thing. We therefore answer very plainly that we desire to do nothing of the sort. If in the foregoing we have on occasion used the word God, no reader is obliged to suppose that our idea agrees with his idea, for we have fully explained what our idea means. We repeat : As my thought at any time, and however engaged, combines several fragmentary thoughts into the unity of one conscious moment, so, we affirm, does the Universal Thought combine the thoughts of all of us into an absolute unity of thought, together with all the objects and all the thoughts about these objects that are, or have been, or will be, or can be, in the Universe. This Universal Thought is what we have ventured, for the sake of convenience, to call God. It is not the God of very much of the traditional theology. It is the God of the idealistic tradition from Plato downwards. Our proof for it is wholly different from those baseless figments of the apologetic books, the design-argument, and the general argument from causality. Since Kant, those arguments must be abandoned by all critical philosophers, and we have indicated something of their weakness. They have been aptly compared to mediæval artillery on a modern battle-field. We accept the comparison. Kant gave to modern philosophy new instruments, and these it is our duty to apply as we can to the old questions that the whole history of thought has been trying to understand. Our special proof for the existence of an Universal Thought has been based, in the foregoing, upon an analysis of the nature of truth and error as necessary conceptions. We do not regard the Universal Thought as in any commonly recognized sense a Creator. A creator would be finite, and his existence would have to be learned from experience. The Universal Thought is infinite, and its existence is proved independently of experience. For the rest, we have insisted that experience furnishes no evidence of single creative powers that are at once unlimited and good. We have however shown how all the Powers that be exist as necessary facts in the Infinite Thought, and how, apart from this thought, nothing is that is. Such is our conception. It is no new one in philosophy. We have tried with no small labor, and after tedious doubting, to make it our own. We have independently given our own reasons for it. And we have asserted that here is an object of infinite religious worth.

And now we must add that we are quite indifferent whether anybody calls all this Theism or Pantheism. It differs from the commoner traditional forms of both. Both usually consider God as a Power, and either leave him off on one side to push things occasionally, or to set them going at the outset, or else identify him with his products. The former way of conceiving God is never more than halfphilosophic. The latter way is apt to degenerate into wholly poetical rhapsodies. We take neither of these ways. For us Causation is a very subordinate idea in philosophy. It expresses only one form of the rational unity of things, and that an imperfect form. The world of the Powers is not yet an universe. Thought must be truer than Power, comprehending all the Powers, and much more besides, in its infinite unity. God as Power would be nothing, or finite. God as Thought can be and is all in all. And if this is philosophy, traditional Theism can do what it wishes to do about the matter.

In short, the present doctrine is the doctrine that in the beginning was the Word, and the Word was with God, and the Word was God. So far, said St.

Augustine, Plato had gone. So far we have gone. Beyond that, said St. Augustine, the truth was not revealed to human wisdom, but only to humble faith. Beyond that, with the rational consequences that we have been able to draw from it in the foregoing, we are frankly agnostic. If any man knows more about the Powers in the world than science has found out by patient examination of the facts, let him rejoice in his knowledge. We are not in possession of such knowledge. We believe in the Conservation of the physical forces, in the Law of Evolution as it is at present and for a limited past time found to express the facts of nature, and in the fact of the Dissipation of Energy. All this we believe as the scientifically probable view, and we do so on the authority of certain students of physical science, who, having examined the facts, seem to agree upon so much as capable of popular exposition. We believe in such other results of science as are known to us. But beyond this nothing as to the Powers in the world is clear to us. We know nothing about individual immortality, nothing about any endless future progress of our species, nothing about the certainty that what men call from without goodness must empirically triumph just here in this little world about us. All that is dark. We know only that the highest Truth is already attained from all eternity in the Infinite Thought, and that in and for that Thought the victory that overcometh the world is once for all won. Whatever happens to our poor selves, we know that the Whole is perfect. And this knowledge gives us peace. We know that our moral Vindicator liveth, and that in his sight all the good that we do is not labor lost.

Yet the purpose of these chapters is not to give at any point a mere negation, even when we speak of the traditional theology. We do not want to exaggerate our quarrel with anybody. If thinkers who accept some traditional form of theology find truth or help in our doctrine, we shall be glad. After all, the religious interest wants, not so much this or that view about some man's special creed, but a foundation for the faith that somehow righteousness is in deepest truth triumphant in the world. If there is no proof, then, as we said in Chapter IX., we must resort to the Postulates. If we can get proof, so much the better.

Thus, however, we have suggested to ourselves another question. These Postulates of Chapter IX., what has become of them now? Are they wholly lost in our insight? No indeed. They remain just what they were, rational forms of our activity, not perfect in their rationality, but constantly valuable to us in our work. The scientific postulates are not superseded, but rather only strengthened, by the insight into the ultimate rationality of things. They become now the assurance that there must be a rational solution to every scientific problem, and that the simplest solution, being the most rational, is the most probable, in case it is actually adequate to all the facts. Just as before, it remains true of us finite beings that our finite external world is at each instant the product of our activity, working with the postulates, upon the material of our sensations. And

that activity remains as before the proper object of a
moral judgment. Only now we see that the highest
form of our activity is likely to be the one most conforming to the truth. What remains true of the
scientific postulates, remains true of the religious
postulates. They are not superseded. For what they
can still do for us is to insist that our idea of the Infinite shall not remain a cold, barren abstraction,
but that we shall appeal to our experience for evidence of what is truly highest and best, and that we
shall then say : " The highest conceptions that I get
from experience of what goodness and beauty are,
the noblest life that I can imagine, the completest
blessedness that I can think of, all these things are
but faint suggestions of a truth that is infinitely realized in the Divine, that knows all truth. Whatever perfection there is suggested in these things,
that He must fully know and experience." Therefore the religious postulates can accompany us everywhere, making all our experience appear to us as an
ever-fresh lesson concerning the mind of God.

The postulates, then, we retain, with the insight.
We abandon, however, the use of these postulates
to demonstrate further special articles of faith as
to supernatural powers or events of any sort. We
know of no miracle save the Infinite himself. And
so we have no interest in many of the forms of popular idealism. To prove that this world is the home
of a Spiritual Life, many good people have been and
are concerned to prove that certain phenomena which
we see about us are in and of themselves direct evidences of the spiritual nature of things. To such

persons a Spirit that is not constantly producing
noteworthy effects, and so getting himself into the
newspapers, would seem unreal.   Therefore, to such
persons Religious Idealism depends for its life and
warmth upon the vividness and the impressiveness
of these phenomenal indications of the action of the
great Spirit.   Such persons, if they have given up
traditional superstitions, still find their delight in
dwelling on the mystery of " vital force," on the occurrence of all sorts of wonderful things, on the theories of occult powers, or of ethereal essences.   To
them one of the best evidences of the spiritual nature of things is the inability of the biologist to
tell us under what conditions life could be produced
from dead matter.   The mysterious nature of nervous action, the influence of the mind upon the
body, and, above all, the occurrence of certain
strange emotional experiences in us, such as the vis-
ions of mystics, these are to them the main proof
that the world is divine and is full of spiritual life.
We do not sympathize with this method of idealism.
We respect its good intentions, but we are unwilling
to look upon it as rationally significant.   For us it
makes absolutely no difference in our faith about
the ultimate spiritual nature of things, whether the
world that we see makes our hair stand on end or
not, or whether the biologists ever come to succeed
in making living matter or not.   That we can make
a fire, does not prove the world less divine.   Nor
would the truth of things be less spiritual, if we
could also manufacture not only protoplasm, but
whole whales or Shakespeares in our laboratories.

31

If we could do so, materialism as a
doctrine would remain just as absurd
Genuine idealism, like the foregoing, is
less whether this or that particular sur
appears in the phenomenal world, since
all knows that the Whole is divine, an
prise. It seeks no confirmation from
ries ; but only for illustrations of rati
for its own part does it venture to d
special workers in science what they s
is not forced to beg Nature to contain
agency, some vague ethereal essence, or
rious and wondrous visible being, who
shall be a guaranty to the gaping on
there exists an Ideal. All this mendic
our view rejects as unworthy of any
thinker. It says, " Look at the facts
Study them as experience gives them.
in their naked commonplace reality. Bu
that the Ideal Divine Life dwells in
throughout their whole boundless realm.

In Plato's " Parmenides," the your
confesses that he sometimes hesitates
there is an Idea for everything, even for
is rebuked for this fear that men may la
He is told that mud also is rational.
must fear nobody's laughter in such a
must see the Divine everywhere. And
must not be going about faithlessly looki
thing that shall be wondrous enough to
say " Here is God."

eth, and that in his sight all the good that we do is not labor lost.

Yet the purpose of these chapters is not to give at any point a mere negation, even when we speak of the traditional theology. We do not want to exaggerate our quarrel with anybody. If thinkers who accept some traditional form of theology find truth or help in our doctrine, we shall be glad. After all, the religious interest wants, not so much this or that view about some man's special creed, but a foundation for the faith that somehow righteousness is in deepest truth triumphant in the world. If there is no proof, then, as we said in Chapter IX., we must resort to the Postulates. If we can get proof, so much the better.

Thus, however, we have suggested to ourselves another question. These Postulates of Chapter IX., what has become of them now? Are they wholly lost in our insight? No indeed. They remain just what they were, rational forms of our activity, not perfect in their rationality, but constantly valuable to us in our work. The scientific postulates are not superseded, but rather only strengthened, by the insight into the ultimate rationality of things. They become now the assurance that there must be a rational solution to every scientific problem, and that the simplest solution, being the most rational, is the most probable, in case it is actually adequate to all the facts. Just as before, it remains true of us finite beings that our finite external world is at each instant the product of our activity, working with the postulates, upon the material of our sensations. And that activity remains as before the proper object of a moral judgment. Only now we see that the highest form of our activity is likely to be the one most conforming to the truth. What remains true of the scientific postulates, remains true of the religious postulates. They are not superseded. For what they can still do for us is to insist that our idea of the Infinite shall not remain a cold, barren abstraction, but that we shall appeal to our experience for evidence of what is truly highest and best, and that we shall then say : " The highest conceptions that I get from experience of what goodness and beauty are, the noblest life that I can imagine, the completest blessedness that I can think of, all these things are but faint suggestions of a truth that is infinitely realized in the Divine, that knows all truth. Whatever perfection there is suggested in these things, that He must fully know and experience." Therefore the religious postulates can accompany us everywhere, making all our experience appear to us as an ever-fresh lesson concerning the mind of God.

The postulates, then, we retain, with the insight. We abandon, however, the use of these postulates to demonstrate further special articles of faith as to supernatural powers or events of any sort. We know of no miracle save the Infinite himself. And so we have no interest in many of the forms of popular idealism. To prove that this world is the home of a Spiritual Life, many good people have been and are concerned to prove that certain phenomena which we see about us are in and of themselves direct evidences of the spiritual nature of things. To such

persons a Spirit that is not constantly producing
noteworthy effects, and so getting himself into the
newspapers, would seem unreal. Therefore, to such
persons Religious Idealism depends for its life and
warmth upon the vividness and the impressiveness
of these phenomenal indications of the action of the
great Spirit. Such persons, if they have given up
traditional superstitions, still find their delight in
dwelling on the mystery of " vital force," on the occurrence of all sorts of wonderful things, on the theories of occult powers, or of ethereal essences. To
them one of the best evidences of the spiritual nature of things is the inability of the biologist to
tell us under what conditions life could be produced
from dead matter. The mysterious nature of nervous action, the influence of the mind upon the
body, and, above all, the occurrence of certain
strange emotional experiences in us, such as the vis-
ions of mystics, these are to them the main proof
that the world is divine and is full of spiritual life.
We do not sympathize with this method of idealism.
We respect its good intentions, but we are unwilling
to look upon it as rationally significant. For us it
makes absolutely no difference in our faith about
the ultimate spiritual nature of things, whether the
world that we see makes our hair stand on end or
not, or whether the biologists ever come to succeed
in making living matter or not. That we can make
a fire, does not prove the world less divine. Nor
would the truth of things be less spiritual, if we
could also manufacture not only protoplasm, but
whole whales or Shakespeares in our laboratories.

If we could do so, materialism as a philosophical doctrine would remain just as absurd as it now is. Genuine idealism, like the foregoing, is utterly careless whether this or that particular surprising thing appears in the phenomenal world, since it once for all knows that the Whole is divine, an eternal surprise. It seeks no confirmation from the laboratories; but only for illustrations of rationality; nor for its own part does it venture to dictate to the special workers in science what they shall find. It is not forced to beg Nature to contain some occult agency, some vague ethereal essence, or some mysterious and wondrous visible being, whose presence shall be a guaranty to the gaping onlooker that there exists an Ideal. All this mendicant idealism our view rejects as unworthy of any clear-headed thinker. It says, " Look at the facts as they are. Study them as experience gives them. Know them in their naked commonplace reality. But know also that the Ideal Divine Life dwells in them and throughout their whole boundless realm."

In Plato's " Parmenides," the young Socrates confesses that he sometimes hesitates to say that there is an Idea for everything, even for mud. He is rebuked for this fear that men may laugh at him. He is told that mud also is rational. Even so we must fear nobody's laughter in such a matter. We must see the Divine everywhere. And therefore we must not be going about faithlessly looking for something that shall be wondrous enough to force us to say " Here is God."

And now, last of all, as the writer bids farewell
to this single lingering fellow-student, he cannot refrain from suggesting to so patient a friend one little thought more concerning the proof that has been
given for the doctrine of these later pages of our
discussion. "Possibly it is all false," the fellow-
student may say. "This fair picture of a Truth that
is also Goodness, may be but another illusion." Be
it so, dear friend, if we have said nothing to convince thee. Perchance all this our later argument
is illusion. Only remember: If it is Error, then,
as we have shown thee, it is Error because and only
because the Infinite knows it to be such. Apart
from that knowledge, our thought would be no error.
At least, then, the Infinite knows what we have at-
tributed to it. If it rejects our ideal, then doubtless
there is something imperfect, not about the Infinite,
but about our Ideal. And so at worst we are like
a child who has come to the palace of the King on
the day of his wedding, bearing roses as a gift to
grace the feast. For the child, waiting innocently
to see whether the King will not appear and praise
the welcome flowers, grows at last weary with watching all day and with listening to harsh words outside
the palace gate, amid the jostling crowd. And so
in the evening it falls fast asleep beneath the great
dark walls, unseen and forgotten; and the wither-
ing roses by and by fall from its lap, and are scattered by the wind into the dusty highway, there to
be trodden under foot and destroyed. Yet all that
happens only because there are infinitely fairer

treasures within the palace than the ignorant child could bring. The King knows of this, yes, and of ten thousand other proffered gifts of loyal subjects. But he needs them not. Rather are all things from eternity his own.